P9-CRW-196

HOLT SCIENCE & TECHNOLOGY

Cells, Heredity, and Classification

HOLT, RINEHART AND WINSTON

A Harcourt Classroom Education Company

Austin • New York • Orlando • Atlanta • San Francisco • Boston • Dallas • Toronto • London

Acknowledgments

Chapter Writers

Katy Z. Allen
Science Writer and Former Biology Teacher
Wayland, Massachusetts

Linda Ruth Berg, Ph.D.
Adjunct Professor–Natural Sciences
St. Petersburg Junior College
St. Petersburg, Florida

Jennie Dusheck
Science Writer
Santa Cruz, California

Mark F. Taylor, Ph.D.
Associate Professor of Biology
Baylor University
Waco, Texas

Lab Writers

Diana Scheidle Bartos
Science Consultant and Educator
Diana Scheidle Bartos, L.L.C.
Lakewood, Colorado

Carl Benson
General Science Teacher
Plains High School
Plains, Montana

Charlotte Blassingame
Technology Coordinator
White Station Middle School
Memphis, Tennessee

Marsha Carver
Science Teacher and Dept. Chair
McLean County High School
Calhoun, Kentucky

Kenneth E. Creese
Science Teacher
White Mountain Junior High School
Rock Springs, Wyoming

Linda Culp
Science Teacher and Dept. Chair
Thorndale High School
Thorndale, Texas

James Deaver
Science Teacher and Dept. Chair
West Point High School
West Point, Nebraska

Frank McKinney, Ph.D.
Professor of Geology
Appalachian State University
Boone, North Carolina

Alyson Mike
Science Teacher
East Valley Middle School
East Helena, Montana

C. Ford Morishita
Biology Teacher
Clackamas High School
Milwaukie, Oregon

Patricia D. Morrell, Ph.D.
Assistant Professor, School of Education
University of Portland
Portland, Oregon

Hilary C. Olson, Ph.D.
Research Associate
Institute for Geophysics
The University of Texas
Austin, Texas

James B. Pulley
Science Editor and Former Science Teacher
Liberty High School
Liberty, Missouri

Denice Lee Sandefur
Science Chairperson
Nucla High School
Nucla, Colorado

Patti Soderberg
Science Writer
The BioQUEST Curriculum Consortium
Beloit College
Beloit, Wisconsin

Phillip Vavala
Science Teacher and Dept. Chair
Salesianum School
Wilmington, Delaware

Albert C. Wartski
Biology Teacher
Chapel Hill High School
Chapel Hill, North Carolina

Lynn Marie Wartski
Science Writer and Former Science Teacher
Hillsborough, North Carolina

Ivora D. Washington
Science Teacher and Dept. Chair
Hyattsville Middle School
Washington, D.C.

Academic Reviewers

Renato J. Aguilera, Ph.D.
Associate Professor
Department of Molecular, Cell, and Developmental Biology
University of California
Los Angeles, California

David M. Armstrong, Ph.D.
Professor of Biology
Department of E.P.O. Biology
University of Colorado
Boulder, Colorado

Alissa Arp, Ph.D.
Director and Professor of Environmental Studies
Romberg Tiburon Center
San Francisco State University
Tiburon, California

Russell M. Brengelman
Professor of Physics
Morehead State University
Morehead, Kentucky

John A. Brockhaus, Ph.D.
Director of Mapping, Charting, and Geodesy Program
Department of Geography and Environmental Engineering
United States Military Academy
West Point, New York

Linda K. Butler, Ph.D.
Lecturer of Biological Sciences
The University of Texas
Austin, Texas

Barry Chernoff, Ph.D.
Associate Curator
Division of Fishes
The Field Museum of Natural History
Chicago, Illinois

Donna Greenwood Crenshaw, Ph.D.
Instructor
Department of Biology
Duke University
Durham, North Carolina

Hugh Crenshaw, Ph.D.
Assistant Professor of Zoology
Duke University
Durham, North Carolina

Joe W. Crim, Ph.D.
Professor of Biology
University of Georgia
Athens, Georgia

Peter Demmin, Ed.D.
Former Science Teacher and Chair
Amherst Central High School
Amherst, New York

Joseph L. Graves, Jr., Ph.D.
Associate Professor of Evolutionary Biology
Arizona State University West
Phoenix, Arizona

William B. Guggino, Ph.D.
Professor of Physiology and Pediatrics
The Johns Hopkins University School of Medicine
Baltimore, Maryland

David Haig, Ph.D.
Assistant Professor of Biology
Department of Organismic and Evolutionary Biology
Harvard University
Cambridge, Massachusetts

Roy W. Hann, Jr., Ph.D.
Professor of Civil Engineering
Texas A&M University
College Station, Texas

Copyright © 2002 by Holt, Rinehart and Winston

All rights reserved. No part of this publication may be reproduced or transmitted in any form or by any means, electronic or mechanical, including photocopy, recording, or any information storage and retrieval system, without permission in writing from the publisher.

Requests for permission to make copies of any part of the work should be mailed to the following address: Permissions Department, Holt, Rinehart and Winston, 10801 N. MoPac Expressway, Austin, Texas 78759.

For permission to reprint copyrighted material, grateful acknowledgment is made to the following sources:

sciLINKS is owned and provided by the National Science Teachers Association. All rights reserved.

The name of the **Smithsonian Institution** and the sunburst logo are registered trademarks of the Smithsonian Institution. The copyright in the Smithsonian Web site and Smithsonian Web site pages are owned by the Smithsonian Institution. All other material owned and provided by Holt, Rinehart and Winston under copyright appearing above.

Copyright © 2000 **CNN** and **CNNfyi.com** are trademarks of Cable News Network LP, LLLP, a Time Warner Company. All rights reserved. Copyright © 2000 Turner Learning logos are trademarks of Turner Learning, Inc., a Time Warner Company. All rights reserved.

Printed in the United States of America

ISBN 0-03-064778-9

1 2 3 4 5 6 7   032   05 04 03 02 01 00

Acknowledgments (cont.)

John E. Hoover, Ph.D.
Associate Professor of Biology
Millersville University
Millersville, Pennsylvania

Joan E. N. Hudson, Ph.D.
Associate Professor of Biological Sciences
Sam Houston State University
Huntsville, Texas

Laurie Jackson-Grusby, Ph.D.
Research Scientist and Doctoral Associate
Whitehead Institute for Biomedical Research
Massachusetts Institute of Technology
Cambridge, Massachusetts

George M. Langford, Ph.D.
Professor of Biological Sciences
Dartmouth College
Hanover, New Hampshire

Melanie C. Lewis, Ph.D.
Professor of Biology, Retired
Southwest Texas State University
San Marcos, Texas

V. Patteson Lombardi, Ph.D.
Research Assistant Professor of Biology
Department of Biology
University of Oregon
Eugene, Oregon

Glen Longley, Ph.D.
Professor of Biology and Director of the Edwards Aquifer Research Center
Southwest Texas State University
San Marcos, Texas

William F. McComas, Ph.D.
Director of the Center to Advance Science Education
University of Southern California
Los Angeles, California

LaMoine L. Motz, Ph.D.
Coordinator of Science Education
Oakland County Schools
Waterford, Michigan

Nancy Parker, Ph.D.
Associate Professor of Biology
Southern Illinois University
Edwardsville, Illinois

Barron S. Rector, Ph.D.
Associate Professor and Extension Range Specialist
Texas Agricultural Extension Service
Texas A&M University
College Station, Texas

Peter Sheridan, Ph.D.
Professor of Chemistry
Colgate University
Hamilton, New York

Miles R. Silman, Ph.D.
Assistant Professor of Biology
Wake Forest University
Winston-Salem, North Carolina

Neil Simister, Ph.D.
Associate Professor of Biology
Department of Life Sciences
Brandeis University
Waltham, Massachusetts

Lee Smith, Ph.D.
Curriculum Writer
MDL Information Systems, Inc.
San Leandro, California

Robert G. Steen, Ph.D.
Manager, Rat Genome Project
Whitehead Institute—Center for Genome Research
Massachusetts Institute of Technology
Cambridge, Massachusetts

Martin VanDyke, Ph.D.
Professor of Chemistry, Emeritus
Front Range Community College
Westminister, Colorado

E. Peter Volpe, Ph.D.
Professor of Medical Genetics
Mercer University School of Medicine
Macon, Georgia

Harold K. Voris, Ph.D.
Curator and Head
Division of Amphibians and Reptiles
The Field Museum of Natural History
Chicago, Illinois

Mollie Walton
Biology Instructor
El Paso Community College
El Paso, Texas

Peter Wetherwax, Ph.D.
Professor of Biology
University of Oregon
Eugene, Oregon

Mary K. Wicksten, Ph.D.
Professor of Biology
Texas A&M University
College Station, Texas

R. Stimson Wilcox, Ph.D.
Associate Professor of Biology
Department of Biological Sciences
Binghamton University
Binghamton, New York

Conrad M. Zapanta, Ph.D.
Research Engineer
Sulzer Carbomedics, Inc.
Austin, Texas

Safety Reviewer

Jack Gerlovich, Ph.D.
Associate Professor
School of Education
Drake University
Des Moines, Iowa

Teacher Reviewers

Barry L. Bishop
Science Teacher and Dept. Chair
San Rafael Junior High School
Ferron, Utah

Carol A. Bornhorst
Science Teacher and Dept. Chair
Bonita Vista Middle School
Chula Vista, California

Paul Boyle
Science Teacher
Perry Heights Middle School
Evansville, Indiana

Yvonne Brannum
Science Teacher and Dept. Chair
Hine Junior High School
Washington, D.C.

Gladys Cherniak
Science Teacher
St. Paul's Episcopal School
Mobile, Alabama

James Chin
Science Teacher
Frank A. Day Middle School
Newtonville, Massachusetts

Kenneth Creese
Science Teacher
White Mountain Junior High School
Rock Springs, Wyoming

Linda A. Culp
Science Teacher and Dept. Chair
Thorndale High School
Thorndale, Texas

Georgiann Delgadillo
Science Teacher
East Valley Continuous Curriculum School
Spokane, Washington

Alonda Droege
Biology Teacher
Evergreen High School
Seattle, Washington

Michael J. DuPré
Curriculum Specialist
Rush Henrietta Junior-Senior High School
Henrietta, New York

Rebecca Ferguson
Science Teacher
North Ridge Middle School
North Richland Hills, Texas

Susan Gorman
Science Teacher
North Ridge Middle School
North Richland Hills, Texas

Gary Habeeb
Science Mentor
Sierra-Plumas Joint Unified School District
Downieville, California

Karma Houston-Hughes
Science Mentor
Kyrene Middle School
Tempe, Arizona

Roberta Jacobowitz
Science Teacher
C. W. Otto Middle School
Lansing, Michigan

Kerry A. Johnson
Science Teacher
Isbell Middle School
Santa Paula, California

M. R. Penny Kisiah
Science Teacher and Dept. Chair
Fairview Middle School
Tallahassee, Florida

Kathy LaRoe
Science Teacher
East Valley Middle School
East Helena, Montana

Jane M. Lemons
Science Teacher
Western Rockingham Middle School
Madison, North Carolina

Scott Mandel, Ph.D.
Director and Educational Consultant
Teachers Helping Teachers
Los Angeles, California

Thomas Manerchia
Former Biology and Life Science Teacher
Archmere Academy
Claymont, Delaware

Maurine O. Marchani
Science Teacher and Dept. Chair
Raymond Park Middle School
Indianapolis, Indiana

Jason P. Marsh
Biology Teacher
Montevideo High School and Montevideo Country School
Montevideo, Minnesota

Edith C. McAlanis
Science Teacher and Dept. Chair
Socorro Middle School
El Paso, Texas

Kevin McCurdy, Ph.D.
Science Teacher
Elmwood Junior High School
Rogers, Arkansas

Kathy McKee
Science Teacher
Hoyt Middle School
Des Moines, Iowa

Acknowledgments continue on page 215.

C Cells, Heredity, and Classification

Skills Development

Process Skills

QuickLabs

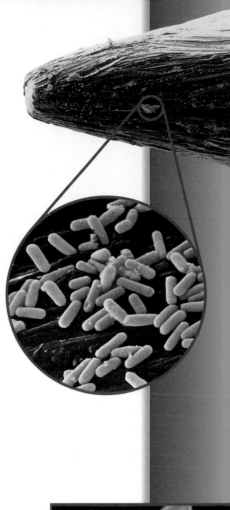

Chapter Labs

Skills Development

Research and Critical Thinking Skills

Connections

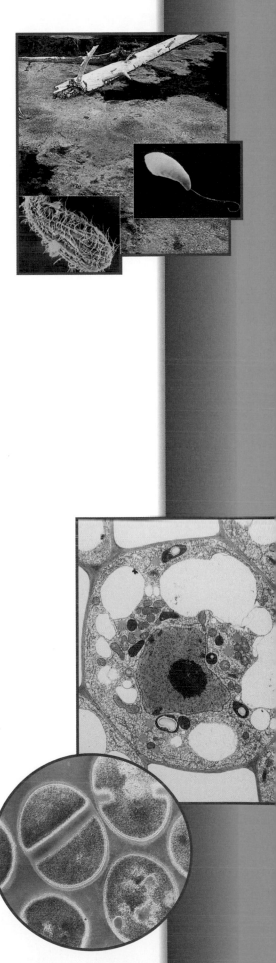

Program Scope and Sequence

Selecting the right books for your course is easy. Just review the topics presented in each book to determine the best match to your district curriculum.

	A MICROORGANISMS, FUNGI, AND PLANTS	**B** ANIMALS
CHAPTER 1	**It's Alive!! Or, Is It?** ❏ Characteristics of living things ❏ Homeostasis ❏ Heredity and DNA ❏ Producers, consumers, and decomposers ❏ Biomolecules	**Animals and Behavior** ❏ Characteristics of animals ❏ Classification of animals ❏ Animal behavior ❏ Hibernation and estivation ❏ The biological clock ❏ Animal communication ❏ Living in groups
CHAPTER 2	**Bacteria and Viruses** ❏ Binary fission ❏ Characteristics of bacteria ❏ Nitrogen-fixing bacteria ❏ Antibiotics ❏ Pathogenic bacteria ❏ Characteristics of viruses ❏ Lytic cycle	**Invertebrates** ❏ General characteristics of invertebrates ❏ Types of symmetry ❏ Characteristics of sponges, cnidarians, arthropods, and echinoderms ❏ Flatworms versus roundworms ❏ Types of circulatory systems
CHAPTER 3	**Protists and Fungi** ❏ Characteristics of protists ❏ Types of algae ❏ Types of protozoa ❏ Protist reproduction ❏ Characteristics of fungi and lichens	**Fishes, Amphibians, and Reptiles** ❏ Characteristics of vertebrates ❏ Structure and kinds of fishes ❏ Development of lungs ❏ Structure and kinds of amphibians and reptiles ❏ Function of the amniotic egg
CHAPTER 4	**Introduction to Plants** ❏ Characteristics of plants and seeds ❏ Reproduction and classification ❏ Angiosperms versus gymnosperms ❏ Monocots versus dicots ❏ Structure and functions of roots, stems, leaves, and flowers	**Birds and Mammals** ❏ Structure and kinds of birds ❏ Types of feathers ❏ Adaptations for flight ❏ Structure and kinds of mammals ❏ Function of the placenta
CHAPTER 5	**Plant Processes** ❏ Pollination and fertilization ❏ Dormancy ❏ Photosynthesis ❏ Plant tropisms ❏ Seasonal responses of plants	
CHAPTER 6		
CHAPTER 7		

Life Science

C CELLS, HEREDITY, & CLASSIFICATION

Cells: The Basic Units of Life
- ❑ Cells, tissues, and organs
- ❑ Populations, communities, and ecosystems
- ❑ Cell theory
- ❑ Surface-to-volume ratio
- ❑ Prokaryotic versus eukaryotic cells
- ❑ Cell organelles

The Cell in Action
- ❑ Diffusion and osmosis
- ❑ Passive versus active transport
- ❑ Endocytosis versus exocytosis
- ❑ Photosynthesis
- ❑ Cellular respiration and fermentation
- ❑ Cell cycle

Heredity
- ❑ Dominant versus recessive traits
- ❑ Genes and alleles
- ❑ Genotype, phenotype, the Punnett square and probability
- ❑ Meiosis
- ❑ Determination of sex

Genes and Gene Technology
- ❑ Structure of DNA
- ❑ Protein synthesis
- ❑ Mutations
- ❑ Heredity disorders and genetic counseling

The Evolution of Living Things
- ❑ Adaptations and species
- ❑ Evidence for evolution
- ❑ Darwin's work and natural selection
- ❑ Formation of new species

The History of Life on Earth
- ❑ Geologic time scale and extinctions
- ❑ Plate tectonics
- ❑ Human evolution

Classification
- ❑ Levels of classification
- ❑ Cladistic diagrams
- ❑ Dichotomous keys
- ❑ Characteristics of the six kingdoms

D HUMAN BODY SYSTEMS & HEALTH

Body Organization and Structure
- ❑ Homeostasis
- ❑ Types of tissue
- ❑ Organ systems
- ❑ Structure and function of the skeletal system, muscular system, and integumentary system

Circulation and Respiration
- ❑ Structure and function of the cardiovascular system, lymphatic system, and respiratory system
- ❑ Respiratory disorders

The Digestive and Urinary Systems
- ❑ Structure and function of the digestive system
- ❑ Structure and function of the urinary system

Communication and Control
- ❑ Structure and function of the nervous system and endocrine system
- ❑ The senses
- ❑ Structure and function of the eye and ear

Reproduction and Development
- ❑ Asexual versus sexual reproduction
- ❑ Internal versus external fertilization
- ❑ Structure and function of the human male and female reproductive systems
- ❑ Fertilization, placental development, and embryo growth
- ❑ Stages of human life

Body Defenses and Disease
- ❑ Types of diseases
- ❑ Vaccines and immunity
- ❑ Structure and function of the immune system
- ❑ Autoimmune diseases, cancer, and AIDS

Staying Healthy
- ❑ Nutrition and reading food labels
- ❑ Alcohol and drug effects on the body
- ❑ Hygiene, exercise, and first aid

E ENVIRONMENTAL SCIENCE

Interactions of Living Things
- ❑ Biotic versus abiotic parts of the environment
- ❑ Producers, consumers, and decomposers
- ❑ Food chains and food webs
- ❑ Factors limiting population growth
- ❑ Predator-prey relationships
- ❑ Symbiosis and coevolution

Cycles in Nature
- ❑ Water cycle
- ❑ Carbon cycle
- ❑ Nitrogen cycle
- ❑ Ecological succession

The Earth's Ecosystems
- ❑ Kinds of land and water biomes
- ❑ Marine ecosystems
- ❑ Freshwater ecosystems

Environmental Problems and Solutions
- ❑ Types of pollutants
- ❑ Types of resources
- ❑ Conservation practices
- ❑ Species protection

Energy Resources
- ❑ Types of resources
- ❑ Energy resources and pollution
- ❑ Alternative energy resources

Scope and Sequence *(continued)*

	F INSIDE THE RESTLESS EARTH	G EARTH'S CHANGING SURFACE
CHAPTER 1	**Minerals of the Earth's Crust** ❑ Mineral composition and structure ❑ Types of minerals ❑ Mineral identification ❑ Mineral formation and mining	**Maps as Models of the Earth** ❑ Structure of a map ❑ Cardinal directions ❑ Latitude, longitude, and the equator ❑ Magnetic declination and true north ❑ Types of projections ❑ Aerial photographs ❑ Remote sensing ❑ Topographic maps
CHAPTER 2	**Rocks: Mineral Mixtures** ❑ Rock cycle and types of rocks ❑ Rock classification ❑ Characteristics of igneous, sedimentary, and metamorphic rocks	**Weathering and Soil Formation** ❑ Types of weathering ❑ Factors affecting the rate of weathering ❑ Composition of soil ❑ Soil conservation and erosion prevention
CHAPTER 3	**The Rock and Fossil Record** ❑ Uniformitarianism versus catastrophism ❑ Superposition ❑ The geologic column and unconformities ❑ Absolute dating and radiometric dating ❑ Characteristics and types of fossils ❑ Geologic time scale	**Agents of Erosion and Deposition** ❑ Shoreline erosion and deposition ❑ Wind erosion and deposition ❑ Erosion and deposition by ice ❑ Gravity's effect on erosion and deposition
CHAPTER 4	**Plate Tectonics** ❑ Structure of the Earth ❑ Continental drifts and sea floor spreading ❑ Plate tectonics theory ❑ Types of boundaries ❑ Types of crust deformities	
CHAPTER 5	**Earthquakes** ❑ Seismology ❑ Features of earthquakes ❑ P and S waves ❑ Gap hypothesis ❑ Earthquake safety	
CHAPTER 6	**Volcanoes** ❑ Types of volcanoes and eruptions ❑ Types of lava and pyroclastic material ❑ Craters versus calderas ❑ Sites and conditions for volcano formation ❑ Predicting eruptions	

Earth Science

H WATER ON EARTH

The Flow of Fresh Water
- ❏ Water cycle
- ❏ River systems
- ❏ Stream erosion
- ❏ Life cycle of rivers
- ❏ Deposition
- ❏ Aquifers, springs, and wells
- ❏ Ground water
- ❏ Water treatment and pollution

Exploring the Oceans
- ❏ Properties and characteristics of the oceans
- ❏ Features of the ocean floor
- ❏ Ocean ecology
- ❏ Ocean resources and pollution

The Movement of Ocean Water
- ❏ Types of currents
- ❏ Characteristics of waves
- ❏ Types of ocean waves
- ❏ Tides

I WEATHER AND CLIMATE

The Atmosphere
- ❏ Structure of the atmosphere
- ❏ Air pressure
- ❏ Radiation, convection, and conduction
- ❏ Greenhouse effect and global warming
- ❏ Characteristics of winds
- ❏ Types of winds
- ❏ Air pollution

Understanding Weather
- ❏ Water cycle
- ❏ Humidity
- ❏ Types of clouds
- ❏ Types of precipitation
- ❏ Air masses and fronts
- ❏ Storms, tornadoes, and hurricanes
- ❏ Weather forecasting
- ❏ Weather maps

Climate
- ❏ Weather versus climate
- ❏ Seasons and latitude
- ❏ Prevailing winds
- ❏ Earth's biomes
- ❏ Earth's climate zones
- ❏ Ice ages
- ❏ Global warming
- ❏ Greenhouse effect

J ASTRONOMY

Observing the Sky
- ❏ Astronomy
- ❏ Keeping time
- ❏ Mapping the stars
- ❏ Scales of the universe
- ❏ Types of telescope
- ❏ Radioastronomy

Formation of the Solar System
- ❏ Birth of the solar system
- ❏ Planetary motion
- ❏ Newton's Law of Universal Gravitation
- ❏ Structure of the sun
- ❏ Fusion
- ❏ Earth's structure and atmosphere

A Family of Planets
- ❏ Properties and characteristics of the planets
- ❏ Properties and characteristics of moons
- ❏ Comets, asteroids, and meteoroids

The Universe Beyond
- ❏ Composition of stars
- ❏ Classification of stars
- ❏ Star brightness, distance, and motions
- ❏ H-R diagram
- ❏ Life cycle of stars
- ❏ Types of galaxies
- ❏ Theories on the formation of the universe

Exploring Space
- ❏ Rocketry and artificial satellites
- ❏ Types of Earth orbit
- ❏ Space probes and space exploration

Scope and Sequence (continued)

	K — INTRODUCTION TO MATTER	L — INTERACTIONS OF MATTER
CHAPTER 1	**The Properties of Matter** ❏ Definition of matter ❏ Mass and weight ❏ Physical and chemical properties ❏ Physical and chemical change ❏ Density	**Chemical Bonding** ❏ Types of chemical bonds ❏ Valence electrons ❏ Ions versus molecules ❏ Crystal lattice
CHAPTER 2	**States of Matter** ❏ States of matter and their properties ❏ Boyle's and Charles's laws ❏ Changes of state	**Chemical Reactions** ❏ Writing chemical formulas and equations ❏ Law of conservation of mass ❏ Types of reactions ❏ Endothermic versus exothermic reactions ❏ Law of conservation of energy ❏ Activation energy ❏ Catalysts and inhibitors
CHAPTER 3	**Elements, Compounds, and Mixtures** ❏ Elements and compounds ❏ Metals, nonmetals, and metalloids (semiconductors) ❏ Properties of mixtures ❏ Properties of solutions, suspensions, and colloids	**Chemical Compounds** ❏ Ionic versus covalent compounds ❏ Acids, bases, and salts ❏ pH ❏ Organic compounds ❏ Biomolecules
CHAPTER 4	**Introduction to Atoms** ❏ Atomic theory ❏ Atomic model and structure ❏ Isotopes ❏ Atomic mass and mass number	**Atomic Energy** ❏ Properties of radioactive substances ❏ Types of decay ❏ Half-life ❏ Fission, fusion, and chain reactions
CHAPTER 5	**The Periodic Table** ❏ Structure of the periodic table ❏ Periodic law ❏ Properties of alkali metals, alkaline-earth metals, halogens, and noble gases	
CHAPTER 6		

Physical Science

M FORCES, MOTION, AND ENERGY	N ELECTRICITY AND MAGNETISM	O SOUND AND LIGHT

Matter in Motion
- ❏ Speed, velocity, and acceleration
- ❏ Measuring force
- ❏ Friction
- ❏ Mass versus weight

Introduction to Electricity
- ❏ Law of electric charges
- ❏ Conduction versus induction
- ❏ Static electricity
- ❏ Potential difference
- ❏ Cells, batteries, and photocells
- ❏ Thermocouples
- ❏ Voltage, current, and resistance
- ❏ Electric power
- ❏ Types of circuits

The Energy of Waves
- ❏ Properties of waves
- ❏ Types of waves
- ❏ Reflection and refraction
- ❏ Diffraction and interference
- ❏ Standing waves and resonance

Forces in Motion
- ❏ Terminal velocity and free fall
- ❏ Projectile motion
- ❏ Inertia
- ❏ Momentum

Electromagnetism
- ❏ Properties of magnets
- ❏ Magnetic force
- ❏ Electromagnetism
- ❏ Solenoids and electric motors
- ❏ Electromagnetic induction
- ❏ Generators and transformers

The Nature of Sound
- ❏ Properties of sound waves
- ❏ Structure of the human ear
- ❏ Pitch and the Doppler effect
- ❏ Infrasonic versus ultrasonic sound
- ❏ Sound reflection and echolocation
- ❏ Sound barrier
- ❏ Interference, resonance, diffraction, and standing waves
- ❏ Sound quality of instruments

Forces in Fluids
- ❏ Properties in fluids
- ❏ Atmospheric pressure
- ❏ Density
- ❏ Pascal's principle
- ❏ Buoyant force
- ❏ Archimedes' principle
- ❏ Bernoulli's principle

Electronic Technology
- ❏ Properties of semiconductors
- ❏ Integrated circuits
- ❏ Diodes and transistors
- ❏ Analog versus digital signals
- ❏ Microprocessors
- ❏ Features of computers

The Nature of Light
- ❏ Electromagnetic waves
- ❏ Electromagnetic spectrum
- ❏ Law of reflection
- ❏ Absorption and scattering
- ❏ Reflection and refraction
- ❏ Diffraction and interference

Work and Machines
- ❏ Measuring work
- ❏ Measuring power
- ❏ Types of machines
- ❏ Mechanical advantage
- ❏ Mechanical efficiency

Light and Our World
- ❏ Luminosity
- ❏ Types of lighting
- ❏ Types of mirrors and lenses
- ❏ Focal point
- ❏ Structure of the human eye
- ❏ Lasers and holograms

Energy and Energy Resources
- ❏ Forms of energy
- ❏ Energy conversions
- ❏ Law of conservation of energy
- ❏ Energy resources

Heat and Heat Technology
- ❏ Heat versus temperature
- ❏ Thermal expansion
- ❏ Absolute zero
- ❏ Conduction, convection, radiation
- ❏ Conductors versus insulators
- ❏ Specific heat capacity
- ❏ Changes of state
- ❏ Heat engines
- ❏ Thermal pollution

Components Listing

Effective planning starts with all the resources you need in an easy-to-use package for each short course.

Directed Reading Worksheets Help students develop and practice fundamental reading comprehension skills and provide a comprehensive review tool for students to use when studying for an exam.

Study Guide Vocabulary & Notes Worksheets and Chapter Review Worksheets are reproductions of the Chapter Highlights and Chapter Review sections that follow each chapter in the textbook.

Science Puzzlers, Twisters & Teasers Use vocabulary and concepts from each chapter of the Pupil's Editions as elements of rebuses, anagrams, logic puzzles, daffy definitions, riddle poems, word jumbles, and other types of puzzles.

Reinforcement and Vocabulary Review Worksheets Approach a chapter topic from a different angle with an emphasis on different learning modalities to help students that are frustrated by traditional methods.

Critical Thinking & Problem Solving Worksheets Develop the following skills: distinguishing fact from opinion, predicting consequences, analyzing information, and drawing conclusions. Problem Solving Worksheets develop a step-by-step process of problem analysis including gathering information, asking critical questions, identifying alternatives, and making comparisons.

Math Skills for Science Worksheets Each activity gives a brief introduction to a relevant math skill, a step-by-step explanation of the math process, one or more example problems, and a variety of practice problems.

Science Skills Worksheets Help your students focus specifically on skills such as measuring, graphing, using logic, understanding statistics, organizing research papers, and critical thinking options.

LAB ACTIVITIES

Datasheets for Labs These worksheets are the labs found in the *Holt Science & Technology* textbook. Charts, tables, and graphs are included to make data collection and analysis easier, and space is provided to write observations and conclusions.

Whiz-Bang Demonstrations Discovery or Making Models experiences label each demo as one in which students discover an answer or use a scientific model.

Calculator-Based Labs Give students the opportunity to use graphing-calculator probes and sensors to collect data using a TI graphing calculator, Vernier sensors, and a TI CBL 2™ or Vernier Lab Pro interface.

EcoLabs and Field Activities Focus on educational outdoor projects, such as wildlife observation, nature surveys, or natural history.

Inquiry Labs Use the scientific method to help students find their own path in solving a real-world problem.

Long-Term Projects and Research Ideas Provide students with the opportunity to go beyond library and Internet resources to explore science topics.

ASSESSMENT

Chapter Tests Each four-page chapter test consists of a variety of item types including Multiple Choice, Using Vocabulary, Short Answer, Critical Thinking, Math in Science, Interpreting Graphics, and Concept Mapping.

Performance-Based Assessments Evaluate students' abilities to solve problems using the tools, equipment, and techniques of science. Rubrics included for each assessment make it easy to evaluate student performance.

TEACHER RESOURCES

Lesson Plans Integrate all of the great resources in the *Holt Science & Technology* program into your daily teaching. Each lesson plan includes a correlation of the lesson activities to the National Science Education Standards.

Teaching Transparencies Each transparency is correlated to a particular lesson in the Chapter Organizer.

Concept Mapping Transparencies, Worksheets, and Answer Key

Give students an opportunity to complete their own concept maps to study the concepts within each chapter and form logical connections. Student worksheets contain a blank concept map with linking phrases and a list of terms to be used by the student to complete the map.

TECHNOLOGY RESOURCES

One-Stop Planner CD-ROM

Finding the right resources is easy with the One-Stop Planner CD-ROM. You can view and print any resource with just the click of a mouse. Customize the suggested lesson plans to match your daily or weekly calendar and your district's requirements. Powerful test generator software allows you to create customized assessments using a databank of items.

The One-Stop Planner for each level includes the following:

- All materials from the Teaching Resources
- Bellringer Transparency Masters
- Block Scheduling Tools
- Standards Correlations
- Lab Inventory Checklist
- Safety Information
- Science Fair Guide
- Parent Involvement Tools
- Spanish Audio Scripts
- Spanish Glossary
- Assessment Item Listing
- Assessment Checklists and Rubrics
- Test Generator

sciLINKS

sciLINKS numbers throughout the text take you and your students to some of the best on-line resources available. Sites are constantly reviewed and updated by the National Science Teachers Association. Special "teacher only" sites are available to you once you register with the service.

go.hrw.com

To access Holt, Rinehart and Winston Web resources, use the home page codes for each level found on page 1 of the Pupil's Editions. The codes shown on the Chapter Organizers for each chapter in the Annotated Teacher's Edition take you to chapter-specific resources.

Smithsonian Institution

Find lesson plans, activities, interviews, virtual exhibits, and just general information on a wide variety of topics relevant to middle school science.

CNNfyi.com

Find the latest in late-breaking science news for students. Featured news stories are supported with lesson plans and activities.

CNN Presents Science in the News Video Library

Bring relevant science news stories into the classroom. Each video comes with a Teacher's Guide and set of Critical Thinking Worksheets that develop listening and media analysis skills. Tapes in the series include:

- Eye on the Environment
- Multicultural Connections
- Scientists in Action
- Science, Technology & Society

Guided Reading Audio CD Program

Students can listen to a direct read of each chapter and follow along in the text. Use the program as a content bridge for struggling readers and students for whom English is not their native language.

Interactive Explorations CD-ROM

Turn a computer into a virtual laboratory. Students act as lab assistants helping Dr. Crystal Labcoat solve real-world problems. Activities develop students' inquiry, analysis, and decision-making skills.

Interactive Science Encyclopedia CD-ROM

Give your students access to more than 3,000 cross-referenced scientific definitions, in-depth articles, science fair project ideas, activities, and more.

ADDITIONAL COMPONENTS

Holt Anthology of Science Fiction

Science Fiction features in the Pupil's Edition preview the stories found in the anthology. Each story begins with a Reading Prep guide and closes with Think About It questions.

Professional Reference for Teachers

Articles written by leading educators help you learn more about the National Science Education Standards, block scheduling, classroom management techniques, and more. A bibliography of professional references is included.

Holt Science Posters

Seven wall posters highlight interesting topics, such as the Physics of Sports, or useful reference material, such as the Scientific Method.

Holt Science Skills Workshop: Reading in the Content Area

Use a variety of in-depth skills exercises to help students learn to read science materials strategically.

Key	
	These materials are blackline masters.
■	All titles shown in green are found in the *Teaching Resources* booklets for each course.

Science & Math Skills Worksheets

The *Holt Science and Technology* program helps you meet the needs of a wide variety of students, regardless of their skill level. The following pages provide examples of the worksheets available to improve your students' science and math skills, whether they already have a strong science and math background or are weak in these areas. Samples of assessment checklists and rubrics are also provided.

In addition to the skills worksheets represented here, *Holt Science and Technology* provides a variety of worksheets that are correlated directly with each chapter of the program. Representations of these worksheets are found at the beginning of each chapter in this Annotated Teacher's Edition. Specific worksheets related to each chapter are listed in the Chapter Organizer. Worksheets and transparencies are found in the softcover *Teaching Resources* for each course.

Many worksheets are also available on the HRW Web site. The address is **go.hrw.com.**

Science Skills Worksheets: Thinking Skills

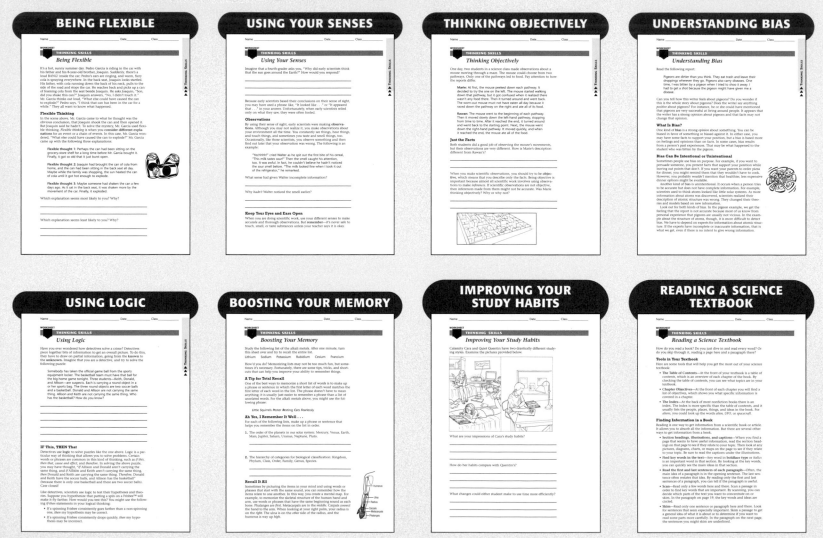

BEING FLEXIBLE

USING YOUR SENSES

THINKING OBJECTIVELY

UNDERSTANDING BIAS

USING LOGIC

BOOSTING YOUR MEMORY

IMPROVING YOUR STUDY HABITS

READING A SCIENCE TEXTBOOK

Science Skills Worksheets: Experimenting Skills

SAFETY RULES!

DOING A LAB WRITE-UP

UNDERSTANDING VARIABLES

WORKING WITH HYPOTHESES

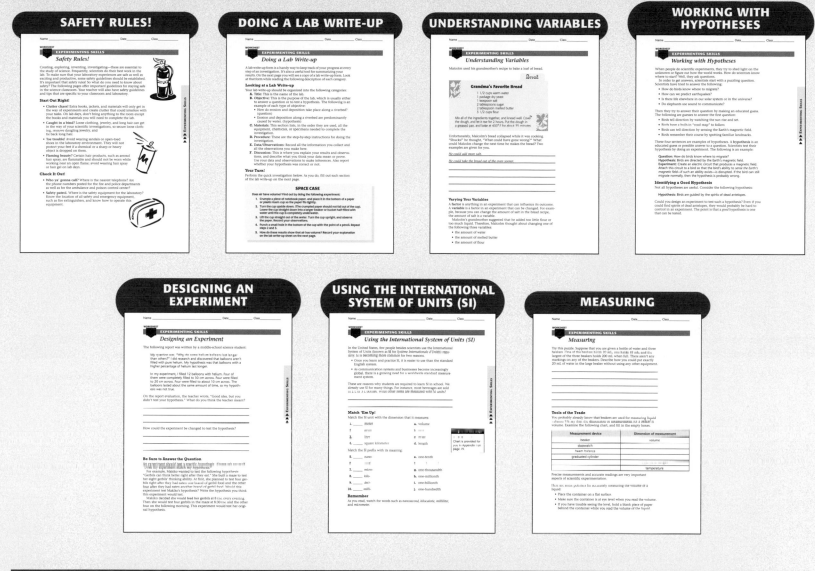

DESIGNING AN EXPERIMENT

USING THE INTERNATIONAL SYSTEM OF UNITS (SI)

MEASURING

Science Skills Worksheets: Researching Skills

CHOOSING YOUR TOPIC

ORGANIZING YOUR RESEARCH

FINDING USEFUL SOURCES

RESEARCHING ON THE WEB

Science & Math Skills Worksheets   **T17**

Science & Math Skills Worksheets (continued)

Science Skills Worksheets: Researching Skills (continued)

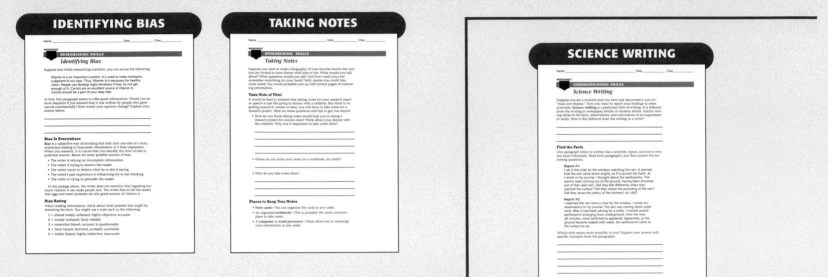

Science Skills Worksheets: Communicating Skills

SCIENCE DRAWING

USING MODELS TO COMMUNICATE

INTRODUCTION TO GRAPHS

GRASPING GRAPHING

INTERPRETING YOUR DATA

RECOGNIZING BIAS IN GRAPHS

MAKING DATA MEANINGFUL

HINTS FOR ORAL PRESENTATIONS

Math Skills for Science

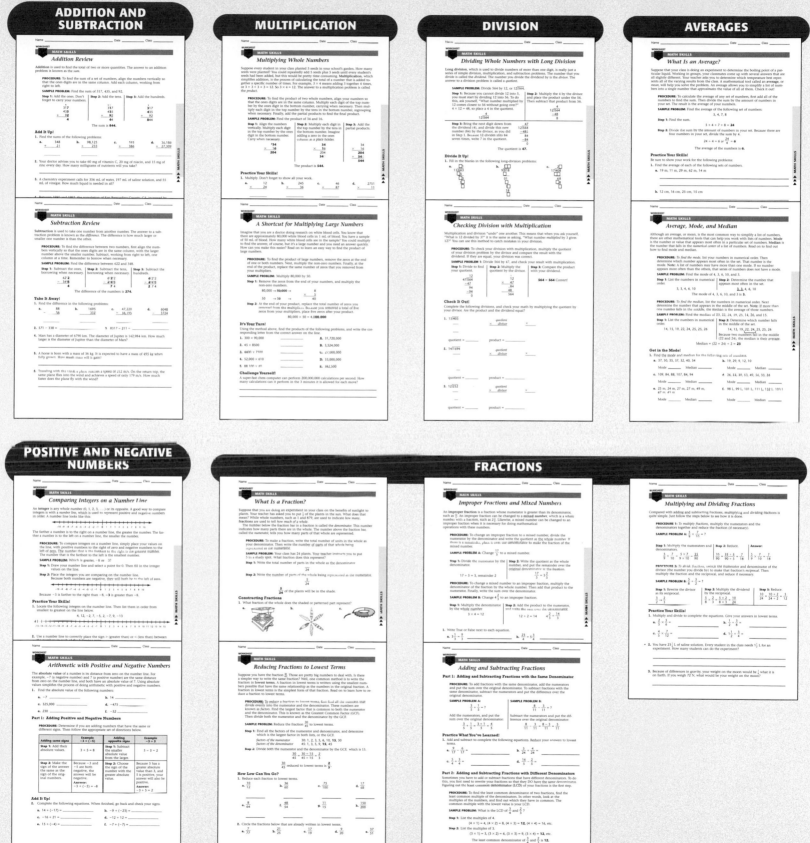

Math Skills for Science (continued)

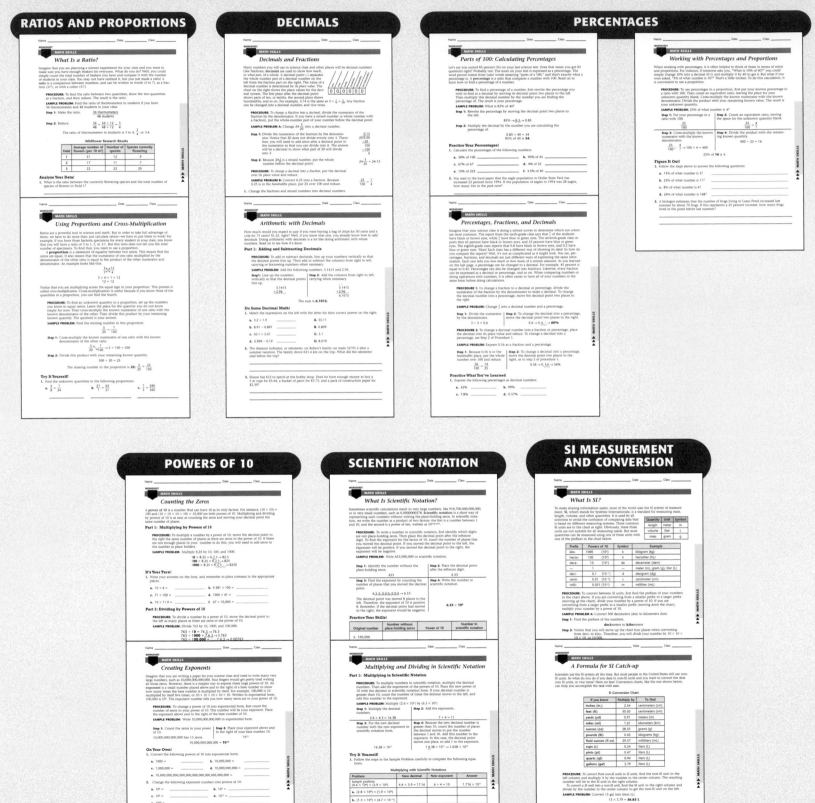

Math Skills for Science (continued)

GEOMETRY

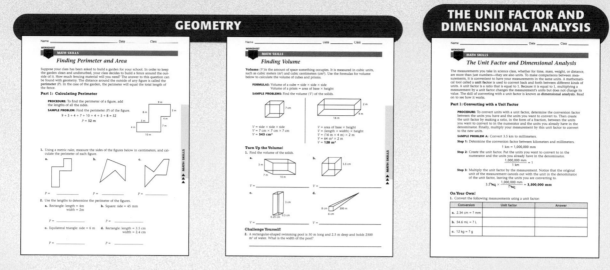

THE UNIT FACTOR AND DIMENSIONAL ANALYSIS

MATH IN SCIENCE: INTEGRATED SCIENCE

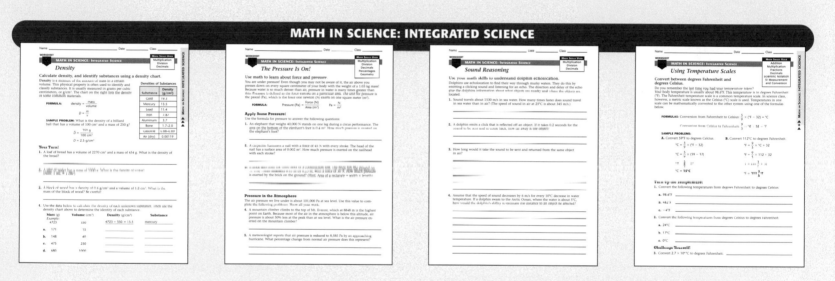

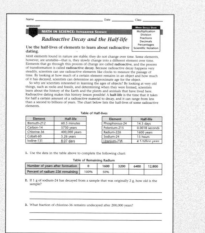

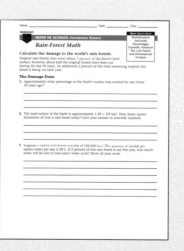

Science & Math Skills Worksheets (continued)

Math Skills for Science (continued)

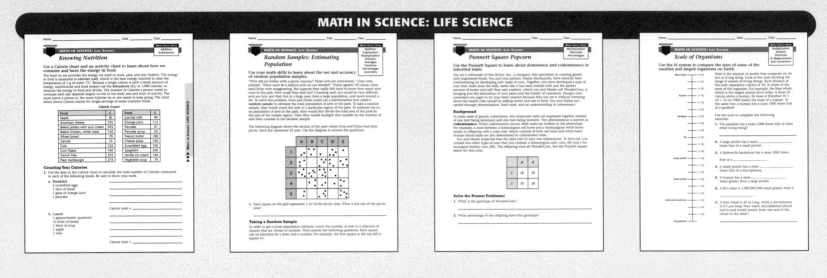

MATH IN SCIENCE: LIFE SCIENCE

Assessment Checklist & Rubrics

The following is just a sample of over 50 checklists and rubrics contained in this booklet.

HOLT SCIENCE & TECHNOLOGY

LIFE SCIENCE
NATIONAL SCIENCE EDUCATION STANDARDS CORRELATIONS

The following lists show the chapter correlation of *Holt Science and Technology: Cells, Heredity, and Classification* with the *National Science Education Standards* (grades 5-8)

UNIFYING CONCEPTS AND PROCESSES

Standard	Chapter Correlation	
Systems, order, and organization Code: UCP 1	Chapter 1	1.1, 1.3
	Chapter 2	2.1, 2.2
	Chapter 3	3.1
	Chapter 4	4.2
	Chapter 6	6.1, 6.2
	Chapter 7	7.1
Evidence, models, and explanation Code: UCP 2	Chapter 1	1.1, 1.2, 1.3
	Chapter 2	2.1
	Chapter 3	3.1, 3.2
	Chapter 4	4.1, 4.2
	Chapter 5	5.1, 5.2, 5.3
	Chapter 6	6.1, 6.3
Change, constancy, and measurement Code: UCP 3	Chapter 1	1.2, 1.3
	Chapter 2	2.1, 2.2
	Chapter 5	5.1, 5.2, 5.3
	Chapter 6	6.1, 6.2
Evolution and equilibrium Code: UCP 4	Chapter 1	1.2, 1.3
	Chapter 2	2.1, 2.2
	Chapter 5	5.1, 5.2
	Chapter 6	6.1
Form and function Code: UCP 5	Chapter 1	1.1, 1.2, 1.3
	Chapter 2	2.2
	Chapter 4	4.1
	Chapter 5	5.1, 5.2
	Chapter 6	6.3
	Chapter 7	7.2

SCIENCE AS INQUIRY

Standard	Chapter Correlation	
Abilities necessary to do scientific inquiry Code: SAI 1	Chapter 1	1.2, 1.3
	Chapter 2	2.1, 2.2, 2.3
	Chapter 3	3.1, 3.2
	Chapter 4	4.1, 4.2
	Chapter 5	5.1, 5.2, 5.3
	Chapter 6	6.1
	Chapter 7	7.1, 7.2
Understandings about scientific inquiry Code: SAI 2	Chapter 1	1.2
	Chapter 2	2.2
	Chapter 3	3.1
	Chapter 4	4.1, 4.2
	Chapter 5	5.1, 5.2
	Chapter 6	6.1, 6.3
	Chapter 7	7.1

SCIENCE & TECHNOLOGY

Standard	Chapter Correlation	
Abilities of technological design Code: ST 1	Chapter 3	3.1
	Chapter 4	4.1
Understandings about science and technology Code: ST 2	Chapter 1	1.2, 1.3
	Chapter 2	2.2
	Chapter 4	4.1, 4.2
	Chapter 5	5.2

SCIENCE IN PERSONAL AND SOCIAL PERSPECTIVES

Standard	Chapter Correlation	
Personal health Code: SPSP 1	Chapter 2	2.2
	Chapter 3	3.1
Populations, resources, and environments Code: SPSP 2	Chapter 5	5.2
Natural hazards Code: SPSP 3	Chapter 6	6.1, 6.2
Risks and benefits Code: SPSP 4	Chapter 1	1.3
	Chapter 2	2.2
	Chapter 4	4.1
Science and technology in society Code: SPSP 5	Chapter 1	1.2, 1.3
	Chapter 2	2.2
	Chapter 3	3.1, 3.2
	Chapter 4	4.1, 4.2
	Chapter 5	5.2

HISTORY AND NATURE OF SCIENCE

Standard	Chapter Correlation	
Science as a human endeavor Code: HNS 1	Chapter 1	1.2, 1.3
	Chapter 4	4.1
	Chapter 5	5.2
	Chapter 6	6.1
	Chapter 7	7.1, 7.2
Nature of science Code: HNS 2	Chapter 1	1.2
	Chapter 3	3.1, 3.2
	Chapter 4	4.1
	Chapter 5	5.1, 5.2, 5.3
	Chapter 6	6.3
	Chapter 7	7.1, 7.2
History of science Code: HNS 3	Chapter 1	1.2, 1.3
	Chapter 3	3.1, 3.2
	Chapter 4	4.1
	Chapter 5	5.2
	Chapter 6	6.1, 6.3
	Chapter 7	7.1

LIFE SCIENCE
NATIONAL SCIENCE EDUCATION CONTENT STANDARDS

STRUCTURE AND FUNCTION IN LIVING SYSTEMS

Standard	Chapter Correlation	
Living systems at all levels of organization demonstrate the complementary nature of structure and function. Important levels of organization for structure and function include cells, organs, tissues, organ systems, whole organisms, and ecosystems. Code: LS 1a	**Chapter 1** **Chapter 4** **Chapter 6**	1.1, 1.2, 1.3 4.1 6.3
All organisms are composed of cells—the fundamental unit of life. Most organisms are single cells; other organisms, including humans, are multicellular. Code: LS 1b	**Chapter 1** **Chapter 6** **Chapter 7**	1.1, 1.2 6.2 7.2
Cells carry on the many functions needed to sustain life. They grow and divide, thereby producing more cells. This requires that they take in nutrients, which they use to provide energy for the work that cells do and to make the materials that a cell or an organism needs. Code: LS 1c	**Chapter 1** **Chapter 2** **Chapter 3**	1.1, 1.2, 1.3 2.1, 2.2, 2.3 3.2
Specialized cells perform specialized functions in multicellular organisms. Groups of specialized cells co-operate to form a tissue, such as a muscle. Different tissues are in turn grouped together and form larger functional units, called organs. Each type of cell, tissue, and organ has a distinct structure and set of functions that serve the organism as a whole. Code: LS 1d	**Chapter 1** **Chapter 3**	1.1, 1.2 3.2
The human organism has systems for digestion, respiration, reproduction, circulation, excretion, movement, control and coordination, and protection from disease. These systems interact with one another. Code: LS 1e	**Chapter 1**	1.1
Disease is a breakdown in structures or functions of an organism. Some diseases are the result of intrinsic failures of the system. Others are the result of damage by infection by other organisms. Code: LS 1f	**Chapter 3** **Chapter 4** **Chapter 7**	3.1 4.2 7.2

REPRODUCTION AND HEREDITY

Standard	Chapter Correlation	
Reproduction is a characteristic of all living systems; because no individual organism lives forever, reproduction is essential to the continuation of every species. Some organisms reproduce asexually. Others reproduce sexually. Code: LS 2a	**Chapter 7**	7.2
In many species, including humans, females produce eggs and males produce sperm. Plants also reproduce sexually—the egg and sperm are produced in the flowers of flowering plants. An egg and sperm unite to begin development of a new individual. The individual receives genetic information from its mother (via the egg) and its father (via the sperm). Sexually produced offspring never are identical to either of their parents. Code: LS 2b	**Chapter 3** **Chapter 4**	3.1, 3.2 4.2
Every organism requires a set of instructions for specifying its traits. Heredity is the passage of these instructions from one generation to another. Code: LS 2c	**Chapter 1** **Chapter 3** **Chapter 4** **Chapter 5** **Chapter 7**	1.2 3.1, 3.2 4.1, 4.2 5.2, 5.3 7.2
Hereditary information is contained in the genes, located in the chromosomes of each cell. Each gene carries a single unit of information. An inherited trait of an individual can be determined by one or by many genes, and a single gene can influence more than one trait. A human cell contains many thousands of different genes. Code: LS 2d	**Chapter 2** **Chapter 3** **Chapter 4**	2.3 3.1, 3.2 4.1, 4.2

REPRODUCTION AND HEREDITY (CONTINUED)

Standard	Chapter Correlation
The characteristics of an organism can be described in terms of a combination of traits. Some traits are inherited and others result from interactions with the environment. Code: LS 2e	**Chapter 3** 3.1 **Chapter 4** 4.1, 4.2

REGULATION AND BEHAVIOR

Standard	Chapter Correlation
All organisms must be able to obtain and use resources, grow, reproduce, and maintain stable internal conditions while living in a constantly changing external environment. Code: LS 3a	**Chapter 1** 1.3 **Chapter 5** 5.1, 5.2 **Chapter 6** 6.1, 6.2
Regulation of an organism's internal environment involves sensing the internal environment and changing physiological activities to keep conditions within the range required to survive. Code: LS 3b	**Chapter 1** 1.2
An organism's behavior evolves through adaptation to its environment. How a species moves, obtains food, reproduces, and responds to danger are based in the species' evolutionary history. Code: LS 3d	**Chapter 5** 5.1, 5.2, 5.3

POPULATIONS AND ECOSYSTEMS

Standard	Chapter Correlation
A population consists of all individuals of a species that occur together at a given place and time. All populations living together and the physical factors with which they interact compose an ecosystem. Code: LS 4a	**Chapter 1** 1.1
Populations of organisms can be categorized by the functions they serve in an ecosystem. Plants and some microorganisms are producers—they make their own food. All animals, including humans, are consumers, which obtain food by eating other organisms. Decomposers, primarily bacteria and fungi, are consumers that use waste materials and dead organisms for food. Food webs identify the relationships among producers, consumers, and decomposers in an ecosystem. Code: LS 4b	**Chapter 6** 6.2
For ecosystems, the major source of energy is sunlight. Energy entering ecosystems as sunlight is transferred by producers into chemical energy through photosynthesis. That energy then passes from organism to organism in food webs. Code: LS 4c	**Chapter 2** 2.2 **Chapter 6** 6.2

DIVERSITY AND ADAPTATIONS OF ORGANISMS

Standard	Chapter Correlation
Millions of species of animals, plants, and microorganisms are alive today. Although different species might look dissimilar, the unity among organisms becomes apparent from an analysis of internal structures, the similarity of their chemical processes, and the evidence of common ancestry. Code: LS 5a	**Chapter 1** 1.2, 1.3 **Chapter 4** 4.1 **Chapter 5** 5.1 **Chapter 8** 8.3 **Chapter 9** 9.1
Biological evolution accounts for the diversity of species developed through gradual processes over many generations. Species acquire many of their unique characteristics through biological adaptation, which involves the selection of naturally occurring variations in populations. Biological adaptations include changes in structures, behaviors, or physiology that enhance survival and reproductive success in a particular environment. Code: LS 5b	**Chapter 1** 1.3 **Chapter 4** 4.2 **Chapter 5** 5.1, 5.2, 5.3 **Chapter 9** 9.2
Extinction of a species occurs when the environment changes and the adaptive characteristics of a species are insufficient to allow its survival. Fossils indicate that many organisms that lived long ago are extinct. Extinction of species is common; most of the species that have lived on Earth no longer exist. Code: LS 5c	**Chapter 5** 5.1, 5.2, 5.3 **Chapter 8** 8.1, 8.2

Master Materials List

For added convenience, Science Kit® provides materials-ordering software on CD-ROM designed specifically for *Holt Science and Technology*. Using this software, you can order complete kits or individual items, quickly and efficiently.

CONSUMABLE MATERIALS	AMOUNT	PAGE
Algae	1 sample	24
Box, large	3	55
Carton, egg	2	115
Charcoal briquette	1	79
Chocolate, candy-coated	75	191
Clay, modeling	2 sticks	103
Cup, plastic	2	33
Cup, plastic	6	186
Elodea sprig	1	3
Gumdrop, black	10	70
Gumdrop, green	10	70
Leaf, fresh	1	103
Marker, various colors	1 pack	25
Marshmallow, large	15	70
Marshmallow, small, colored	50	190
Marshmallow, small, white	50	190
Paper, adding-machine	1 roll	131
Paper, construction, various colors	5 sheets	94
Paper, tracing	1 sheet	79
Paper, white	1 sheet	79, 94
Paper, white	2 sheets	25

CONSUMABLE MATERIALS	AMOUNT	PAGE
Pencil, assorted, colored	4	25
Pipe cleaner	3	70
Plaster of Paris	300 mL	103
Plastic wrap, clear, approx. 1 x 2 ft	1 sheet	34
Plate, paper	1	103
Poster board, colored	1	94
Poster board, white	1	94, 184
Potato	3	186
Rice	1/4 lb	115
Salt	1 box	186
Shell	1	103
Sugar, granulated	1/4 cup	33
Swab, cotton	1	14
Tape, masking	25–50 cm	62, 145, 159
Tape, transparent	4 cm	79, 184
Toothpick, green	6	70
Toothpick, red	6	70
Water, distilled	4 L	186
Yeast, active, dry-baking	1 packet	33
Yogurt	1 cup	14

Nonconsumable Equipment	Amount	Page
Bag, large, paper	1	94
Bag, medium, paper or plastic	14	70
Bead, set of 3 different colors	5 sets	34
Bowl, large, plastic	1	34
Box, sand, 2 x 3 m	1	122
Cloth, colored, 50 x 50 cm	1	190
Container, plastic with lid	1	150
Coverslip, plastic	1	3, 14, 24
Eyedropper, plastic	1	24
Gloves, various styles	5 pairs	55
Hat, various styles	5	55
Magnifying lens	1	79
Meterstick	1	122
Microscope, compound	1	3, 14, 24
Microscope, slide, plastic	1	3, 14, 24
Penny	100	150
Pin, map	15	70
Pushpin, blue	10	70

Nonconsumable Equipment	Amount	Page
Pushpin, green	10	70
Quarter	2	62
Ruler, metric	1	33, 122
Sand	approx. 20 lb	122
Sand, fine	1 lb	184
Scale (or balance)	1	184
Scale, bathroom	1	46
Scarf, various styles	5	55
Scissors	1	70, 94, 184
Shoe, various styles	10	159
Stirring rod	1	33
Stopwatch	1	190
Tape measure	1	46
Test tube	2	33
Test-tube rack	1	33
Tweezers	1	3

Answers to Concept Mapping Questions

The following pages contain sample answers to all of the concept mapping questions that appear in the Chapter Reviews. Because there is more than one way to do a concept map, your students' answers may vary.

CHAPTER 1 Cells: The Basic Units of Life

CHAPTER 2 The Cell in Action

CHAPTER 3 Heredity

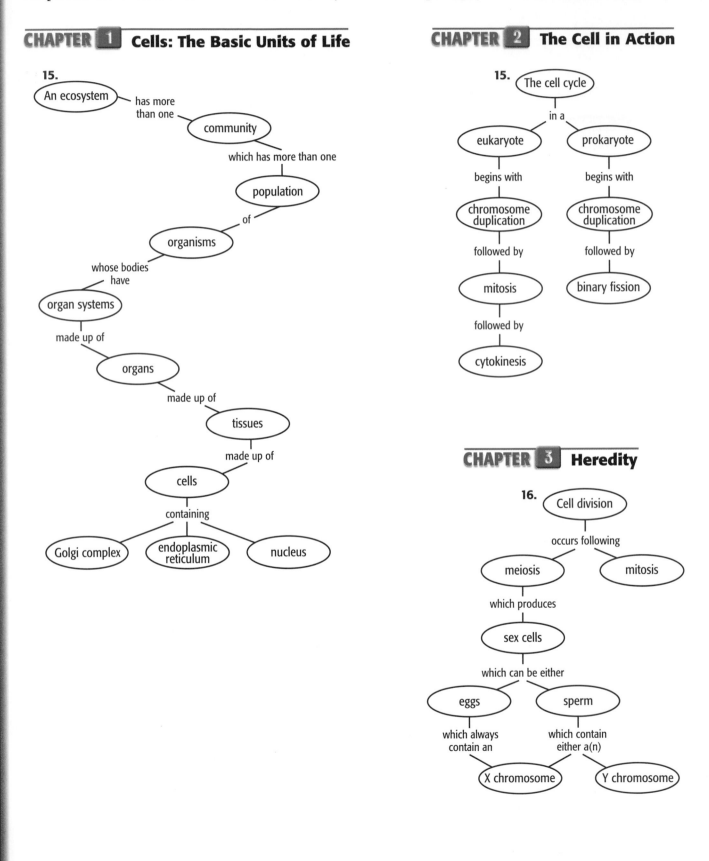

CHAPTER 4 Genes and Gene Technology

14.

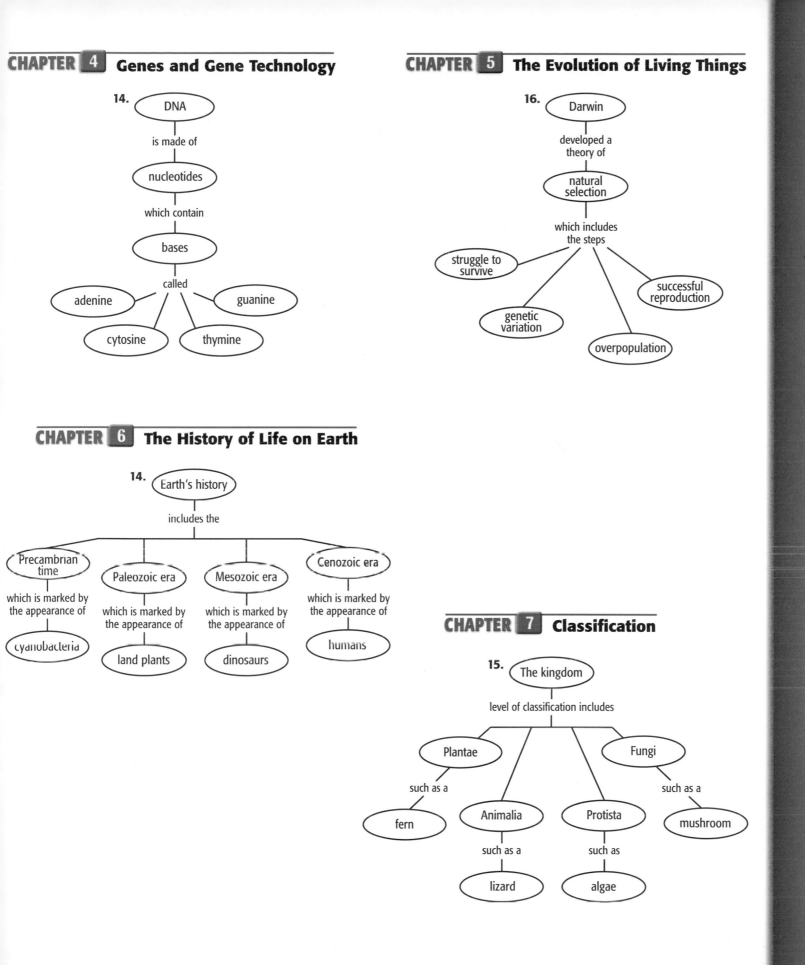

DNA
is made of
nucleotides
which contain
bases
called
adenine guanine
cytosine thymine

CHAPTER 5 The Evolution of Living Things

16.

Darwin
developed a theory of
natural selection
which includes the steps
struggle to survive
genetic variation
overpopulation
successful reproduction

CHAPTER 6 The History of Life on Earth

14.

Earth's history
includes the
Precambrian time
Paleozoic era
Mesozoic era
Cenozoic era

which is marked by the appearance of
cyanobacteria

which is marked by the appearance of
land plants

which is marked by the appearance of
dinosaurs

which is marked by the appearance of
humans

CHAPTER 7 Classification

15.

The kingdom
level of classification includes
Plantae
Animalia
Protista
Fungi

such as a
fern

such as a
lizard

such as
algae

such as a
mushroom

To the Student

This book was created to make your science experience interesting, exciting, and fun!

Go for It!
Science is a process of discovery, a trek into the unknown. The skills you develop using *Holt Science & Technology*—such as observing, experimenting, and explaining observations and ideas—are the skills you will need for the future. There is a universe of exploration and discovery awaiting those who accept the challenges of science.

Science & Technology
You see the interaction between science and technology every day. Science makes technology possible. On the other hand, some of the products of technology, such as computers, are used to make further scientific discoveries. In fact, much of the scientific work that is done today has become so technically complicated and expensive that no one person can do it entirely alone. But make no mistake, the creative ideas for even the most highly technical and expensive scientific work still come from individuals.

Activities and Labs
The activities and labs in this book will allow you to make some basic but important scientific discoveries on your own. You can even do some exploring on your own at home! Here's your chance to use your imagination and curiosity as you investigate your world.

Keep a ScienceLog

In this book, you will be asked to keep a type of journal called a ScienceLog to record your thoughts, observations, experiments, and conclusions. As you develop your ScienceLog, you will see your own ideas taking shape over time. You'll have a written record of how your ideas have changed as you learn about and explore interesting topics in science.

Know "What You'll Do"

The "What You'll Do" list at the beginning of each section is your built-in guide to what you need to learn in each chapter. When you can answer the questions in the Section Review and Chapter Review, you know you are ready for a test.

Check Out the Internet

You will see this *sciLINKS* logo throughout the book. You'll be using *sci*LINKS as your gateway to the Internet. Once you log on to *sci*LINKS using your computer's Internet link, type in the *sci*LINKS address. When asked for the keyword code, type in the keyword for that topic. A wealth of resources is now at your disposal to help you learn more about that topic.

In addition to *sci*LINKS you can log on to some other great resources to go with your text. The addresses shown below will take you to the home page of each site.

---

internet connect

This textbook contains the following on-line resources to help you make the most of your science experience.

Visit **go.hrw.com** for extra help and study aids matched to your textbook. Just type in the keyword HG2 HOME.

*sci*LINKS
NSTA

Visit **www.scilinks.org** to find resources specific to topics in your textbook. Keywords appear throughout your book to take you further.

 Smithsonian Institution®
Internet Connections

Visit **www.si.edu/hrw** for specifically chosen on-line materials from one of our nation's premier science museums.

Visit **www.cnnfyi.com** for late-breaking news and current events stories selected just for you.

Chapter Organizer

CHAPTER ORGANIZATION	TIME MINUTES	OBJECTIVES	LABS, INVESTIGATIONS, AND DEMONSTRATIONS
Chapter Opener pp. 2–3	45	National Standards: UCP 4, HNS 1, LS 1b, 5b	**Start-Up Activity,** What Are Plants Made Of? p. 3
Section 1 **Organization of Life**	90	▶ Explain how life is organized, from a single cell to an ecosystem. ▶ Describe the difference between unicellular organisms and multicellular organisms. UCP 1, 2, 5, LS 1a–1e, 4a	
Section 2 **The Discovery of Cells**	90	▶ State the parts of the cell theory. ▶ Explain why cells are so small. ▶ Calculate a cell's surface-to-volume ratio. ▶ List the advantages of being multicellular. ▶ Explain the difference between prokaryotic cells and eukaryotic cells. UCP 3–5, SAI 1, 2, ST 2, SPSP 5, HNS 1–3, LS 1a–1d, 2c, 3b, 5a; Labs UCP 2, 3, SAI 1	**Demonstration,** Membranes, p. 11 in ATE **QuickLab,** Do Bacteria Taste Good? p. 14 **Making Models,** Elephant-Sized Amoebas? p. 184 **Datasheets for LabBook,** Elephant-Sized Amoebas?
Section 3 **Eukaryotic Cells: The Inside Story**	90	▶ Explain the function of each part of a eukaryotic cell. ▶ Describe the differences between animal cells and plant cells. UCP 2–5, ST 2, SPSP 4, 5, HNS 1, 3, LS 1a, 1c, 3a, 5a, 5b; Labs UCP 1, SAI 1	**Demonstration,** Cell Walls, p. 17 in ATE **Discovery Lab,** Cells Alive! p. 24 **Datasheets for LabBook,** Cells Alive! **Skill Builder,** Name That Part! p. 25 **Datasheets for LabBook,** Name That Part! **Labs You Can Eat,** The Incredible Edible Cell **Whiz-Bang Demonstrations,** Grand Strand **Long-Term Projects & Research Ideas,** Ewe Again, Dolly?

See page **T23** *for a complete correlation of this book with the*

NATIONAL SCIENCE EDUCATION STANDARDS.

TECHNOLOGY RESOURCES

Guided Reading Audio CD English or Spanish, Chapter 1

One-Stop Planner CD-ROM with Test Generator

 **CNN.** **Science, Technology & Society,** Flavor Cells, Segment 3
 Treating Pets with Laser Light, Segment 4

Chapter 1 • Cells: The Basic Units of Life

CLASSROOM WORKSHEETS, TRANSPARENCIES, AND RESOURCES	SCIENCE INTEGRATION AND CONNECTIONS	REVIEW AND ASSESSMENT
Directed Reading Worksheet **Science Puzzlers, Twisters & Teasers**		
Directed Reading Worksheet, Section 1 **Transparency 7,** From Cell to Organism **Reinforcement Worksheet,** An Ecosystem	**Chemistry Connection,** p. 6 **Real-World Connection,** p. 7 in ATE **Connect to Earth Science,** p. 7 in ATE	**Homework,** p. 5 in ATE **Section Review,** p. 8 **Quiz,** p. 8 in ATE **Alternative Assessment,** p. 8 in ATE
Directed Reading Worksheet, Section 2 **Transparency 8,** Surface-to-Volume Ratio **Math Skills for Science Worksheet,** What Is a Ratio? **Math Skills for Science Worksheet,** Finding Perimeter and Area **Math Skills for Science Worksheet,** Finding Volume	**Connect to Astronomy,** p. 10 in ATE **Real-World Connection,** p. 10 in ATE **Math and More,** Surface Area, p. 12 in ATE **MathBreak,** Surface-to-Volume Ratio, p. 13 **Apply,** p. 13 **Connect to Earth Science,** p. 13 in ATE **Connect to Earth Science,** p. 14 in ATE **Health Watch:** The Scrape of the Future, p. 31	**Self-Check,** p. 11 **Self-Check,** p. 14 **Section Review,** p. 15 **Quiz,** p. 15 in ATE **Alternative Assessment,** p. 15 in ATE
Directed Reading Worksheet, Section 3 **Transparency 260,** Structural Formulas **Critical Thinking Worksheet,** Cellular Construction **Transparency 9,** Organelles and Their Functions **Transparency 10,** Comparing Animal and Plant Cells **Reinforcement Worksheet,** Building a Eukaryotic Cell	**Connect to Physical Science,** p. 18 in ATE **Multicultural Connection,** p. 20 in ATE **Multicultural Connection,** p. 21 in ATE **Across the Sciences:** Battling Cancer with Pigs' Blood and Laser Light, p. 30	**Homework,** pp. 17, 19, 22 in ATE **Self-Check,** p. 18 **Section Review,** p. 23 **Quiz,** p. 23 in ATE **Alternative Assessment,** p. 23 in ATE

END-OF-CHAPTER REVIEW AND ASSESSMENT

Chapter Review in Study Guide
Vocabulary and Notes in Study Guide
Chapter Tests with Performance-Based Assessment, Chapter 1 Test
Chapter Tests with Performance-Based Assessment, Performance-Based Assessment 1
Concept Mapping Transparency 3

---

internet connect

 Holt, Rinehart and Winston On-line Resources
go.hrw.com

For worksheets and other teaching aids related to this chapter, visit the HRW Web site and type in the keyword: **HSTCEL**

SCiLINKS **NSTA** **National Science Teachers Association**
www.scilinks.org

Encourage students to use the _sci_LINKS numbers listed in the internet connect boxes to access information and resources on the **NSTA** Web Site.

Chapter Resources & Worksheets

Visual Resources

TEACHING TRANSPARENCIES

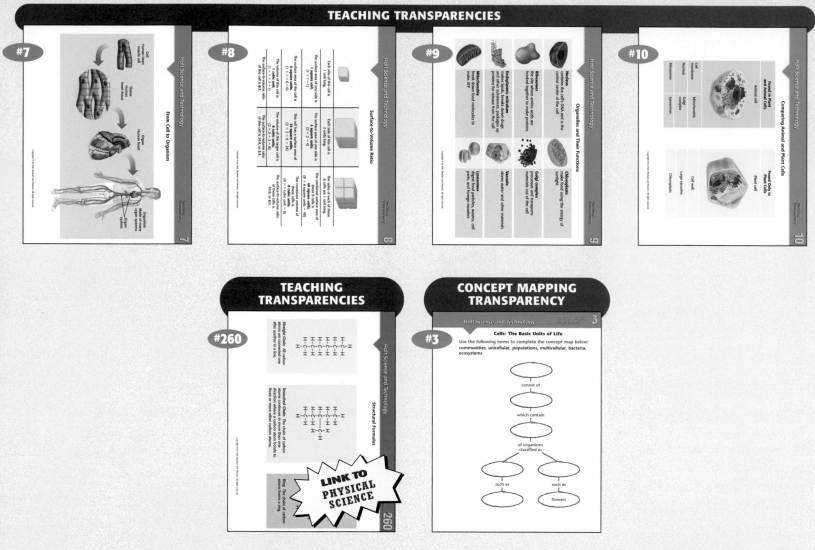

TEACHING TRANSPARENCIES

CONCEPT MAPPING TRANSPARENCY

Meeting Individual Needs

DIRECTED READING

REINFORCEMENT & VOCABULARY REVIEW

SCIENCE PUZZLERS, TWISTERS & TEASERS

Review & Assessment

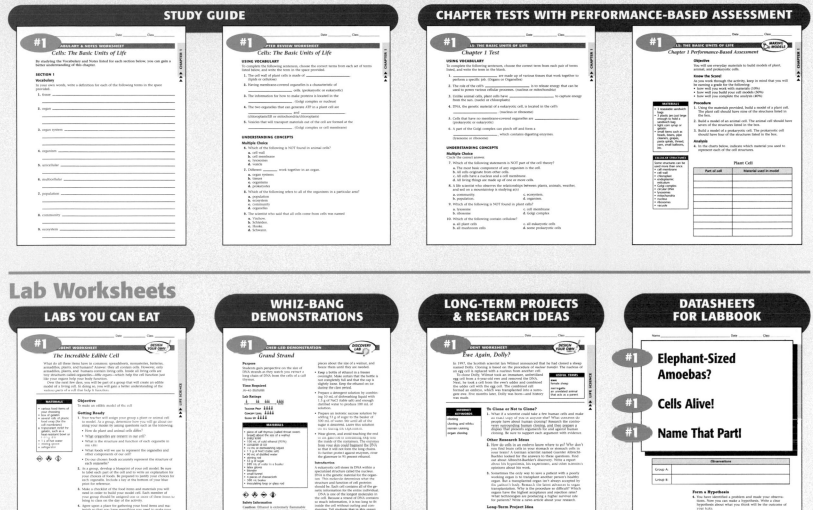

STUDY GUIDE

CHAPTER TESTS WITH PERFORMANCE-BASED ASSESSMENT

Lab Worksheets

LABS YOU CAN EAT

WHIZ-BANG DEMONSTRATIONS

LONG-TERM PROJECTS & RESEARCH IDEAS

DATASHEETS FOR LABBOOK

Applications & Extensions

CRITICAL THINKING & PROBLEM SOLVING

SCIENCE TECHNOLOGY

Chapter Background

SECTION 1

Organization of Life

▶ In a Heartbeat

The heart will function properly only if the cells that form the connective tissue and muscle perform their jobs in coordination. Scientists can use an enzyme to dissolve an embryonic heart into its individual cells. When placed in a dish, these cells, called myocytes, will continue to beat, although out of sync with each other. After a couple of days, sheets of interconnected cells form and they beat in unison. Why? Openings develop between cells that touch, and their cytoplasms connect, allowing the cells to communicate directly with each other.

▶ Organs: Delicate Workhorses

The most frequently transplanted organ is the kidney, followed by the liver, heart, and lung. Most transplants must be done within a few hours after the organ is removed from a donor because organs are too delicate to survive current long-term storage procedures.

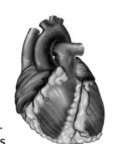

- Cryobiologists, scientists who study how life systems tolerate low temperatures, are studying the possibility of storing organs and organ systems at subfreezing temperatures. They are investigating the fluids that keep insects alive during subfreezing temperatures, hoping this knowledge can be applied to human organs.

IS THAT A FACT!

- ➤ In 1931, a doctor removed a patient's parathyroid glands in error. These glands control the amount of calcium in the blood, which in turn regulates the heart. As a last-ditch effort to save the patient, a cow's parathyroid glands were ground up and injected into the patient. The patient recuperated and lived another 30 years with similar treatments.

- ➤ Researchers are studying hypnosis as a weapon against cancer. Individuals with cancer are hypnotized to help them manage their pain. Data suggest that this treatment also helps patients live considerably longer.

SECTION 2

The Discovery of Cells

▶ Microtomy

The development of high-magnification microscopes required that the preparation of specimens for viewing also become more sophisticated. Microtomy used to refer only to specimen cutting because a microtome is the instrument used to slice tissue sections. Today microtomy refers collectively to the art of preparing specimens by any number of techniques. When microscopic organisms are viewed as wholemounts, they are preserved, stained, dried (alcohol removes the water), and made transparent with clove or cedar oil. Then the organism is mounted in a drop of resin on a glass slide and covered with a piece of glass only 0.005 mm thick.

▶ Physiology and the Cell Theory

The development of the cell theory aided research in other fields. In the mid-1800s, French physiologist Claude Bernard proposed that plants and animals are composed of sets of control mechanisms that work to maintain the internal conditions necessary for life. He recognized that a mammal can sustain a constant body temperature regardless of the outside temperature. Today we recognize this ability as homeostasis. But at the time no one knew what the "organized sets of control mechanisms" were. The discovery of cells, and how their many components function to sustain life in an organism, gave credence to Bernard's position.

IS THAT A FACT!

➤ Aeolid nudibranchs are mollusks that eat hydroids, small polyps that have protective stinging cells. The nudibranchs' digestive systems carefully sort out the hydroids' stinging cells and send them to the protective tentacles on their own backs.

SECTION 3

Eukaryotic Cells: The Inside Story

▶ "Protein" Therapy

As scientists delved deeper into the cell, they moved past the initial stages of merely identifying its structures to asking, "What do these organelles do?" and "How do they do it?" Decades of investigation have produced "gene therapy," which refers to the use of a cell's genetic material to cure disease. It might be more appropriate to call this rapidly expanding field of science "protein therapy."

• The gene can be thought of as a blueprint for the proteins essential to life. People with Duchenne's muscular dystrophy lack dystrophin, an essential muscle protein that maintains the structure of muscle cells. Researchers have been able to remove the harmful genetic components of a virus and replace them with the gene for dystrophin. Their plan is to inject the dystrophin gene (the gene that codes for the dystrophin protein) directly into the muscles of Duchenne's patients and trick the body into maintaining healthy muscle.

▶ Cell Scientists

Microbiologists study the characteristics of bacteria and other microorganisms to understand how they interact with people, plants, and animals. Virologists investigate viruses, which are active only inside a living cell. Mycologists study fungi, which include molds, and yeast. Environmental microbiologists inspect the water in rivers and lakes. Those in agriculture are concerned with organisms that affect soil quality.

▶ Mitochondrial Diseases

Mitochondrial diseases are a group of illnesses caused by malfunctioning mitochondria. The problem can be with either the genes of the mitochondria or the genes of the cell. Any activity or organ that requires energy is affected by these diseases. Because the brain requires huge amounts of energy to function, it often suffers in people who have a mitochondrial disease. Other commonly affected areas are muscles, including the heart; organs, such as the kidneys; and bone marrow.

▶ Cell Walls

Every culture in the world relies in some way on the cell walls of dead organisms. Materials such as thatch, reed, and wood are composed of cell walls that remain after an organism has died.

For background information about teaching strategies and issues, refer to the *Professional Reference for Teachers.*

CHAPTER 1

Cells: The Basic Units of Life

Pre-Reading Questions

Students may not know the answers to these questions before reading the chapter, so accept any reasonable response.

Suggested Answers

1. A cell is a membrane-covered structure that contains the items necessary to carry out life processes. Cells are found in all living things.

2. Cells allow life processes to occur. Cells are small because a large surface-to-volume ratio allows them to easily exchange food and wastes with the environment.

CHAPTER 1

Cells: The Basic Units of Life

Pre-Reading Questions

1. What is a cell, and where are cells found?

2. Why are there cells, and why are they so small?

TINY DEFENDERS

Invading bacteria have entered your body. These foreign cells are about to make you sick. But wait—your white blood cells come to the rescue! In this microscopic image, a white blood cell is reaching out its "arm" (called a *pseudopod*) to destroy a bacterium. In this chapter, you will learn about bacteria, blood cells, and other cells in your body.

2

⬛ internet**connect**

go.hrw.com
HRW On-line Resources
go.hrw.com
For worksheets and other teaching aids, visit the HRW Web site and type in the keyword: **HSTCEL**

SC*LINKS*
NSTA
www.scilinks.com
Use the *sci*LINKS numbers at the end of each chapter for additional resources on the **NSTA** Web site.

Smithsonian Institution®
www.si.edu/hrw
Visit the Smithsonian Institution Web site for related on-line resources.

CNNfyi.com
www.cnnfyi.com
Visit the CNN Web site for current events coverage and classroom resources.

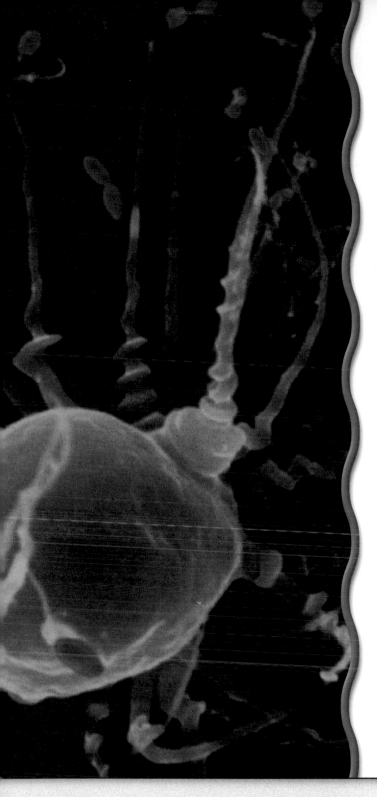

START-UP Activity

WHAT ARE PLANTS MADE OF?

All living things, including plants, are made of cells. What do plant cells look like? Do this activity to find out.

Procedure

1. Tear off a small leaf near the tip of an **Elodea sprig.**

2. Using **tweezers,** place the whole leaf in a drop of **water** on a **microscope slide.**

3. Place a **coverslip** on top of the water drop. Put one edge on the slide, then slowly lower the coverslip over the drop to prevent air bubbles.

4. Place the slide on your **microscope.** Find the cells. You may have to use the highest powered lens to see them.

5. Draw a picture of what you see.

Analysis

6. Describe the shape of the *Elodea* cells. Are they all the same?

7. Do you think your cells look like *Elodea* cells? Explain your answer.

3

START-UP Activity

WHAT ARE PLANTS MADE OF?

MATERIALS
FOR EACH STUDENT:
• water
• plastic microscope slide
• *Elodea* sprig
• tweezers
• plastic coverslip
• microscope

Safety Caution

Remind students to review all safety cautions and icons before beginning this lab activity.

Answers to START-UP Activity

6. Students should see that all the cells share similar structures but may not be exactly the same.

7. Accept all reasonable responses. Plant cells differ from human body cells, but they share many similar structures.

Focus

Organization of Life

In this section, students will learn that a cell is the smallest unit of life. In most multicellular organisms, groups of cells form tissues that compose organs. Two or more organs can interact to form an organ system. Students will also learn that organisms can be further organized into populations, communities, and ecosystems.

🎯 Bellringer

On the board or overhead viewer, write the following questions:

> Why can't you use your teeth to breathe? Why can't you use your arm muscles to digest food?

Have students answer these questions in their ScienceLog.

1 Motivate

ACTIVITY

Concept Mapping Divide the class into small groups. Provide each group with pictures of tissues, organs, and organ systems. Have the students arrange the pictures into concept maps. Encourage them to notice unusual relationships between organs. For example, the stomach and the heart may seem very different, but both are made of muscle tissue, and both function by holding and moving substances through their cavities.

Terms to Learn

tissue	multicellular
organ	population
organ system	community
organism	ecosystem
unicellular	

What You'll Do

◆ Explain how life is organized, from a single cell to an ecosystem.
◆ Describe the difference between unicellular organisms and multicellular organisms.

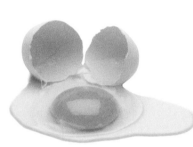

Figure 1 *The first cell of a chicken is one of the largest cells in the world.*

Directed Reading Worksheet Section 1

Organization of Life

Imagine that you are going on a trip to Mars. In your suitcase, you should pack everything you will need in order to survive. What would you pack? To start, you'd need food, oxygen, and water. And that's just the beginning. You would probably need a pretty big suitcase, wouldn't you? Actually, you have all of these items inside your body's cells. A cell is smaller than the period at the end of this sentence, yet a single cell has all the items necessary to carry out life's activities.

Every living thing has at least one cell. Many living things exist as a single cell, while others have trillions of cells. To get an idea of what a living thing with nearly 100 trillion cells looks like, just look in the mirror!

Cells: Starting Out Small

Most cells are too small to be seen without a microscope, but you might have one of the world's largest cells in your refrigerator. To find out what it is, see **Figure 1**. The first cell of a chicken is yellow with a tiny white dot in it, and it is surrounded by clear, jellylike fluid called egg white. The white dot divides over and over again to form a chick. The yellow yolk (from the first cell) and the egg white provide nutrients for the developing chick's cells. Like a chicken, you too began as a single egg cell. Look at **Figure 2** to see some of the early stages of your development.

Not all of your cells look or act the same. You have about 200 different kinds of cells, and each type is specialized to do a particular job. Some are bone cells, some are blood cells, and others are skin cells. When someone looks at all of those cells together, they see you.

Figure 2 *You began as a single cell. But after many cell divisions, you are now made of about 100 trillion cells.*

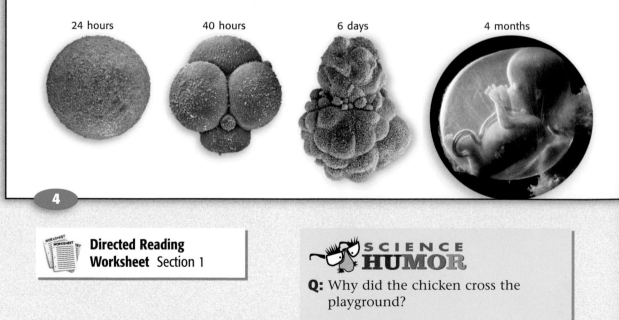

24 hours   40 hours   6 days   4 months

🐭 SCIENCE HUMOR

Q: Why did the chicken cross the playground?

A: to get to the other slide

Tissues: Cells Working in Teams

When you look closely at your clothes, you can see that threads have been grouped together (woven) to make cloth that has a function. In the same way, cells are grouped together to make a tissue that has a function. A **tissue** is a group of cells that work together to perform a specific job in the body. The material around and between the cells is also part of the tissue. Some examples of tissues in your body are shown in **Figure 3.**

Organs: Teams Working Together

When two or more tissues work together to perform a specific job, the group of tissues is called an **organ.** Some examples of organs are your stomach, intestines, heart, lungs, and skin. That's right; even your skin is an organ because it contains different kinds of tissues. To get a closer look, see **Figure 4.**

Plants also have different kinds of tissues that work together. A leaf is a plant organ that contains tissue that traps light energy to make food. Other examples of plant organs are stems and roots.

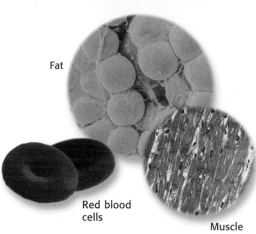
Fat

Red blood cells

Muscle

Figure 3 *Blood, fat, and muscle cells are just a few of the many cells that make tissues in your body.*

Figure 4 *The skin is the body's largest organ. An average-sized person's skin has a mass of about 4.5 kg.*

BRAIN FOOD

The part of the skin, hair, and nails that you can see is dead tissue! Isn't it strange to think that we put so much effort into making sure our dead cells look nice?

IS THAT A FACT!

In your lifetime you will shed about 18 kg (almost 40 lb) of dead skin.

2 Teach

DISCUSSION

Muscles Ask students to list all the ways they use their muscles. Responses will probably include walking, riding a bike, swimming, and throwing or kicking a ball. Explain that muscles are also involved in swallowing food (tongue), digestion (stomach), and blinking eyes (eyelids). Sometimes muscles act voluntarily (jumping), and sometimes they act involuntarily (the heart beating).

MISCONCEPTION /// ALERT \\\

Hair and fingernails grow out of specialized skin cells. Even though they grow continuously, both are composed of dead cells along with a protein called *keratin*. If they were alive and contained nerve cells, like the deep skin layers, haircuts and manicures would be quite painful.

Homework

Writing Not all living things have the same kinds of tissues and organs. Yet all must perform similar life processes. Have students research and compare the structures a fish uses to breathe with those that a human uses. Their report should also answer the question, "What parts of the human and fish respiratory systems are similar?" (Even though a fish has gills and a human has lungs, both have cells that exchange and transport oxygen and carbon dioxide.)

2 Teach, continued

MEETING INDIVIDUAL NEEDS

Learners Having Difficulty
To help students understand the levels of organization within an organism, instruct them to write the following headings on the board:

> Cell, Tissue, Organ, Organ system

Tell students to write these headings across the top of their paper and list at least two examples of each under the headings. Then ask students to share their information with their classmates.

USING THE FIGURE

Writing Have students write an expanded caption for **Figure 5.** They should read additional references for information describing the functions of the leaf, stem, and root organ systems. Then have them identify systems in the human body, if any, that perform similar functions.

RETEACHING

Writing A great way to learn something is to teach it to someone else. Have students write a letter to a friend explaining how cells, tissues, organs, and organ systems are all related.

PORTFOLIO

Answer to Activity
Accept all reasonable responses.

Chemistry
CONNECTION

On the surface of every person's cells are special proteins that act like identification cards. When a person gets an organ transplant, the cells of the new organ must have most of the same "ID cards" as the person's cells. If too many are different, the person's body will try to reject the new organ.

Activity

A school system's job is to educate students at all levels. The different schools (elementary, middle, and high school) are like the different organs within an organ system. Groups of teachers at each school work together to teach a specific grade level. If each group of teachers can be thought of as tissue, what would that make each individual teacher? What other examples can you use to represent the parts of an organ system? Explain your answer.

TRY at HOME

6

internet**connect**

SCI**LINKS**
NSTA

TOPIC: Organization of Life
GO TO: www.scilinks.org
*sci*LINKS **NUMBER:** HSTL055

Organ Systems: A Great Combination

Organs work together in groups to perform particular jobs. These groups are called **organ systems.** Each system has a specific job to do in the body. For example, your digestive system's job is to break down food into very small particles so it can be used by all of your body's cells. Your nervous system's job is to transmit information back and forth between your brain and the other parts of your body. Organ systems in plants include leaf systems, root systems, and stem systems.

Your body has several organ systems. The digestive system is shown in **Figure 5.** Each organ in the digestive system has a job to do. A particular organ is able to do its job because of the different tissues within it.

The organs in an organ system depend on each other. If any part of the system fails, the whole system is affected. And failure of one organ system can affect other organ systems. Just think of what would happen if your digestive system stopped converting food to energy. None of the other organ systems would have energy to function.

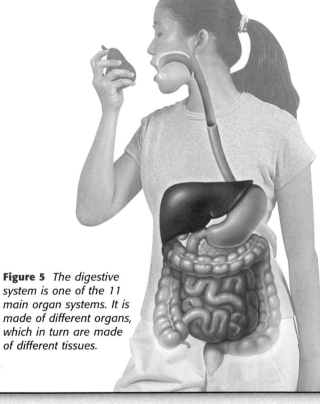

Figure 5 *The digestive system is one of the 11 main organ systems. It is made of different organs, which in turn are made of different tissues.*

IS THAT A FACT!

An elephant's trunk is constructed of 135 kg (300 lb) of hair, skin, connective tissue, nerves, and muscles. The muscle tissue is composed of 150,000 tiny subunits of muscle, each coordinated with the others to enable an elephant to drink, breathe, grab, and greet its friends.

Organisms: Independent Living

Anything that can live on its own is called an **organism.** All organisms are made up of at least one cell. If a single cell is living on its own, it is called a **unicellular** organism. Most unicellular organisms are so small that you need to use a microscope to see them. Some different kinds of unicellular organisms are shown in **Figure 6.**

You are a **multicellular** organism. This means that you can exist only as a group of cells and that most of your cells can survive only if they remain a part of your body. When you fall down on a sidewalk and scrape your knee, the cells you leave behind on the sidewalk are not able to live on their own. **Figure 7** shows how your cells work together to make a multicellular organism.

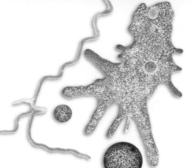

Figure 6
Unicellular organisms come in a wide variety of shapes and sizes.

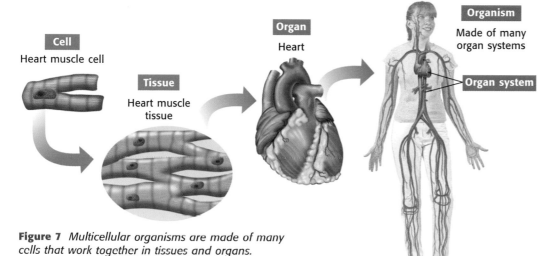

Figure 7 *Multicellular organisms are made of many cells that work together in tissues and organs.*

Cell — Heart muscle cell
Tissue — Heart muscle tissue
Organ — Heart
Organism — Made of many organ systems
Organ system

The Big Picture

Although unicellular organisms and multicellular organisms can live on their own, they usually do not live alone. Organisms interact with each other in many different ways.

Populations A group of organisms that are of the same kind and that live in the same area make up a **population.** All of the ladybird beetles living in the forest shown in **Figure 8** make up the ladybird beetle population of that forest. All of the red oak trees make up the forest's red oak population.

Figure 8 *A population is made up of all of the individuals of the same kind that live in the same area.*

REAL-WORLD CONNECTION

Your skin cells depend on other body cells for nutrients and oxygen, which is why they cannot live independently of your body. When someone suffers a serious burn and no longer has a protective covering of skin cells, scientists can grow skin for them in a laboratory. They take healthy skin cells, mix them with collagen proteins from cow skin, and suspend them in a nutrient solution. These new cells are applied to the burned skin as a bandage while the damaged skin heals.

CONNECT TO EARTH SCIENCE

Populations are sometimes joined or divided by Earth's physical features, such as mountains, rivers, and islands. The islands of Madagascar and Comoro, off the east coast of Africa, are home to 50 species of lemurs, a type of primate. The lemurs are geographically isolated, so while they are quite diverse on Madagascar and Comoro, there are no other wild populations of lemurs anywhere else in the world. Speciation as a result of geographic isolation is not limited to islands. Species can form when populations are divided for thousands of years by mountains, rivers, and other barriers.

WEIRD SCIENCE

Living on your own doesn't mean you can't cooperate with others. On coral reefs, a group of striped fish called cleaner wrasses attract fish that are infested with parasites to an area on the reef. The infested fish lie still while wrasses eat the parasites and fungi off their body.

internet connect

SCiLINKS NSTA

TOPIC: Populations, Communities, and Ecosystems
GO TO: www.scilinks.org
*sci*LINKS NUMBER: HSTL060

Teaching Transparency 7
"From Cell to Organism"

Reinforcement Worksheet
"An Ecosystem"

3 Extend

Going Further

Writing Have students write promotional materials that encourage cells to join an organ or organ system or to remain a single cell. For example, a single cell might have independence but lack the help it needs to do its work. A tissue provides a cell with helpers that have similar interests, but it requires cooperation and good "inter-cellular skills."

PORTFOLIO

4 Close

Quiz

1. What is the relationship between your digestive system, stomach, and intestines? (The digestive system is an organ system. The stomach and intestines are organs that are parts of the digestive system.)

2. The blood cells in your body are alive, are genetically similar to each other, and can be found in the same location (inside your body). Are these cells a population? (No. A population consists of organisms that are capable of living independently. Blood cells cannot live outside the body.)

Alternative Assessment

Concept Mapping Have students choose a human organ system and identify its component organs. Then ask students to describe the function of these organs and their relationship to one another in a concept map.

Figure 9 *The fox, flowers, and trees are all part of a forest community.*

Communities Two or more different populations living in the same area make up a **community.** The populations of foxes, oak trees, lizards, flowers, and other organisms in a forest are all part of a forest community, as shown in **Figure 9.** Your hometown is a community that includes all of the people, dogs, cats, and other organisms living there.

Ecosystems The community and all of the nonliving things that affect it, such as water, soil, rocks, temperature, and light, make up an **ecosystem.** Ecosystems on land are called *terrestrial* ecosystems, and they include forests, deserts, prairies, and your own backyard. Ecosystems in water are called *aquatic* ecosystems, and they include rivers, ponds, lakes, oceans, and even aquariums. The community in Figure 10 lives in a terrestrial ecosystem.

SECTION REVIEW

1. Complete the following sentence: *Cells* are related to ? in the same way that ? are related to *organ systems.*

2. How do the cells of unicellular organisms differ from the cells of multicellular organisms?

3. **Applying Concepts** Use the picture of an aquarium below to answer the following questions:
   a. How many *different* kinds of organisms are visible?
   b. How many populations are visible?
   c. How many communities are visible?

internet**connect**

*sci*LINKS.
NSTA

TOPIC: Organization of Life & Populations, Communities, and Ecosystems
GO TO: www.scilinks.org
*sci*LINKS NUMBER: HSTL055, HSTL060

8

▼ Answers to Section Review

1. tissues, organs

2. The cells of unicellular organisms can survive on their own, but the cells of multicellular organisms must remain a part of the organism's body to survive.

3. a. 8; don't forget to count the plants.
   b. 8
   c. 1; the community includes all the living things in the aquarium.

Terms to Learn

cell membrane	prokaryotic
organelles	eukaryotic
cytoplasm	bacteria
nucleus	

What You'll Do

◆ State the parts of the cell theory.
◆ Explain why cells are so small.
◆ Calculate a cell's surface-to-volume ratio.
◆ List the advantages of being multicellular.
◆ Explain the difference between prokaryotic cells and eukaryotic cells.

The Discovery of Cells

Most cells are so tiny that they are not visible to the naked eye. So how did we find out that cells are the basic unit of all living things? What would make someone think that a rabbit or a tree or a person is made up of tiny parts that cannot be seen? Actually, the first person to see cells was not even looking for them.

Seeing the First Cells

In 1665, a British scientist named Robert Hooke was trying to find something interesting that he could show to other scientists at a meeting. Earlier, he had built a crude microscope that allowed him to look at very tiny objects. One day he decided to look at a thin slice of cork, a soft plant tissue found in the bark of trees like the ones shown in **Figure 10.** To his amazement, the cork looked like hundreds of little boxes, which he described as looking like a honeycomb. He named these tiny boxes *cells,* which means "little rooms" in Latin.

Although Hooke did not realize it, these boxes were actually the outer layers of the cork cells that were left behind after the cells died. Later, he looked at thin slices of plants and saw that they too were made of tiny cells. Some of them were even filled with "juice" (those were living cells). Hooke's microscope and drawings of cork cells are shown in **Figure 11.**

Hooke also used his microscope to look at feathers, fish scales, and the eyes of house flies, but he spent most of his time looking at plants and fungi. Since plant and fungal cells had walls that were easier to see, Hooke thought that cells were found only in those types of organisms and not in animals.

Figure 10 *Cork is a soft material found in trees. Cork cells were the first cells seen with a microscope.*

Figure 11 *This is the compound microscope that Hooke used to see the first cells. Hooke made a drawing of the cork cells that he saw.*

SCIENCE HUMOR

Q: What did Robert Hooke say to his stockbroker?

A: Cell! Cell!

Focus

The Discovery of Cells

This section introduces students to the internal structures of a cell. They will learn about the parts of a cell and why cells are so small. Finally, they will learn the differences and similarities between prokaryotic and eukaryotic cells.

Bellringer

Write the following on the board or overhead projector:

Why weren't cells discovered until 1665? What invention made their discovery possible? Write your answers in your ScienceLog. (Cells weren't discovered until 1665 because most cells are too small to be seen with the naked eye. The microscope is the invention that made their discovery possible.)

1 Motivate

ACTIVITY

Modeling Cell Discovery
Before beginning this section, have students model Robert Hooke's discovery. Divide the class into small groups, and provide each group with a microscope and a prepared slide of cork cells. Have them describe and sketch their observations in their ScienceLog.

Directed Reading Worksheet Section 2

CONNECT TO
ASTRONOMY

Both biologists and astronomers use magnifiers. Biologists use microscopes to see things that are too small to see with the unaided eye. Astronomers use telescopes to see planets, moons, and stars that are huge but too far away to view otherwise. The first telescope was made by a Dutchman named Hans Lipperhey in 1608. In 1609, the Italian scientist Galileo became the first to use a telescope for astronomy. He discovered four moons orbiting the planet Jupiter. Ask students to write a list of words that have the prefixes *micro-* and *tele-* and to use those examples to define those prefixes. **Sheltered English**

REAL-WORLD CONNECTION

The yeast used in baking is a relative of single-celled eukaryotes living among lots of other organisms in the air around us. It was probably an accidental discovery that wheat dough exposed to air for a length of time would rise and, when baked, produce bread. Sourdough breads require the right combination of yeast and bacteria in the dough, and strains of native yeast vary regionally the same way many other organisms do. Sourdough from San Francisco has its own characteristic taste because bakers there use a yeast that is most common in the air around that city.

LabBook PG 184
Elephant-Sized Amoebas?

Figure 12 *Leeuwenhoek saw unicellular organisms similar to these, which are found in pond scum.*

Elephant-sized "animalcules"? Find out for yourself on LabBook page 184!

10

Seeing Cells in Other Life-Forms

In 1673, a few years after Hooke made his observations, a Dutch merchant named Anton van Leeuwenhoek (LAY vuhn hook) used one of his own handmade microscopes to get a closer look at pond scum, similar to that shown in **Figure 12.** He was amazed to see many small creatures swimming around in the slimy ooze; he named the creatures *animalcules,* which means "little animals."

Leeuwenhoek also looked at blood he took from different animals and tartar he scraped off their teeth and his own. He observed that blood cells in fish, birds, and frogs are oval-shaped, while those in humans and dogs are flatter. He was the first person to see bacteria, and he discovered that the yeasts used to make bread dough rise are actually unicellular organisms.

The Cell Theory

After Hooke first saw the cork cells, almost two centuries passed before anyone realized that cells are present in *all* living things. Matthias Schleiden, a German scientist, looked at many slides of plant tissues and read about what other scientists had seen under the microscope. In 1838, he concluded that all plant parts are made of cells.

The next year, Theodor Schwann, a German scientist who studied animals, stated that all animal tissues are made of cells. Not long after that, Schwann wrote the first two parts of what is now known as the *cell theory:*

- **All organisms are composed of one or more cells.**
- **The cell is the basic unit of life in all living things.**

About 20 years later, in 1858, Rudolf Virchow, a German doctor, saw that cells could not develop from anything except other cells. He then wrote the third part of the cell theory:

- **All cells come from existing cells.**

WEIRD SCIENCE

Scientists have discovered that enzymes in spinach cells can decompose explosives and reduce them to less-toxic byproducts. The process can be done at room temperature and does not require any special equipment. If field tests of this technique are successful, the tiny proteins of these microscopic cells will help safely eliminate a 500,000-ton stockpile of explosives around the country.

Cell Similarities

Cells come in many different shapes and sizes and perform a wide variety of functions, but they all have the following things in common:

Cell Membrane All cells are surrounded by a **cell membrane.** This membrane acts as a barrier between the inside of the cell and the cell's environment. It also controls the passage of materials into and out of the cell. **Figure 13** shows the outside of a cell.

Hereditary Material Part of the cell theory states that all cells are made from existing cells. When new cells are made, they receive a copy of the hereditary material of the original cells. This material is *DNA* (deoxyribonucleic acid). It controls all of the activities of a cell and contains the information needed for that cell to make new cells.

Cytoplasm and Organelles All cells have chemicals and structures that enable the cell to live, grow, and reproduce. The structures are called **organelles.** Although all cells have organelles, they don't all have the same kind. Some organelles are surrounded by membranes, but others are not. The cell in **Figure 14** has membrane-covered organelles. The chemicals and structures of a cell are surrounded by fluid. This fluid and almost everything in it are collectively called the **cytoplasm** (SIET oh PLAZ uhm).

Small Size Almost all cells are too small to be seen with the naked eye. You are made up of 100 trillion cells, and it would take 50 of these cells just to cover up the dot on the letter *i*.

Self-Check

Why do all cells need DNA? *(See page 216 to check your answer.)*

Figure 13 *The cell membrane holds the contents of the cell together.*

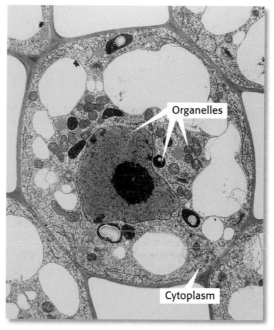

Figure 14 *This cell has many organelles. These organelles are surrounded by membranes.*

Organelles

Cytoplasm

IS THAT A FACT!

The largest cell in the world is the yolk of an ostrich egg. It's the size of a baseball.

Answer to Self-Check

Cells need DNA to control cell processes and to make new cells.

READING STRATEGY

Prediction Guide Have students respond to the following statement before reading this page: Blood cells are completely different from bone cells (true/false). Ask students to explain the reasons for their answer. Have students evaluate their answer after they read the page.

DEMONSTRATION

Membranes

MATERIALS

- wire mesh food strainer
- 250 mL of sand
- 250 mL of water
- 250 mL of gravel similar to that used to line fish tanks
- 250 mL of marbles or large pebbles
- pan to place under strainer

Place each material in the strainer, and have students observe and explain the results. Tell students that the cell membrane functions somewhat like the strainer. It lets some materials pass through, but not others. Explain also that the process works in both directions.

MISCONCEPTION
ALERT

The physical relationship between molecules and cells is often confusing to students. Molecules are not alive; they are much smaller and fit inside of cells.

Prediction Guide Before reading this page, ask students to choose one of the following reasons for why they think cells are so small:

1. There isn't enough microscopic food available for them.

2. There isn't enough room in a multicellular organism.

3. another reason (ask for suggestions)

Have students evaluate their answer after they read the page.

MATH and MORE

Surface Area The following problem simplifies the principle of surface-to-volume ratio because it concerns a one-dimensional figure. Give each student a sheet of $\frac{1}{4}$ in. grid paper. Tell them to outline a rectangle 4 squares wide and 5 squares long. What is the area of this rectangle? ($4 \times 5 = 20$ squares)

Now tell students to outline another rectangle that is twice as big, 8 squares wide and 10 squares long. What is the area of the second rectangle? ($8 \times 10 = 80$ squares)

Next ask students to calculate the perimeter, or "surface area," of each rectangle.
($5 + 5 + 4 + 4 = 18$)
($10 + 10 + 8 + 8 = 36$)

How did doubling the size of the rectangle affect its internal area? How did it affect its surface area? (The internal area quadrupled: $80 \div 20 = 4$. The surface area only doubled: $36 \div 18 = 2$.)

Giant Amoeba Eats New York City

This is not a headline you are likely to ever see. Why not? Amoebas consist of only a single cell. Most amoebas can't even grow large enough to be seen without a microscope. That's because as a cell gets larger, it needs more food and produces more waste. Therefore, more materials must be able to move into and out of the cell through the cell membrane.

Surface-to-Volume Ratio To keep up with these demands, a growing cell needs a larger surface area through which to exchange materials. As the cell's volume increases, its outer surface grows too. But the volume of a cell (the amount a cell will hold) increases at a faster rate than the area of its outer surface. If a cell gets too large, its surface will have too few openings to allow enough materials into and out of it.

To understand why the volume of a cell increases faster than its surface area, look at the table below. The *surface-to-volume ratio* is the area of a cell's outer surface in relation to its volume. The surface-to-volume ratio decreases as cell size increases. Increasing the number of cells but not their size maintains a high surface-to-volume ratio.

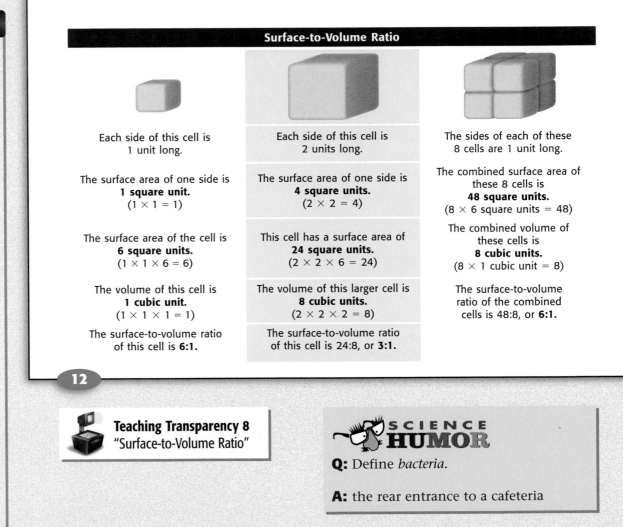

Surface-to-Volume Ratio

Each side of this cell is 1 unit long.

The surface area of one side is **1 square unit**.
($1 \times 1 = 1$)

The surface area of the cell is **6 square units**.
($1 \times 1 \times 6 = 6$)

The volume of this cell is **1 cubic unit**.
($1 \times 1 \times 1 = 1$)

The surface-to-volume ratio of this cell is **6:1**.

Each side of this cell is 2 units long.

The surface area of one side is **4 square units**.
($2 \times 2 = 4$)

This cell has a surface area of **24 square units**.
($2 \times 2 \times 6 = 24$)

The volume of this larger cell is **8 cubic units**.
($2 \times 2 \times 2 = 8$)

The surface-to-volume ratio of this cell is 24:8, or **3:1**.

The sides of each of these 8 cells are 1 unit long.

The combined surface area of these 8 cells is **48 square units**.
(8×6 square units $= 48$)

The combined volume of these cells is **8 cubic units**.
(8×1 cubic unit $= 8$)

The surface-to-volume ratio of the combined cells is 48:8, or **6:1**.

12

📺 **Teaching Transparency 8** "Surface-to-Volume Ratio"

SCIENCE HUMOR

Q: Define *bacteria*.

A: the rear entrance to a cafeteria

The Benefits of Being Multicellular Do you know now why you are made up of many tiny cells instead of one large cell? A single cell as big as you are would have an incredibly small surface-to-volume ratio. The cell could not survive because its outer surface would be too small to allow in the materials it would need. Multicellular organisms grow by producing more small cells, not larger cells. The elephant in **Figure 15** has cells that are the same size as yours.

Many Kinds of Cells In addition to being able to grow larger, multicellular organisms are able to do lots of other things because they are made up of different kinds of cells. Just as there are teachers who are specialized to teach and mechanics who are specialized to work on cars, different cells are specialized to perform different jobs. A single cell cannot do all the things that many different cells can do. Having many different cells that are specialized for specific jobs allows multicellular organisms to perform more functions than unicellular organisms.

The different kinds of cells can form tissues and organs with different functions. People have specialized cells, such as muscle cells, eye cells, and brain cells, so they can walk, run, watch a movie, think, and do many other activities. If you enjoy doing many different things, be glad you are not a single cell.

Figure 15 An elephant is larger than a human because it has more cells, not larger cells.

MATH BREAK

Surface-to-Volume Ratio
The shape of a cell can affect its surface-to-volume ratio. Examine the cells below, and answer the questions that follow:

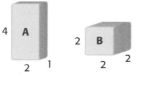

1. What is the surface area of Cell A? of Cell B?
2. What is the volume of Cell A? of Cell B?
3. Which of the two cells pictured here has the greater surface-to-volume ratio?

A Pet *Paramecium*
Imagine that you have a pet *Paramecium*, a type of unicellular organism. In order to properly care for your pet, you have to figure out how much you need to feed it. The dimensions of your *Paramecium* are roughly 125 μm × 50 μm × 20 μm. If seven food molecules can enter through each square micrometer of surface every minute, how many molecules can it eat in 1 minute? If your pet needs one food molecule per cubic micrometer of volume every minute to survive, how much would you have to feed it every minute?

CONNECT TO
EARTH SCIENCE

The work of paleontologists helps us understand the antiquity of unicellular and multicellular life on Earth. Part of their work includes determining the ages of the rocks that contain fossils. But paleontologists can also learn about Earth's past climate by asking questions about life-forms, such as, "Was the organism a marine plant or an animal?"

Answers to MATHBREAK

1. 28 square units; 24 square units
2. 8 cubic units; 8 cubic units
3. Cell *A*'s surface-to-volume ratio is the largest, at 28:8. (Even though Cell *A* has a larger surface area, the two cells have the same volume.)

 Math Skills Worksheet
"What Is a Ratio?"

 Math Skills Worksheet
"Finding Perimeter and Area"

 Math Skills Worksheet
"Finding Volume"

Answers to APPLY
- The surface area of the pet is 19,500 μm², so it can eat 136,500 molecules of food every minute.
- The volume of the pet is 125,000 μm³. If it needs one food molecule for every cubic micrometer, then it needs to be fed 125,000 food molecules every minute to survive.

Answers to Self-Check

1. The surface-to-volume ratio decreases as the cell size increases.

2. A eukaryotic cell has a nucleus and membrane-covered organelles.

─── **CONNECT TO** ───
EARTH SCIENCE

Astronomers are interested in the work of scientists who investigate bacteria and other microscopic organisms in Earth's crust. Microbiologists have drilled deep into the crust and found microbes nearly 3 km below the surface, where the temperature is 75°C (167°F). Because other planets have surface conditions similar to the harsh environment within the Earth's crust, astronomers believe it may be possible for microbes to live elsewhere in the solar system. Have students research and write a brief report on the conditions in Earth's crust and learn about the organisms that live there.

QuickLab

MATERIALS

FOR EACH STUDENT:
• cotton swab
• yogurt with active culture
• plastic microscope slide
• water
• plastic coverslip
• microscope

Answer to QuickLab

Drawings should depict rod-shaped bacteria.

internetconnect

SCI**LINKS**
NSTA

TOPIC: Prokaryotic Cells
GO TO: www.scilinks.org
sciLINKS NUMBER: HSTL065

✓ Self-Check

1. As a cell grows larger, what happens to its surface-to-volume ratio?

2. What does a eukaryotic cell have that a prokaryotic cell does not?

(See page 216 to check your answer.)

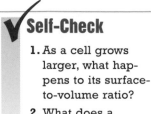

QuickLab

Do Bacteria Taste Good?

If they're the kind found in yogurt, they taste great! Using a **cotton swab,** put a small dot of **yogurt** on a **plastic microscope slide.** Add a drop of **water,** and use the cotton swab to stir. Add a **plastic coverslip,** and examine the slide using a **microscope.** Draw what you see.

The masses of rod-shaped bacteria feed on the sugar in milk (lactose) and convert it into lactic acid. Lactic acid causes milk to thicken, which makes yogurt!

Two Types of Cells

The many different kinds of cells that exist can be divided into two groups. As you have already learned, all cells have DNA. In one group, cells have a **nucleus,** which is a membrane-covered organelle that holds the cells' DNA. In the other group, the cells' DNA is not contained in a nucleus. Cells that do not have a nucleus are **prokaryotic** (proh KAR ee AH tik), and cells that have a nucleus are **eukaryotic** (yoo KAR ee AH tik).

Prokaryotic Cells Prokaryotic cells are also called **bacteria.** They are the world's smallest cells, and they do not have a nucleus. A prokaryotic cell's DNA is one long, circular molecule shaped sort of like a rubber band.

Bacteria do not have any membrane-covered organelles, but they do have tiny, round organelles called *ribosomes.* These organelles work like little factories to make proteins.

Most bacteria are covered by a hard cell wall outside a softer cell membrane. Think of the membrane pressing against the wall as an inflated balloon pressing against the inside of a glass jar. But unlike the balloon and jar, the membrane and the wall allow food and waste molecules to pass through. **Figure 16** shows a generalized view of a prokaryotic cell.

Bacteria were probably the first type of cells on Earth. The oldest fossils ever found are of prokaryotic cells. Scientists have estimated these fossils to be 3.5 billion years old.

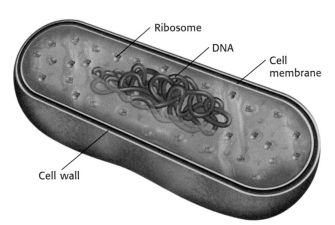

Figure 16 *Prokaryotic cells do not have a nucleus or any other membrane-covered organelles. The circular DNA is bunched up in the cytoplasm.*

14

WEIRD SCIENCE

In 1969, the *Apollo 12* crew retrieved a space probe from the moon that had been launched nearly three years earlier. In the probe's camera, NASA scientists found a stowaway. The bacterium *Streptococcus mitis* had traveled to the moon and back. Despite the rigors of space travel, more than two and a half years of radiation exposure, and freezing temperatures, the *Streptococcus mitis* was successfully reconstituted.

Eukaryotic Cells Eukaryotic cells are more complex than prokaryotic cells. Although most eukaryotic cells are about 10 times larger than prokaryotic cells, they still have a high enough surface-to-volume ratio to survive. Fossil evidence suggests that eukaryotic cells first appeared about 2 billion years ago. All living things that are not bacteria are made of one or more eukaryotic cells. This includes plants, animals, fungi, and protists.

Eukaryotic cells have a nucleus and many other membrane-covered organelles. An advantage of having the cell divided into compartments is that it allows many different chemical processes to occur at the same time. A generalized eukaryotic cell is shown in **Figure 17.**

There is more DNA in eukaryotic cells than in prokaryotic cells, and it is stored in the nucleus. Instead of being circular, the DNA molecules in eukaryotic cells are linear.

All eukaryotic cells have a cell membrane, and some of them have a cell wall. Those that have cell walls are found in plants, fungi, and some unicellular organisms. The tables below summarize the differences between eukaryotic and prokaryotic cells.

Nucleus

Figure 17 Eukaryotic cells contain a nucleus and many other organelles.

Prokaryotic Cells	Eukaryotic Cells
No nucleus	Nucleus
No membrane covered organelles	Membrane-covered organelles
Circular DNA	Linear DNA
Bacteria	All other cells

Science CONNECTION

A new way to cure sick cells? See page 30.

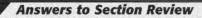
SECTION REVIEW

1. What are the three parts of the cell theory?

2. What do all cells have in common?

3. What are two advantages of being multicellular?

4. If a unicellular organism has a cell wall, ribosomes, and circular DNA, is it eukaryotic or prokaryotic?

5. **Applying Concepts** Which has the greater surface-to-volume ratio, a tennis ball or a basketball? Explain your answer. What could be done to increase the surface-to-volume ratio of both?

internet connect

SCI LINKS
NSTA

TOPIC: Prokaryotic Cells
GO TO: www.scilinks.org
*sci*LINKS NUMBER: HSTL065

15

3 Extend

RESEARCH

Writing Muscle cramps that occur during or after exercise may be caused in part by lactic acid buildup within the muscle cells. Have students write a report that explains what happens in muscle cells to cause this condition.

PORTFOLIO

4 Close

Quiz

1. When Robert Hooke saw "juice" in some cells, what was he looking at? (cytoplasm)

2. Why did Hooke think cells existed only in plants and fungi and not in animals? (Plant and fungal cells have cell walls. Hooke's microscope wasn't strong enough to view the more delicate cell membranes of animal cells.)

ALTERNATIVE ASSESSMENT

Writing Divide the students into groups, and assign two or three vocabulary words to each group. Tell students to write a descriptive statement about each word without using the word in the sentence. Each group challenges the other groups to guess the word described. For example, "The fluid inside a cell" is the definition. "What is cytoplasm?" is the correct response.

▼ *Answers to Section Review*

1. All organisms are composed of one or more cells; the cell is the basic unit of life in all living things; all cells come from existing cells.

2. All cells have a cell membrane, hereditary material (DNA), cytoplasm, and organelles, and they are almost always small.

3. Multicellular organisms can grow larger and have cells that are specialized for different tasks.

4. Cells with circular DNA are prokaryotic.

5. The tennis ball would have the greater surface-to-volume ratio. Flattening the balls would increase the surface-to-volume ratio by decreasing their volume.

Eukaryotic Cells: The Inside Story

In this section, students will learn the names and functions of organelles in a eukaryotic cell. They will learn which organelles enable a cell to make proteins, produce energy, transport and store materials, and prepare to divide. Finally, they will learn the difference between plant and animal cells.

🔔 Bellringer

On the board or overhead projector, write the following:

List three differences between prokaryotic and eukaryotic cells. (Prokaryotic cells have circular DNA, no nucleus, and no membrane-covered organelles. Eukaryotic cells have linear DNA, a nucleus, and membrane-covered organelles.)

1 Motivate

DISCUSSION

Cellular Activity Ask students if they can feel the flurry of activity within their cells that keeps them alive. (No.)

Ask how they know their cells are working. (They can breathe, digest food, and move.)

Explain that there is a tendency to consider life processes as activities performed only by whole organisms. What we sometimes forget is that the plant or animal can do these things only because its *cells* are doing these things.

Terms to Learn

cell wall
ribosome
endoplasmic
   reticulum
mitochondria

chloroplast
Golgi complex
vesicle
vacuole
lysosome

What You'll Do

◆ Explain the function of each part of a eukaryotic cell.
◆ Describe the differences between animal cells and plant cells.

Eukaryotic Cells: The Inside Story

For a long time after the discovery of cells, scientists did not really know what cells were made of. Cells are so small that the details of their structure could not be seen until better methods of magnifying and staining were developed. We now know that cells are very complex, especially eukaryotic cells. Everything, from the structures covering the cells to the organelles inside them, performs a task that helps to keep the cells alive.

Holding It All Together

All cells have outer coverings that separate what is inside the cell from what is outside. One kind of covering, called the cell membrane, surrounds all cells. Some cells have an additional layer outside the cell membrane called the cell wall.

Cell Membrane All cells are covered by a cell membrane. The job of the cell membrane is to keep the cytoplasm inside, to allow nutrients in and waste products out, and to interact with things outside the cell. In **Figure 18,** you can see a close-up view of the cell membrane of a cell that has had its top half cut away.

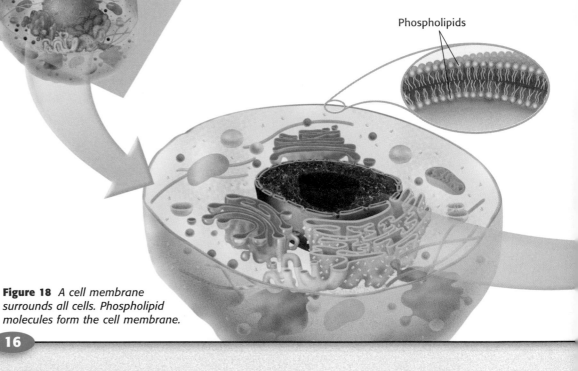

Phospholipids

Figure 18 *A cell membrane surrounds all cells. Phospholipid molecules form the cell membrane.*

16

MISCONCEPTION ///ALERT\\\

Students often think of cells as flat. Pictures, and even viewing cells in a microscope, can reinforce that misconception. The fact that cells are three-dimensional is often overlooked. **Sheltered English**

Cell Wall

The cells of plants and algae have a hard cell wall made of cellulose. The **cell wall** provides strength and support to the cell membrane. When too much water enters or leaves a plant cell, the cell wall can prevent the membrane from tearing. The strength of billions of cell walls in plants enables a tree to stand tall and its limbs to defy gravity. When you are looking at dried hay, sticks, and wooden boards, you are seeing the cell walls of dead plant cells. The cells of fungi, such as mushrooms, toadstools, mold, and yeasts, have cell walls made of a chemical similar to that found in the hard covering of insects. **Figure 19** shows a cross section of a generalized plant cell and a close-up view of the cell wall.

The Cell's Library

The largest and most visible organelle in a eukaryotic cell is the nucleus. The word *nucleus* means "kernel" or "nut" (maybe it does look sort of like a nut inside a piece of candy). As you can see in **Figure 20,** the nucleus is covered by a membrane through which materials can pass.

The nucleus has often been called the control center of the cell. As you know, it stores the DNA that has information on how to make all of the cell's proteins. Almost every chemical reaction that is important to the cell's life involves some kind of protein. Sometimes a dark spot can be seen inside the nucleus. This spot is called a *nucleolus,* and it looks like a small nucleus inside the big nucleus. The nucleolus stores the materials that will be used later to make ribosomes in the cytoplasm.

Cell wall

Cell membrane

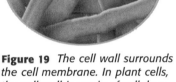

Figure 19 *The cell wall surrounds the cell membrane. In plant cells, the cell wall is made of cellulose fibers.*

DNA

Nucleolus

Nuclear membrane

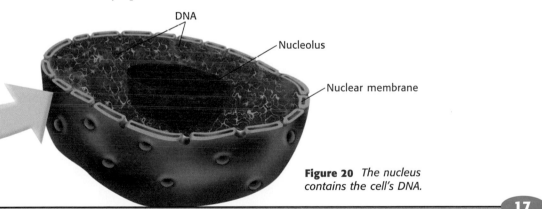

Figure 20 *The nucleus contains the cell's DNA.*

17

2) Teach

DEMONSTRATION

Cell Walls With a stick, a mushroom, and your own hand, you can illustrate the difference between a rigid cell wall and a flexible cell membrane like that found in human skin cells. Bend the stick, and it will break. Bend the mushroom, and it will come apart. Make a fist, and your skin stretches to accommodate the flexing of muscles and bone joints. If we had rigid cell walls like plants, we would find it extremely difficult to move.
 Sheltered English

MEETING INDIVIDUAL NEEDS

Writing **Advanced Learners**
 Because all multicellular plants and animals are composed of eukaryotic cells, stress that the eukaryotic cell can be an entity in itself, not just a component of a larger organism. Have students research one-celled eukaryotic organisms, like a yeast or a one-celled protist, and compare them with eukaryotic cells that are part of a multicellular plant or animal. Students should include drawings, and record their findings in their ScienceLog.

PORTFOLIO

Directed Reading Worksheet Section 3

Homework

PORTFOLIO

Poster Project Have students investigate red blood cells and create a poster comparing the red blood cell with the cheek skin cell. (RBCs are the only cells in the human body that do not have a nucleus or mitochondria. Without a nucleus they cannot divide and reproduce. They live for only about 120 days, but new ones are made by bone marrow at the rate of up to 200 billion per day.)

Writing **Advanced Learners**

Have students write a science fiction story about an animal whose cells are invaded by chloroplasts. Students should describe how that animal's life processes would be affected and how that animal would use this unusual occurrence to its advantage. Encourage students to write about an animal other than a mammal.

Answer to Self-Check

Cell walls surround the cell membranes of some cells. All cells have cell membranes, but not all cells have cell walls. Cell walls give structure to some cells.

CONNECT TO
PHYSICAL SCIENCE

Biophysics uses tools and techniques of physics to study the life processes of cells. Biophysicists are interested in the relationship between a molecule's structure and its function. Sophisticated techniques, such as electron microscopy, X-ray diffraction, magnetic resonance spectroscopy, and electrophoresis, allow them to study the structure of proteins, nucleic acids, and even parts of cells, such as ribosomes. Use the following Teaching Transparency to illustrate molecular structure.

Teaching Transparency 260
"Structural Formulas"

LINK TO PHYSICAL SCIENCE

Protein Factories

Proteins, the building blocks of all cells, are made up of chemicals known as *amino acids*. These amino acids are hooked together to make proteins at very small organelles called **ribosomes.** Ribosomes are the smallest but most abundant organelles. *All* cells have ribosomes because all cells need protein to live. Unlike most other organelles, ribosomes are not covered with a membrane.

The Cell's Delivery System

Eukaryotic cells have an organelle called the endoplasmic (EN doh PLAZ mik) reticulum (ri TIK yuh luhm), which is shown in **Figure 21.** The **endoplasmic reticulum,** or ER, is a membrane-covered compartment that makes lipids and other materials for use inside and outside the cell. It is also the organelle that breaks down drugs and certain other chemicals that could damage the cell. The ER is the internal delivery system of a cell. Substances in the ER can move from one place to another through its many tubular connections, sort of like cars moving through tunnels.

The ER looks like flattened sacks stacked side by side or a cloth folded back and forth. Some ER may be covered with ribosomes that make its surface look rough. The proteins made at those ribosomes pass into the ER. Later the proteins are released from the ER for use elsewhere.

Self-Check

What is the difference between a cell wall and a cell membrane? *(See page 216 to check your answer.)*

Ribosome

Endoplasmic reticulum

Mitochondria

Figure 21 *The ER is made up of flattened compartments and tubes. Ribosomes are attached to some of the ER.*

Endoplasmic reticulum

18

WEIRD SCIENCE

Scientists at the University of New Mexico have created artificial muscles that are twice as strong as the real thing. Pending government approval, these artificial muscles may be implanted to replace paralyzed tissue in people with serious injuries.

The Cell's Power Plants

In today's world, we use many sources of energy, such as oil, gas, and nuclear power. We need this energy to heat our homes, fuel our cars, and cook our food. Cells also need energy to function. Where do they get it?

Mitochondria Inside all cells, food molecules are "burned" (broken down) to release energy. The energy is transferred to a special molecule that the cell uses to get work done. As you learned earlier, this molecule is called ATP.

ATP can be made at several locations in eukaryotic cells, but most of it is produced at bean-shaped organelles called **mitochondria** (MIET oh KAHN dree uh), shown in **Figure 22.** These organelles are surrounded by two membranes. The inner membrane, which has many folds in it, is where most of the ATP is made.

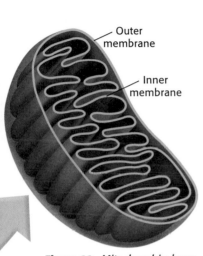

Mitochondria can work only if they have oxygen. The reason you breathe air is to make sure your mitochondria have the oxygen they need to make ATP. Highly active cells, such as those in the heart and liver, may have thousands of mitochondria, while other cells may have only a few.

Figure 22 *Mitochondria have two membranes. The inner membrane has many folds.*

Chloroplasts Plants and algae have an additional kind of energy-converting organelle, called a **chloroplast,** which is shown in **Figure 23.** Chloroplasts have two membranes and structures that look like stacks of coins. These are flattened, membrane-covered sacs that contain an important chemical called chlorophyll. Chlorophyll is what makes chloroplasts green. The energy of sunlight is trapped by chlorophyll and used to make sugar. This process is called *photosynthesis.* The sugar that is produced is used by mitochondria to make ATP. You will learn more about photosynthesis in a later chapter.

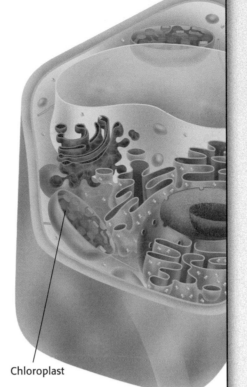

Chloroplast

Figure 23 *Chloroplasts, found in plant cells, also have two membranes. The inner membrane forms stacks of flattened sacs.*

Outer membrane

Inner membrane

19

IS THAT A FACT!

Nerve cells, called *neurons,* are the longest cells in the human body. They can be more than 1 m long.

MEETING INDIVIDUAL NEEDS

Learners Having Difficulty
Arrange students in pairs. Tell each pair to draw a plant or animal eukaryotic cell based on information presented in the text. Instruct them not to label the cell's parts. Then have them exchange drawings with another pair and put the proper labels on their classmates' picture. Finally, have each group of two pairs compare and discuss their work.

Homework

Making Models Invite the class to make edible cells at home and bring them to class. They can decorate a muffin, a cracker, a piece of pita bread, an English muffin, a pizza, or any other base they like and decorate their choice with edible organelles. Before they eat their creations, they should show them to the rest of the class and explain the way they've represented the cell's structure in food. Pictures of the edible cells can be displayed in the classroom. **Sheltered English**

ACTIVITY

Making Models
Have the students create a cell using a shoe box for the cell wall. Any material readily available can be used for the cell parts. Parts can be hung on a string, glued to the box, or attached by any method the student chooses. The boxes can be displayed in the classroom. **Sheltered English**

Multicultural CONNECTION

Camillo Golgi was born in 1843 in a small town called Corteno, in the northern Italian province of Lombardy. He received a medical degree in 1865. Although he was a psychiatrist, he was interested in the microscopic nature of the nervous system. He discovered the "black reaction," which is a method of staining tissue with silver nitrate so it can be viewed clearly with a microscope. In 1897, using this method, he saw the cellular structures we know today as the Golgi complex. Golgi died at the age of 83.

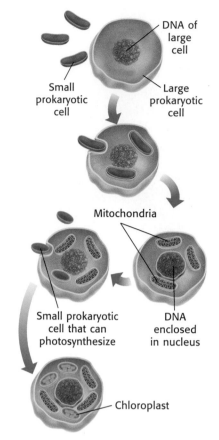

Figure 24 *Mitochondria and chloroplasts may have originated from energy-producing ancestors that were engulfed by larger cells.*

Where Did They Come From? Many scientists believe that mitochondria and chloroplasts originated as prokaryotic cells that were "eaten" by larger cells. Instead of being digested, the bacteria survived. **Figure 24** shows how bacteria might have become the ancestors of mitochondria and chloroplasts.

What evidence do scientists have that this theory is correct? The first piece of evidence is that mitochondria and chloroplasts are about the same size as bacteria. The second is that both are surrounded by *two membranes*. If the theory is correct, the outer membrane was created when the bacteria were engulfed by the larger cells. Other evidence supports this theory. Mitochondria and chloroplasts have the same kind of ribosomes and circular DNA as bacteria. They also divide like bacteria.

The Cell's Packaging Center

When proteins and other materials need to be processed and shipped out of a eukaryotic cell, the job goes to an organelle called the **Golgi complex.** This structure is named after Camillo Golgi, the Italian scientist who first identified it.

The Golgi complex looks like the ER, but it is located closer to the cell membrane. The Golgi complex of a cell is shown in **Figure 25.** Lipids and proteins from the ER are delivered to the Golgi complex, where they are modified for different functions. The final products are enclosed in a piece of the Golgi complex's membrane that pinches off to form a small compartment. This small compartment transports its contents to other parts of the cell or outside of the cell.

Golgi complex

Figure 25 *The Golgi complex processes, packages, and transports materials sent to it from the ER.*

SCIENTISTS AT ODDS

Many scientists did not believe Golgi's claims about the Golgi complex. They thought he just saw tiny globs of the staining material. The existence of the Golgi complex was finally confirmed in the mid-1950s with the aid of the electron microscope.

The Cell's Storage Centers

All eukaryotic cells have membrane-covered compartments called **vesicles.** Some of them form when part of the membrane pinches off the ER or Golgi complex. Others are formed when part of the cell membrane surrounds an object outside the cell. This is how white blood cells engulf other cells in your body, as shown in **Figure 26.**

Vacuoles Most plant cells have a very large membrane-covered chamber called a **vacuole,** as shown in **Figure 27.** Vacuoles store water and other liquids. Vacuoles that are full of water help support the cell. Some plants wilt when their cell vacuoles lose water. If you want crispy lettuce for a salad, all you need to do is fill up the vacuoles by leaving the lettuce in water overnight. Have you ever wondered what makes roses red and violets blue? It is a colorful liquid stored inside vacuoles. Vacuoles also contain the juices you associate with oranges and other fruits.

Some unicellular organisms that live in freshwater environments have a problem with too much water entering the cell. They have a special structure called a contractile vacuole that can squeeze excess water out of the cell. It works in much the same way that a pump removes water from inside a boat.

Figure 26 *The smaller cell is a yeast cell that is being engulfed by a white blood cell.*

Vacuole

Figure 27 *This plant cell's vacuole is the large structure in the middle of the cell shown in blue. Vacuoles are usually the largest organelles in a plant cell.*

21

IS THAT A FACT!

The vacuoles in grapes hold so much juice that they must dry in the sun for several weeks before they become raisins. A grape loses about three-fourths of its original weight in the process.

Multicultural CONNECTION

Dr. Jewell Plummer Cobb, a cell biologist, was the first African American woman to be named president of a university in the California university system. Before she was named president of California State University at Fullerton in 1981, Dr. Cobb researched and helped explain how pigment cells normally function and how they change when they become cancerous. Dr. Cobb also taught at Sarah Lawrence College in New York and later at Rutgers University in New Jersey, where she also served as Dean. Throughout her career as a research biologist and university administrator, Dr. Cobb has demonstrated a deep commitment to research and education.

MEETING INDIVIDUAL NEEDS

Learners Having Difficulty
You can make a demonstration model of a vacuole within a cell by filling a balloon with water or air and putting it inside a clear-plastic storage bag. Show that the vacuole is part of the cell and is distinct within the cell. You can demonstrate that cells are full of motion and activity by moving the balloon around inside the bag.
Sheltered English

Critical Thinking Worksheet
"Cellular Construction"

USING THE FIGURE

Have students refer to **Figure 29** and the chart below it to create their own drawing of a cell. But instead of drawing realistic images, tell them to draw an object that provides a visual clue about the organelle's job. For example, the Golgi complex, which transports materials, might be a car or a bus.
 Sheltered English

Homework

The organelles in a cell are rebelling against the nucleus. They all think they work too hard and want to take a vacation. Have students write a dialog between the nucleus and the other organelles. Tell them to help each organelle present a case for why it needs a rest and then have the nucleus explain what would happen if even one of them took two weeks off.

Teaching Transparency 9
"Organelles and Their Functions"

Teaching Transparency 10
"Comparing Animal and Plant Cells"

Reinforcement Worksheet
"Building a Eukaryotic Cell"

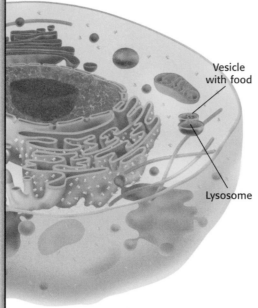

Vesicle with food

Lysosome

Figure 28 *This lysosome is pouring enzymes into a vesicle that contains food particles. The digested food molecules are released into the cytoplasm for use by the cell.*

Packages of Destruction

What causes most of the cells of a caterpillar to dissolve into ooze inside a cocoon? What causes the tail of a tadpole to shrink and then disappear? Lysosomes, that's what!

Lysosomes are special vesicles in animal cells that contain enzymes. When a cell engulfs a particle and encloses it in a vesicle, lysosomes bump into these vesicles and pour enzymes into them. This is illustrated in **Figure 28.** The particles in the vesicles are digested by the enzymes.

Lysosomes destroy worn-out or damaged organelles. They also get rid of waste materials and protect the cell from foreign invaders.

Sometimes lysosome membranes break, and the enzymes spill into the cytoplasm, killing the cell. This is what must happen for a tadpole to become a frog. Lysosomes cause the cells in a tadpole's tail to die and dissolve as the tadpole becomes a frog. Lysosomes played a similar role in your development! Before you were born, lysosomes caused the destruction of cells that formed the webbing between your fingers. Lysosome destruction of cells may also be one of the factors that contribute to the aging process in humans.

Organelles and Their Functions		
Nucleus contains the cell's DNA and is the control center of the cell		**Chloroplasts** make food using the energy of sunlight
Ribosomes the site where amino acids are hooked together to make proteins		**Golgi complex** processes and transports materials out of the cell
Endoplasmic reticulum makes lipids, breaks down drugs and other substances, packages up proteins for release from the cell		**Vacuole** stores water and other materials
Mitochondria break down food molecules to make ATP		**Lysosomes** digest food particles, wastes, cell parts, and foreign invaders

22

internet connect

SC*LINKS*
NSTA

TOPIC: Eukaryotic Cells
GO TO: www.scilinks.org
*sci*LINKS NUMBER: HSTL070

IS THAT A FACT!

Some tadpoles are three years old before they become frogs. The tadpole of the American bullfrog may take as long as 36 months before leaping to adulthood.

Plant or Animal?

How can you tell the difference between a plant cell and an animal cell? They both have a cell membrane, and they both have nuclei, ribosomes, mitochondria, endoplasmic reticula, Golgi complexes, and lysosomes. But plant cells have things that animal cells do not have: a cell wall, chloroplasts, and a large vacuole. You can see the differences between plant and animal cells in **Figure 29.**

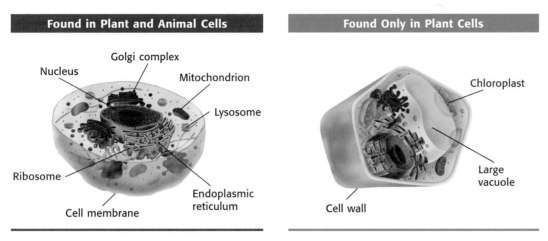

Found in Plant and Animal Cells

Golgi complex
Nucleus
Mitochondrion
Lysosome
Ribosome
Cell membrane
Endoplasmic reticulum

Found Only in Plant Cells

Chloroplast
Large vacuole
Cell wall

Figure 29 *Animal and plant cells have some structures in common, but they also have some that are unique.*

SECTION REVIEW

1. How does the nucleus control the cell's activities?

2. Which of the following would not be found in an animal cell: mitochondria, cell wall, chloroplast, ribosome, endoplasmic reticulum, Golgi complex, large vacuole, DNA, chlorophyll?

3. Use the following words in a sentence: oxygen, ATP, breathing, and mitochondria.

4. **Applying Concepts** You have the job of giving new names to different things in a city. The new names have to be parts of a eukaryotic cell. Write down some things you would see in a city. Assign the name of a cell part that is most appropriate to their function. Explain your choices.

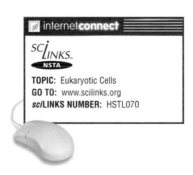

internet connect

SC**LINKS**
NSTA

TOPIC: Eukaryotic Cells
GO TO: www.scilinks.org
sci LINKS NUMBER: HSTL070

▼ Answers to Section Review

1. It contains the information on how to make the cell's proteins, which are involved in just about all the chemical activities of a cell.

2. cell wall, chloroplast, large vacuole, chlorophyll

3. Possible answer: Breathing supplies oxygen, which is needed by mitochondria to make ATP.

4. Answers will vary. Accept all reasonable responses.

GOING FURTHER

Writing Students now know that plant cells are a bit different from animal cells because of things such as cell walls and chloroplasts. But scientists group plantlike and animal-like organisms together and call them *protists.* Some protists are single-celled, like bacteria. Have students research and report on the differences between bacteria and protists. Encourage them to use additional resources to find information about protists and the two kingdoms of bacteria. Have them prepare a report on their findings.

PORTFOLIO

4 Close

Quiz

1. Every cell needs a membrane. Why? (A membrane is needed to keep the cytoplasm inside, to help transport nutrients and waste products, and to interact with things outside the cell.)

2. What would be the negative effects of a cell's not having lysosomes? (The cell would not be able to break down food molecules, get rid of wastes, get rid of damaged cells, or protect itself from invasion by foreign matter.)

ALTERNATIVE ASSESSMENT

Have students draw two cells, one plant and one animal. They should use one color to label all the structures common to both types of cells and another color to label all the structures that are different. **Sheltered English**

Discovery Lab

Cells Alive!
Teacher's Notes

Time Required

One 45-minute class period

Lab Ratings

EASY ————————→ HARD

TEACHER PREP 🦺
STUDENT SET-UP 🦺
CONCEPT LEVEL 🦺
CLEAN UP 🦺

MATERIALS

The materials listed on the student page are enough for a group of 3–4 students. You may wish to collect the algae ahead of time so they are available for students when they begin the lab. Be sure to keep the algae in a warm, damp place out of direct sunlight; a closed plastic bag with water sprayed into it is ideal.

Safety Caution

Remind students to review all safety cautions and icons before beginning this lab activity.

 Datasheets for LabBook

Terry Rakes
Elmwood Junior High School
Rogers, Arkansas

Discovery Lab

Cells Alive!

You probably have used a microscope to look at single-celled organisms such as those shown on this page. Single-celled organisms can be found in pond water. In the following exercise, you will look at *Protococcus*—algae that form a greenish stain on tree trunks, wooden fences, flowerpots, and buildings.

MATERIALS

- *Protococcus* (or other algae)
- microscope
- eyedropper
- water
- microscope slide and coverslip

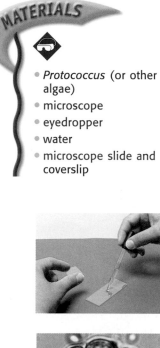

Protococcus

Procedure

1 Locate some *Protococcus*. Scrape a small sample into a container. Bring the sample to the classroom, and make a wet mount of it as directed by your teacher. If you can't find *Protococcus* outdoors, look for algae on the glass in an aquarium. Such algae may not be *Protococcus*, but they will be a very good substitute.

Euglena   *Amoeba*   *Paramecium*

2 Set the microscope on low power to examine the algae. Draw the cells that you see.

3 Switch to high power to examine a single cell. Draw the cell.

4 You probably will notice that each cell contains several chloroplasts. Label a chloroplast on your drawing. What is the function of the chloroplast?

5 Another structure that should be clearly visible in all the algae cells is the nucleus. Find the nucleus in one of your cells, and label it on your drawing. What is the function of the nucleus?

6 What does the cytoplasm look like? Describe any movement you see inside the cells.

Analysis

7 Are *Protococcus* single-celled organisms or multicellular organisms?

8 How are *Protococcus* different from amoebas?

24

Answers

4. Chloroplasts are the parts of the cell that are responsible for photosynthesis.

5. The nucleus of a cell controls most of the activities that take place in that cell and contains the hereditary information.

6. The cytoplasm is a clear gel-like substance that fills the cell and surrounds the organelles.

7. *Protococcus* is a genus composed of single-celled algae.

8. Many answers are possible, but the following are most likely: *Protococcus* cannot move about like amoebas can; unlike amoebas, they are green and they photosynthesize.

Skill Builder Lab

Name That Part!

Plant cells and animal cells have many organelles and other parts in common. For example, both plant and animal cells contain a nucleus and mitochondria. But plant cells and animal cells differ in several ways. In this exercise, you will investigate the similarities and differences between animal cells and plant cells.

MATERIALS

- colored pencils or markers
- white, unlined paper

Plant cell

Procedure

1. Using colored pencils or markers and white, unlined paper, trace or draw the plant cell and the animal cell shown below. Draw each cell on a separate sheet of paper. You may color each organelle a different color.

2. Label the parts of each cell.

3. Below each drawing, list all the parts that you labeled and describe their function.

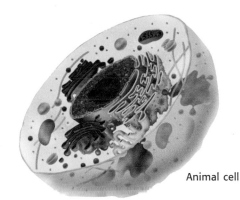

Animal cell

Analysis

4. List at least four structures that plant cells and animal cells have in common.

5. List three structures that plant cells have that animal cells do not have.

25

Datasheets for LabBook

Martha Kisiah
Fairview Middle School
Tallahassee, Florida

Skill Builder Lab

Name That Part!
Teacher's Notes

Time Required
One 40-minute class period

Lab Ratings

EASY ——————→ HARD

TEACHER PREP ▲
STUDENT SET-UP ▲
CONCEPT LEVEL ▲
CLEAN UP ▲

Answers

2. Have students label the following parts: Golgi complex, cytoplasm, nucleus, nucleolus, nuclear membrane, cell membrane, mitochondria, endoplasmic reticulum, vacuole, cell wall, chloroplast, lysosome.

3. **Golgi complex**—area that stores and packages chemicals
cytoplasm—materials between nucleus and cell membrane
nucleus—control center containing genetic information
nucleolus—spherical body in the nucleus
nuclear membrane—membrane surrounding the nucleus
cell membrane—membrane surrounding the cytoplasm and the organelles
mitochondria—releases energy from nutrients
endoplasmic reticulum—location of ribosomal attachment and part of the cell's internal transport system
vacuole—bubblelike storage structure
cell wall—stiff outer covering of a plant cell
chloroplast—plastid that stores chlorophyll used in photosynthesis
lysosome—digests large particles

4. Any four structures are correct except the following: centriole, vacuole, cell wall, chloroplast.

5. vacuole, cell wall, chloroplast

Chapter Highlights

Chapter Highlights

VOCABULARY DEFINITIONS

SECTION 1

tissue a group of similar cells that work together to perform a specific job in the body

organ a combination of two or more tissues that work together to perform a specific function in the body

organ system a group of organs working together to perform body functions

organism anything that can independently carry out life processes

unicellular made of a single cell

multicellular made of many cells

population a group of individuals of the same species that live together in the same area at the same time

community all of the populations of different species that live and interact in an area

ecosystem a community of organisms and their nonliving environment

SECTION 2

cell membrane a phospholipid layer that covers a cell's surface and acts as a barrier between the inside of a cell and the cell's environment

organelles structures within a cell, sometimes surrounded by a membrane

cytoplasm cellular fluid surrounding a cell's organelles

nucleus membrane-covered organelle found in eukaryotic cells that contains a cell's DNA and serves as a control center for the cell

prokaryotic describes a cell that does not have a nucleus or any other membrane-covered organelles; also called bacteria

eukaryotic describes a cell that has a nucleus

bacteria extremely small single-celled organisms without a nucleus; prokaryotic cells

---

SECTION 1

Vocabulary

  tissue (p. 5)
  organ (p. 5)
  organ system (p. 6)
  organism (p. 7)
  unicellular (p. 7)
  multicellular (p. 7)
  population (p. 7)
  community (p. 8)
  ecosystem (p. 8)

Section Notes

- The cell is the smallest unit of life on Earth. Organisms can be made up of one or more cells.

- In multicellular organisms, groups of cells can work together to form tissue. Organs are formed from different tissues and work together with other organs in organ systems.

- The same kind of organisms living together in the same place at the same time make up a population. Different populations living together in the same area make up a community. An ecosystem includes the community and an area's nonliving parts, such as the water and soil.

SECTION 2

Vocabulary

  cell membrane (p. 11)
  organelles (p. 11)
  cytoplasm (p. 11)
  nucleus (p. 14)
  prokaryotic (p. 14)
  eukaryotic (p. 14)
  bacteria (p. 14)

Section Notes

- The cell theory states that all organisms are made of cells, the cell is the basic unit of life, and all cells come from other cells.

- All cells have a cell membrane, DNA, cytoplasm, and organelles. Most cells are too small to be seen with the naked eye.

☑ Skills Check

Math Concepts

SURFACE-TO-VOLUME RATIO You can determine the surface-to-volume ratio of a cell or other object by dividing surface area by the volume. To determine the surface-to-volume ratio of the rectangle at left, you must first determine the surface area. Surface area is the total area of all the sides. This rectangle has two sides with an area of 6 cm × 3 cm, two sides with an area of 3 cm × 2 cm, and two sides with an area of 6 cm × 2 cm.

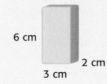

6 cm

2 cm

3 cm

surface area = 2(6 cm × 3 cm) + 2(3 cm × 2 cm) + 2(6 cm × 2 cm) = 72 cm²

Next you need to find the volume. The volume is determined by multiplying the length of the three sides.

volume = 6 cm × 3 cm × 2 cm = 36 cm³

To find surface-to-volume ratio, you divide the surface area by the volume:

$$\frac{72}{36} = 2$$

So the surface-to-volume ratio of this rectangle is 2:1.

Lab and Activity Highlights

Cells Alive!   PG 24

Name That Part!   PG 25

Elephant-Sized Amoebas?   PG 184

Datasheets for LabBook
(blackline masters for these labs)

SECTION 2

- Materials that cells need to take in or release must pass through the cell membrane.

- The surface-to-volume ratio is a comparison of the cell's outer surface to the cell's volume. A cell's surface-to-volume ratio decreases as the cell grows.

  - Eukaryotes have linear DNA enclosed in a nucleus and membrane-covered organelles. Prokaryotic cells have circular DNA and organelles that are not covered by membranes.

Labs

Elephant-Sized Amoebas?
(p. 184)

SECTION 3

Vocabulary

cell wall (p. 17)
ribosome (p. 18)
endoplasmic reticulum (p. 18)
mitochondria (p. 19)
chloroplast (p. 19)
Golgi complex (p. 20)
vesicle (p. 21)
vacuole (p. 21)
lysosome (p. 22)

Section Notes

- All cells have a cell membrane that surrounds the contents of the cell. Some cells have a cell wall outside their membrane.

- The nucleus is the control center of the eukaryotic cell. It contains the cell's DNA.

- Ribosomes are the sites where amino acids are strung together to form proteins. Ribosomes are not covered by a membrane.

- The endoplasmic reticulum (ER) and the Golgi complex are membrane-covered compartments in which materials are made and processed before they are transported to other parts of the cell or out of the cell.

- Mitochondria and chloroplasts are energy-producing organelles.

- Vesicles and vacuoles are membrane-covered compartments that store material. Vacuoles are found in plant cells. Lysosomes are vesicles found in animal cells.

SECTION 3

cell wall a structure that surrounds the cell membrane of some cells and provides strength and support to the cell membrane

ribosome a small organelle in cells where proteins are made from amino acids

endoplasmic reticulum a membrane-covered cell organelle that produces lipids, breaks down drugs and other substances, and packages proteins for delivery out of the cell

mitochondria cell organelles surrounded by two membranes that break down food molecules to make ATP

chloroplast an organelle found in plant and algae cells where photosynthesis occurs

Golgi complex the cell organelle that modifies, packages, and transports materials out of the cell

vesicle a membrane-covered compartment in a eukaryotic cell that forms when part of the cell membrane surrounds an object and pinches off

vacuole a large membrane-covered structure found in plant cells that serve as storage containers for water and other liquids

lysosome a special vesicle in cells that digests food particles, wastes, and foreign invaders

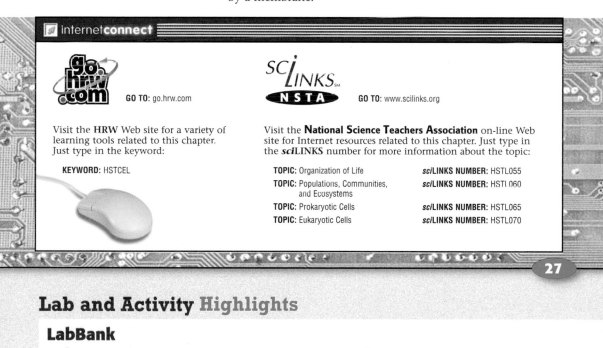

internet connect

GO TO: go.hrw.com

Visit the **HRW** Web site for a variety of learning tools related to this chapter. Just type in the keyword:

KEYWORD: HSTCEL

SCI**LINKS**
N S T A

GO TO: www.scilinks.org

Visit the **National Science Teachers Association** on-line Web site for Internet resources related to this chapter. Just type in the *sci*LINKS number for more information about the topic:

TOPIC: Organization of Life	*sci*LINKS NUMBER: HSTL055
TOPIC: Populations, Communities, and Ecosystems	*sci*LINKS NUMBER: HSTL060
TOPIC: Prokaryotic Cells	*sci*LINKS NUMBER: HSTL065
TOPIC: Eukaryotic Cells	*sci*LINKS NUMBER: HSTL070

27

Lab and Activity Highlights

LabBank

 Labs You Can Eat, The Incredible Edible Cell

Whiz-Bang Demonstrations, Grand Strand

 Long-Term Projects & Research Ideas, Ewe Again, Dolly?

 Vocabulary Review Worksheet

 Blackline masters of these Chapter Highlights can be found in the **Study Guide.**

Chapter Review
Answers

USING VOCABULARY

1. cellulose
2. eukaryotic
3. nucleus
4. mitochondria/chloroplasts
5. Golgi complex

UNDERSTANDING CONCEPTS

Multiple Choice

6. a
7. b
8. c
9. a
10. c
11. c

Short Answer

12. Cells must be small to have a large surface-to-volume ratio.
13. Mitochondria have a double membrane, possess their own ribosomes, contain circular DNA, divide like bacteria, and are about the same size as bacteria.
14. Answers should paraphrase the following points: all organisms are composed of one or more cells; the cell is the basic unit of life in all living things; all cells come from existing cells.

Concept Mapping Transparency 3

Chapter Review

USING VOCABULARY

To complete the following sentences, choose the correct term from each pair of terms listed below:

1. The cell wall of plant cells is made of __?__. (*lipids* or *cellulose*)

2. Having membrane-covered organelles is a characteristic of __?__ cells. (*prokaryotic* or *eukaryotic*)

3. The information for how to make proteins is located in the __?__. (*Golgi complex* or *nucleus*)

4. The two organelles that can generate ATP in a plant cell are __?__ and __?__. (*chloroplasts/ER* or *mitochondria/chloroplasts*)

5. Vesicles that will transport materials out of the cell are formed at the __?__. (*Golgi complex* or *cell membrane*)

UNDERSTANDING CONCEPTS

Multiple Choice

6. Which of the following is *not* found in animal cells?
   a. cell wall
   b. cell membrane
   c. lysosomes
   d. vesicle

7. Different __?__ work together in an organ.
   a. organ systems
   b. tissues
   c. organisms
   d. prokaryotes

8. Which of the following refers to all of the organisms in a particular area?
   a. population
   b. ecosystem
   c. community
   d. organelles

9. The scientist who said that all cells come from cells was named
   a. Virchow.
   b. Schleiden.
   c. Hooke.
   d. Schwann.

10. Which of the following are *not* covered by a membrane?
    a. Golgi complex
    b. mitochondria
    c. ribosomes
    d. none of the above

11. Which of the following contain enzymes that can break down particles in vesicles?
    a. mitochondria
    b. endoplasmic reticulum
    c. lysosomes
    d. none of the above

Short Answer

12. Why are most cells so small?

13. What five characteristics of mitochondria suggest that they may have originated as bacteria?

14. In your own words, list the three parts of the cell theory.

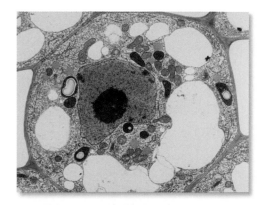

Concept Mapping

15. Use the following terms to create a concept map: ecosystem, cells, organisms, Golgi complex, organ systems, community, organs, endoplasmic reticulum, nucleus, population, tissues.

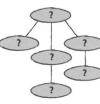

CRITICAL THINKING AND PROBLEM SOLVING

Write one or two sentences to answer the following questions:

16. Explain how the nucleus can control what happens in a lysosome.

17. Even though cellulose is not made at ribosomes, explain how ribosomes in a plant cell are important to the formation of a cell wall.

MATH IN SCIENCE

18. Assume that three food molecules per cubic unit of volume per minute is required for the cell below to survive. If one molecule can enter through each square unit of surface per minute, this cell is

a. too big and would starve.
b. too small and would starve.
c. at a size that would allow it to survive.

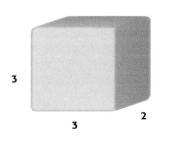

3

3   2

INTERPRETING GRAPHICS

Look at the cell diagrams below, and answer the questions that follow:

Cell A

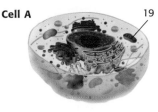
19

Cell B

21

19. Name the organelle labeled "19" in Cell A.

20. Is Cell A a bacterial cell, a plant cell, or an animal cell? Explain your answer.

21. What is the name and function of the organelle labeled "21" in Cell B?

22. Is Cell B a prokaryotic cell or a eukaryotic cell? Explain your answer.

Reading Check-up

Take a minute to review your answers to the Pre-Reading Questions found at the bottom of page 2. Have your answers changed? If necessary, revise your answers based on what you have learned since you began this chapter.

Concept Mapping

15. An answer to this exercise can be found at the front of this book.

CRITICAL THINKING AND PROBLEM SOLVING

16. The nucleus controls the production of proteins. The enzymes needed to break down materials in a lysosome are proteins.

17. Enzymes are used to make cellulose, and enzymes are proteins. All proteins are made at ribosomes.

MATH IN SCIENCE

18. a. too big and would starve

INTERPRETING GRAPHICS

19. mitochondrion
20. Animal; it is not a bacteria because it has a nucleus, and it is not a plant because it has no cell wall.
21. vacuole; storage of water and other materials
22. eukaryotic, because it has a nucleus

Blackline masters of this Chapter Review can be found in the **Study Guide.**

Battling Cancer With Pigs' Blood and Laser Light

Background

Students may want to know more about the traditional forms of cancer treatment. Some common therapies are chemotherapy, radiation treatment, and surgery. These are often used in combination to combat a single cancer. Although these treatments are highly effective on many forms of cancer, there are side effects that accompany them. For instance, chemotherapy and radiation treatments are generally toxic to the human body, causing side effects that can even be life threatening. Side effects include nausea, diarrhea, hair loss, organ failure, and bone marrow toxicity. Also, many cancer treatments lower a patient's ability to fight other diseases.

Chemotherapy is usually administered intravenously and is designed to interrupt the growth of cancer cells at different points in their development. For instance, one drug is effective on cancer cells during their division stage, while another attacks the cancer in its growth phase. Radiation treatments use high-energy beams of X rays and gamma rays to destroy cancerous tissues. The radiation impairs the cells' ability to multiply. Unfortunately, many forms of cancer are resistant to these treatments, and doctors continually seek new and better ways to cure cancer.

ACROSS THE SCIENCES

LIFE SCIENCE • PHYSICAL SCIENCE

Battling Cancer with Pigs' Blood and Laser Light

What do you get when you cross pigs' blood and laser beams? Would you believe a treatment for cancer? Medical researchers have developed an effective new cancer treatment called *photodynamic therapy,* or PDT. It combines high-energy laser beams with a light-sensitive drug derived from pigs' blood to combat the deadly disease.

▲ Blood from pigs provides substances used to help treat cancer.

Pigs' Blood to the Rescue

The first step in PDT involves a light-sensitive substance called *porphyrin.* Porphyrins are natural chemicals found in red blood cells that bind to lipoproteins, which carry cholesterol in our blood. All cells use lipoproteins in their cell membranes. But cells that divide quickly, like cancer cells, make membranes faster than normal cells. Since they use more lipoproteins, they also accumulate more porphyrins.

Scientists have developed a synthetic porphyrin, called Photofrin®, made from natural porphyrins found in pigs' blood. Photofrin can absorb energy from light. When Photofrin is injected into a patient's bloodstream, it acts the same way natural porphyrins do—it becomes part of the cell membranes formed by cancer cells. A short time later, the patient visits a surgeon's office for step two of PDT, zapping the diseased tissue with a laser beam.

Hitting the Target

A surgeon threads a long, thin laser-tipped tube into the cancerous area where the Photofrin has accumulated. When the laser beam hits the cancerous tissue, Photofrin absorbs the light energy. Then, in a process similar to photosynthesis, Photofrin releases oxygen. The type of oxygen released damages the proteins, lipids, nucleic acids, and other components of cancer cells. This damage kills off cancer cells in the treated area but doesn't kill healthy cells. Photofrin is more sensitive to certain wavelengths of light than are natural porphyrins. And the intense beam of laser light can be precisely focused on the cancerous tissue without affecting nearby healthy tissue.

An Alternative?

PDT is an important medical development because it kills cancer cells without many of the harmful side effects caused by other cancer therapies, such as chemotherapy. However, PDT does have some side effects. Until the drug wears off, in about 30 days, the patient is susceptible to severe sunburn. Researchers are working to develop a second-generation drug, called BPD (benzoporphyrin derivative), that will have fewer side effects and respond to different wavelengths of lasers. BPD is also being tested for use in certain eye diseases and as a treatment for psoriasis.

Find Out for Yourself

▶ Do some research to find out why scientists used pigs' blood to create Photofrin.

Answer to Find Out for Yourself

Researchers used pigs' blood because it is similar to human blood and is available in the large quantities necessary for research.

Health WATCH

The Scrape of the Future

What did you do the last time you scraped your knee? You probably put a bandage on it, and before you realized it your knee was as good as new. Bandages serve as barriers that help prevent infection and further injury. But what if there were such a thing as a living bandage that actually helped your body heal? It sounds like science fiction, but it's not!

The Main Factor

An injury to the skin, such as a scraped knee, triggers skin cells to produce and release a steady stream of proteins that heal the injury. These naturally occurring proteins are called *human growth factors,* or just *growth factors.* Growth factors specialize in rebuilding the body. Some reconstruct connective tissue that provides structure for new skin, some help rebuild blood vessels in a wounded area, and still others stimulate the body's immune system. Thanks to growth factors, scraped skin usually heals in just a few days.

Help from a Living Bandage

Unfortunately, healing isn't always an easy, natural process. Someone with a weakened immune system may be unable to produce enough growth factors to heal a wound properly. For example, someone with severe burns may have lost the ability in the burned area to produce the proteins necessary to rebuild healthy tissues. In these cases, using manufactured human growth factors can greatly assist the healing process.

▲ Dr. Daniel Smith holds the GEBB that he designed.

Recent advances in bioengineering can help people whose immune system prevents them from healing naturally. The Genetically Engineered Biological Bandage (GEBB) is a special bandage that is actually a bag of living skin cells taken from donors. The cells' DNA is manipulated to produce human growth factors. The GEBB is about 1 cm thick and consists of three layers: a thin gauze layer; a thin, permeable membrane; and a dome-shaped silicone bag containing the growth factors. The bandage is applied to the wound just as a normal bandage is, with the gauze layer closest to the injury. The growth factors leave the silicone bag through the membrane and pass through the gauze into the wound. There they act on the wound just as the body's own growth factors would.

Time-Release Formula

The GEBB also helps heal wounds more quickly. It maximizes the effectiveness of growth hormones by releasing them at a constant rate over 3 to 5 days.

Because the GEBB imitates the body's own healing processes, other versions of the living bandage will likely be used in the future to treat a variety of wounds and skin conditions, such as severe acne.

Think About It

► Can you think of other advances in medical technology, such as eyeglasses or a hearing aid, that mimic or enhance what the human body does naturally?

Background

Skin is a naturally healing tissue helped by growth factors. Bones, muscles, blood, and many major organs, including the liver and lungs, can also heal and repair major damage with the help of the body's own growth factors. Nerve cells, including those in the spinal cord and brain, are less able to recover from damage.

Scientists are studying how nerves grow and what growth factors are involved in hopes of discovering a way to promote healing in people who suffer from nerve cell damage.

31

Answers to Think About It

Answers will vary, but there are mechanical voices; artificial muscles; wheelchairs that respond to breath commands; hearing aids; glasses; and artificial hips, hands, legs, and even hearts.

Chapter Organizer

CHAPTER ORGANIZATION	TIME MINUTES	OBJECTIVES	LABS, INVESTIGATIONS, AND DEMONSTRATIONS
Chapter Opener pp. 32–33	45	National Standards: UCP 3, SAI 1, SPSP 5, LS 1b	**Start-Up Activity,** Cells in Action, p. 33
Section 1 **Exchange with the Environment**	120	▶ Explain the process of diffusion. ▶ Describe how osmosis occurs. ▶ Compare passive transport with active transport. ▶ Explain how large particles get into and out of cells. UCP 1–4, LS 1c; Labs UCP 2, SAI 1	**QuickLab,** Bead Diffusion, p. 34 **Demonstration,** Membrane Model, p. 34 in ATE **Demonstration,** Crossing Membranes, p. 35 in ATE **Interactive Explorations CD-ROM,** The Nose Knows *A Worksheet is also available in the Interactive Explorations Teacher's Edition.* **Design Your Own,** The Perfect Taters Mystery, p. 186 **Datasheets for LabBook,** The Perfect Taters Mystery **Inquiry Labs,** Fish Farms in Space **Whiz-Bang Demonstrations,** It's in the Bag!
Section 2 **Cell Energy**	120	▶ Describe photosynthesis and cellular respiration. ▶ Compare cellular respiration with fermentation. UCP 1, 3–5, SAI 2, ST 2, SPSP 4–5, LS 1c, 4c; Labs SAI 1, SPSP 1, LS 1c	**Demonstration,** Light Response, p. 38 in ATE **Skill Builder,** Stayin' Alive! p. 46 **Datasheets for LabBook,** Stayin' Alive!
Section 3 **The Cell Cycle**	120	▶ Explain how cells produce more cells. ▶ Discuss the importance of mitosis. ▶ Explain how cell division differs in animals and plants. SAI 1, LS 1c, 2d	**Labs You Can Eat,** The Mystery of the Runny Gelatin **Whiz-Bang Demonstration,** Stop Picking on My Enzyme **Long-Term Projects & Research Ideas,** Taming the Wild Yeast

*See page **T23** for a complete correlation of this book with the*

NATIONAL SCIENCE EDUCATION STANDARDS.

TECHNOLOGY RESOURCES

Guided Reading Audio CD
English or Spanish, Chapter 2

 CNN Science, Technology & Society,
Radioactive Medicine, Segment 5

One-Stop Planner CD-ROM
with Test Generator

 Interactive Explorations CD-ROM
CD 3, Exploration 1, The Nose Knows

Science Discovery Videodiscs
Image and Activity Bank with Lesson Plans:
Outside and Inside

CLASSROOM WORKSHEETS, TRANSPARENCIES, AND RESOURCES	SCIENCE INTEGRATION AND CONNECTIONS	REVIEW AND ASSESSMENT
Directed Reading Worksheet **Science Puzzlers, Twisters & Teasers**		
Directed Reading Worksheet, Section 1 **Transparency 11**, Passive and Active Transport **Transparency 12**, Endocytosis **Transparency 12**, Exocytosis **Reinforcement Worksheet**, Into and Out of the Cell	**Math and More**, p. 35 in ATE	**Self-Check**, p. 35 **Homework**, p. 36 in ATE **Section Review**, p. 37 **Quiz**, p. 37 in ATE **Alternative Assessment**, p. 37 in ATE
Directed Reading Worksheet, Section 2 **Transparency 243**, Solar Heating Systems **Transparency 13**, Photosynthesis and Respiration: What's the Connection? **Reinforcement Worksheet**, Activities of the Cell **Critical Thinking Worksheet**, A Celluloid Thriller	**Connect to Physical Science**, p. 39 in ATE **Connect to Physical Science**, p. 40 in ATE **Apply**, p. 41 **Chemistry Connection**, p. 39 **Across the Sciences**: Electrifying News About Microbes, p. 52	**Homework**, p. 40 in ATE **Section Review**, p. 41 **Quiz**, p. 41 in ATE **Alternative Assessment**, p. 41 in ATE
Directed Reading Worksheet, Section 3 **Math Skills for Science Worksheet**, Creating Exponents **Science Skills Worksheet**, Using Models to Communicate **Transparency 14**, The Cell Cycle: Phases of Mitosis **Reinforcement Worksheet**, This Is Radio KCEL	**MathBreak**, Cell Multiplication, p. 42 **Math and More**, p. 43 in ATE **Holt Anthology of Science Fiction**, *Contagion*	**Self-Check**, p. 43 **Homework**, p. 44 in ATE **Section Review**, p. 45 **Quiz**, p. 45 in ATE **Alternative Assessment**, p. 45 in ATE

internet connect

go.hrw.com **Holt, Rinehart and Winston On-line Resources**
go.hrw.com

For worksheets and other teaching aids related to this chapter, visit the HRW Web site and type in the keyword: **HSTACT**

SCLINKS NSTA **National Science Teachers Association**
www.scilinks.org

Encourage students to use the *sci*LINKS numbers listed in the internet connect boxes to access information and resources on the **NSTA** Web site.

END-OF-CHAPTER REVIEW AND ASSESSMENT

Chapter Review in Study Guide
Vocabulary and Notes in Study Guide
Chapter Tests with Performance-Based Assessment, Chapter 2 Test
Chapter Tests with Performance-Based Assessment, Performance-Based Assessment 2
Concept Mapping Transparency 4

Chapter Resources & Worksheets

Visual Resources

TEACHING TRANSPARENCIES

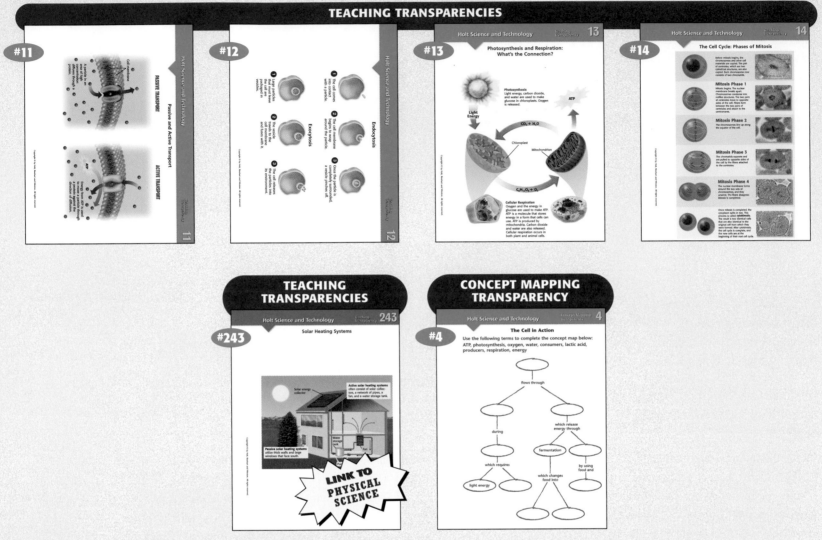

TEACHING TRANSPARENCIES

CONCEPT MAPPING TRANSPARENCY

Meeting Individual Needs

DIRECTED READING

REINFORCEMENT & VOCABULARY REVIEW

SCIENCE PUZZLERS, TWISTERS & TEASERS

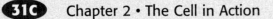

Chapter 2 • The Cell in Action

Review & Assessment

STUDY GUIDE

CHAPTER TESTS WITH PERFORMANCE-BASED ASSESSMENT

Lab Worksheets

INQUIRY LABS

LONG-TERM PROJECTS & RESEARCH IDEAS

LABS YOU CAN EAT

WHIZ-BANG DEMONSTRATIONS

DATASHEETS FOR LABBOOK

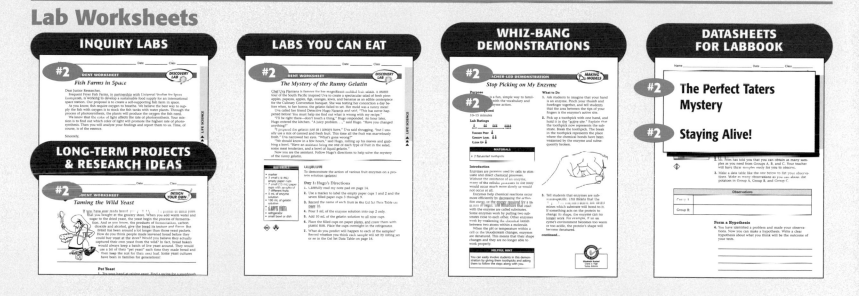

Applications & Extensions

CRITICAL THINKING & PROBLEM SOLVING

SCIENCE TECHNOLOGY

INTERACTIVE EXPLORATIONS

SECTION 1

Exchange with the Environment

▶ **Endocytosis**

There are three different mechanisms of endocytosis: pinocytosis, phagocytosis, and receptor-mediated endocytosis. These processes allow a substance to enter a cell without passing through the cell membrane. The type of material involved determines which method is used.

- Large particles such as bacteria enter the cell by phagocytosis. The host cell changes shape, and the membrane sends out projections called pseudopods, meaning "false feet," which surround the particle, bringing it inside the cell.

- In receptor-mediated endocytosis, receptors on the membrane that are specific for a given substance bind to the substance before the endocytotic process begins. This method is used during cholesterol metabolism.

- In pinocytosis, the cell membrane surrounds the substance and forms a vesicle to bring the material into the cell. Pinocytosis usually involves material that is dissolved in water.

▶ **Reverse Osmosis**

Reverse osmosis is a process that forces water across semipermeable membranes under high pressure. The high pressure reverses the natural tendency of the solutes on the concentrated side of the membrane to pass through to the less-concentrated side. In this way water passing through the membrane is purified.

IS THAT A FACT!

- ➤ The largest single-celled organism that ever lived was a protozoa that measured 20 cm in diameter. It is now extinct.

SECTION 2

Cell Energy

▶ **Jan Baptista van Helmont (1580–1644)**

Van Helmont was a Belgian chemist, physiologist, and physician who coined the word *gas.* He was the first scientist to comprehend the existence of gases separate from the atmospheric air. Although he didn't know that it was carbon dioxide, van Helmont stated that the *spiritus sylvestre,* or "wild spirit," emitted by burning charcoal was the same as that given off by fermenting grape juice. He applied chemistry to the study of physiological processes, and for this he is known as the "father of biochemistry."

- Joseph Priestly (1733–1804) was an English clergyman and physical scientist who was one of the discoverers of oxygen. He also observed that light was vital for plant growth and that green leaves released oxygen.

- Jan Ingenhousz (1730–1799), a Dutch-born British physician and scientist, discovered photosynthesis.

▶ **Carotenoids and Photosynthesis**

Carotenoids are responsible for the orange colors in plants. Their presence is usually masked by chlorophyll. They are sensitive to wavelengths of light to which chlorophyll cannot respond. Carotenoids can absorb the light waves and transfer the energy to chlorophyll, which then incorporates that energy into the photosynthetic pathway.

IS THAT A FACT!

- Cellular respiration was discovered in 1937 by German biochemist Hans Krebs (1900–1981). The Krebs cycle is a series of chemical reactions that are essential to metabolic activities in all living organisms.

SECTION 3

The Cell Cycle

▶ Cytogenetics

Cytogeneticists study the role of human chromosomes in health and disease. Chromosome studies can reveal abnormalities such as whether a person is carrying the genetic material for a genetically linked disease.

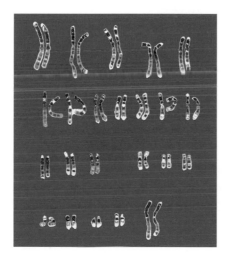

▶ Cell Division

The frequency of cell division varies a great deal. Fruit-fly embryo cells divide about every 8 minutes. Human liver cells may not divide for up to 1 year. Scientists are still trying to determine what orchestrates growth and regulates cell division. This information would help scientists understand diseases of unregulated cell division, such as cancer.

IS THAT A FACT!

- Cell division occurs at least 10 million times every second in an adult human body.

- DNA and chromosomes are related but are not the same thing. A chromosome is made up of DNA that has been wound up and organized with proteins that hold it all together. For much of the cell cycle, DNA is loose and not very visible.

▶ Cell Adhesion

Blood cells exist individually in the body, but most other cells are connected to each other. Usually this involves special adhesion proteins, such as adherins, cadherins, catenins, and integrins. These proteins connect adjoining cells by physically locking the cells together, fastening one cell to the next. Sometimes these junctions are outside the cell, and sometimes they are inside. Adherence proteins can span the cell membranes and connect the inside of one cell to the inside of its neighbor cell.

IS THAT A FACT!

- In a healthy body, cells reproduce at exactly the same rate at which they die. However, some agents make cells reproduce uncontrollably, causing a disease known as cancer. One of these carcinogenic agents is ultraviolet radiation, which is emitted by the sun and ultraviolet lamps. People who spend excessive amounts of time in the sun run the risk of developing skin cancer.

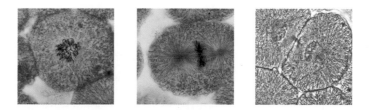

For background information about teaching strategies and issues, refer to the *Professional Reference for Teachers.*

CHAPTER

2

The Cell in Action

Pre-Reading Questions

Students may not know the answers to these questions before reading the chapter, so accept any reasonable response.

Suggested Answers

1. Answers will vary but should reflect knowledge of diffusion, osmosis, endocytosis, active transport, and exocytosis.

2. Cells use food to make energy through respiration and fermentation.

3. Eukaryotic cells divide using mitosis and cytokinesis. Prokaryotic cells divide by binary fission. Every division doubles the number of cells.

Pre-Reading Questions

1. How do water, food, and wastes get into and out of a cell?

2. How do cells use food molecules?

3. How does one cell produce many cells?

A Copier Machine

These cells are from the growing tip of a plant root. In order to grow, the plant is producing many new cells. When plant cells divide, the cell copies its genetic material. The cell then undergoes mitosis. Mitosis is the process that ensures that each new cell ends up with the correct complement of chromosomes. All the different stages of mitosis can be seen in this tissue.

📨 internet**connect**

HRW On-line Resources

go.hrw.com

For worksheets and other teaching aids, visit the HRW Web site and type in the keyword: **HSTACT**

www.scilinks.com

Use the *sci*LINKS numbers at the end of each chapter for additional resources on the **NSTA** Web site.

Smithsonian Institution®

www.si.edu/hrw

Visit the Smithsonian Institution Web site for related on-line resources.

CNNfyi.com

www.cnnfyi.com

Visit the CNN Web site for current events coverage and classroom resources.

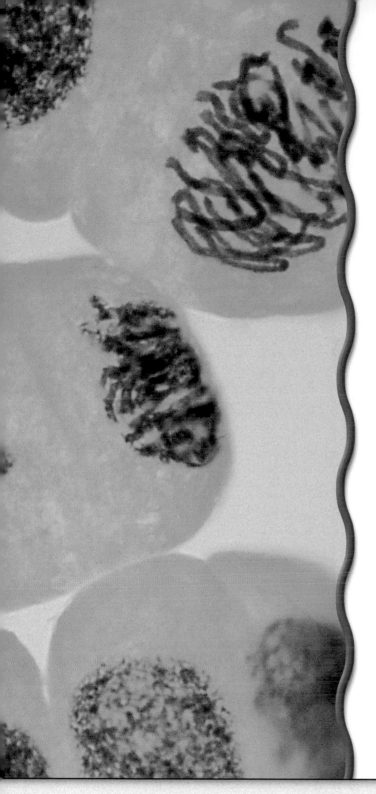

START-UP Activity

CELLS IN ACTION

Yeasts are fungi that are used in baking. Yeast cells break down sugar molecules to release energy. In the process, a gas called carbon dioxide (CO_2) is produced. Bubbles of CO_2 cause the bread dough to rise. The amount of CO_2 produced depends on how much sugar is broken down.

Procedure

1. Pour **4 mL of a sugar solution** into **a cup** that contains **10 mL of** a **yeast-and-water mixture.** Mix the two liquids with a **stirring rod.**

2. Pour the contents into a **small test tube.**

3. Place a slightly **larger test tube** over the small test tube. The top of the small test tube should touch the bottom of the larger test tube. Quickly turn both test tubes over. Use a **ruler** to measure the height of the fluid in the large test tube.

4. Place the test tubes in a **test-tube rack** and do not disturb them. After 20 minutes, measure the height of the liquid in the larger test tube again.

Analysis

5. What is the difference between the first height measurement and the second?

6. What do you think caused the change in the height of the fluid?

33

START-UP Activity

CELLS IN ACTION

MATERIALS

FOR EACH STUDENT:
- small plastic cup
- yeast-and-water mixture
- small plastic test tube
- sugar solution
- stirring rod
- large plastic test tube
- test-tube rack
- ruler

Safety Caution

Remind students to review all safety cautions and icons before beginning this lab activity. Students should wear safety goggles at all times and wash their hands when they are finished. Students should not taste the solutions.

Teacher's Notes

The yeast suspension is prepared by mixing one package of dry yeast in 250 mL of water. The sugar solution is prepared by dissolving 30 mL (2 tbsp) of sugar in 100 mL of water. Some students can put their vials on ice and others can put them in a warm place, and others can leave them in a warm place overnight. In this way, students can see how temperature can affect the metabolism of yeast cells.

Answers to START-UP Activity

5. Answers will vary. Students should subtract the first measurement from the second measurement.

6. When the yeast cells released the energy in sugar, the CO_2 that the cells produced increased the volume of air in the smaller tube and pushed more yeast-and-sugar mixture into the larger tube, increasing the height of the liquid in the larger tube.

Focus

Exchange with the Environment

This section explains the processes involved in the exchange of materials between a cell and its environment. Students will learn about diffusion and osmosis, which is the diffusion of water across the cell membrane. Finally, students will compare and contrast active and passive transport and learn how large particles move into and out of cells.

🔔 Bellringer

Writing Write the following on the board or the overhead projector:

Which of the following best describes a living cell:

a. a building block

b. a living organism

c. a complex factory

d. all of the above

Have students write a paragraph in their ScienceLog defending their choice.

1 Motivate

DEMONSTRATION

Membrane Model Blow soap bubbles in front of the class. Explain that soap bubbles have several properties that are similar to biological membranes. One property is flexibility. The components of soap film and the cell membrane move around freely. Both soap bubbles and membranes are self-sealing. If two bubbles or membranes collide, they fuse. If one is cut in half, two smaller but whole bubbles or membranes form.
Sheltered English

Terms to Learn

diffusion   active transport
osmosis   endocytosis
passive transport exocytosis

What You'll Do

◆ Explain the process of diffusion.
◆ Describe how osmosis occurs.
◆ Compare passive transport with active transport.
◆ Explain how large particles get into and out of cells.

Quick**Lab**

Bead Diffusion

Arrange three groups of **colored beads** on the bottom of a **plastic bowl.** Each group should have five beads of the same color. Stretch some **clear plastic wrap** tightly over the top of the bowl. Gently shake the bowl for 10 seconds while watching the beads. How is the scattering of the beads like the diffusion of particles? How is it different from the diffusion of particles?

34

Quick**Lab**

MATERIALS

FOR EACH GROUP:
• three groups of colored beads
• plastic bowl
• clear plastic wrap

Exchange with the Environment

What would happen to a factory if its power were shut off or its supply of raw materials never arrived? What if it couldn't get rid of its garbage? The factory would stop functioning. Like a factory, a cell must be able to obtain energy and raw materials and get rid of wastes.

The exchange of materials between a cell and its environment takes place at the cell's membrane. To understand how materials move into and out of the cell, you need to know about diffusion, a process that affects the movement of particles.

What Is Diffusion?

What happens if you pour dye into a container of solid gelatin? At first, it is easy to see where the gelatin ends and the dye begins. But over time the line between the two layers will become blurry, as shown in **Figure 1.** Why? Dye and gelatin, like all matter, are made up of tiny particles. The particles are always moving and colliding with each other. The mixing of the different particles causes the layers to blur. This occurs whether matter is in the form of a gas, liquid, or solid.

Figure 1 *The particles of the dye and the gelatin slowly begin to mix because of diffusion.*

Particles naturally travel from areas where they are crowded to areas where they are less crowded. **Diffusion** is the movement of particles from an area where their concentration is high to an area where their concentration is low. This movement can occur across cell membranes or outside of cells. Cells do not need to use any energy for diffusion of particles to occur.

Answers to QuickLab

The beads moved from areas where the colors were more concentrated to areas where they were less concentrated. Eventually, the different-colored beads were mixed somewhat evenly. The mixing of the beads required the use of the students' energy and also occurred much more quickly than diffusion normally occurs.

Diffusion of Water All organisms need water to live. The cells of living organisms are surrounded by and filled with fluids that are made mostly of water. The diffusion of water through the cell membrane is so important to life processes that it has been given a special name—**osmosis.**

Water, like all matter, is made up of small particles. Pure water has the highest possible concentration of water particles. To lower this concentration, you simply mix water with something else, such as food coloring, sugar, or salt. **Figure 2** shows what happens when osmosis occurs between two different concentrations of water.

The Cell and Osmosis As you have learned, water particles will move from areas of high concentration to areas of lower concentration. This concept is especially important when you look at it in relation to your cells.

For example, **Figure 3** shows the effects of different concentrations of water on a red blood cell. As you can see, osmosis takes place in different directions depending on the concentration of water surrounding the cell. Fortunately for you, your red blood cells are normally surrounded by blood plasma, which is made up of water, salts, sugars, and other particles in the same concentration as they exist inside the red blood cells.

The cells of plants also take in and release water by osmosis. This is why a wilted plant or even a wilted stalk of celery will become firm again if given water.

Self-Check

What would happen to a grape if you placed it in a dish of pure water? in water mixed with a large amount of sugar? *(See page 216) to check your answer.)*

Figure 2 *This container is divided by a barrier. Particles of water are small enough to pass through the barrier, but the particles of food coloring are not.*

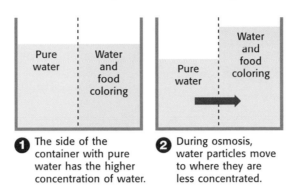

❶ The side of the container with pure water has the higher concentration of water.

❷ During osmosis, water particles move to where they are less concentrated.

This cell has a normal shape because the concentration of water in the cell is the same as the concentration outside the cell.

This cell is in pure water. It is gaining water because the concentration of water particles is lower inside the cell than outside.

Figure 3 *The shape of these red blood cells is affected by the concentration of water outside the cell.*

35

internetconnect

SC**LINKS**
NSTA

TOPIC: Osmosis
GO TO: www.scilinks.org
*sci***LINKS NUMBER:** HSTL075

Answers to Self-Check

In pure water, the grape would absorb water and swell up. In water mixed with a large amount of sugar, the grape would lose water and shrink.

MATH and MORE

Gases diffuse approximately 10,000 times faster in air than in water. If a gas diffuses to fill a room completely in 6 minutes, how long would it take the gas to fill a similar volume of still water? (60,000 minutes) How many hours would that be? (1,000 hours) How many days? (41.67 days)

DEMONSTRATION
Crossing Membranes

MATERIALS
• plastic sandwich bag
• twist tie
• tincture of iodine
• cornstarch
• 500 mL beakers (2)
• eyedropper
• graduated cylinder

Fill one beaker with 250 mL of water. Add 20 drops of iodine. Fill a second beaker with 250 mL water, and stir in 15 mL (1 tbsp) of cornstarch. Pour one-half of the starch-and-water mixture into the plastic bag. Secure the top of the bag with the twist tie. If any starch-and-water mixture spills onto the outside of the bag, rinse it off. Place the bag in the iodine-water mixture. Check immediately for any changes. Look again after 30 minutes. Iodine is used to test for the presence of starch and will turn the starch-and-water mixture black. The iodine particles are small enough to move through the tiny holes in the plastic bag, but the starch molecules are too large.   Sheltered English

Directed Reading Worksheet Section 1

LabBook PG 186
The Perfect Taters Mystery

ACTIVITY

Odor Diffusion One day prior to doing this activity, prepare the following:

MATERIALS

FOR EACH GROUP:
- small container with tight-fitting lid (one per pair of students)
- cotton ball for each container
- several strong-smelling liquids, such as vanilla, garlic oil, and eucalyptus

Soak a cotton ball in one of the liquids. Place the cotton ball in a container, and cover the container with a lid. Repeat until all containers have a soaked cotton ball.

Ask students if they can detect what is inside. If not, instruct students how to safely investigate the odors in the bottle. Have them hold the container 30 cm in front of their face and waft the air above the container toward their nose. Instruct them never to sniff directly from a container. Tell them to remove the lids, and ask them what they smell.

Explain that the cotton balls were soaked in aromatic fluids and that those fluids vaporized and diffused from the area of greatest concentration (the cotton ball) and moved to the area of lesser concentration (the air). **Sheltered English**

Teaching Transparency 11 "Passive and Active Transport"

LabBook

Help solve The Perfect Taters Mystery on page 186 of the LabBook!

Moving Small Particles

Many particles, such as water and oxygen, can diffuse directly through the cell membrane, which is made of phospholipid molecules. These particles can slip through the molecules of the membrane in part because of their small size. However, not all of the particles a cell needs can pass through the membrane in this way. For example, sugar and amino acids aren't small enough to squeeze between the phospholipid molecules, and they are also repelled by the phospholipids in the membrane. They must travel through protein "doorways" located in the cell membrane in order to enter or leave the cell.

Particles can travel through these proteins either by passive transport or by active transport. **Passive transport,** shown in **Figure 4,** is the diffusion of particles through the proteins. The particles move from an area of high concentration to an area of low concentration. The cell does not need to use any energy to make this happen.

Active transport, shown in **Figure 5,** is the movement of particles through proteins against the normal direction of diffusion. In other words, particles are moved from an area of low concentration to an area of high concentration. The cell must use energy to make this happen. This energy comes from the molecule ATP, which stores energy in a form that cells can use.

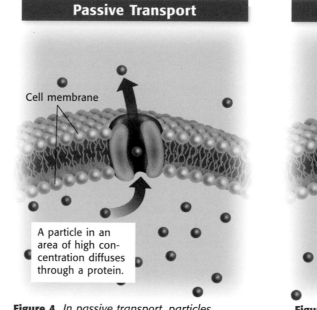

Passive Transport

Cell membrane

A particle in an area of high concentration diffuses through a protein.

Figure 4 *In passive transport, particles travel through proteins from areas of high concentration to areas of low concentration.*

36

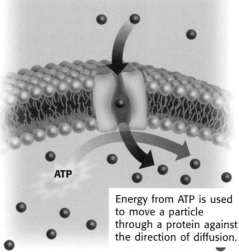

Active Transport

ATP

Energy from ATP is used to move a particle through a protein against the direction of diffusion.

Figure 5 *In active transport, cells use energy to move particles from areas of low concentration to areas of high concentration.*

Homework

Writing Ask students to describe how each of the following materials would get through a cell membrane and into a cell. Which of the materials require active transport?

a. pure water

b. sugar entering a cell that already contains a high concentration of particles

c. sugar entering a cell that has a low concentration of particles

d. a large protein

(b, d)

Moving Large Particles

Diffusion, passive transport, and active transport are good methods of moving small particles into and out of cells, but what about moving large particles? The cell membrane has two ways of accomplishing this task: *endocytosis* and *exocytosis*.

Endocytosis In **endocytosis,** the cell membrane surrounds a particle and encloses it in a vesicle. This is how large particles, such as other cells, can be brought into a cell, as shown in **Figure 6.**

1 The cell comes into contact with a particle.

2 The cell membrane begins to wrap around the particle.

3 Once the particle is completely surrounded, a vesicle pinches off.

Figure 6 Endocytosis *means "within the cell."*

Exocytosis When a large particle must be removed from the cell, the cell uses a different process. In **exocytosis,** vesicles are formed at the endoplasmic reticulum or Golgi complex and carry the particles to the cell membrane, as shown in **Figure 7.**

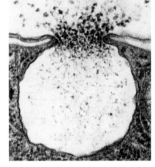 

1 Large particles that must leave the cell are packaged in vesicles.

2 The vesicle travels to the cell membrane and fuses with it.

3 The cell releases the particles into its environment

Figure 7 Exocytosis *means "outside the cell."*

SECTION REVIEW

1. During diffusion, how do particles move?

2. How does a cell take in large particles? How does a cell expel large particles?

3. **Making Inferences** The transfer of glucose into a cell does not require ATP. What type of transport supplies a cell with glucose? Explain your answer.

internet **connect**

SC**LINKS**
NSTA

TOPIC: Osmosis
GO TO: www.scilinks.org
*sci*LINKS NUMBER: HSTL075

▼ **Answers to Section Review**

1. During diffusion, particles move from areas of high concentration to areas of low concentration.

2. Large particles are taken in by endocytosis and expelled by exocytosis.

3. Passive transport supplies a cell with glucose. Passive transport doesn't require the use of energy. Inform students who have trouble answering the question that glucose is a type of sugar.

RESEARCH

Writing Have students write a brief biography of Albert Claude (1898–1983), who used the electron microscope to study cells. (He shared the 1974 Nobel Prize for physiology or medicine with his student George Palade and with Christian de Duve.)

4) Close

Quiz

1. What part of the cell do materials pass through to get into and out of the cell? (the cell membrane)

2. What is osmosis? (the diffusion of water through the cell membrane)

ALTERNATIVE ASSESSMENT

Writing Have students write an instruction manual that tells a cell how to transport both a large molecule and a small molecule through the cell membrane.

Teaching Transparency 12 "Endocytosis" "Exocytosis"

Reinforcement Worksheet "Into and Out of the Cell"

Interactive Explorations CD-ROM "The Nose Knows"

SECTION 2

Focus

Cell Energy

This section introduces energy and the cell. Students learn about solar energy and the process of photosynthesis. Finally, students learn about cellular respiration and fermentation.

🔔 Bellringer

Ask students to make a list in their ScienceLog of all the reasons why a cell might need energy. Remind students that there are many types of cells doing many different jobs.

1 Motivate

DEMONSTRATION

Light Response Cut out a square from black construction paper. Fold the square over a plant leaf of a common house-plant, such as a geranium. Affix the square with a paper clip. Be sure the leaf does not receive any sunlight. Leave the leaf covered for about 1 week. Remove the black square. The leaf will be much paler than the other leaves. In the absence of sunlight, chlorophyll is depleted and not replenished. Thus, the leaf's green color will have faded.
Sheltered English

Directed Reading Worksheet Section 2

READING WARM-UP

Terms to Learn

photosynthesis
cellular respiration
fermentation

What You'll Do

◆ Describe photosynthesis and cellular respiration.
◆ Compare cellular respiration with fermentation.

Cell Energy

Why do you get hungry? Feeling hungry is your body's way of telling you that your cells need energy. Your cells and the cells of all organisms use energy to carry out the chemical activities that allow them to live, grow, and reproduce.

From Sun to Cell

Nearly all of the energy that fuels life comes from the sun. Plants are able to capture light energy from the sun and change it into food through a process called **photosynthesis.** The food that plants make supplies them with energy and also becomes a source of energy for the organisms that eat the plants. Without plants and other producers, consumers would not be able to live.

Photosynthesis Plants have molecules in their cells that absorb the energy of light. These molecules are called *pigments*. Chlorophyll, the main pigment used in photosynthesis, gives plants their green color. In the cells of plants, chlorophyll is found in chloroplasts, which are shown in **Figure 8.**

Plants use the energy captured by chlorophyll to change carbon dioxide (CO_2) and water (H_2O) into food, the simple sugar glucose ($C_6H_{12}O_6$). Glucose is a carbohydrate. When plants make glucose, they are converting the sun's energy into a form of energy that can be stored. The energy in glucose is used by the plant's cells, and some of it may be stored in the form of other carbohydrates or lipids. Photosynthesis also produces oxygen (O_2). Photosynthesis can be summarized by the following equation:

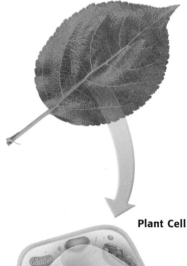

Plant Cell

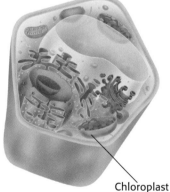

Chloroplast

$$6CO_2 + 6H_2O + \text{light energy} \rightarrow C_6H_{12}O_6 + 6O_2$$

Carbon dioxide Water Glucose Oxygen

Figure 8 *During photosynthesis, plant cells use the energy in sunlight to make food (glucose) from carbon dioxide and water. Photosynthesis takes place in chloroplasts.*

SCIENTISTS AT ODDS

In the 1800s, scientists were reluctant to change their belief that life came from a special "life force." Rudolf Virchow (1821–1902), a German scientist studying cells, believed strongly that life was a physical property of cells, not a mysterious life force. His way of thinking became known as mechanistic because life, it seemed, could be described as the sum of all the physical mechanisms of the cell. Those who clung to the life-force theory were known as vitalists. The mechanists battled the vitalists for 75 years before the cell theory became widely accepted. Today the mechanist view is still dominant in the study of biology.

Getting Energy from Food

The food you eat has to be broken down so that the energy it contains can be converted into a form your cells can use. In fact, all organisms must break down food molecules in order to release the stored energy. There are two ways to do this. One way uses oxygen and is called **cellular respiration.** The other way does not use oxygen and is called **fermentation.**

Cellular Respiration The word *respiration* means "breathing," but cellular respiration is not the same thing as breathing. Breathing supplies your cells with the oxygen they need to perform cellular respiration. Breathing also rids your body of carbon dioxide, which is a waste product of cellular respiration.

Most organisms, such as the cow in **Figure 9,** use cellular respiration to obtain energy from food. During cellular respiration, food (glucose) is broken down into CO_2 and H_2O, and energy is released. A lot of the energy is stored in the form of ATP. ATP is the molecule that supplies energy to fuel the activities of cells. Most of the energy released, however, is in the form of heat. In some organisms, including yourself, this heat helps to maintain the body's temperature.

In the cells of eukaryotes, cellular respiration takes place in mitochondria. The process of cellular respiration is summarized in the equation below. Does this equation remind you of the equation for photosynthesis? The diagram on the next page shows how photosynthesis and respiration are related.

$$C_6H_{12}O_6 + 6O_2 \longrightarrow 6CO_2 + 6H_2O + \text{energy (ATP)}$$

| Glucose | Oxygen | Carbon dioxide | Water |

Chemistry CONNECTION

When the Earth was young, its atmosphere lacked oxygen. The first forms of life used fermentation to gain energy. After organisms evolved the ability to photosynthesize, about 3 billion years ago, the oxygen they produced was added to the atmosphere.

Mitochondria

Animal Cell

Figure 9 *The mitochondria in the cells of this cow will use cellular respiration to release the energy stored in the grass.*

39

SCIENCE HUMOR

Q: How do cells communicate with each other?

A: by cellular phone

2) Teach

GROUP ACTIVITY

Writing Divide the class into groups of three or four. Have each group write the story of a carbon atom as it is used throughout time. Stories should begin with a molecule of carbon dioxide. What plant uses it for photosynthesis? What animals swallow it and use it to fuel respiration? Have students share their stories if time allows.

CONNECT TO PHYSICAL SCIENCE

Conventional solar heating is a much simpler process than photosynthesis. The sun's energy heats either the house itself, or it heats water, which then circulates through the house. If students have ever felt the warm water from a hose that has been left in the sun, they have felt stored solar energy. Use Teaching Transparency 243 to illustrate how solar energy can be used to heat a home.

Teaching Transparency 243 "Solar Heating Systems" LINK TO PHYSICAL SCIENCE

internetconnect

SCiLINKS NSTA
TOPIC: Cell Energy
GO TO: www.scilinks.org
*sci*LINKS NUMBER: HSTL080

USING THE FIGURE

Refer students to the diagram on this page. Ask students to answer the following questions: What happens to the ATP? Where does the ATP go? How is ATP used by the cell? How is the cell's use of CO_2 and H_2O analogous to people's recycling of paper and glass bottles?

CONNECT TO PHYSICAL SCIENCE

Scientists have developed new solar cells that simulate photo- synthesis more closely than traditional solar cells do. Just as plant cells use energy from the sun to change water and carbon dioxide into energy-rich sugars, these new solar cells use the sun's energy to convert water into energy-rich hydrogen gas, which can be used as fuel. As in plants, the byproduct of this process is clean oxygen.

Teaching Transparency 13
"Photosynthesis and Respiration: What's the Connection?"

Reinforcement Worksheet
"Activities of the Cell"

Critical Thinking Worksheet
"A Celluloid Thriller"

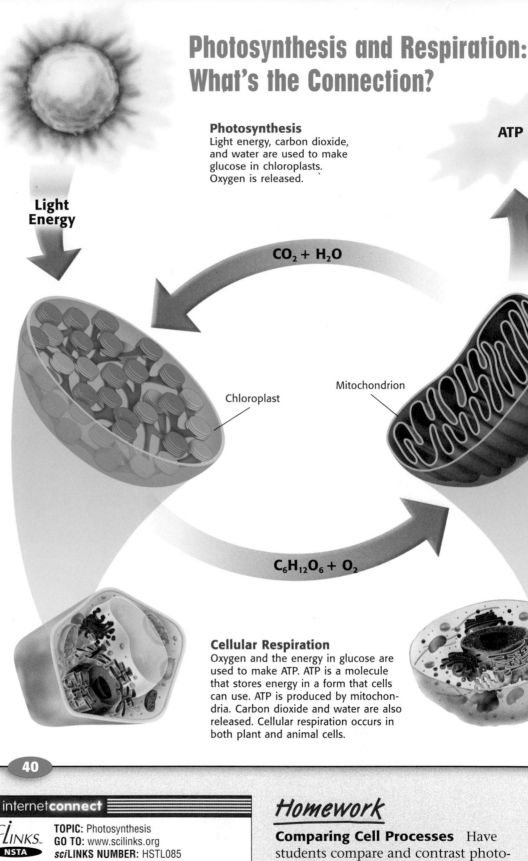

Photosynthesis and Respiration: What's the Connection?

Photosynthesis
Light energy, carbon dioxide, and water are used to make glucose in chloroplasts. Oxygen is released.

ATP

Light Energy

$CO_2 + H_2O$

Chloroplast

Mitochondrion

$C_6H_{12}O_6 + O_2$

Cellular Respiration
Oxygen and the energy in glucose are used to make ATP. ATP is a molecule that stores energy in a form that cells can use. ATP is produced by mitochon- dria. Carbon dioxide and water are also released. Cellular respiration occurs in both plant and animal cells.

40

internetconnect

SCILINKS
NSTA

TOPIC: Photosynthesis
GO TO: www.scilinks.org
*sci*LINKS NUMBER: HSTL085

Homework

Comparing Cell Processes Have students compare and contrast photo- synthesis and respiration. Ask students to use diagrams to display their com- parisons. Encourage students to share their diagrams with their classmates.

Fermentation Have you ever run so far that you started to feel a burning sensation in your muscles? Well, sometimes your muscle cells can't get the oxygen they need to produce ATP by cellular respiration. When this happens, they use the process of fermentation. Fermentation leads to the production of a small amount of ATP and products from the partial breakdown of glucose.

There are two major types of fermentation. The first type occurs in your muscles. It produces lactic acid, which contributes to muscle fatigue after strenuous activity. This type of fermentation also occurs in the muscle cells of other animals and in some types of fungi and bacteria. The second type of fermentation occurs in certain types of bacteria and in yeast. This type of fermentation is described in **Figure 10.**

Figure 10 *Yeast cells make carbon dioxide and alcohol during the fermentation of sugar. The carbon dioxide causes bubbles to form in bread.*

APPLY

Fantasy Island

You have been given the assignment of restoring life to a barren island. What types of organisms would you put on the island? If you want to have animals on the island, what other organisms must be on the island as well? Explain your answer.

SECTION REVIEW

1. Why are producers important to the survival of all other organisms?

2. How do the processes of photosynthesis and cellular respiration relate to each other?

3. What does breathing have to do with cellular respiration?

4. How are respiration and fermentation similar? How are they different?

5. **Identifying Relationships** In which cells would you expect to find the greater number of mitochondria: cells that are very active or cells that are not very active? Why?

---

internet connect

SCI LINKS
NSTA

TOPIC: Cell Energy, Photosynthesis
GO TO: www.scilinks.org
sci INKS NUMBER: HSTL080, HSTL085

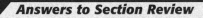

▼ **Answers to Section Review**

1. Producers harness energy in sunlight to produce food (glucose). This food becomes an energy source for producers and for the organisms that consume them.

2. Photosynthesis uses light energy, carbon dioxide, and water to produce glucose and oxygen. Respiration uses the products of photosynthesis to make ATP, carbon dioxide, and water.

3. Breathing supplies the oxygen that cells need for cellular respiration.

4. Both processes release the energy stored in food. Respiration requires oxygen, but fermentation does not.

5. Active cells would have more mitochondria because they have a greater need for energy.

---

3) Extend

GOING FURTHER

Tell students that plants are often referred to as the "lungs of the Earth." Ask students to reflect on this idea and to prepare a presentation for the class. Suggest that students research rain forests as an example of Earth's "lungs" and explain their contribution to the health of the planet.

Answer to APPLY

Answers will vary. Plants must be on the island in order to provide a source of food and energy for the animals.

4) Close

Quiz

Ask students whether the following statements are true or false.

1. Plants and animals capture their energy from the sun. (false)

2. Cellular respiration describes how a cell breathes. (false)

3. Fermentation produces ATP and lactic acid. (true)

ALTERNATIVE ASSESSMENT

Concept Mapping Have students draw a concept map of energy transfer using the following images:

sunshine; tree, for firewood; sugar cane; yeast consuming sugar, making bread rise; person chopping firewood, for baking oven; person eating bread

Students should note on their map which organisms use photosynthesis, which use respiration, and which use fermentation.
Sheltered English

The Cell Cycle

This section introduces the life cycle of a cell. Students will learn how cells reproduce and the importance of mitosis. Finally, students will learn how cell division differs in plants and animals.

 **Bellringer**

On the board or an overhead projector, write the following:

> Biology is the only science in which multiplication means the same thing as division.

Have students explain this sentence in their ScienceLog. (When cells divide, they are multiplying.)

Answer to MATHBREAK

After 24 hours, 16 cells will have formed from Cell *A*, and 8 cells will have formed from Cell *B*. Cell *A* will have formed 8 more cells than Cell *B*.

1 Motivate

ACTIVITY

Making Models Have pairs of students use string for the cell membrane and pieces of pipe cleaners for chromosomes to demonstrate the basic steps of mitosis, as described in this section. Sheltered English

 Directed Reading Worksheet Section 3

SECTION 3
READING WARM-UP

Terms to Learn

cell cycle	chromatids
chromosome	centromere
binary fission	mitosis
homologous chromosomes	cytokinesis

What You'll Do

◆ Explain how cells produce more cells.
◆ Discuss the importance of mitosis.
◆ Explain how cell division differs in animals and plants.

MATH BREAK

Cell Multiplication

It takes Cell *A* 6 hours to complete its cell cycle and produce two cells. The cell cycle of Cell *B* takes 8 hours. How many more cells would be formed from Cell *A* than from Cell *B* in 24 hours?

Figure 11 *Bacteria reproduce by pinching in two.*

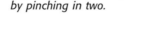
internet connect

SCILINKS
NSTA
TOPIC: Microbes
GO TO: www.scilinks.org
*sci*LINKS NUMBER: HSTL095

The Cell Cycle

In the time that it takes you to read this sentence, your body will have produced millions of new cells! Producing new cells allows you to grow and replace cells that have died. For example, the environment in your stomach is so acidic that the cells lining it must be replaced every few days!

The Life of a Cell

As you grow, you pass through different stages in life. Similarly, your cells pass through different stages in their life cycle. The life cycle of a cell is known as the **cell cycle.**

The cell cycle begins when the cell is formed and ends when the cell divides and forms new cells. Before a cell divides, it must make a copy of its DNA. DNA contains the information that tells a cell how to make proteins. The DNA of a cell is organized into structures called **chromosomes.** In some organisms, chromosomes also contain protein. Copying chromosomes ensures that each new cell will be able to survive.

How does a cell make more cells? Well, that depends on whether the cell is prokaryotic or eukaryotic.

Making More Prokaryotic Cells Prokaryotic cells (bacteria) and their DNA are not very complex. Bacteria have ribosomes and a single, circular molecule of DNA, but they don't have any membrane-covered organelles. Because of this, cell division in bacteria is fairly simple. It is called **binary fission,** which means "splitting into two parts." Each of the resulting cells contains one copy of the DNA. Some of the bacteria in **Figure 11** are undergoing binary fission.

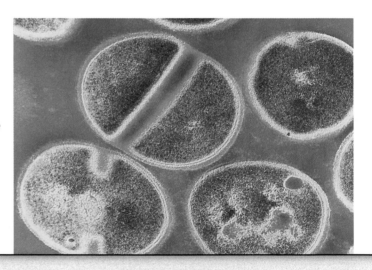

IS THAT A FACT!

Before sophisticated microscopes were available, scientists could not see cells pinching and dividing. Many believed that cells came into existence spontaneously—as though crystallizing out of bodily fluids.

Eukaryotic Cells and Their DNA Eukaryotic cells are usually much larger and more complex than prokaryotic cells. Because of this, eukaryotic cells have a lot more DNA. The chromosomes of eukaryotes contain DNA and proteins.

The number of chromosomes in the cells of eukaryotes differs from one kind of organism to the next and has nothing to do with the complexity of an organism. For example, fruit flies have 8 chromosomes, potatoes have 48, and humans have 46. **Figure 12** shows the 46 chromosomes of a human body cell lined up in pairs. These pairs are made up of similar chromosomes known as **homologous** (hoh MAHL uh guhs) **chromosomes.**

Making More Eukaryotic Cells The eukaryotic cell cycle includes three main stages. In the first stage, the cell grows and copies its organelles and chromosomes. During this time, the strands of DNA and proteins are like loosely coiled pieces of thread. After each chromosome is duplicated, the two copies are called **chromatids.** Chromatids are held together at a region called the **centromere.** The chromatids each twist and coil and condense into an X shape, as shown in **Figure 13.** After this happens, the cell enters the second stage of the cell cycle.

In the second stage, the chromatids separate. The complicated process of chromosome separation is **mitosis.** Mitosis ensures that each new cell receives a copy of each chromosome. Mitosis can be divided into four phases, as shown on the following pages.

In the third stage of the cell cycle, the cell divides and produces two cells that are identical to the original cell. Cell division will be discussed after mitosis has been described.

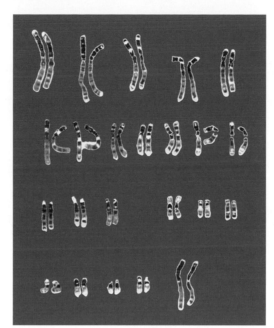
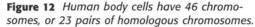

Figure 12 *Human body cells have 46 chromosomes, or 23 pairs of homologous chromosomes.*

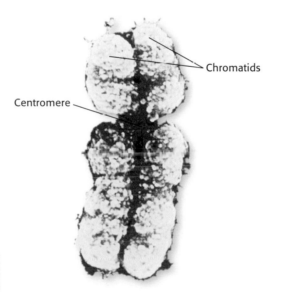

Chromatids

Centromere

Figure 13 *Two strands of DNA and protein coiled together to form this duplicated chromosome, which consists of two chromatids.*

> ✔ **Self-Check**
>
> After duplication, how many chromatids are there in a pair of homologous chromosomes? *(See page 216 to check your answer.)*

WEIRD SCIENCE

A fern called *Ophioglossum reticulatum* has 1,260 chromosomes per cell, more than any other organism.

READING STRATEGY

Prediction Guide Have students guess whether the following statement is true or false before reading this page:

> The number of chromosomes in eukaryotic cells differs because some organisms are more complex than others. (false)

Have students evaluate their answer after they read the page.

MATH and MORE

Have students make a bar graph to represent the following information:

Cell Type A divides every 3 hours; Cell Type B divides every 6 hours; and Cell Type C divides every 8 hours. If you start with one cell of each type, how many A, B, and C cells will be produced in a 24-hour period? On a graph, compare the number of cells produced by each type. (Cell A, 256; Cell B, 16; Cell C, 8)

Math Skills Worksheet "Creating Exponents"

Answer to Self-Check

After duplication, there are four chromatids—two from each of the homologous chromosomes.

internetconnect

SCILINKS NSTA

TOPIC: The Cell Cycle
GO TO: www.scilinks.org
*sci*LINKS NUMBER: HSTL090

ACTIVITY

Making Models To help students visualize cells, have them work in small groups to make three-dimensional models of plant and animal cells. Have students use different colors of clay to represent the nucleus, the chloroplasts, the mitochondria, and the cytoplasm. Students can use aluminum foil for cell walls and can use plastic wrap as cell membranes.

Next have students model mitosis. Tell them to base their model on the illustrations on pages 44 and 45. Students could use curly noodles or packaging "popcorn" to represent the four chromosomes. **Sheltered English**

MEETING INDIVIDUAL NEEDS

Advanced Learners Have students research in high school or college texts to find the names of the four phases of mitosis (prophase, metaphase, anaphase, and telophase) and the name of the time between cell divisions (interphase). Students should put this information on a circular diagram illustrating the cell cycle. **Sheltered English**

Homework

Cells and Diseases Most human diseases can be examined at the cellular level. Viruses take over cellular functions. Bacteria can cause infections and produce toxins that irritate or destroy our cells. Other diseases affect cellular function. Have students research and prepare an oral presentation on a disease that interests them, noting the kinds of cells affected by the disease.

Mitosis and the Cell Cycle

The diagram below shows the cell cycle and the phases of mitosis in an animal cell. Although mitosis is a continuous process, it can be divided into the four phases that are shown and described. As you know, different types of living things have different numbers of chromosomes. In this diagram, only four chromosomes are shown to make it easier to see what's happening.

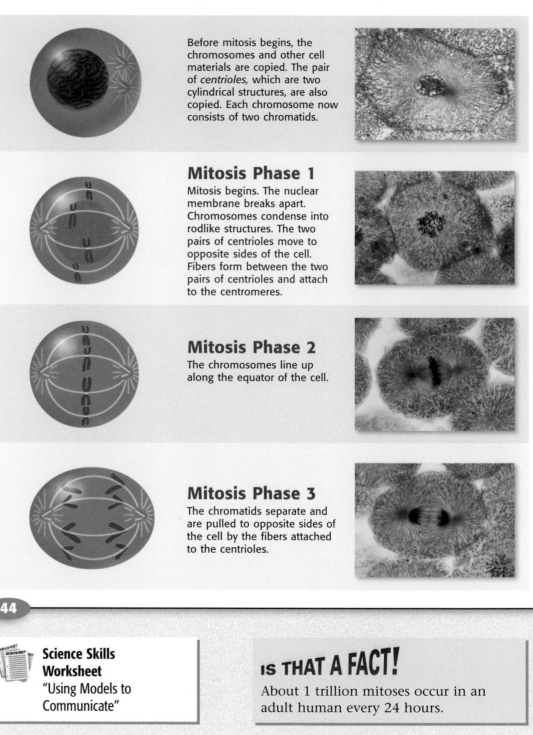

Before mitosis begins, the chromosomes and other cell materials are copied. The pair of *centrioles,* which are two cylindrical structures, are also copied. Each chromosome now consists of two chromatids.

Mitosis Phase 1

Mitosis begins. The nuclear membrane breaks apart. Chromosomes condense into rodlike structures. The two pairs of centrioles move to opposite sides of the cell. Fibers form between the two pairs of centrioles and attach to the centromeres.

Mitosis Phase 2

The chromosomes line up along the equator of the cell.

Mitosis Phase 3

The chromatids separate and are pulled to opposite sides of the cell by the fibers attached to the centrioles.

44

Science Skills Worksheet "Using Models to Communicate"

IS THAT A FACT!
About 1 trillion mitoses occur in an adult human every 24 hours.

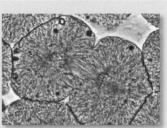

Mitosis Phase 4

The nuclear membrane forms around the two sets of chromosomes, and they unwind. The fibers disappear. Mitosis is completed.

Once mitosis is completed, the cytoplasm splits in two. This process is called **cytokinesis.** The result is two identical cells that are also identical to the original cell from which they were formed. After cytokinesis, the cell cycle is complete, and the new cells are at the beginning of their next cell cycle.

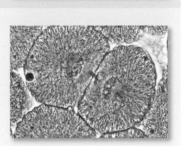

More About Cytokinesis In animal cells and other eukaryotes that do not have cell walls, division of the cytoplasm begins at the cell membrane. The cell membrane begins to pinch inward to form a groove, which eventually pinches all the way through the cell, and two daughter cells are formed. Cytokinesis in an animal cell is shown above.

Eukaryotic cells that have a cell wall, such as the cells of plants, algae, and fungi, do things a little differently. In these organisms, a *cell plate* forms in the middle of the cell and becomes the new cell membranes that will separate the two new cells. After the cell is split in two, a new cell wall forms between the two membranes. Cytokinesis in a plant cell is shown in **Figure 14.**

Cell plate

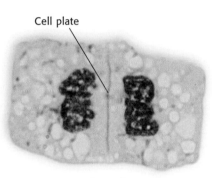

Figure 14 *When plant cells divide, a cell plate forms and the cell is split in two.*

SECTION REVIEW

1. How are binary fission and mitosis similar? How are they different?

2. Why is it important for chromosomes to be copied before cell division?

3. How does cytokinesis differ in animals and plants?

4. **Applying Concepts** What would happen if cytokinesis occurred without mitosis?

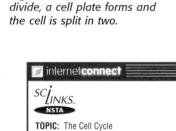

internetconnect

SCI*LINKS*
NSTA

TOPIC: The Cell Cycle
GO TO: www.scilinks.org
*sci***LINKS NUMBER:** HSTL090

▼ **Answers to Section Review**

1. Both processes lead to the production of two identical cells. Mitosis is the division of the nucleus in a eukaryotic cell. Binary fission is the division of a prokaryotic (bacterial) cell, which does not possess a nucleus.

2. Two copies of the chromosomes must be present before cell division because each of the two new cells needs to have a copy.

3. Animal cells pinch in two, and plant cells form a cell plate to divide into two cells.

4. One of the new cells would not have a set of chromosomes.

GOING FURTHER

Writing Have students research the role of mitosis in cancer and write a report based on their research. Their reports should include a discussion of the goals of various cancer treatments, such as radiation, chemotherapy, and surgery.

4 **Close**

Quiz

1. What is cell division? (It is the process by which cells reproduce themselves.)

2. How do prokaryotic cells make more cells? (binary fission)

3. How do eukaryotic cells make more cells? (mitosis and cytokinesis)

ALTERNATIVE ASSESSMENT

Writing Have students write and illustrate the biography of a cell. It can be humorous or serious, but it should include accurate descriptions of how materials are transported in and out of the cell and of the processes involved in cell reproduction.

PORTFOLIO

Teaching Transparency 14 "The Cell Cycle: Phases of Mitosis"

Reinforcement Worksheet "This Is Radio KCEL"

Section 3 • The Cell Cycle **45**

Staying Alive!
Teacher's Notes

Time Required

One 45-minute class period

Lab Ratings

EASY ────────────► HARD

TEACHER PREP	🧪
STUDENT SET-UP	🧪
CONCEPT LEVEL	🧪
CLEAN UP	🧪

MATERIALS

The materials listed on the student page are enough for one group of 5–6 students. You may wish to have your students use a calculator to complete this activity.

Preparation Notes

Some students may consider their height and weight to be personal and won't want to weigh and measure themselves with the others in the class. Give these students the option of using the data of a fictional person, such as one of the following:

Jenny	80 lb	4 ft	age 11
Ben	65 lb	3 ft	age 12
Carlos	110 lb	5 ft 2 in.	age 11
Alexa	120 lb	4 ft 6 in.	age 12
Tasheika	90 lb	4 ft 6 in.	age 13

Skill Builder Lab

Staying Alive!

Every second of your life, your body's trillions of cells take in, use, and store energy. They repair themselves, reproduce, and get rid of waste. Together, these processes are called metabolism. Your cells use the food that you eat to provide the energy you need to stay alive.

Your basal metabolic rate (BMR) is a measurement of the energy that your body needs to carry out all the basic life processes while you are at rest. These processes include breathing, keeping your heart beating, and keeping your body's temperature stable. Your BMR is influenced by your gender, your age, and many other things. Your BMR may be different from everyone else's, but it is normal for you. In this activity, you will find the amount of energy, measured in Calories, you need every day in order to stay alive.

MATERIALS

- bathroom scale
- tape measure

Procedure

1 Find your weight on a bathroom scale. If the scale measures in pounds, convert your weight in pounds to your mass in kilograms. To convert your weight in pounds (lb) to mass in kilograms (kg), multiply the number of pounds by 0.454 kg/lb.

Example: If Carlos weighs 125 lb, his mass in kilograms is:

$$125 \text{ lb} \times \frac{0.454 \text{ kg}}{\text{lb}} = 56.75 \text{ kg}$$

2 Use a tape measure to find your height. If the tape measures in inches, convert your height in inches to height in centimeters. To convert your height in inches (in.) to your height in centimeters (cm), multiply the number of inches by 2.54 cm/in.

Example: If Carlos is 62 in. tall, his height in centimeters is:

$$62 \text{ in.} \times \frac{2.54 \text{ cm}}{\text{in.}} = 157.48 \text{ cm}$$

3 Now that you know your height and mass, use the appropriate formula on the next page to get a close estimate of your BMR. Your answer will give you an estimate of the number of Calories your body needs each day just to stay alive.

46

Datasheets for LabBook

Kathy LaRoe
East Valley Middle School
East Helena, Montana

Calculating Your BMR

Females	Males
65 + (10 × your mass in kilograms) + (1.8 × your height in centimeters) − (4.7 × your age in years)	66 + (13.5 × your mass in kilograms) + (5 × your height in centimeters) − (6.8 × your age in years)

4 Your metabolism is also influenced by how active you are. Talking, walking, and playing games all take more energy than being at rest. To get an idea of how many Calories your body needs each day to stay healthy, select the lifestyle that best describes yours from the table below. Then multiply your BMR by the activity factor.

Activity Factors

Activity	Activity lifestyle	Factor
Moderately inactive	normal, everyday activities	1.3
Moderately active	exercise 3 to 4 times a week	1.4
Very active	exercise 4 to 6 times a week	1.6
Extremely active	exercise 6 to 7 times a week	1.8

Analysis

5 In what way could you compare your whole body to a single cell? Explain your answer.

6 Does an increase in activity increase your BMR? Does an increase in activity increase your need for Calories? Explain your answers.

7 If you are moderately inactive, how many more Calories would you need if you began to exercise every day?

Going Further

The best energy sources are those that supply the correct amount of Calories for your lifestyle and also provide the nutrients you need. Research in the library or on the Internet to find out which kinds of foods are the best energy sources for you. How does your list of best energy sources compare with your diet?

List everything you eat and drink in one day. Find out how many Calories are in each item, and find the total number of Calories you have consumed. How does this number of Calories compare with the number of Calories you need each day for all your activities?

Lab Notes

Some students will think their basal metabolic rate, or BMR, is impossibly low. Emphasize that the BMR is the number of Calories a body needs just to keep the heart beating, the lungs breathing, and the cells respiring. It is not the number of Calories a person needs for an active lifestyle. Of course, a person can consume fewer than that number of Calories for a day, or even for a few days, without dying. Explain that the Calories required to live during starvation conditions are obtained from stored fat. When there is no more fat, then the energy comes from muscle tissue. Under extreme conditions of starvation, the body even begins to shut down some organ functions that use energy but that are not required for survival, such as the uterine cycle in women. Some students may ask why the BMR numbers are so much higher in males than in females. Explain that before puberty, the numbers are much closer together. But as boys approach puberty, they generally develop a higher muscle-to-fat ratio than girls do. Cellular respiration for muscle tissue requires more energy than for fat tissue.

47

Answers

5. Just as each cell needs energy on a small scale, your body requires energy on a much larger scale.

6. Technically, the BMR does not change with activity. It is the minimum amount of energy a person needs to stay alive. Activity requires that more energy be added to the BMR, thereby increasing the need for Calories.

7. Students should multiply their own BMR by 1.3, then multiply their BMR by 1.8. Students should subtract the smaller number from the larger number. This represents the additional Calories per day a person would expend shifting from a moderately inactive state to an extremely active one.

Chapter Highlights

Chapter Highlights

VOCABULARY DEFINITIONS

SECTION 1

diffusion the movement of particles from an area where their concentration is high to an area where their concentration is low

osmosis the diffusion of water across a cell membrane

passive transport the diffusion of particles through proteins in the cell membrane from areas where the concentration of particles is high to areas where the concentration of particles is low

active transport the movement of particles through proteins in the cell membrane against the direction of diffusion; requires cells to use energy

endocytosis the process in which a cell membrane surrounds a particle and encloses it in a vesicle to bring it into the cell

exocytosis the process used to remove large particles from a cell; during exocytosis, a vesicle containing the particles fuses with the cell membrane

SECTION 2

photosynthesis the process by which plants capture light energy from the sun and convert it into sugar

cellular respiration the process of producing ATP from oxygen and glucose; releases carbon dioxide as a waste product

fermentation the breakdown of sugars to make ATP in the absence of oxygen

---

SECTION 1

Vocabulary

diffusion *(p. 34)*

osmosis *(p. 35)*

passive transport *(p. 36)*

active transport *(p. 36)*

endocytosis *(p. 37)*

exocytosis *(p. 37)*

Section Notes

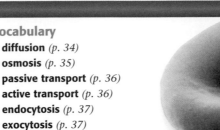

- A cell can survive only if food molecules are taken into the cell and waste materials are removed. Materials enter and leave the cell by passing through the cell membrane. The cell membrane allows some materials to pass through but prevents others.

- A cell does not need to use energy to move particles from regions of high concentration to regions of low concentration. This type of movement is called diffusion.

- Osmosis is the diffusion of water through a membrane.

- Some substances enter and leave a cell by passing through proteins. During passive transport, substances diffuse through proteins. During active transport, substances are moved from areas of low concentration to areas of high concentration. The cell must supply energy for active transport to occur.

- Particles that are too large to pass easily through the membrane can enter a cell by a process called endocytosis. Large particles can leave a cell by exocytosis.

Labs

The Perfect Taters Mystery *(p. 186)*

☑ Skills Check

Math Concepts

CELL CYCLE It takes 4 hours for a cell to complete its cell cycle and produce 2 cells. How many cells can be produced from this cell in 12 hours? First you must determine how many cell cycles will occur in 12 hours:

12 hours/4 hours = 3

The number of cells doubles after each cycle:

Cycle 1	1 cell × 2 = 2 cells
Cycle 2	2 cells × 2 = 4 cells
Cycle 3	4 cells × 2 = 8 cells

Therefore, after 3 cell cycles (12 hours), 8 cells will have been produced from the original cell.

Visual Understanding

MITOSIS The process of mitosis can be confusing, but looking at illustrations can help. Look at the illustrations of the cell cycle on pp. 44 and 45. Read the label for each phase, and look at the illustrations and photographs for each. Look for the cell structures that are described in the label. Trace the movement of chromosomes through each step. By carefully studying the labels and pictures, you can better understand mitosis.

48

Lab and Activity Highlights

Stayin' Alive! `PG 46`

The Perfect Taters Mystery `PG 186`

Datasheets for LabBook
(blackline masters for these labs)

SECTION 2

Vocabulary

photosynthesis *(p. 38)*

cellular respiration *(p. 39)*

fermentation *(p. 39)*

Section Notes

- The sun is the ultimate source of almost all energy needed to fuel the chemical activities of organisms. Most producers use energy from sunlight to make food during the process known as photosynthesis. This food then becomes a source of energy for the producers and for the consumers that eat the producers.

- Cells use cellular respiration or fermentation to release the energy from food to make ATP. Cellular respiration requires oxygen, but fermentation does not.

SECTION 3

Vocabulary

cell cycle *(p. 42)*

chromosome *(p. 42)*

binary fission *(p. 42)*

homologous chromosomes *(p. 43)*

chromatids *(p. 43)*

centromere *(p. 43)*

mitosis *(p. 43)*

cytokinesis *(p. 45)*

Section Notes

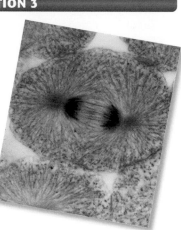

- The life cycle of a cell is called the cell cycle. The cell cycle begins when the cell is formed and ends when the cell divides to produce two new cells. Prokaryotic cells produce new cells by binary fission. Eukaryotic cells produce new cells by mitosis and cytokinesis.

- Before mitosis, the chromosomes are copied. During mitosis, chromatids separate, and two new nuclei are formed. During cytokinesis, the cell divides.

internet connect

GO TO: go.hrw.com

Visit the **HRW** Web site for a variety of learning tools related to this chapter. Just type in the keyword:

KEYWORD: HSTACT

SCI LINKS NSTA

GO TO: www.scilinks.org

Visit the **National Science Teachers Association** on-line Web site for Internet resources related to this chapter. Just type in the *sci*LINKS number for more information about the topic:

TOPIC: Osmosis   *sci*LINKS NUMBER: HSTL075
TOPIC: Cell Energy   *sci*LINKS NUMBER: HSTL080
TOPIC: Photosynthesis   *sci*LINKS NUMBER: HSTL085
TOPIC: The Cell Cycle   *sci*LINKS NUMBER: HSTL090
TOPIC: Microbes   *sci*LINKS NUMBER: HSTL095

49

VOCABULARY DEFINITIONS, *continued*

SECTION 3

cell cycle the life cycle of a cell; in eukaryotes it consists of chromosome duplication, mitosis, and cytokinesis

chromosome coiled structure of DNA and protein that forms in the cell nucleus during cell division

binary fission the simple cell division in which one cell splits into two; used by bacteria

homologous chromosomes chromosomes with matching information

chromatids identical copies of a chromosome

centromere the region that holds chromatids together when a chromosome is duplicated

mitosis nuclear division in eukaryotic cells in which each cell receives a copy of the original chromosomes

cytokinesis the process in which cytoplasm divides after mitosis

 Vocabulary Review Worksheet

Blackline masters of these Chapter Highlights can be found in the **Study Guide.**

Lab and Activity Highlights

LabBank

 Inquiry Labs, Fish Farms in Space

Whiz-Bang Demonstrations
- It's in the Bag!
- Stop Picking on My Enzyme

Labs You Can Eat, The Mystery of the Runny Gelatin

 Long-Term Projects & Research Ideas, Taming the Wild Yeast

Interactive Explorations CD-ROM

CD 3, Exploration 1, "The Nose Knows"

UNDERSTANDING VOCABULARY

1. osmosis
2. exocytosis
3. photosynthesis
4. cellular respiration
5. mitosis, cytokinesis

UNDERSTANDING CONCEPTS

Multiple Choice

6. c
7. c
8. b
9. d
10. a
11. c

Short Answer

12. Cells need chloroplasts for photosynthesis and need mitochondria for respiration.
13. At the beginning of mitosis, each chromosome consists of two chromatids.
14. The first stage is cell growth and copying of DNA (duplication). The second stage is mitosis, and the third stage is cytokinesis (cell division).

Chapter Review

USING VOCABULARY

To complete the following sentences, choose the correct term from each pair of terms listed below:

1. The diffusion of water through the cell membrane is called __?__. *(osmosis or active transport)*

2. A cell can remove large particles during __?__. *(exocytosis or endocytosis)*

3. Plants use __?__ to make glucose. *(cellular respiration or photosynthesis)*

4. During __?__, food molecules are broken down to form CO_2 and H_2O and release large amounts of energy. *(cellular respiration or fermentation)*

5. In eukaryotes, __?__ creates two nuclei, and __?__ creates two cells. *(cytokinesis or mitosis)*

UNDERSTANDING CONCEPTS

Multiple Choice

6. When particles are moved through a membrane from a region of low concentration to a region of high concentration, the process is called
   a. diffusion.
   b. passive transport.
   c. active transport.
   d. fermentation.

7. An organism with chloroplasts is a
   a. consumer.   c. producer.
   b. prokaryote.   d. centromere.

8. What is produced by mitosis?
   a. two identical cells
   b. two nuclei
   c. chloroplasts
   d. two different cells

9. Before the energy in food can be used by a cell, it must first be transferred to molecules of
   a. proteins.
   b. carbohydrates.
   c. DNA.
   d. ATP.

10. Which one of the following does not perform mitosis?
    a. prokaryotic cell
    b. human body cell
    c. eukaryotic cell
    d. plant cell

11. Which of the following would form a cell plate during the cell cycle?
    a. human cell
    b. prokaryotic cell
    c. plant cell
    d. all of the above

Short Answer

12. What cell structures are needed for photosynthesis? for respiration?

13. How many chromatids are present in a chromosome at the beginning of mitosis?

14. What are the three stages of the cell cycle in a eukaryotic cell?

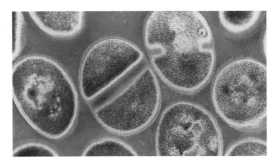

Concept Mapping

15. Use the following terms to create a concept map: chromosome duplication, cytokinesis, prokaryote, mitosis, cell cycle, binary fission, eukaryote.

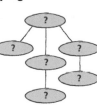

CRITICAL THINKING AND PROBLEM SOLVING

Write one or two sentences to answer the following questions:

16. Which one of the plants below was given water mixed with salt, and which one was given pure water? Explain how you know, and be sure to use the word *osmosis* in your answer.

17. Why would your muscle cells need to be supplied with more food when there is a lack of oxygen than when there is plenty of oxygen present?

18. A parent cell has 10 chromosomes before dividing.
   a. Will the cell go through binary fission or mitosis and cytokinesis to produce new cells?
   b. How many chromosomes will each new cell have after the parent cell divides?

MATH IN SCIENCE

19. A cell has six chromosomes at the beginning of its cell cycle. How many chromatids will line up at the equator of the cell during mitosis?

INTERPRETING GRAPHICS

Look at the cell below to answer the following questions:

20. Is the cell prokaryotic or eukaryotic?

21. In what stage of the cell cycle is this cell?

22. How many chromatids are present? How many pairs of homologous chromosomes are present?

23. How many chromosomes will be present in each of the new cells after the cell divides?

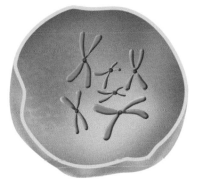

 **Reading Check-up**

Take a minute to review your answers to the Pre-Reading Questions found at the bottom of page 32. Have your answers changed? If necessary, revise your answers based on what you have learned since you began this chapter.

51

Concept Mapping Transparency 4

Blackline masters of this Chapter Review can be found in the **Study Guide.**

Concept Mapping

15. An answer to this exercise can be found at the front of this book.

CRITICAL THINKING AND PROBLEM SOLVING

16. The wilted plant on the right was given salt water. Osmosis occurred, and water in the plant moved into the soil, where the concentration of water was lower.

17. When there is plenty of oxygen, the cells can get energy from cellular respiration. When there is a lack of oxygen, the cell must use fermentation, which doesn't produce as much energy. For fermentation to produce more energy, more food would be required.

18. **a.** The cell is a eukaryotic cell and will go through mitosis and cytokinesis. Prokaryotic cells have only one chromosome.
   b. Each new cell will receive a copy of each chromosome, so each will have 10 chromosomes.

MATH IN SCIENCE

19. Each chromosome will duplicate before mitosis, so $6 \times 2 = 12$ chromatids.

INTERPRETING GRAPHICS

20. The cell is eukaryotic because it shows sister chromatids linked at centromeres.

21. The cell is in mitosis because the chromosomes have already duplicated.

22. There are 12 chromatids. There are three pairs of homologous chromosomes.

23. There will be six chromosomes in each new cell.

Background

The release of energy from food is called *cellular respiration.* Cellular respiration takes place in two stages, resulting in the storage of energy in ATP *(adenosine triphosphate)* molecules.

In the microbial battery, scientists harvest some of this energy and transfer it into electricity that can be readily used.

One of the benefits of the microbial battery is its ability to make use of waste products. Ask students to consider the effect this might have on the energy demands of nations that have limited access to fossil fuels.

ACROSS THE SCIENCES

LIFE SCIENCE • PHYSICAL SCIENCE

Electrifying News About Microbes

Your car is out of fuel, and there isn't a service station in sight. No problem! Your car's motor runs on electricity supplied by trillions of microorganisms—and they're hungry. You pop a handful of sugar cubes into the tank along with some fresh water, and you're on your way. The microbes devour the food and produce enough electricity to get you home safely.

A "Living" Battery

Sound far-fetched? Peter Bennetto and his team of scientists at King's College, in London, don't think so. Chemists there envision "living" batteries that will someday operate everything from wristwatches to entire towns. Although cars won't be using batteries powered by bacteria anytime soon, the London scientists have demonstrated that microorganisms can convert food into usable electrical energy. One test battery that is smaller than 0.5 cm^2 kept a digital clock operating for a day.

Freeing Electrons

For nearly a century, scientists have known that living things produce and use electric charges. But only in the last few decades have they figured out the chemical processes that produce these tiny electric charges. As part of their normal activities, living cells break down starches and sugars, and these chemical reactions release electrons. Scientists produce electricity by harvesting these free electrons from single-celled organisms, such as bacteria.

Bennetto and his colleagues have developed a list of foods that matches the carbohydrates, such as table sugar and molasses, with the microorganisms that digest them the most efficiently. Bennetto explains that there are lazy bacteria and efficient bacteria. An efficient microbe can convert more than 90 percent of its food into compounds that will fuel an

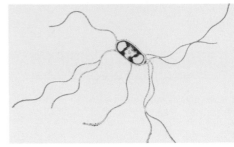

▲ *Bacteria like this can convert carbohydrates to electrical energy.*

electric reaction. A less efficient microbe converts 50 percent or less of its food into electron-yielding compounds.

Feed Them Leftovers

One advantage that batteries powered by microbes have over generators is that microbes do not require nonrenewable resources, such as coal or oil. Microbes can produce electricity by consuming pollutants, such as certain byproducts from the milk and sugar industries. And since the microorganisms reproduce constantly, no battery charging is necessary; just give the battery a bacteria change from time to time. For now, the London scientists are content to speculate on the battery's potential. Other specialists, such as electrical engineers, are needed to make this technology practical.

Project Idea

▶ Imagine that you manage a government agency and you are asked to provide funds for research on batteries powered by microbes. Think of some of the benefits of developing "living batteries." Are there any problems you can think of? As a class, decide whether you would fund the research.

52

Answer to Project Idea

Answers will vary, but students should recognize the two sides to investing in new discoveries. New technologies are risky, but solutions to scientific problems often begin as far-fetched ideas.

Science Fiction

"Contagion"
by Katherine MacLean

A quarter mile from their spaceship, the *Explorer*, a team of doctors walk carefully along a narrow forest trail. Around them, the forest looks like an Earth forest in the fall—the leaves are green, copper, purple, and fiery red. But it isn't fall. And the team is not on Earth.

Minos is enough like Earth to be the home of another colony of humans. But Minos might also be home to unknown organisms that could cause severe illness or death among the *Explorer*'s crew. These diseases might be enough like Earth diseases to be contagious, yet just different enough to be extremely difficult to treat.

Something large moves among the shadows—it looks like a man. When he suddenly steps out onto the trail, he is taller than any of them, lean and muscled, and darkly tanned with bright red hair. Even more amazing, he speaks.

"Welcome to Minos. The mayor sends greetings from Alexandria."

And so we, and the crew of the *Explorer*, meet red-haired Patrick Mead. According to Patrick, there was once a colony of humans on Minos. About two years after the colony arrived, a terrible plague swept through the colony and killed everyone except the Mead family. But, Patrick tells them, the plague has never come back and there are no other contagions on Minos.

Or are there? What has Patrick hidden from the crew of the *Explorer*? Read Katherine MacLean's "Contagion" in the *Holt Anthology of Science Fiction* to find out.

53

Further Reading If students enjoyed this story, suggest some of Katherine MacLean's other works, such as the following:

The Missing Man (novella), Bart Books, 1988

The Diploids (short story collection), Gregg Press, 1981

The Man in the Bird Cage (novel), Ace Books, 1971

SCIENCE FICTION
"Contagion"
by Katherine MacLean

When they arrive on the previously unknown planet Minos, the crew of the Earth ship Explorer *immediately admire their friendly, strong, healthy, and handsome host. But could he carry a deadly disease?*

Teaching Strategy

Reading Level This is a relatively long story, containing quite a few medical terms. Students may find it challenging.

Background

About the Author Katherine MacLean's desire to write science fiction comes from an interest in combining her lifelong interests in psychology, biology, and history. In her short story collection, *The Diploids*, she applies the methods of experimentation used in physics and chemistry to anthropology and psychology. Much like "Contagion," many of these stories suggest that scientists have a choice; if they pursue science correctly, their discoveries and insights will change human interactions for the better. In one of her most famous stories, "The Snowball Effect," MacLean warns against the dangers of amateurs delving into science where only experts should venture.

MacLean's stories have appeared in many anthologies and magazines. In addition, MacLean has written several novels. In 1971 MacLean's unique blending of the sciences won her a Nebula Award for her novella *The Missing Man*.

Chapter Organizer

CHAPTER ORGANIZATION	TIME MINUTES	OBJECTIVES	LABS, INVESTIGATIONS, AND DEMONSTRATIONS
Chapter Opener pp. 54–55	45	National Standards: UCP 2, 4, LS 1d, 2c	**Start-Up Activity,** Clothing Combos, p. 55
Section 1 **Mendel and His Peas**	90	▶ Explain the experiments of Gregor Mendel. ▶ Explain how genes and alleles are related to genotypes and phenotypes. ▶ Use the information in a Punnett square. UCP 1, 2, SAI 1, 2, ST 1, 2, SPSP 1, 5, HNS 2, 3, LS 1f, 2b–2e; Labs UCP 2, SAI 1, HNS 2, LS 2b, 2c, 2e	**Demonstration,** Flower Dissection, p. 59 in ATE **QuickLab,** Take Your Chances, p. 62 **Making Models,** Bug Builders, Inc., p. 70 **Datasheets for LabBook,** Bug Builders, Inc. **Design Your Own,** Tracing Traits, p. 188 **Datasheets for LabBook,** Tracing Traits
Section 2 **Meiosis**	90	▶ Explain the difference between mitosis and meiosis. ▶ Describe how Mendel's ideas are supported by the process of meiosis. ▶ Explain the difference between male and female sex chromosomes. UCP 2, SAI 1, SPSP 5, HNS 2, 3, LS 1c, 1d, 2a–2d	**Demonstration,** Modeling Meiosis, p. 66 in ATE **Long-Term Projects & Research Ideas,** Portrait of a Dog

See page **T23** *for a complete correlation of this book with the*

NATIONAL SCIENCE EDUCATION STANDARDS.

TECHNOLOGY RESOURCES

Guided Reading Audio CD
English or Spanish, Chapter 3

One-Stop Planner CD-ROM
with Test Generator

 CNN Science, Technology & Society,
BioDiesel, Segment 6
Bioengineered Plants, Segment 8

Chapter 3 • Heredity

CLASSROOM WORKSHEETS, TRANSPARENCIES, AND RESOURCES	SCIENCE INTEGRATION AND CONNECTIONS	REVIEW AND ASSESSMENT
Directed Reading Worksheet **Science Puzzlers, Twisters & Teasers**		
Directed Reading Worksheet, Section 1 **Transparency 293,** White Light Is Separated by a Prism **Science Skills Worksheet,** Finding Useful Sources **Math Skills for Science Worksheet,** What Is a Ratio? **Math Skills for Science Worksheet,** Punnett Square Popcorn **Transparency 15,** Punnett Square: *PP* × *pp* Cross **Transparency 15,** Punnett Square: *Pp* × *Pp* Cross **Reinforcement Worksheet,** Dimples and DNA **Critical Thinking Worksheet,** A Bittersweet Solution	**Connect to Physical Science,** p. 58 in ATE **Multicultural Connection,** p. 58 in ATE **MathBreak,** Understanding Ratios, p. 60 **Math and More,** p. 60 in ATE **Apply,** p. 63 **Science, Technology, and Society:** Mapping the Human Genome, p. 76	**Homework,** pp. 56, 59, 62 in ATE **Section Review,** p. 63 **Quiz,** p. 63 in ATE **Alternative Assessment,** p. 63 in ATE
Directed Reading Worksheet, Section 2 **Transparency 16,** Meiosis in Eight Easy Steps: A **Transparency 17,** Meiosis in Eight Easy Steps: B **Transparency 18,** Meiosis and Mendel	**Cross-Disciplinary Focus,** p. 66 in ATE **Health Watch:** Lab Rats with Wings, p. 77	**Self-Check,** p. 67 **Homework,** p. 68 in ATE **Section Review,** p. 69 **Quiz,** p. 69 in ATE **Alternative Assessment,** p. 69 in ATE

internet connect

go.hrw.com
Holt, Rinehart and Winston On-line Resources
go.hrw.com

For worksheets and other teaching aids related to this chapter, visit the HRW Web site and type in the keyword: **HSTHER**

SCiLINKS
NSTA
National Science Teachers Association
www.scilinks.org

Encourage students to use the *sci*LINKS numbers listed in the internet connect boxes to access information and resources on the **NSTA** Web site.

END-OF-CHAPTER REVIEW AND ASSESSMENT

Chapter Review in Study Guide
Vocabulary and Notes in Study Guide
Chapter Tests with Performance-Based Assessment, Chapter 3 Test
Chapter Tests with Performance-Based Assessment, Performance-Based Assessment 3
Concept Mapping Transparency 5

Chapter Resources & Worksheets

Visual Resources

TEACHING TRANSPARENCIES

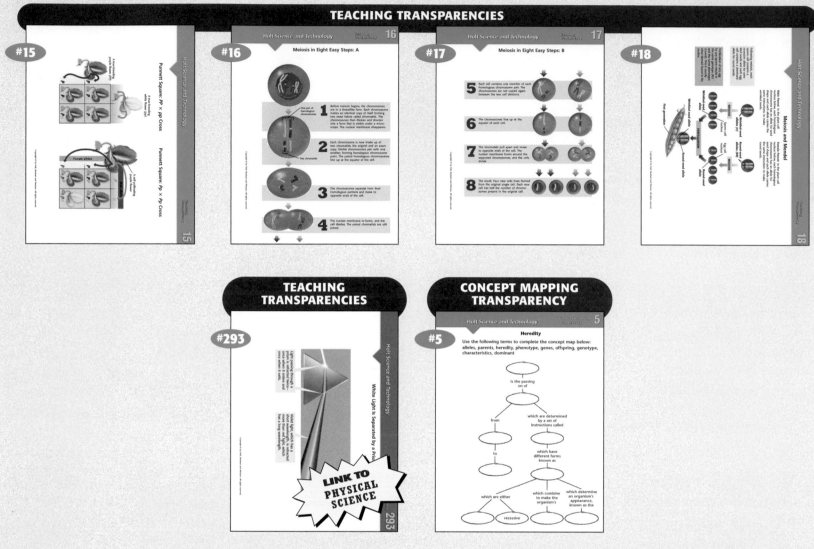

#15

Punnett Square: *PP* × *pp* Cross

Punnett Square: *Pp* × *Pp* Cross

#16 — Meiosis in Eight Easy Steps: A

#17 — Meiosis in Eight Easy Steps: B

#18 — Meiosis and Mendel

TEACHING TRANSPARENCIES

#293 — White Light Is Separated by a Prism

LINK TO PHYSICAL SCIENCE

CONCEPT MAPPING TRANSPARENCY

#5 — Heredity

Use the following terms to complete the concept map below: alleles, parents, heredity, phenotype, genes, offspring, genotype, characteristics, dominant

Meeting Individual Needs

DIRECTED READING

#3 — DIRECTED READING WORKSHEET

Heredity

Chapter Introduction

As you begin this chapter, answer the following.

1. Read the title of the chapter. List three things that you already know about this subject.

2. Write two questions about this subject that you would like answered by the time you finish this chapter.

3. How does the title of the Start-Up Activity relate to the subject of the chapter?

Section 1: Mendel and His Peas (p. 56)

4. You don't look exactly like anyone else, unless you are an identical twin. Why do you think that is true?

Why Don't You Look Like a Rhinoceros? (p. 56)

5. How does heredity explain why you don't look like a rhinoceros?

REINFORCEMENT & VOCABULARY REVIEW

#3 — REINFORCEMENT WORKSHEET

Dimples and DNA

Complete this worksheet after you have finished reading Chapter 6, Section 1.

In humans, dimpled cheeks are a dominant trait, with a genotype of *DD* or *Dd*. Nondimpled cheeks are a recessive trait, with a genotype of *dd*.

1. Imagine that Parent A, with the genotype *DD*, has dimpled cheeks. Parent B has the genotype *dd* and does not have dimpled cheeks.

The Punnett square below diagrams the cross between Parent A and Parent B. Complete the Punnett square. (The first square has been done for you. You may want to refer to How to Make a Punnett square in your text.)

Parent A

	D	D
d	Dd	
d		

Parent B

2. A Punnett square shows what genotypes are possible for the offspring of a certain cross. What genotypes are possible for the offspring of Parent A and Parent B?

3. Each of the four squares of a Punnett square represents a 25 percent probability that the offspring will have that particular genotype. What is the probability that the offspring of Parent A and Parent B will have dimpled cheeks?

#3 — VOCABULARY REVIEW WORKSHEET

Vocabulary Garden

After you finish Chapter 6, give this puzzle a try!

Write the word or phrase being described below in the appropriate space on the next page.

1. Chromosomes that are the same size and shape
2. Carry genes that determine the sex of offspring
3. Genes that govern the same characteristic
4. The inherited combination of alleles
5. Process that results in two identical cells
6. The transmission of characteristics from one generation to the next
7. Cell division that produces sex cells
8. Trait that faded away in Mendel's first experiment
9. Tool used to visualize all the possible combinations of alleles from parents
10. Trait that always appeared in Mendel's first experiment
11. A true-_____ plant always produces offspring with the same trait as the parent.
12. A self-_____ plant contains both male and female reproductive structures.
13. Male sex cells
14. Female sex cells
15. An organism's inherited appearance
16. The mathematical likelihood that an event will occur
17. Located on chromosomes

SCIENCE PUZZLERS, TWISTERS & TEASERS

#3 — SCIENCE PUZZLERS, TWISTERS & TEASERS

Heredity

Put on Your Rhyming Genes

1. Fill in the blanks in each of the following rhymes to complete these catchy jingles about heredity.

a. With an "X" from my mom Gail
And a "Y" from my dad Dale
It should be clear that I'm a _____

b. As you surely know from your reading,
A pair of dominant or recessive alleles
Makes you _____

c. Your genes, indeed, would be tough to steal:
Those thieves would be very aggressive
They may grab a dominant _____
Though some thieves steal only _____

The PUNnett Square

2. These puns are bound to make you groan. Fill in the blanks with words from the chapter.

a. If you have blue _____ does that mean that you're bound to be sad?

b. Ouch! You just stepped on _____

Review & Assessment

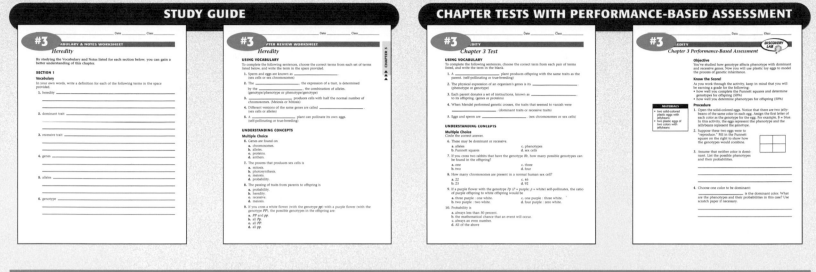

STUDY GUIDE

#3 VOCABULARY & NOTES WORKSHEET
Heredity

By studying the Vocabulary and Notes listed for each section below, you can gain a better understanding of this chapter.

SECTION 1
Vocabulary
In your own words, write a definition for each of the following terms in the space provided.

1. heredity

2. dominant trait

3. recessive trait

4. genes

5. alleles

6. genotype

#3 CHAPTER REVIEW WORKSHEET
Heredity

USING VOCABULARY
To complete the following sentences, choose the correct terms from each set of terms listed below, and write the term in the space provided.

1. Sperm and eggs are known as _____ (sex cells or sex chromosomes)

2. The _____, the expression of a trait, is determined by the _____, the combination of alleles. (genotype/phenotype or phenotype/genotype)

3. _____ produces cells with half the normal number of chromosomes. (Meiosis or Mitosis)

4. Different versions of the same gene are called _____. (sex cells or alleles)

5. A _____ plant can pollinate its own eggs. (self-pollinating or true-breeding)

UNDERSTANDING CONCEPTS
Multiple Choice

6. Genes are found on
   a. chromosomes.
   b. alleles.
   c. proteins.
   d. anthers.

7. The process that produces sex cells is
   a. mitosis.
   b. photosynthesis.
   c. meiosis.
   d. probability.

8. The passing of traits from parents to offspring is
   a. probability.
   b. heredity.
   c. recessive.
   d. meiosis.

9. If you cross a white flower (with the genotype *pp*) with a purple flower (with the genotype *PP*), the possible genotypes in the offspring are:
   a. *PP* and *pp*.
   b. all *Pp*.
   c. all *PP*.
   d. all *pp*.

CHAPTER TESTS WITH PERFORMANCE-BASED ASSESSMENT

#3 Heredity
Chapter 3 Test

USING VOCABULARY
To complete the following sentences, choose the correct term from each pair of terms listed, and write the term in the blank.

1. A _____ plant produces offspring with the same traits as the parent. (self-pollinating or true-breeding)

2. The physical expression of an organism's genes is its _____. (phenotype or genotype)

3. Each parent donates a set of instructions, known as _____, to its offspring. (genes or proteins)

4. When Mendel performed genetic crosses, the traits that seemed to vanish were _____. (dominant traits or recessive traits)

5. Eggs and sperm are _____. (sex chromosomes or sex cells)

UNDERSTANDING CONCEPTS
Multiple Choice
Circle the correct answer.

6. These may be dominant or recessive.
   a. alleles
   b. Punnett squares
   c. phenotypes
   d. sex cells

7. If you cross two rabbits that have the genotype *Bb*, how many possible genotypes can be found in the offspring?
   a. one
   b. two
   c. three
   d. four

8. How many chromosomes are present in a normal human sex cell?
   a. 22
   b. 23
   c. 46
   d. 92

9. If a purple flower with the genotype *Pp* (*P* = purple; *p* = white) self-pollinates, the ratio of purple offspring to white offspring would be
   a. three purple : one white.
   b. two purple : two white.
   c. one purple : three white.
   d. four purple : zero white.

10. Probability is
   a. always less than 50 percent.
   b. the mathematical chance that an event will occur.
   c. always an even number.
   d. All of the above

#3 Heredity
Chapter 3 Performance-Based Assessment — **DISCOVERY LAB**

Objective
You've studied how genotype affects phenotype with dominant and recessive genes. Now you will use plastic toy eggs to model the process of genetic inheritance.

Know the Score!
As you work through the activity, keep in mind that you will be earning a grade for the following:
• how well you complete the Punnett squares and determine genotypes for offspring (50%)
• how well you determine phenotypes for offspring (50%)

MATERIALS
• two solid-colored plastic eggs with jellybeans
• two plastic eggs of two colors with jellybeans

Procedure
1. Open the solid-colored eggs. Notice that there are two jellybeans of the same color in each egg. Assign the first letter of each color as the genotype for the egg. For example, B = blue. In this activity, the eggs represent the phenotype and the jellybeans represent the genotype.

2. Suppose these two eggs were to "reproduce." Fill in the Punnett square on the right to show how the genotypes would combine.

3. Assume that neither color is dominant. List the possible phenotypes and their probabilities.

4. Choose one color to be dominant: _____ is the dominant color. What are the phenotypes and their probabilities in this case? Use scratch paper if necessary.

Lab Worksheets

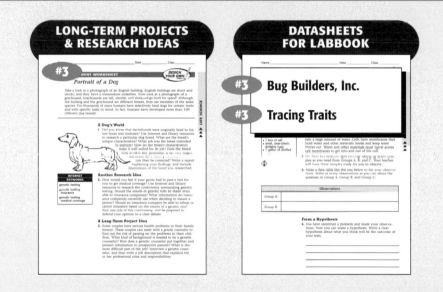

LONG-TERM PROJECTS & RESEARCH IDEAS

#3 STUDENT WORKSHEET — **DESIGN YOUR OWN**
Portrait of a Dog

Take a look at a photograph of an English bulldog. English bulldogs are short and stocky, and they have a tremendous underbite. Now look at a photograph of a greyhound. Greyhounds are tall, slender, and sleek—dogs built for speed! Although the bulldog and the greyhound are different breeds, they are members of the same species. For thousands of years humans have selectively bred dogs for certain traits and with specific tasks in mind. In fact, humans have developed more than 100 different dog breeds!

A Dog's World
1. Did you know that dachshunds were originally bred to follow foxes into foxholes? Use Internet and library resources to research a particular dog breed. What are the breed's unique characteristics? What job was the breed intended to perform? How do the breed's characteristics make it well suited for its job? Does the breed still perform any job today, or is its role purely as a pet or show animal? Can they be corrected? Write a report explaining your findings, and include illustrations of the breed you researched.

INTERNET KEYWORDS
genetic testing
genetic testing insurance
genetic testing medical coverage

Another Research Idea
2. How would you feel if your genes had to pass a test for you to get medical coverage? Use Internet and library resources to research the controversy surrounding genetic testing. Should the results of genetic tests be made available to insurance companies? What information do insurance companies currently use when deciding to insure a person? Should an insurance company be able to refuse or cancel insurance based on the results of a genetic test? Pick one side of this controversy, and be prepared to defend your opinion in a class debate.

A Long-Term Project Idea
3. Some couples have serious health problems in their family history. These couples can meet with a genetic counselor to find out the risk of passing on the problems to their children. What kind of background is needed to be a genetic counselor? How does a genetic counselor put together and present information to prospective parents? What is the most difficult part of the job? Interview a genetic counselor, and then write a job description that explains his or her professional roles and responsibilities.

DATASHEETS FOR LABBOOK

#3 Bug Builders, Inc.

#3 Tracing Traits

tain a large amount of water. Cells have membranes that hold water and other materials inside and keep some things out. Water and other materials must travel across cell membranes to get into and out of the cell.

2. Use tape and one pen you will be sitting in more complex as you need from Groups A, B, and C. Your teacher will have these samples ready for you to observe.

3. Make a data table like the one below to list your observations. Write as many observations as you can about the potatoes in Group A, Group B, and Group C.

Observations	
Group A:	
Group B:	

Form a Hypothesis
4. You have identified a problem and made your observations. Now you can make a hypothesis. Write a clear hypothesis about what you think will be the outcome of your tests.

Applications & Extensions

CRITICAL THINKING & PROBLEM SOLVING

#3 CRITICAL THINKING WORKSHEET
A Bittersweet Solution

Dr. Ivanna B. Famus, a plant geneticist, has a small laboratory on the island of Kaupul, where she is trying to improve the fruit yield of local plants. She claims this is possible by combining the genes of local plants with those of the infamous Phooey plant of Harbuschamango. The Phooey plant grows very quickly and produces huge fruit that are rarely attacked by insects because of their extremely bitter taste. Her first experiments were conducted on the island's orange trees and kiwi vines.

Here are the results from her first lab experiment:
• 80 percent of the orange trees grew more quickly; the oranges were larger and tasted bitter.
• 20 percent of the kiwi fruit grew more quickly and tasted bitter.

Some of the island's inhabitants are opposed to Dr. Famus's experiments. They believe the introduction of a new plant hybrid could affect the plant and animal life of their island. One native Kaupulian said, "That geneticist is gonna mess up our island's ecosystem!"

Making Observations
1. How does the phenotype of the hybrid orange tree differ from the phenotype of the original orange trees?

2. What traits were dominant in Dr. Famus's new orange trees? Explain your answer.

SCIENCE TECHNOLOGY

#6 Science in the News: Critical Thinking Worksheets
Segment 6
BioDiesel

#8 _____ fuel from algae is a renewable or a nonrenewable resource?

2. Name the biggest environmental advantage of using fuel extracted from algae.

3. What do you think are the main environmental conditions algae need in order to grow?

4. What do you see as the biggest limitation to **CNN**

SECTION 1

Mendel and His Peas

▶ **Gregor Mendel**
In 1843, in the city of Brünn, Austria (which is now Brno, a city in the Czech Republic), Gregor Mendel (1822–1884) entered a monastery. In 1865, Mendel published the results of his garden-pea experiments. Although Mendel's ideas are wide-spread today, few scientists took notice of his work during his lifetime. Mendel presented his findings in two lectures, and he had only 40 copies of his work made. Because there were no computers or photocopy machines during Mendel's time, his findings were not distributed to many scientists.

- When Mendel was elected abbot of the monastery in 1868, his duties prevented him from visiting scientists and attending conferences where he could have discussed his results. It was not until 1900, when Mendel's work was rediscovered by scientists in Holland, Germany, and Austria-Hungary, that his theories gained general acceptance in the scientific community.

- Mendel's observations were used to justify Darwin's theory of evolution by natural selection. Mendel's ideas are considered to be the foundation of modern genetics.

IS THAT A FACT!

- From 1856 to 1863, while studying inheritance, Mendel grew almost 30,000 pea plants!

- Mendel also made contributions to beekeeping, horticulture, and meteorology. In 1877, Mendel became interested in weather and began issuing weather reports to local farmers.

- Punnett squares are named after their inventor, R. C. Punnett. Punnett explored inheritance by crossing different breeds of chickens in the early 1900s, soon after Mendel's work was rediscovered.

▶ **Pollination**
Pollen can be transferred between plants by wind, insects, and a variety of animals. Some common pollinators are bees, butterflies, moths, flies, bats, and birds. Animals are attracted to the color of the flower, the patterns found on the petals, or the flower's fragrance. Pollen is an excellent food for some animals.

SECTION 2

Meiosis

▶ **Chromosomes**
Chromosomes are composed of genes, the sequences of DNA that provide the instructions for making all the proteins in an organism. During cell division, the duplicated chromosomes separate so that one copy of each chromosome is present in the two new cells.

IS THAT A FACT!

- Male bees have only half the number of chromosomes that female bees have.

▶ **Walther Flemming**
Walther Flemming (1843–1905), a German physician and anatomist, was the first to use a microscope and

special dyes to study cell division. Flemming used the term *mitosis* to describe the process he observed.

▶ Mitosis

In mitosis, a cell divides to form two identical cells. The steps of the process are similar in almost all living organisms. In addition to enabling growth, mitosis allows organisms to replace cells that have died or malfunctioned. Mitosis can take anywhere from a few minutes to a few hours, and it may be affected by characteristics of the environment, such as light and temperature.

▶ Meiosis

In humans, meiosis is very different in males and females. In males, meiosis results in four similar sperm cells. In females, however, only one functional egg is produced. The other three resulting cells, which are known as *polar bodies,* contain the same amount of genetic material as the functional egg but do not mature.

▶ Genetic Disorders

A genetic disorder results from an inherited disruption in an organism's DNA. These inherited disruptions can take several forms, including a change in the number of chromosomes and the deletion or duplication of entire chromosomes or parts of chromosomes. Often the change responsible for a disorder is the alteration of

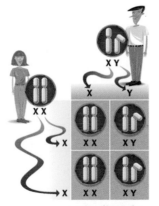

a single specific gene. However, some genetic disorders result from several of these genetic alterations occurring simultaneously. Diseases resulting from these alterations cause a wide variety of physical malfunctions and developmental problems.

- Hemophilia is an inherited blood disorder affecting about one person in 10,000. People with hemophilia are genetically unable to produce the blood proteins necessary to form blood clots. As a result, cuts and bruises considered unthreatening to anyone else can be dangerous for hemophiliacs. The clotting factors missing in people with hemophilia are now widely available and can be self-administered.

- Cystic fibrosis (CF) is a disease for which one in 31 Americans carries a recessive trait. If two of these people have children together, there is a 25 percent chance that any child born to them will have the disease. CF affects the intestinal, bronchial, and sweat glands. In people with CF, these glands secrete thick, sticky fluids that are difficult for the body to process, impeding breathing and digestion. Modern medical treatment has extended the median age for people with CF to about 30 years, an enormous improvement in just a few decades.

- Rubinstein-Taybi syndrome (RTS) is a complex genetic disorder whose characteristics include broad thumbs and toes, mental retardation, and distinctive facial features. This wide range of characteristics is believed to be linked to any one of a number of mutations in a gene responsible for providing the body with a protein called CBP. CBP is thought to be vital to the body's delicate metabolism. Because CBP greatly influences body processes, people with a problem producing CBP have a wide range of difficulties. Children with RTS can benefit from proper nutrition and early intervention with therapies and special education.

For background information about teaching strategies and issues, refer to the *Professional Reference for Teachers.*

Heredity

 Pre-Reading Questions

Students may not know the answers to these questions before reading the chapter, so accept any reasonable response.

Suggested Answers

1. Humans do not all look alike because we have a huge variety of genes that are combined differently in each of us.

2. A baby will be a boy if he has one X sex chromosome and one Y sex chromosome. A baby will be a girl if she has two X sex chromosomes.

Heredity

Sections

Pre-Reading Questions

1. Why don't all humans look exactly alike?
2. What determines whether a human baby will be a boy or a girl?

54

INDIAN PAINTBRUSHES

What do you notice about the red and yellow flowers in this photo? Besides their color, these flowers look very much alike. This similarity is because the flowers are of the same kind of plant, called Indian Paintbrush. Many things about the way a plant looks, including flower color, is determined by the plant's genes. These plants have different genes for flower color. In this chapter, you will learn about genes and about how differences in genes are important to evolution.

internet**connect**

HRW On-line Resources

go.hrw.com

For worksheets and other teaching aids, visit the HRW Web site and type in the keyword: **HSTHER**

SCiLINKS NSTA

www.scilinks.com

Use the *sci*LINKS numbers at the end of each chapter for additional resources on the **NSTA** Web site.

Smithsonian Institution

www.si.edu/hrw

Visit the Smithsonian Institution Web site for related on-line resources.

CNNfyi.com

www.cnnfyi.com

Visit the CNN Web site for current events coverage and classroom resources.

CLOTHING COMBOS

In this activity, your class will investigate how traits from parents can be joined to make so many different combinations in children.

Procedure

1. The entire class should use **three boxes.** One box contains **five hats.** One box contains **five gloves,** and one box contains **five scarves.**

2. Without looking in the boxes, five of your classmates will select one item from each box. Lay the items on the table. Repeat this process, five students at a time, until the entire class has picked "an outfit." Record what hat, scarf, and glove each student chose.

Analysis

3. Were any two outfits exactly alike? Do you think you saw all of the possible combinations? Explain your answer.

4. Choose a partner. Using the pieces of clothing you and your partner selected from the box, how many different combinations could you make by giving a third person one hat, one glove, and one scarf?

5. How is step 4 like parents passing traits to their children?

6. Based on this activity, why do you think parents often have children who look very different from each other?

55

CLOTHING COMBOS

MATERIALS
FOR EACH GROUP: • box with 5 hats • box with 5 scarves • box with 5 gloves

Safety Caution

Infestations of head lice are a common problem in schools. Sharing hats would, of course, be inadvisable during such a period. Jackets or sweatshirts could be substituted for hats in this exercise.

Answers to START-UP Activity

3. Answers will vary. There should be many different combinations. It is unlikely that students will see all of the possible combinations.

4. 8

5. You are choosing hats, scarves, and gloves randomly. Traits are passed from parent to offspring randomly as well. By combining the traits of two parents, there are many possible combinations of traits in the offspring.

6. Answers will vary. The number of possible genetic combinations is huge because we have so many genes.

Focus

Mendel and His Peas

This section introduces the genetic experiments of Gregor Mendel. Students explore how flowering plants are fertilized and how the offspring are affected by different crosses. Students also learn to use a Punnett square to predict the results of genetic crosses.

🎙️ Bellringer

Pose the following questions to your students:

Some people have brown eyes, some have blue, and some have green. Some people have earlobes attached directly to their head, while others have earlobes that hang loose. Where do people get these different traits? How are they passed from one generation to the next? Write your thoughts in your ScienceLog.

1) Motivate

ACTIVITY

Creating Tables Ask students to notice the differences in eye color, hair color, and earlobes among their classmates. Have them count the number of students with each trait and make a data table for each trait. The tables for eye color and earlobes will each have two columns. Have students calculate the ratios of attached to unattached earlobes and brown to blue eyes. Students may have eyes that are a color other than blue or brown, and this could be noted in a third column. (Note: A class of students is not a scientific sample and may not yield statistically significant results.)

Terms to Learn

heredity	alleles
dominant trait	genotype
recessive trait	phenotype
genes	probability

What You'll Do

- ◆ Explain the experiments of Gregor Mendel.
- ◆ Explain how genes and alleles are related to genotypes and phenotypes.
- ◆ Use the information in a Punnett square.

Activity

Imagine that you are planning to meet your pen pal at the airport, but you have never met. How would you describe yourself? Would you say that you are tall or short, have curly hair or straight hair, have brown eyes or green eyes? Make a list. Put a check mark next to traits you think you inherited.

TRY at HOME

Lab Book PG 188

Tracing Traits

Mendel and His Peas

There is no one else in the world exactly like you. You are unique. But what sets you apart? If you look around your classroom, you'll see that you share many physical characteristics with your classmates. For example, you all have skin instead of scales and a noticeable lack of antennae. You are a human being very much like all of your fellow human beings.

Yet you are different from everyone else in many ways. The people you most resemble are your parents and your brothers and sisters. But you probably don't look exactly like them either. Read on to find out why this is so.

Why Don't You Look Like a Rhinoceros?

The answer to this question seems simple: Neither of your parents is a rhinoceros. But there's more to this answer than meets the eye. As it turns out, **heredity,** or the passing of traits from 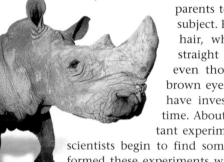 parents to offspring, is a very complicated subject. For example, you might have curly hair, while both of your parents have straight hair. You might have blue eyes, even though both of your parents have brown eyes. How does this happen? People have investigated this question for a long time. About 150 years ago, some very important experiments were performed that helped scientists begin to find some answers. The person who performed these experiments was Gregor Mendel.

Who Was Gregor Mendel?

Gregor Mendel was born in 1822 in Heinzendorf, Austria. Growing up on his family's farm, Mendel learned a lot about cultivating flowers and fruit trees. After completing his studies at a university, he entered a monastery. He worked in the monastery garden, where he was able to use plants to study the way traits are passed from parents to offspring. **Figure 1** shows an illustration of Mendel in the monastery garden.

Figure 1 Gregor Mendel

Homework

✏️ *Writing* What rhinoceroses look like is also genetically determined and varied. There are five species of rhinoceros, ranging in length from 2.5 m (8 ft) to 4.3 m (almost 14 ft). Have interested students research and give a written report on the rhinos alive today and the ones we know about from fossils.

Unraveling the Mystery

From his experiences breeding plants, Mendel knew that sometimes the patterns of inheritance seemed simple and sometimes they did not. Mendel wanted to find out why.

Mendel was interested in the way traits are passed from parents to offspring. For example, sometimes a trait that appeared in one generation did not show up in any of the offspring in the next generation. In the third generation, though, the trait showed up again. Mendel noticed similar patterns in people, plants, and many other living things.

To simplify his investigation, Mendel decided to study only one kind of organism. He had already done studies using the garden pea plant, so he chose this as his subject.

How Do You Like Your Peas? Garden peas were a good choice for several reasons. These plants grow quickly, they are usually self-pollinating, and they come in many varieties. A *self-pollinating plant* contains both male and female reproductive structures, like the flower in **Figure 2**. Therefore, pollen from one flower or plant can fertilize the eggs of the same flower or the eggs of another flower on the same plant. **Figure 3** illustrates the parts of a flower and how fertilization takes place in plants.

Figure 2 *This photograph of a flower shows the male and female reproductive structures.*

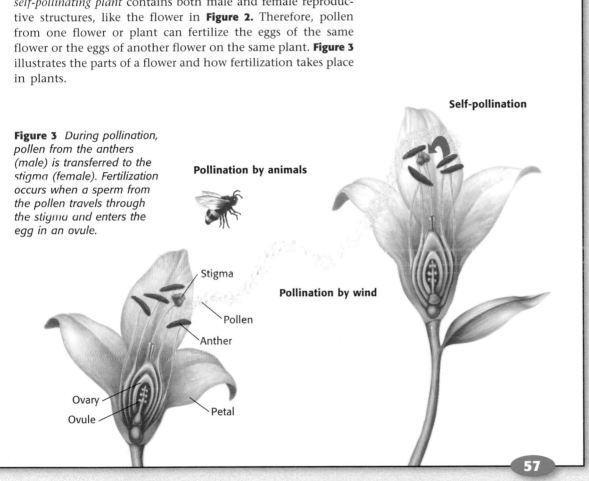

Figure 3 *During pollination, pollen from the anthers (male) is transferred to the stigma (female). Fertilization occurs when a sperm from the pollen travels through the stigma and enters the egg in an ovule.*

Pollination by animals

Pollination by wind

Self-pollination

Stigma

Pollen

Anther

Ovary

Ovule

Petal

2 Teach

USING THE FIGURES

Discuss the physical processes involved in the fertilization of the flowers illustrated in **Figure 3.** The flower on the right can be fertilized by another flower or can fertilize itself. Compare this figure with **Figure 5,** and point out that removing the anthers from the flower makes it impossible for the plant to self-pollinate.
  Sheltered English

DISCUSSION

Scientific Method Have students identify the steps of the scientific method in Mendel's work.

- **Ask a question**—How are traits inherited?
- **Form a hypothesis**—Inheritance has a pattern.
- **Test the hypothesis**—Cross true-breeding plants and offspring.
- **Analyze the results**—Identify patterns in inherited traits.
- **Draw conclusions**—Traits are inherited in predictable patterns.

What step did Mendel omit? (Hint: Why was his work overlooked for so long?) (communicate the results)

Directed Reading Worksheet Section 1

57

IS THAT A FACT!

Although Mendel was brilliant, he had difficulty learning from scientific texts. In the monastery gardens, Mendel explored the scientific ideas he had trouble with in school. While trying to grow better peas, he discovered genetics, an entirely new field of science!

internet connect

SCiLINKS
NSTA

TOPIC: Gregor Mendel
GO TO: www.scilinks.org
*sci*LINKS NUMBER: HSTL105

Learners Having Difficulty
Ask students the following questions: What other traits might vary among flowers of the same species? Why do traits vary among individuals of the same species? Can any traits of a plant's offspring be predicted? Sheltered English

CONNECT TO
PHYSICAL SCIENCE

Flower colors vary widely, from white to nearly black. White flowers reflect the entire visible spectrum of light. Flowers displaying other colors absorb all the visible wavelengths except for the colors that we see on them. A red rose absorbs all the visible wavelengths of light except red, which is why it appears red to us. Use the following Teaching Transparency to illustrate how white light is composed of all the colors of the rainbow.

Teaching Transparency 293
"White Light Is Separated by a Prism"

LINK TO PHYSICAL SCIENCE

Multicultural
CONNECTION

Writing Throughout history, cultures have developed different interpretations of how traits are inherited between generations. Social prohibitions have helped cultures avoid genetic interbreeding. Have interested students write a research report to share with the class.

Science Skills Worksheet
"Finding Useful Sources"

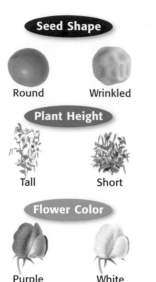

Seed Shape

Round   Wrinkled

Plant Height

Tall   Short

Flower Color

Purple   White

Figure 4 *These are some of the plant characteristics that Mendel studied.*

Peas Be My Podner

Mendel chose to study only one characteristic, such as plant height or pea color, at a time. That way, he could understand the results. Mendel chose plants that had two forms for each of the characteristics he studied. For example, for the characteristic of plant height, one form always produced tall plants, and the other form always produced short plants. Some of the characteristics investigated by Mendel are shown in **Figure 4.** The two different traits of each characteristic are also shown.

True-Breeding Plants Mendel was very careful to use plants that were true breeding for each of the traits he was studying. When a *true-breeding plant* self-pollinates, it will always produce offspring with the same trait the parent plant has. For example, a tall true-breeding plant will always produce offspring that are tall.

Mendel decided to find out what would happen if he crossed two plants that had different forms of a single trait. To do this, he used a method known as *cross-pollination*. In cross-pollination, the anthers of one plant are removed so that the plant cannot self-pollinate. Then pollen from another plant is used to fertilize the plant without anthers. This way, Mendel could select which pollen would fertilize which plant. This technique is illustrated in **Figure 5.**

Pollen is transferred.

A plant that produces wrinkled seeds

Anther

A plant that produces round seeds

Stigma   Anthers are removed.

Figure 5 *Mendel removed the anthers from a plant that produced round seeds. Then he used pollen from a plant that produced wrinkled seeds to fertilize the plant that produced round seeds.*

58

internet**connect**

SCI**LINKS** NSTA
TOPIC: Heredity
GO TO: www.scilinks.org
*sci***LINKS NUMBER:** HSTL110

WEIRD SCIENCE

Environmental stimuli can sometimes affect flower color. Hydrangeas growing in acidic soil produce blue flowers. If the soil is made alkaline, the same plants will produce pink flowers.

Mendel's First Experiment

In his first experiment, Mendel performed crosses to study seven different characteristics. Each of the crosses was between the two traits of each characteristic. The results of the cross between plants that produce round seeds and plants that produce wrinkled seeds are shown in **Figure 6.** The offspring from this cross are known as the *first generation*. Do the results surprise you? What do you think happened to the trait for wrinkled seeds?

Mendel got similar results for each of the crosses that he made. One trait always appeared, and the other trait seemed to vanish. Mendel chose to call the trait that appeared the **dominant trait.** The other trait seemed to recede into the background, so Mendel called this the **recessive trait.** To find out what might have happened to the recessive trait, Mendel decided to perform another experiment.

Mendel's Second Experiment

Mendel allowed the first generation from each of the seven crosses to self-pollinate. This is also illustrated in Figure 6. This time the plant with the dominant trait for seed shape (which is round) was allowed to self-pollinate. As you can see, the recessive trait for wrinkled seeds showed up again.

Mendel performed this same experiment on the two traits of each of the seven characteristics. No matter which characteristic Mendel investigated, when the first generation was allowed to self-pollinate, the recessive trait reappeared.

Figure 6 *A plant that produces wrinkled seeds is fertilized with pollen from a plant that produces round seeds.*

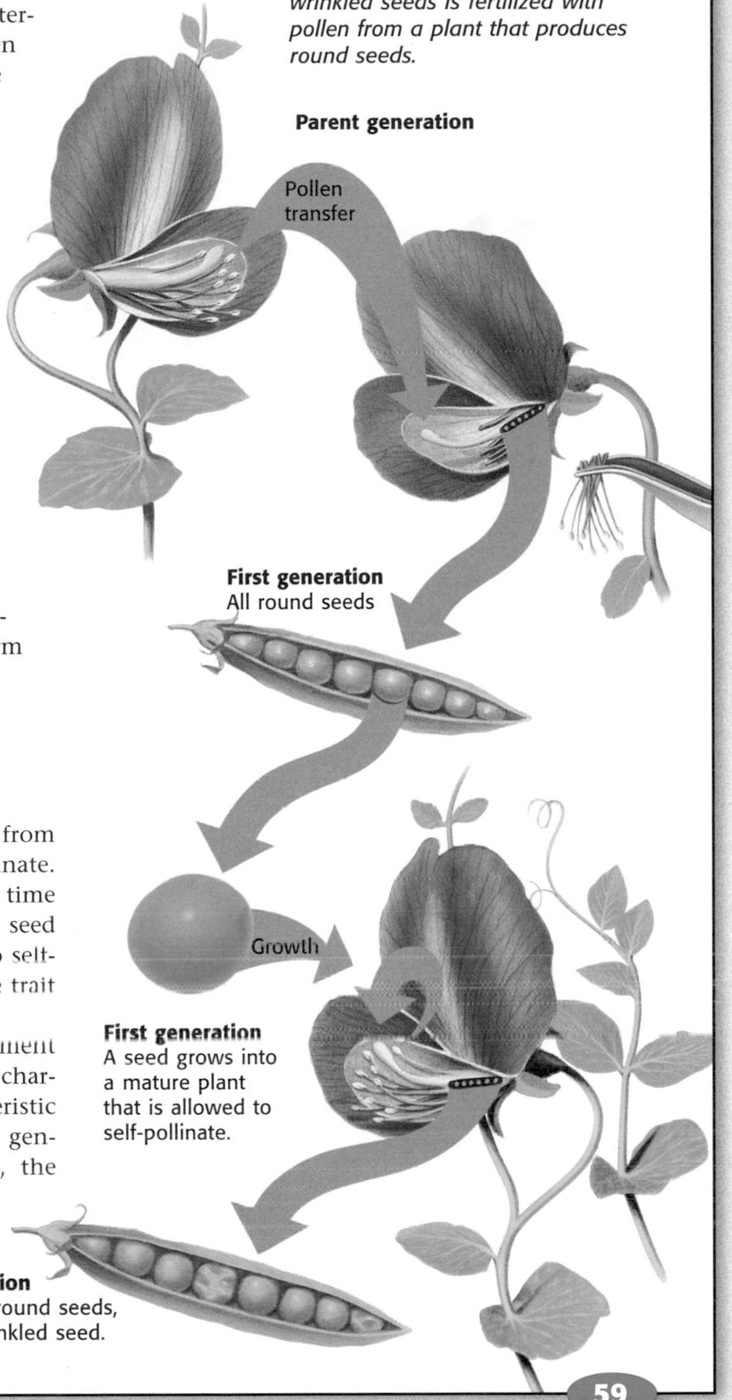

Parent generation

Pollen transfer

First generation
All round seeds

Growth

First generation
A seed grows into a mature plant that is allowed to self-pollinate.

Second generation
For every three round seeds, there is one wrinkled seed.

59

GROUP ACTIVITY

Mendelian Crosses Give each student a purple bead and a white bead, and ask them to perform a Mendelian cross. Tell students to begin with the first generation with the allele combination *Pp*. Have students randomly "pollinate" with 10 other members of the class. To "pollinate," students should pair up and shake all four beads together. Without looking, each student should choose one bead. The two beads selected will determine the genotype of the offspring. Have them do this 10 times. Students should record the genotype for each pollination. Have students tally the results and determine the ratio of white-flowering plants to purple-flowering plants resulting from the matches.

DEMONSTRATION

Flower Dissection Obtain a flower that has anthers and a stigma, such as a pea flower, a tulip, or a lily. Be careful: Pollen can stain clothing and cause allergic reactions. Dissect the flower, and show students the anthers and the stigma. Could this flower self-pollinate? (Yes; it has both anthers and a stigma.)

Demonstrate how Mendel removed the anthers of his flowers and then used a small brush to transfer pollen from plant to plant. Sheltered English

Homework

Poster Project Have students create posters to illustrate Mendel's first and second experiments. Have each student demonstrate one of the seven traits Mendel studied. Encourage students to use materials such as flowers, yellow and green seeds, or wrinkled and round peas. Each project should clearly identify the parents, the first generation, and the second generation. (This activity can also be done with seven groups, one for each trait.) Sheltered English

internetconnect

SCLINKS
NSTA

TOPIC: Dominant and Recessive Traits
GO TO: www.scilinks.org
*sci*LINKS NUMBER: HSTL115

USING THE TABLE

As seen in the table on this page, Mendel used at least 580 plants for each trait he studied. Why did Mendel work with such large samples? (Because Mendel was studying probability, larger samples increased the accuracy of his results.)

Would his data have been different if he had used much smaller samples? (Yes; the data would probably have been less accurate.)

MATH and MORE

Ratios are commonly used to compare two values. For instance, ratios are often used to express speeds, such as 55 km/h, and prices, such as 79 cents/kg. In these examples, the ratios are 55:1 and 79:1.

 Math Skills Worksheet "What Is a Ratio?"

Answer to MATHBREAK

The ratio of nougat-filled chocolates to caramel-filled chocolates is 18:6, or $\frac{18}{6}$, which can be reduced to $\frac{3}{1}$. This can be rewritten as 3:1 or 3 to 1.

Math Skills Worksheet "Punnett Square Popcorn"

$\div \ 5 \ \div \ \Omega \ \le \ \infty \ +_\Omega \ ^\surd \ 9 \ _\infty \ ^\le \ \Sigma \ 2$

MATH BREAK

Understanding Ratios

A ratio is a way to compare two numbers by using division. The ratio of plants with purple flowers to plants with white flowers can be written as 705 to 224 or 705:224. This ratio can be reduced, or simplified, by dividing the first number by the second as follows:

$$\frac{705}{224} = \frac{3.15}{1}$$

which is the same thing as a ratio of 3.15:1. For every three plants with purple flowers, there will be roughly one plant with white flowers. Try this problem:

In a box of chocolates, there are 18 nougat-filled chocolates and 6 caramel-filled chocolates. What is the ratio of nougat-filled chocolates to caramel-filled chocolates?

A Different Point of View

Mendel then did something that no one else had done before: He decided to count the number of plants with each trait that turned up in the second generation. He hoped that this might help him explain his results. Take a look at Mendel's actual results, shown in the table below.

Mendel's Results				
Characteristic	Dominant trait		Recessive trait	Ratio
Flower color	705 purple		224 white	3.15:1
Seed color	6,002 yellow		2,001 green	?
Seed shape	5,474 round		1,850 wrinkled	?
Pod color	428 green		152 yellow	?
Pod shape	882 smooth		299 bumpy	?
Flower position	651 along stem		207 at tip	?
Plant height	787 tall		277 short	?

As you can see, the recessive trait showed up again, but not as often as the dominant trait showed up. Mendel decided to calculate the *ratio* of dominant traits to recessive traits for each characteristic. Follow in Mendel's footsteps by calculating the dominant-to-recessive ratio for each characteristic. (If you need help, check out the MathBreak at left.) Can you find a pattern among the ratios?

Ratios for Mendel's Results

The reduced ratios of dominant to recessive traits in Mendel's specimens are as follows:

Flower color	3.15:1
Seed color	3.00:1
Seed shape	2.96:1
Pod color	2.82:1
Pod shape	2.95:1
Flower position	3.14:1
Plant height	2.84:1

Answer to the question at the bottom of the student page

All the ratios can be rounded off to 3:1.

A Brilliant Idea

Mendel realized that his results could be explained only if each plant had two sets of instructions for each characteristic. Each parent donates one set of instructions, now known as **genes,** to the offspring. The fertilized egg would then have two forms of the same gene for every characteristic—one from each parent. The two forms of a gene are known as **alleles.**

The Proof Is in the Punnett Square To understand Mendel's conclusions, we'll use a diagram called a Punnett square. A *Punnett square* is used to visualize all the possible combinations of alleles from the parents. Dominant alleles are symbolized with capital letters, and recessive alleles are symbolized with lowercase letters. Therefore, the alleles for a true-breeding purple-flowered plant are written as *PP.* The alleles for a true-breeding white-flowered plant are written as *pp.* The cross between these two parent plants, as shown in **Figure 7,** is then written as *PP* × *pp.* The squares contain the allele combinations that could occur in the offspring. The inherited combination of alleles is known as the offspring's **genotype.**

Figure 7 shows that all of the offspring will have the same genotype: *Pp.* The dominant allele, *P,* in each genotype ensures that all of the offspring will be purple-flowered plants. An organism's appearance is known as its **phenotype.** The recessive allele, *p,* may be passed on to the next generation.

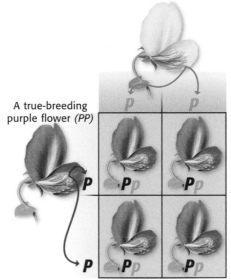

A true-breeding white flower *(pp)*

A true-breeding purple flower *(PP)*

Figure 7 *The possible allele combinations in the offspring for this cross are all the same:* **Pp.**

How to Make a Punnett Square

Draw a square, and divide it into four sections. Next, write the letters that represent alleles from one parent along the top of the box. Write the letters that represent alleles from the other parent along the side of the box.

The cross shown at right is between a plant that produces only round seeds, **RR,** and a plant that produces only wrinkled seeds, **rr.** Follow the arrows to see how the inside of the box was filled. The resulting alleles inside the box show all the possible genotypes for the offspring from this cross. What would the phenotypes for these offspring be?

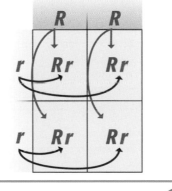

SCIENCE HUMOR

Q: What do you get when you cross a bridge with a bicycle?

A: to the other side

Answer to How to Make a Punnett Square

All the phenotypes would be round.

61

RETEACHING

Ratios If students have difficulty calculating ratios, review fractions using this demonstration. Display three pennies and one nickel, and ask students the following questions:

How many coins are there in all? (four) What fraction of the coins are pennies? ($\frac{3}{4}$)

What fraction of the coins are nickels? ($\frac{1}{4}$)

How many pennies and nickels are there? (three pennies and one nickel)

What is the ratio of pennies to nickels? (3 to 1)

Sheltered English

MISCONCEPTION ALERT

Not all inherited traits follow the examples studied by Mendel. For instance, a cross between a red horse and a white horse can produce a horse with both red and white hair. Such a horse is said to have a roan coat. This is an example of codominance. In this and similar cases, both alleles are equally dominant, so the model developed by Mendel does not apply.

Teaching Transparency 15 "Punnett Square: *PP* × *pp* Cross"

3 Extend, continued

Homework

Punnett Squares Have students create Punnett squares for the different crosses in Mendel's experiments. Students should include the phenotype and genotype of the parents and offspring.

MATERIALS

FOR EACH GROUP:
• masking tape
• 2 quarters

Answers to QuickLab

Students should find that they get the *bb* combination about $\frac{1}{4}$, or 25 percent, of the time. The more trials there are, the closer the probability will be to 25 percent. Note that each coin represents one parent's alleles. For example, the female parent has the alleles *B* and *b*. The probability that the offspring will inherit either of these alleles from the female parent is $\frac{1}{2}$, or 50 percent. The same is true for the male parent. The probability of throwing two *b* alleles in a row is calculated as follows: $\frac{1}{2} \times \frac{1}{2} = \frac{1}{4}$, and $\frac{1}{4} \times 100 = 25$ percent.

 Teaching Transparency 15
"Punnett Square: *Pp* × *Pp* Cross"

 Reinforcement Worksheet
"Dimples and DNA"

Critical Thinking Worksheet
"A Bittersweet Solution"

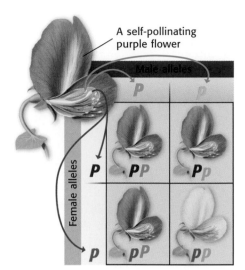
A self-pollinating purple flower

Male alleles

Female alleles

Figure 8 *This Punnett square shows the possible results from the cross **Pp** × **Pp**.*

Take Your Chances

You have two guinea pigs you would like to breed. Each has brown fur and the genotype **Bb.** What are the chances that their offspring will have white fur with the genotype **bb?** Try this to find out. Stick a piece of **masking tape** on both sides of **two quarters.** Label one side of each quarter with a capital **B** and the other side with a lowercase **b.** Toss both coins 50 times, making note of your results each time. How many times did you get the **bb** combination? What is the probability that the next toss will result in **bb?**

TRY at HOME

More Evidence In Mendel's second experiment, he allowed the first-generation plants to self-pollinate. **Figure 8** shows a self-pollination cross of a first-generation plant with the genotype *Pp*. The parental alleles in the cross indicate that the egg and sperm can contain either a *P* allele or a *p* allele.

What might the genotypes of the offspring be? Notice that one square shows the *Pp* combination, while another shows the *pP* combination. These are exactly the same genotype, even though the letters are written in a different order. The other possible genotypes in the offspring are *PP* and *pp*. The combinations *PP*, *Pp*, and *pP* have the same phenotype—purple flowers—because they each contain at least one dominant allele (*P*). Only one combination, *pp*, produces plants with white flowers. The ratio of dominant to recessive is 3:1, just as Mendel calculated from his data.

What Are the Chances?

It's important to understand that offspring are equally likely to inherit either allele from either parent. Think of a coin toss. There's a 50 percent chance you'll get heads and a 50 percent chance you'll get tails. Like the toss of a coin, the chance of inheriting one allele or another is completely random.

Probability The mathematical chance that an event will occur is known as **probability.** Probability is usually expressed as a fraction or percentage. If you toss a coin, the probability of tossing tails is $\frac{1}{2}$. This means that half the number of times you toss a coin, you will get tails. To express probability as a percentage, divide the numerator of the fraction by the denominator, and then multiply the answer by 100.

$$\frac{1}{2} \times 100 = 50\%$$

To find the probability that you will toss two heads in a row, multiply the probability of the two events.

$$\frac{1}{2} \times \frac{1}{2} = \frac{1}{4}$$

The percentage would be $1 \div 4 \times 100$, which equals 25 percent.

Many ordinary fruits and vegetables carry recessive genes for bizarre traits. For instance, a recessive gene in tomatoes causes the skin to be covered with fuzzy hair!

62

62

Chapter 3 • Heredity

APPLY

Curly Eared Cats

A curly eared cat, like the one at right, mated with a cat that had normal ears. If half the kittens had the genotype **Cc** and curly ears, and the other half had the genotype **cc** and normal ears, which was the allele for curly ears?

What was the genotype of each parent? (**Hint:** Use a Punnett square to fill in the genotypes of the offspring, and then work backward.)

Genotype Probability The same method is used to calculate the probability that an offspring will inherit a certain genotype. For a pea plant to inherit the white flower trait, it must receive a **p** allele from each parent. There is a 50 percent chance of inheriting either allele from either parent. So the probability of inheriting two **p** alleles from a **Pp** × **Pp** cross is $\frac{1}{2} \times \frac{1}{2}$. This equals $\frac{1}{4}$ or 25 percent.

Gregor Mendel—Gone but Not Forgotten Good ideas are often overlooked or misunderstood when they first appear. This was the fate of Gregor Mendel's ideas. In 1865, he published his findings for the scientific community. Unfortunately, his work didn't get much attention. It wasn't until after his death, more than 30 years later, that Mendel finally got the recognition he deserved. Once Mendel's ideas were rediscovered and understood, the door was opened to modern genetics.

SECTION REVIEW

1. The allele for a cleft chin, **C**, is dominant among humans. What would be the results from a cross between a woman with the genotype **Cc** and a man with the genotype **cc**? Create a Punnett square showing this cross.

2. Of the possible combinations you found in question 1, what is the ratio of offspring with a cleft chin to offspring without a cleft chin?

3. **Applying Concepts** The Punnett square at right shows the possible combinations of alleles for fur color in rabbits. Black fur, **B**, is dominant over white fur, **b.** Given the combinations shown, what are the genotypes of the parents?

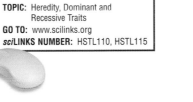

internet**connect**
*sci*LINKS NSTA

TOPIC: Heredity, Dominant and Recessive Traits
GO TO: www.scilinks.org
*sci***LINKS NUMBER:** HSTL110, HSTL115

63

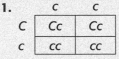

Answers to Section Review

1.

	c	c
C	Cc	Cc
c	cc	cc

2. 1:1

3. BB, bb

4 Close

Answers to APPLY

The dominant allele is the allele for curly ears, *C.* The parents' genotypes were *Cc* (curly ears) and *cc* (normal ears).

Quiz

For rabbits, the allele for black fur, *B*, is dominant over the allele for white fur, *b.* Suppose two black parents have four bunnies—three black and one white.

1. What are the genotypes of the parents? (The parents both have the recessive allele, so they are both genotype *Bb.*)

2. What are the possible genotypes of all four siblings? (The white bunny has genotype *bb*, and the black bunnies may be *BB* or *Bb.*)

ALTERNATIVE ASSESSMENT

Ask students to imagine two animal parents with different genetic traits. Have them assign three characteristics to each parent, such as tall or short and red-nosed or blue-nosed. For each pair of characteristics, have students choose one as dominant and the other as recessive. Students should use Punnett squares to determine the possible first-generation genotypes and phenotypes for each trait in a cross between the two parents. Then have students choose two genotypes for each characteristic from the first generation and create a Punnett square showing the possible second-generation genotypes and phenotypes resulting from that cross.

Focus

Meiosis

This section discusses chromosomes, describes the process of meiosis, and explains the difference between meiosis and mitosis. The section explains how meiosis supports Mendel's findings and concludes with a discussion of sex chromosomes and how sex is determined.

Bellringer

Ask students to write a sentence for each of the following terms:

heredity, genotype, and phenotype

(**Heredity** is the passing on of traits from parents to offspring.

The combination of an organism's alleles is its **genotype.**

The way that an organism looks is known as its **phenotype.**)

1 Motivate

DISCUSSION

Inherited Traits Lead a class discussion about traits that are passed from parents to their children. Have the students list examples of traits that "run in families" and that could be genetically determined. (Answers may include traits such as hair color; a tendency to develop diseases, such as diabetes and some forms of cancer; or personality traits, such as shyness.)

Ask students to think about how traits are inherited. For example, some traits are carried by one sex, and some diseases are said to "skip a generation." Explain that this section will introduce the physical processes that determine genetic inheritance.

SECTION 2
READING WARM-UP

Terms to Learn

sex cells
homologous chromosomes
meiosis
sex chromosomes

What You'll Do

◆ Explain the difference between mitosis and meiosis.
◆ Describe how Mendel's ideas are supported by the process of meiosis.
◆ Explain the difference between male and female sex chromosomes.

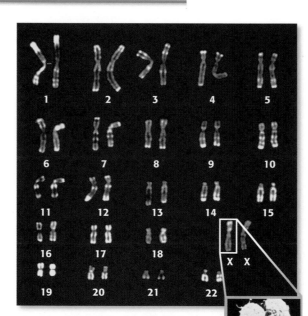

Figure 9 *Human body cells have 46 chromosomes, or 23 pairs of homologous chromosomes. One member of a pair of homologous chromosomes is shown at right.*

64

Meiosis

In the early 1900s, scientists began doing experiments similar to those done by Gregor Mendel. Excited by their findings, they searched for similar results obtained by others. They came across Mendel's forgotten paper and realized that their discoveries were not new; Mendel had made the same observation 35 years earlier. However, genes were still a mystery. Where were they located, and how did they pass information from one cell to another? Understanding reproduction was the first step in finding the answers to these questions.

Two Kinds of Reproduction

You know that there are two types of reproduction: asexual reproduction and sexual reproduction.

One Makes Two In *asexual reproduction,* only one parent cell is needed for reproduction. First, the internal structures of the cell are copied by a process known as mitosis. The parent cell then divides, producing new cells that are exact copies of the parent cell. Most single-celled organisms reproduce in this way. Most of the cells in your body also divide this way.

Two Make One A different type of reproduction is used to make a new human being or a new pea plant. In *sexual reproduction,* two parent cells join together to form a new individual. The parent cells, known as **sex cells,** are different from ordinary body cells. Human body cells, for example, have 46 chromosomes (or 23 pairs), as shown in **Figure 9.** The chromosomes in each pair are called **homologous** (hoh MAHL uh guhs) **chromosomes.** But human sex cells have only 23 chromosomes—half the usual number. Male sex cells are called *sperm.* Female sex cells are called *eggs,* or ova. Each sperm and each egg has only one of the chromosomes from each homologous pair.

internetconnect

SCILINKS
NSTA

TOPIC: Cell Division
GO TO: www.scilinks.org
*sci*LINKS NUMBER: HSTL120

Science BІᴼᴼpers

In 1918, a prominent scientist miscounted the number of chromosomes in a human cell. He counted 48. For almost 40 years, scientists thought this number was correct. In fact, it wasn't until 1956 that chromosomes were correctly counted and found to be only 46.

Less Is More Why is it important that sex cells have half the usual number of chromosomes? When an egg and a sperm join to form a new individual, each parent donates one half of a homologous pair of chromosomes. This ensures that the offspring will receive a normal number of chromosomes in each body cell. Each body cell must have an entire set of 46 chromosomes in order to grow and function properly.

Meiosis to the Rescue Sex cells are made during meiosis, a copying process that is different from mitosis. **Meiosis** (mie OH sis) produces new cells with half the usual number of chromosomes. When the sex cells are made, the chromosomes are copied once, and then the nucleus divides twice. The resulting sperm and eggs have half the number of chromosomes found in a normal body cell.

Meanwhile, Back at the Lab

What does all of this have to do with the location of genes? Not long after Mendel's paper was rediscovered, a young graduate student named Walter Sutton made an important observation. Sutton was studying sperm cells in grasshoppers. Sutton knew of Mendel's studies, which showed that the egg and sperm must each contribute the same amount of information to the offspring. That was the only way the 3:1 ratio found in the second generation could be explained. Sutton also knew from his own studies that although eggs and sperm were different, they did have something in common: their chromosomes were located inside a nucleus. Using his observations of meiosis, his understanding of Mendel's work, and some creative thinking, Sutton proposed something very important:

Genes are located on chromosomes!

And Sutton was correct, as it turned out. The steps of meiosis are outlined on the next two pages. But first, let's review mitosis so that you can compare the two processes.

Mitosis Revisited

1 Inside a typical cell: each of the long strands (chromosomes) makes a copy of itself.

2 Each chromosome consists of two identical copies called chromatids. The chromosomes thicken and shorten.

3 The nuclear membrane dissolves. The chromosomes line up along the equator (center) of the cell.

4 The chromatids pull apart.

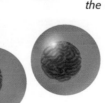
5 The nuclear membrane forms around the separated chromatids. The chromosomes unwind, and the cell divides.

6 The result: two identical copies of the original cell.

65

READING STRATEGY

Prediction Guide Before students read the passage about meiosis, ask them whether the following statements are true or false. Students will discover the answers as they explore Section 2.

- Mitosis is the only type of cell division. (false)
- Only sex cells undergo meiosis. (true)
- Sex cells contain half the number of chromosomes as other body cells. (true)

USING THE FIGURES

Use the graphical representations of mitosis and meiosis in this section to describe what happens in each type of division. On the board, draw two identical cells, each containing four chromosomes. Label one cell "Mitosis," and label the other "Meiosis." Have students describe what happens in each stage of mitosis and illustrate the stages on the board. (Using colored chalk might help distinguish between the dividing chromosomes.) Repeat the process for meiosis. Point out that in this case mitosis results in two identical cells, each containing four chromosomes, while meiosis results in four cells, each containing two chromosomes. **Sheltered English**

IS THAT A FACT!

In human males, meiosis and sperm production take about 9 weeks. It's a continuous process that begins at puberty. In females, meiosis and egg production begin before birth. The process stops abruptly, however, and does not begin again until a girl enters puberty. Until a woman reaches menopause, one egg each month resumes meiosis and finishes its development. Therefore, the meiosis of a single egg may take up to 50 years to complete!

Directed Reading Worksheet Section 2

DEMONSTRATION

Modeling Meiosis Select all cards that are the same color, and shuffle them. Each card will represent one chromosome. Tell students that two cards of the same number or face—for example, a queen of spades and a queen of clubs—represent homologous chromosomes. Next pair up the cards according to face or number. Make two piles; each pile should contain one of a pair. Ask students what this division represents. (the separation of homologous chromosomes into two cells)

Emphasize that this activity models only the first cell division of meiosis. Stress that after the second cell division of meiosis, each new cell will have half the number of chromosomes. Sheltered English

CROSS-DISCIPLINARY FOCUS

Theater Students may enjoy watching a choreographed dance or skit that walks them methodically through the steps of meiosis. Have interested students design the skit or dance, and allow them time to perform it. This can be a very effective way to present this difficult material. Sheltered English

Teaching Transparency 16 "Meiosis in Eight Easy Steps: A"

Meiosis in Eight Easy Steps

The diagram on these two pages shows each stage of meiosis. Read about each step as you look at the diagram. Different types of living things have different numbers of chromosomes. In this diagram, only four chromosomes are shown.

One pair of homologous chromosomes

Two chromatids

1 Before meiosis begins, the chromosomes are in a threadlike form. Each chromosome makes an identical copy of itself, forming two exact halves called *chromatids.* The chromosomes then thicken and shorten into a form that is visible under a microscope. The nuclear membrane disappears.

2 Each chromosome is now made up of two chromatids, the original and an exact copy. Similar chromosomes pair with one another, forming *homologous chromosome pairs.* The paired homologous chromosomes line up at the equator of the cell.

3 The chromosomes separate from their homologous partners and move to opposite ends of the cell.

4 The nuclear membrane re-forms, and the cell divides. The paired chromatids are still joined.

66

 SCIENCE HUMOR

Q: If human sex cells are created by meiosis, how are cat sex cells produced?

A: by meowsis

 WEIRD SCIENCE

In some species of animals, there is only one gender! For instance, all desert whiptail lizards *(Cnemidophorus neomexicanus)* are female. Eggs are produced through parthenogenesis, and the unfertilized eggs develop into females that are genetically identical to their mother.

5 Each cell contains one member of each homologous chromosome pair. The chromosomes are not copied again between the two cell divisions.

6 The chromosomes line up at the equator of each cell.

7 The chromatids pull apart and move to opposite ends of the cell. The nuclear membrane forms around the separated chromosomes, and the cells divide.

8 The result: Four new cells have formed from the original single cell. Each new cell has half the number of chromosomes present in the original cell.

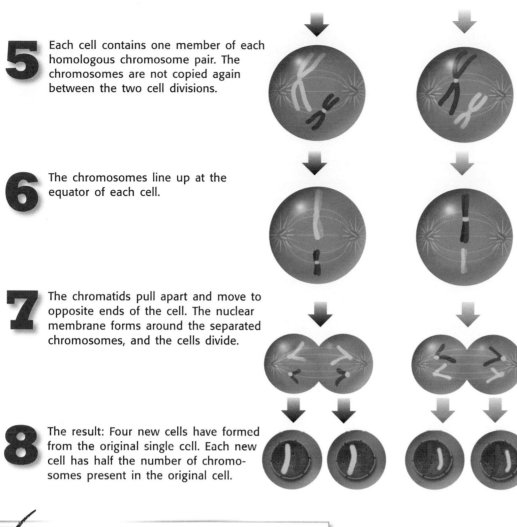

✓ Self-Check

1. How many chromosomes are in the original single cell in the diagram on page 66?

2. How many homologous pairs are shown in the original cell?

3. How many times do the chromosomes make copies of themselves during meiosis? How many times do cells divide during meiosis?

4. How many chromosomes are present in each cell at the end of meiosis? at the end of mitosis?

(See page 216 to check your answers.)

internet**connect**

sci**LINKS**
NSTA

TOPIC: Cell Division
GO TO: www.scilinks.org
*sci*LINKS **NUMBER:** HSTL120

Scientists have bred watermelons that have an extra set of chromosomes. These watermelons are sterile, and their seeds do not develop. The result is seedless watermelons.

MEETING INDIVIDUAL NEEDS

Advanced Learners

Using high school or college texts, have students find the names of each stage of meiosis. Students should use this information to make a poster of meiosis. They can also compare the process of meiosis and mitosis.

ACTIVITY

Concept Mapping Have students use the new terms in this section to create a concept map.

Teaching Transparency 17 "Meiosis in Eight Easy Steps: B"

67

Answers to Self-Check

1. four

2. two

3. They make copies of themselves once. They divide twice.

4. Two, or half the number of chromosomes in the parent are present at the end of meiosis. After mitosis, there would be four chromosomes, the same number as in the parent cell.

INDEPENDENT PRACTICE

Writing Have each student write a ScienceLog entry to chronicle the events of a chromosome containing an allele for a specific trait. Have the student describe the chromosome's role in the parent organism, the first-generation offspring, and the second-generation offspring. Descriptions should define whether the trait is dominant or recessive and should include an analysis of the factors that determine the genotype and phenotype of the parent and the offspring.

USING THE FIGURE

Draw a Punnett square for the cross *RR* × *rr*, shown in **Figure 10.** Then draw another Punnett square for the first generation cross, *Rr* × *Rr*. How many genotypes are possible from the second cross? What are they? What are the possible phenotypes from the second cross? (One genotype is possible from the first cross, *Rr*. Three genotypes are possible for the second cross: *RR*, *Rr* (*rR*), and *rr*. The two possible phenotypes are wrinkled seeds, *rr* and round seeds, *RR*, *Rr*.)

MISCONCEPTION ///ALERT\\\\

A common misconception is that many types of cells undergo meiosis. Make sure students understand that meiosis occurs *only* during sex-cell formation.

Meiosis and Mendel

As Walter Sutton realized, the steps in meiosis explain Mendel's findings. **Figure 10** illustrates what happens to a pair of homologous chromosomes during meiosis and fertilization. The cross is between a plant that is true breeding for round seeds and a plant that is true breeding for wrinkled seeds.

Figure 10 *Meiosis helps explain Mendel's findings.*

Male Parent In the plant cell nucleus below, each homologous chromosome has an allele for seed shape and each allele carries the same instructions: to make wrinkled seeds.

Female Parent In the plant cell nucleus below, each homologous chromosome has an allele for seed shape and each allele carries the same instruction: to make round seeds.

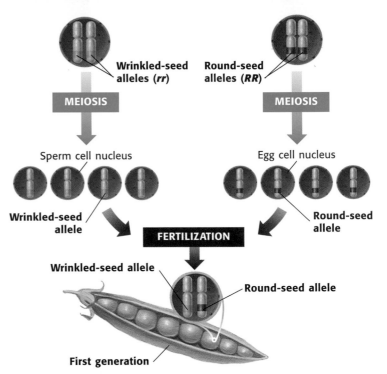

Following **meiosis**, each sperm cell contains a recessive allele for wrinkled seeds and each egg cell contains a dominant allele for round seeds.

Fertilization of any egg by any sperm results in the same genotype (*Rr*) and the same phenotype (round). This is exactly what Mendel found in his studies.

Each fertilized egg in the first generation contained one dominant allele and one recessive allele for seed type. Only one genotype was possible because all sperm formed during meiosis contained the wrinkled-seed allele and all eggs contained the round-seed allele. When the first generation was allowed to self-pollinate, the possible genotypes changed. There are three genotype possibilities for this cross: *RR*, *Rr*, and *rr*.

68

Teaching Transparency 18 "Meiosis and Mendel"

Homework

PORTFOLIO **Making Models** Have students use markers, yarn, glue, and poster board to make a poster illustrating the process of meiosis. Each step of the process should include the sex chromosomes. The posters should demonstrate an understanding of meiosis, of sex cells, of sex chromosomes, and of sex determination. Sheltered English

Male or Female?

There are many ways that different organisms become male or female. To see how this happens in humans, examine **Figure 11.** Then look back at Figure 9, on page 64. Each figure shows the chromosomes in human body cells. Which chromosome photograph is from a female, and which is from a male? Here's a hint: Females have 23 matched pairs, while males have 22 matched pairs and one unmatched pair.

Sex Chromosomes The chromosomes in Figure 11 are from a male, and the chromosomes in Figure 9 are from a female. **Sex chromosomes** carry genes that determine whether the offspring is male or female. In humans, females have two X chromosomes (the matching pair), and males have one X chromosome and one Y chromosome (the unmatched pair).

During meiosis, one of each of the chromosome pairs ends up in a sex cell. This is also true of the sex chromosomes. Females have two X chromosomes in each body cell. When meiosis produces the egg cells, each egg contains one X chromosome. Males have both an X chromosome and a Y chromosome in each body cell. During meiosis, these chromosomes separate, so each sperm cell contains either an X or a Y chromosome. An egg fertilized by a sperm with an X chromosome will produce a female. If the sperm contains a Y chromosome, the offspring will be male. This is illustrated in **Figure 12.**

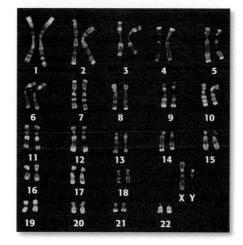

Figure 11 Are these chromosomes from a male or female? How can you tell?

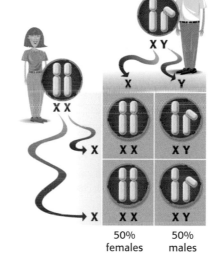

Figure 12 Egg and sperm combine to form either the XX or XY combination.

X Y

X X

X

X X   X Y

X

X X   X Y

50% females   50% males

SECTION REVIEW

1. Explain the difference between sex cells and sex chromosomes.

2. If there are 14 chromosomes in pea plant cells, how many chromosomes are present in a sex cell of a pea?

3. **Interpreting Illustrations** Examine the illustration at right. Does it show a stage of mitosis or meiosis? How can you tell?

69

---

4) Close

Answers to Male or Female?

The chromosomes shown in **Figure 9** are from a female; the chromosomes shown in **Figure 11** are from a male.

Answer to question in Figure 11

Male; there are 22 matched pairs, and the last pair is *XY*.

Quiz

Ask students whether these statements are true or false.

1. Men and women have entirely different kinds of chromosomes. (false)

2. Men and women have a different number of chromosomes. (false)

3. You can tell the difference between men and women just by looking at a photograph of their chromosomes. (true)

ALTERNATIVE ASSESSMENT

Writing Have students write a description of sex cells and how they are produced in their ScienceLog. (Sex cells are produced by meiosis, in which the chromosomes are copied once and the cells divide twice. The final cells each have half the number of chromosomes of the original. Two sex cells—an egg cell and a sperm cell—combine to create one cell with the same total number of chromosomes as a typical body cell.)

▼ **Answers to Section Review**

1. Each sex cell (egg or sperm) contains half of all the chromosomes, including one sex chromosome. The sex chromosomes contain genes that determine whether an offspring will be a male or a female.

2. seven

3. Meiosis; in meiosis, the chromatids stay together when the homologous chromosomes separate, as shown in the illustration.

Making Models Lab

Bug Builders, Inc.
Teacher's Notes

Time Required
Two 45-minute class periods

Lab Ratings

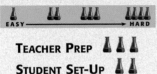
EASY ——————————→ HARD

TEACHER PREP 🧪🧪🧪
STUDENT SET-UP 🧪🧪
CONCEPT LEVEL 🧪🧪🧪
CLEAN UP 🧪

MATERIALS

You will need 14 small brown-paper bags—two sacks for each characteristic listed on this page. Each bag will contain either the mother's alleles or the father's alleles. Cut 1 in. squares of paper to represent alleles. Use a different color paper for each trait (seven colors).

Safety Caution
Remind students to review all safety cautions and icons before beginning this lab activity.

Datasheets for LabBook

CLASSROOM TESTED & APPROVED

Kathy LaRoe
East Valley Middle School
East Helena, Montana

Bug Builders, Inc.

Imagine that you are a designer for a toy company that makes toy bugs. The president of Bug Builders, Inc., wants new kinds of the wildly popular Space Bugs, but he wants to use the bug parts that the company already has. It's your job to come up with new bugs. You have studied how traits are passed from one generation to the next. You will use this knowledge to come up with new combinations of traits and to build the bug parts in new ways. Model A and Model B, shown on this page, will act as the "parent" bugs.

MATERIALS

- 14 allele sacks (supplied by your teacher)
- large marshmallows (head and body segments)
- red and green toothpicks (antennae)
- green and blue pushpins (noses)
- pipe cleaners (tails)
- green and black gumdrops (feet)
- map pins (eyes)
- scissors

Ask a Question

① What are the possible genotypes and phenotypes for the offspring of a cross between Model A and Model B?

Collect Data

② Your teacher will have fourteen allele sacks for the class—two for each characteristic. The sacks will hold slips of paper with capital or lowercase letters printed on them. Take one piece of paper from each sack. (Remember: Capital letters are dominant alleles, and lowercase letters are recessive alleles.) For each characteristic, one allele sack carries the alleles from "Mom" and one allele sack carries the alleles from "Dad." After you have recorded the alleles you have drawn, place the slips of paper back into the sacks.

Model A ("Mom")
- red antennae
- 3 body segments
- curly tail
- 2 pairs of legs
- green nose
- black feet
- 3 eyes

Model B ("Dad")
- green antennae
- 2 body segments
- straight tail
- 3 pairs of legs
- blue nose
- green feet
- 2 eyes

70

3. Make a table like the one below in your ScienceLog or on a computer. Fill in the first two columns with the alleles you picked in step 2. Next, fill in the third column with the genotype of the new model ("Baby").

Bug Family Traits				
Trait	Model A "Mom" allele	Model B "Dad" allele	New model "Baby" genotype	New model "Baby" phenotype
Antennae color				
Number of body segments				
Tail shape				
Number of leg pairs				
Nose color				
Foot color				
Number of eyes				

DO NOT WRITE IN BOOK

4. Use the data at right to fill in the last column of the table.

5. Now that you have your table filled out, you are ready to pick the parts that you need to build your bug.

Analyze the Results

6. Take a class poll of the traits of the offspring. What are the ratios for each trait?

Genotypes and Phenotypes	
RR or *Rr* = red antennae	*rr* = green antennae
SS or *Ss* = 3 body segments	*ss* = 2 body segments
CC or *Cc* = curly tail	*cc* = straight tail
LL or *Ll* = 3 pairs of legs	*ll* = 2 pairs of legs
BB or *Bb* = blue nose	*bb* = green nose
GG or *Gg* = green feet	*gg* = black feet
EE or *Ee* = 2 eyes	*ee* = 3 eyes

Draw Conclusions

7. What are the possible genotypes of the parents? How many different genotypes are possible in the offspring?

Going Further

Find a mate for your "Baby" bug. What are the possible genotypes and phenotypes of the offspring from this match?

71

Preparation Notes

This lab will take some preparation time, but it is well worth the effort for a genetics-reinforcement lesson.

1. Cut enough squares so that each student will have two alleles for each characteristic. You must have an equal number of both dominant and recessive alleles.

2. Half the squares for each characteristic should be marked with capital letters to indicate dominant alleles. The other half should be marked with lowercase letters to indicate recessive alleles.

3. Label each paper bag with one of the seven characteristics. Place both dominant and recessive alleles in their corresponding paper bag.

4. Have students draw one allele from each sack.

Going Further

Answers will vary. Have students use Punnett squares to explore possible genotypes.

Answers

1. 128; two forms of each of seven characteristics
   $2 \times 2 \times 2 \times 2 \times 2 \times 2 \times 2 = 2^7 = 128$

6. Student ratios should be similar to the ratios determined when the alleles were selected by the teacher.

7. Answers will vary. Have students construct Punnett squares using the parental traits. Except for the results obtained by parental genotypes that are all homozygous recessive, the student will see other possibilities for genotypes and phenotypes from the same parents.

Chapter Highlights

VOCABULARY DEFINITIONS

SECTION 1

heredity the passing of traits from parent to offspring

dominant trait a trait observed when at least one dominant allele for a characteristic is inherited

recessive trait a trait that is apparent only when two recessive alleles for the characteristic are inherited

genes segments of DNA that carry hereditary instructions located on chromosomes and passed from parent to offspring

alleles alternative forms of a gene that govern the same characteristics

genotype the inherited combination of alleles

phenotype an organism's inherited appearance

probability the mathematical chance that an event will occur

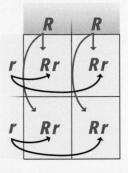

Chapter Highlights

SECTION 1

Vocabulary

heredity (p. 56)
dominant trait (p. 59)
recessive trait (p. 59)
genes (p. 61)
alleles (p. 61)
genotype (p. 61)
phenotype (p. 61)
probability (p. 62)

Section Notes

- Heredity is the passing of traits from parents to offspring.

- Traits are inherited forms of characteristics.

- Gregor Mendel used pea plants to study heredity.

- Mendel's pea plants were self-pollinating. They contained both male and female reproductive structures. They were also true breeding, always producing offspring with the same traits as the parents.

- Offspring inherit two sets of instructions for each characteristic, one set from each parent.

- The sets of instructions are known as genes.

- Different versions of the same gene are known as alleles.

- If both the dominant allele and the recessive allele are inherited for a characteristic, only the dominant allele is expressed.

- Recessive traits are apparent only when two recessive alleles for the characteristic are inherited.

- A genotype is the combination of alleles for a particular trait.

- A phenotype is the physical expression of the genotype.

- Probability is the mathematical chance that an event will occur. It is usually expressed as a fraction or as a percentage.

Labs

Tracing Traits (p. 188)

☑ Skills Check

Math Concepts

RATIOS A jar contains 24 green marbles and 96 red marbles. There are 4 red marbles for every 1 green marble.

$$\frac{96}{24} = \frac{4}{1}$$

This can also be written as follows:

$$4:1$$

Visual Understanding

PUNNETT SQUARES
A Punnett square can help you visualize all the possible combinations of alleles passed from parents to offspring. See page 61 to review how Punnett squares are made.

	R	R
r	Rr	Rr
r	Rr	Rr

Lab and Activity Highlights

Bug Builders, Inc. PG 70

Tracing Traits PG 188

 Datasheets for LabBook
(blackline masters for these labs)

SECTION 2

Vocabulary

sex cells *(p. 64)*

homologous chromosomes
(p. 64)

meiosis *(p. 65)*

sex chromosomes *(p. 69)*

Section Notes

- Genes are located on chromosomes.

- Most human cells contain 46 chromosomes, or 23 pairs.

- Each pair contains one chromosome donated by the mother and one donated by the father. These pairs are known as homologous chromosomes.

- Meiosis produces sex cells, eggs and sperm.

- Sex cells have half the usual number of chromosomes.

- Sex chromosomes contain genes that determine an offspring's sex.

- Human females have two X chromosomes, and males have one X chromosome and one Y chromosome.

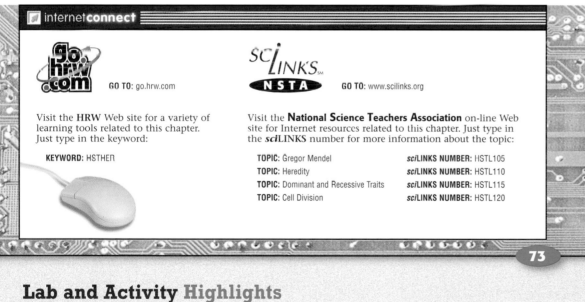

SECTION 2

sex cells eggs or sperm; a sex cell carries half the number of chromosomes found in other body cells

homologous chromosomes chromosomes with matching information

meiosis cell division that produces sex cells

sex chromosomes chromosomes that carry genes that determine the sex of offspring

Vocabulary Review Worksheet

Blackline masters of these Chapter Highlights can be found in the **Study Guide.**

---

internet connect

GO TO: go.hrw.com

Visit the **HRW** Web site for a variety of learning tools related to this chapter. Just type in the keyword:

KEYWORD: HSTHER

SCLINKS
N S T A

GO TO: www.scilinks.org

Visit the **National Science Teachers Association** on-line Web site for Internet resources related to this chapter. Just type in the *sci*LINKS number for more information about the topic:

TOPIC: Gregor Mendel   *sci*LINKS NUMBER: HSTL105
TOPIC: Heredity   *sci*LINKS NUMBER: HSTL110
TOPIC: Dominant and Recessive Traits   *sci*LINKS NUMBER: HSTL115
TOPIC: Cell Division   *sci*LINKS NUMBER: HSTL120

73

Lab and Activity Highlights

LabBank

Long-Term Projects & Research Ideas,
Portrait of a Dog

Chapter Review

USING VOCABULARY

1. sex cells

2. phenotype, genotype

3. Meiosis

4. alleles

5. self-pollinating

To complete the following sentences, choose the correct term from each pair of terms listed below:

1. Sperm and eggs are known as ___?___. (*sex cells* or *sex chromosomes*)

2. The ___?___, the expression of a trait, is determined by the ___?___, the combination of alleles. (*genotype* or *phenotype*)

3. ___?___ produces cells with half the normal number of chromosomes. (*Meiosis* or *Mitosis*)

4. Different versions of the same genes are called ___?___. (*sex cells* or *alleles*)

5. A ___?___ plant can pollinate its own eggs. (*self-pollinating* or *true-breeding*)

UNDERSTANDING CONCEPTS

Multiple Choice

6. a

7. c

8. b

9. b

10. c

11. c

12. c

Short Answer

13. Females have two X chromosomes. Males have one X and one Y chromosome.

14. Sample answer: A recessive trait is a genetic trait that is expressed only if there are two recessive alleles for the gene. A recessive trait is not expressed if an allele for a dominant trait is present.

15. Sex cells have half the number of chromosomes as other body cells.

Concept Mapping

16. An answer to this exercise can be found at the front of this book.

CRITICAL THINKING AND PROBLEM SOLVING

17. The trait for blue eyes must be determined by a recessive allele. Brown must be dominant to blue. So both parents must carry the blue recessive allele, and a blue recessive allele must have been passed on to the child from both parents.

18. Meiosis is important for reproduction because it ensures that the characteristic number of chromosomes will not be doubled when an egg and a sperm come together.

UNDERSTANDING CONCEPTS

Multiple Choice

6. Genes are found on
   a. chromosomes.
   b. alleles.
   c. proteins.
   d. anthers.

7. The process that produces sex cells is
   a. mitosis.
   b. photosynthesis.
   c. meiosis.
   d. probability.

8. The passing of traits from parents to offspring is
   a. probability.
   b. heredity.
   c. recessive.
   d. meiosis.

9. If you cross a white flower (with the genotype *pp*) with a purple flower (with the genotype *PP*), the possible genotypes in the offspring are:
   a. *PP* and *pp*.
   b. all *Pp*.
   c. all *PP*.
   d. all *pp*.

10. For the above cross, what would the phenotypes be?
    a. all white
    b. all tall
    c. all purple
    d. $\frac{1}{2}$ white, $\frac{1}{2}$ purple

11. In meiosis,
    a. the chromosomes are copied twice.
    b. the nucleus divides once.
    c. four cells are produced from a single cell.
    d. All of the above

12. Probability is
    a. always expressed as a ratio.
    b. a 50% chance that an event will occur.
    c. the mathematical chance that an event will occur.
    d. a 3:1 chance that an event will occur.

Short Answer

13. Which sex chromosomes do females have? Which do males have?

14. In your own words, give a one- or two-sentence definition of the term *recessive trait*.

15. How are sex cells different from other body cells?

19. No; true-breeding plants always produce the same trait. If Mendel had not used true-breeding plants, then he would have seen much more variation in traits. He would not have been able to tell whether traits were dominant or recessive because there would not have been reproducible ratios of dominant to recessive traits.

Concept Mapping Transparency 5

Concept Mapping

16. Use the following terms to create a concept map: meiosis, eggs, cell division, X chromosome, sex cells, sperm, mitosis, Y chromosome.

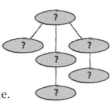

CRITICAL THINKING AND PROBLEM SOLVING

Write one or two sentences to answer the following questions:

17. If a child has blue eyes and both her parents have brown eyes, what does that tell you about the trait for blue eyes? Explain your answer.

18. Why is meiosis important for sexual reproduction?

19. Gregor Mendel used only true-breeding plants. If he had used plants that were not true breeding, do you think he would have discovered dominant and recessive traits? Why or why not?

MATH IN SCIENCE

20. Assume that **Y** is the dominant allele for yellow seeds and **y** is the recessive allele for green seeds. What is the probability that a pea plant with the genotype **Yy** crossed with a pea plant with the genotype **yy** will have offspring with the genotype **yy**?

INTERPRETING GRAPHICS

Examine the Punnett square below, and then answer the following questions:

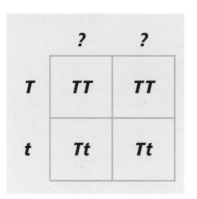

	?	?
T	**TT**	**TT**
t	**Tt**	**Tt**

21. What is the unknown genotype?

22. If **T** represents the allele for tall pea plants, and **t** represents the allele for short pea plants, what is the phenotype of each parent and of the offspring?

23. If each of the offspring were allowed to self-fertilize, what are the possible genotypes in the next generation?

24. What is the probability of each genotype in item 23?

Reading Check up

Take a minute to review your answers to the Pre-Reading Questions found at the bottom of page 54. Have your answers changed? If necessary, revise your answers based on what you have learned since you began this chapter.

MATH IN SCIENCE

20. The probability of inheriting a y allele from the Yy plant is $\frac{1}{2}$. The probability of inheriting a y allele for the yy plant is $\frac{1}{1}$. Therefore, the probability that the offspring will inherit the yy genotype is $\frac{1}{1} \times \frac{1}{2}$, or 50 percent. These results can be visualized by using a Punnett square.

INTERPRETING GRAPHICS

21. *TT*

22. All the parents and offspring are tall pea plants.

23. Students should make two new Punnett squares. Self fertilization of *TT (TT × TT)* will yield offspring of all *TT*. Self fertilization of *Tt (Tt × Tt)* will yield offspring of *TT, Tt,* and *tt*.

24. *TT* has a 100 percent probability with a *TT* parent and a 25 percent probability with a *Tt* parent. *Tt* has a 50 percent probability with a *Tt* parent, and a 0 percent probability with a *TT* parent. The genotype *tt* has a 25 percent probability with a *Tt* parent, and a 0 percent probability with a *TT* parent.

Blackline masters of this Chapter Review can be found in the **Study Guide**.

Science, Technology, and Society

Mapping the Human Genome

Answer to What Do You Think?

The Human Genome Project has spawned a flurry of debate over ethical, social, and legal issues surrounding the use of genetic information. Students have been asked to further investigate these issues. Some issues students may wish to consider include the following:

1. **Genetic privacy** Insurance companies may require genetic testing before offering health insurance. Should insurance companies be allowed to see a person's genetic profile when deciding to provide an otherwise healthy person medical insurance? Employers may choose not to hire people who may become sick. Are people entitled to keep their genetic profiles private?

2. **Ownership of genetic information** Many researchers are rushing to sequence and patent genes. Sometimes scientists patent genes even when they do not know what proteins these genes code for. When researchers patent and claim rights to genetic information, they limit its use by other scientists. Patenting genetic information, however, encourages competition and more-frequent discoveries. Should scientists be able to patent genetic information?

Scientists with the United States Department of Energy and National Institutes of Health are in the midst of what may be the most ambitious scientific research project ever—the Human Genome Project (HGP). These researchers want to create a map of all the genes found on human chromosomes. The body's complete set of genetic instructions is called the genome. Scientists hope this project will provide valuable information that may help prevent or even cure many genetic diseases.

Whose Genes Are These?

You might be wondering whose genome the scientists are decoding. Actually, it doesn't matter because each person is unique in only about 1 percent of his or her genetic material. The scientists' goal is to identify how tiny differences in that 1 percent of DNA make each of us who we are, and to understand how some changes can cause disease.

Genetic Medicine

The tiny changes that can cause disease, called mutations, are often inherited. Once scientists determine the normal order of our genes, doctors may be able to use this information to help detect mutations in patients. Then doctors would be able to warn patients of an increased risk of a disease before any symptoms appear! For example, a doctor's early warning about a genetic risk of high cholesterol would give a person a chance to eat healthier and exercise more before any serious symptoms were detectable.

Advancing Technology

Scientists organizing the HGP hope to have a complete and accurate sequence of the human

▲ *This scientist is performing one of the many steps involved in the research for the Human Genome Project.*

genome—estimated to have between 50,000 and 100,000 genes—by 2003. One day in the future, scientists may even be able to provide people with a healthy gene to replace a mutated one. This technique, called gene therapy, may eventually be the cure for many genetic diseases.

What Do You Think?

▶ Despite the medical advancements the Human Genome Project will bring, many people continue to debate ethical, social, and legal issues surrounding this controversial project. Look into these issues, and discuss them with your classmates!

76

3. **Perfect babies** Doctors can test developing fetuses for some genetic problems. Should they be able to replace bad genes? Should parents be able to manipulate the genetic information so their children will have a desired eye color or hair color? When should physicians be allowed to change a baby's genetic information, and when shouldn't they?

Health WATCH

Lab Rats with Wings

What's less than 1 mm in length, can be extremely annoying when buzzing around your kitchen, and sometimes grows legs out of its eyes? The answer is *Drosophila melanogaster*—better known as the fruit fly because it feeds on fruit. This tiny insect has played a big role in helping us understand many illnesses, especially those that occur at certain stages of human development. Scientists use fruit flies to find out more about diseases and disorders such as cancer, Alzheimer's disease, muscular dystrophy, and Down's syndrome.

Why a Fly?

Fruit flies are some scientists' favorite research animal. Scientists can raise several generations of fruit flies in just a few months. Because fruit flies have only a two-week life cycle, scientists can alter a fruit-fly gene as part of an experiment and then see the results very quickly.

Another advantage to using these tiny animals is their small size. Thousands of fruit flies can be raised in a relatively small space.

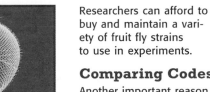

▲ *This is what a normal fruit fly looks like under a scanning electron microscope.*

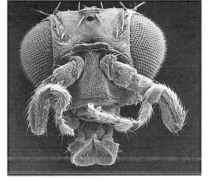

▲ *This fruit fly has legs growing out of its eyes!*

Researchers can afford to buy and maintain a variety of fruit fly strains to use in experiments.

Comparing Codes

Another important reason for using these "lab rats with wings" is that their genetic code is relatively simple and well understood. Fruit flies have 12,000 genes, whereas humans have more than 70,000. Nonetheless, many fruit-fly genes are similar in function to human genes, and scientists have learned to manipulate them to produce genetic mutations. Scientists who study these mutations gain valuable information about genetic mutations in humans. Without fruit flies, some human genetic problems that we now have important information about—such as basal cell carcinoma cancer—might have taken many more years and many more dollars to study.

Where Do You Draw the Line?

▶ Do you think it is acceptable for scientists to perform research on fruit flies? What about on rats, mice, and rabbits? Have a debate with your classmates about conducting scientific experiments on other species.

77

Answers to Where Do You Draw The Line?
Answers will vary, but students should be aware that animals are used in biological research. Scientists have learned a great deal using animal models. Many scientists who work with animals take great care to minimize animal suffering during the experiments. In recent years, other models—such as computer models and cultured cells—have become available and can be used as substitutes for animals in some experiments.

HEALTH WATCH
Lab Rats with Wings

Teaching Strategy

This activity has two objectives. First, it will allow the students to obtain a better grasp of the relationship a gene has to other body structures, such as cells or organs. Second, it will give students a better understanding of what is meant by the word *mutation* in the fruit-fly article.

For this activity to work, students must understand what blueprints are. Explain that blueprints are sheets of paper that have sketches of all the aspects of the house to be built. These plans are followed precisely in order to build the house. Show students sample blueprints, and point out all the dimensional information they contain.

Next present an analogy to the students using the following representations:

body = city
organ = neighborhood
cell of organ = house in
   neighborhood
chromosomes in cell =
   blueprints for house in
   neighborhood
gene on chromosome = part of
   blueprints that gives instructions for certain aspect of
   house (like dimensions of the
   master bedroom or direction
   in which a door will open)

Chapter Organizer

CHAPTER ORGANIZATION	TIME MINUTES	OBJECTIVES	LABS, INVESTIGATIONS, AND DEMONSTRATIONS
Chapter Opener pp. 78–79	45	National Standards: UCP 2, SAI 1, LS 1f, 2c–2e	**Start-Up Activity,** Fingerprint Your Friends, p. 79
Section 1 **What Do Genes Look Like?**	90	▶ Describe the basic structure of the DNA molecule. ▶ Explain how DNA molecules can be copied. ▶ Explain some of the exceptions to Mendel's heredity principles. UCP 2, 5, SAI 1, 2, ST 1, 2, SPSP 4, 5, HNS 1–3, LS 1a, 2c–2e, 5a; Labs UCP 2, 5, HNS 1, LS 1a	**Demonstration,** p. 85 in ATE **Making Models,** Base-Pair Basics, p. 94 **Datasheets for LabBook,** Base-Pair Basics
Section 2 **How DNA Works**	90	▶ Explain the relationship between genes and proteins. ▶ Outline the basic steps in making a protein. ▶ Define *mutation,* and give an example. ▶ Evaluate the information in a pedigree. UCP 1, 2, SAI 1, 2, ST 2, SPSP 5, LS 1f, 2b–2e, 5b	**QuickLab,** Mutations, p. 91 **Interactive Explorations CD-ROM,** DNA Pawprints *A **Worksheet** is also available in the **Interactive Explorations Teacher's Edition.*** **Long-Term Projects & Research Ideas,** The Anti-freeze Protein

See page **T23** for a complete correlation of this book with the

NATIONAL SCIENCE EDUCATION STANDARDS.

TECHNOLOGY RESOURCES

Guided Reading Audio CD English or Spanish, Chapter 4

One-Stop Planner CD-ROM with Test Generator

Interactive Explorations CD-ROM CD 3, Exploration 8, DNA Pawprints

CNN. Science, Technology & Society, Developing the Perfect Pepper, Segment 9

Science Discovery Videodiscs Science Sleuths: Twins or Not?

Chapter 4 • Genes and Gene Technology

CLASSROOM WORKSHEETS, TRANSPARENCIES, AND RESOURCES	SCIENCE INTEGRATION AND CONNECTIONS	REVIEW AND ASSESSMENT
Directed Reading Worksheet **Science Puzzlers, Twisters & Teasers**		
Directed Reading Worksheet, Section 1 **Transparency 19,** DNA Structure **Math Skills for Science Worksheet,** A Shortcut for Multiplying Large Numbers **Science Skills Worksheet,** Science Drawing **Transparency 20,** Incomplete Dominance	**Real-World Connection,** p. 81 in ATE **MathBreak,** Genes and Bases, p. 83 **Math and More,** p. 83 in ATE **Cross-Disciplinary Focus,** p. 84 in ATE **Scientific Debate:** DNA on Trial, p. 100	**Homework,** pp. 80, 85 in ATE **Self-Check,** p. 83 **Section Review,** p. 87 **Quiz,** p. 87 in ATE **Alternative Assessment,** p. 87 in ATE
Directed Reading Worksheet, Section 2 **Transparency 21,** The Making of a Protein **Transparency 167,** The Formation of Smog **Transparency 22,** An Example of Substitution **Transparency 23,** Pedigree **Reinforcement Worksheet,** DNA Mutations **Critical Thinking Worksheet,** The Perfect Parrot	**Math and More,** p. 89 in ATE **Meteorology Connection,** p. 90 **Connect to Earth Science,** p. 90 in ATE **Cross-Disciplinary Focus,** p. 91 in ATE **Apply,** p. 92 **Cross-Disciplinary Focus,** p. 92 in ATE **Holt Anthology of Science Fiction,** *Moby James*	**Self-Check,** p. 89 **Section Review,** p. 93 **Quiz,** p. 93 in ATE **Alternative Assessment,** p. 93 in ATE

internet**connect**

go.hrw.com **Holt, Rinehart and Winston On-line Resources**
go.hrw.com

For worksheets and other teaching aids related to this chapter, visit the HRW Web site and type in the keyword: **HSTDNA**

SCI**LINKS** NSTA **National Science Teachers Association**
www.scilinks.org

Encourage students to use the *sci*LINKS numbers listed in the internet connect boxes to access information and resources on the **NSTA** Web site.

END-OF-CHAPTER REVIEW AND ASSESSMENT

Chapter Review in Study Guide
Vocabulary and Notes in Study Guide
Chapter Tests with Performance-Based Assessment, Chapter 4 Test
Chapter Tests with Performance-Based Assessment, Performance-Based Assessment 4
Concept Mapping Transparency 6

Chapter Resources & Worksheets

Visual Resources

TEACHING TRANSPARENCIES

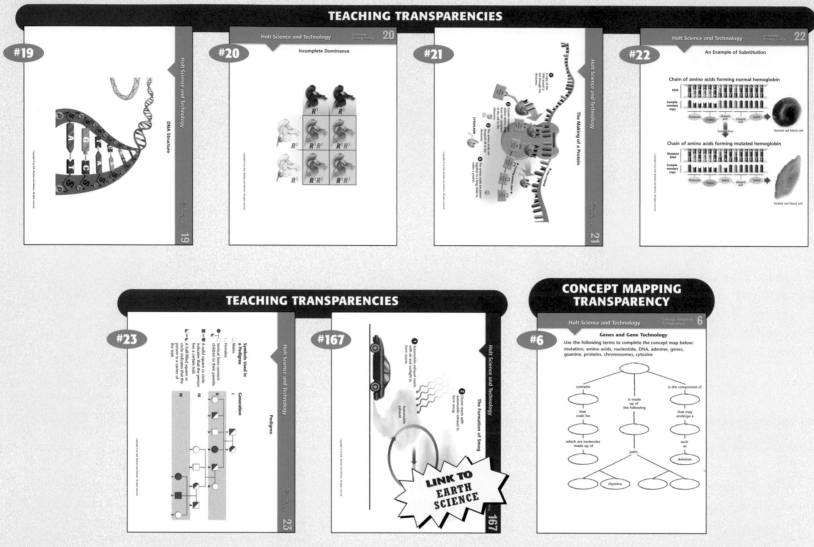

#19 — DNA Structure — Holt Science and Technology — 19

#20 — Holt Science and Technology — Incomplete Dominance — 20

#21 — The Making of a Protein — Holt Science and Technology — 21

#22 — Holt Science and Technology — An Example of Substitution — 22

Chain of amino acids forming normal hemoglobin

normal red blood cell

Chain of amino acids forming mutated hemoglobin

Sickled red blood cell

TEACHING TRANSPARENCIES

#23 — Pedigree — Holt Science and Technology — 23

#167 — The Formation of Smog — Holt Science and Technology — 167

LINK TO EARTH SCIENCE

CONCEPT MAPPING TRANSPARENCY

#6 — Holt Science and Technology — Concept Mapping Transparency 6

Genes and Gene Technology

Use the following terms to complete the concept map below: mutation, amino acids, nucleotide, DNA, adenine, genes, guanine, proteins, chromosomes, cytosine

Meeting Individual Needs

DIRECTED READING

#4 — DIRECTED READING WORKSHEET — *Genes and Gene Technology*

Chapter Introduction

As you begin this chapter, answer the following.

1. Read the title of the chapter. List three things that you already know about this subject.

2. Write two questions about this subject that you would like answered by the time you finish this chapter.

Section 1: What Do Genes Look Like? (p. 80)

3. Where are the chromosomes found in most cells?
   a. the nucleus   c. the DNA
   b. the genes   d. the ribosomes

4. _____ make up chromosomes.

The Pieces of the Puzzle (p. 80)

5. What two functions must the gene material be able to carry out?

REINFORCEMENT & VOCABULARY REVIEW

#4 — REINFORCEMENT WORKSHEET — *DNA Mutations*

Complete this worksheet after reading Chapter 7, Section 2.

DNA is made up of nucleotides. Each nucleotide is made up of a sugar, a phosphate, and a base. There are four bases that can occur in DNA: adenine, cytosine, thymine, and guanine. Remember that adenine and thymine are complementary and form pairs, and cytosine and guanine are complementary and form pairs.

1. Below is half of a section of DNA that has been split apart and is ready to copy itself. Write the appropriate letter in the space provided to build the DNA's new complementary strand.

G _____
T _____
A _____
A _____
C _____
T _____
C _____
T _____

2. Sometimes mistakes happen when the DNA is being copied. These mistakes, or mutations, change the order of the bases in DNA. There are three kinds of mutations that can occur in DNA: deletion, insertion, and substitution.
   a. Below is an original sequence of bases in DNA and the sequence of bases after a mutation has occurred. On the original base sequence, show where the mutation has occurred by circling the appropriate base pair, and write what type of mutation it is in the space provided.

base sequence in original cell DNA / base sequence in a cell with mutated DNA

#4 — VOCABULARY REVIEW WORKSHEET — *Unraveling Genes*

Solve the clues and unscramble the letters to fill in the blanks. Use the letters in the squares as well as the final clue, to unravel the secret message.

1. Substance which carries our genetic material: NAD
2. Subunits of DNA: DISTONEUCLE
3. Nucleotide base: ENIDANE
4. The complement of number 3: TIEHYMN
5. Nucleotide base known as G: NUANIGE
6. Complement of number 5: YOSTINCE
7. Shape of a DNA molecule (two words): EXELLIDOBUH
8. Organelle which manufactures proteins: MOOSERIB
9. Mistake which occurs in DNA: UNMATIOT
10. Agents which cause DNA mistakes: UNGATEM
11. A tool for tracing a trait through a family: DEEPIGIRE
12. A technique used to manipulate individual genes: (two words) NEETIEGGINGBEECINNER

SCIENCE PUZZLERS, TWISTERS & TEASERS

#4 — SCIENCE PUZZLERS, TWISTERS & TEASERS — *Genes and Gene Technology*

Green Gene

1. On the planet Dyejob, green hair is a recessive trait. Great Grandma and Great Grandpa Berg both have green hair. So do their three children. They were surprised to find that three of their grandchildren have green hair too, even though all of their great-grandchildren have black hair. The Bergs concluded that their grandson Bobby must be a carrier of the green hair gene. Shown below is the pedigree of the Berg family. The solid shapes represent the family members with green hair. The pedigree does not show who is a carrier of the gene. Using the pedigree, answer the following questions.

The Bergs

a. Which, if any, of Bobby's three sisters are carriers of the gene for green hair as well?

b. Beth does not have green hair. Is Beth a carrier? Explain.

c. Bunny, who has blond hair, is a carrier of the green hair gene. She claims to be the long lost child of Great Grandma and Great Grandpa Berg. Should they include her as a daughter in their will? Explain.

Chapter 4 • Genes and Gene Technology

Review & Assessment

STUDY GUIDE

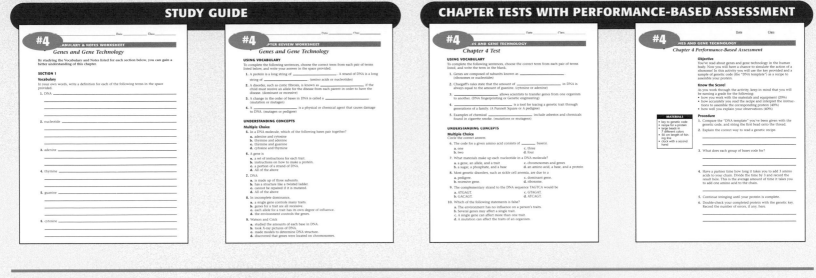

#4 VOCABULARY & NOTES WORKSHEET
Genes and Gene Technology

#4 CHAPTER REVIEW WORKSHEET
Genes and Gene Technology

CHAPTER TESTS WITH PERFORMANCE-BASED ASSESSMENT

#4 GENES AND GENE TECHNOLOGY
Chapter 4 Test

#4 GENES AND GENE TECHNOLOGY
Chapter 4 Performance-Based Assessment

Lab Worksheets

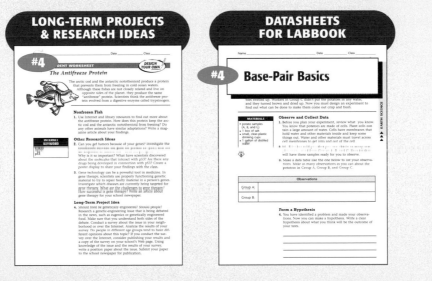

LONG-TERM PROJECTS & RESEARCH IDEAS

#4 STUDENT WORKSHEET
The Antifreeze Protein

DATASHEETS FOR LABBOOK

#4 Base-Pair Basics

Applications & Extensions

CRITICAL THINKING & PROBLEM SOLVING

#4 CRITICAL THINKING WORKSHEET
The Perfect Parrot

SCIENCE TECHNOLOGY

#9 Science in the News: Critical Thinking Worksheets
Segment 9
Developing the Perfect Pepper

INTERACTIVE EXPLORATIONS

#3-8 Exploration B Worksheet
DNA Pawprints

SECTION 1

What Do Genes Look Like?

▶ DNA

In 1869, long before the time of Watson and Crick, a 22-year-old Swiss scientist isolated DNA from a cell nucleus. Unfortunately, he had no idea of its function, much less of its role in inheritance. It was not until 75 years later, in 1944, that an American geneticist named Oswald T. Avery found evidence that DNA is the carrier of genetic information.

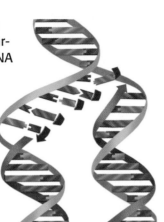

IS THAT A FACT!

- ☛ Human DNA consists of about 3 billion base pairs.

- ☛ If you could print a book with all the genetic information carried in just one human cell, it would be 500,000 pages long.

- ☛ The uncoiled DNA in the nucleus of a human body cell is about 2 m long. The DNA in chromosomes is so tightly coiled that the 46 chromosomes from a human body cell would be only about 0.00032 cm long if they were lined up end to end!

▶ Eye Color

Eye color is a trait that is influenced by the presence of melanin, a dark pigment, in the iris. People whose eyes have the least pigment have blue eyes, and people whose eyes have the most pigment have brown eyes. Scientists

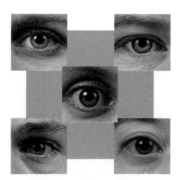

think that the number of alleles present for eye pigment control eye color. For example, one allele is thought to contribute to a medium blue eye color, while as many as eight alleles may contribute to dark brown eye color.

SECTION 2

How DNA Works

▶ Cracking the Genetic Code

In the 1960s, scientists cracked the genetic code—the translation between codons, the three base sequences and amino acids. They have found that the genetic code is universal in almost all living organisms. If a codon aligns with a particular amino acid in humans, the same codon aligns with the same amino acid in bacteria. This similarity suggests that all life-forms have a common evolutionary ancestor.

▶ Mutations and Natural Selection

The discovery that changes in DNA can lead to new traits supports Darwin's theory of evolution by natural selection. When an environment changes, mutations may enhance an organism's chances of survival in the new conditions. For example, a certain mutation makes houseflies resistant to DDT but also reduces their growth rate. Originally, this mutation was harmful, but after DDT became part of the environment of many houseflies, the mutation helped the flies survive. By the process of natural selection, the mutation was spread throughout the fly population.

▶ Amino Acids

Of the known amino acids, 20 are necessary for human growth and metabolism. The human body can manufacture 10 of these. The other 10, which are called the essential amino acids, must be obtained from plant or animal proteins in the diet. Foods containing all the essential amino acids include eggs, milk, seafood, and meat. Legumes, grains, nuts, and seeds contain many of the essential amino acids.

▶ Protein Synthesis

It took many years for scientists to determine how protein is synthesized in the cell. The discovery that DNA's nucleotide sequence corresponds to a certain amino acid sequence was a key step in unlocking this mystery. This link was conclusively proven by Charles Yanofsky and Sydney Brenner in 1964.

- The genetic sequences used to make proteins can be compared to sentences. Where each three-letter "word" in the genetic "sentence" starts and stops is very important for constructing a protein. For example, suppose the sentence to code for a particular protein read "PAT SAW THE FAT CAT." If you start just one base pair too late, the sentence would read "ATS AWT HEF ATC AT," which is meaningless.

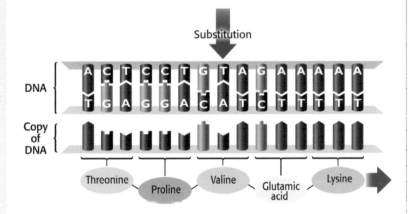

► Huntington's Disease

Huntington's disease is a hereditary degenerative brain disease caused by a dominant allele. People affected by Huntington's often display peculiar, dancelike movements. In the United States, many cases of Huntington's disease can be traced back to two brothers. The two men immigrated to North America from England in the 1600s because their family was accused of witchcraft. Apparently, they were persecuted because of their strange behaviors, which are now understood to be symptoms of Huntington's disease.

► Chimeras

Genetically engineered hybrid creatures are often called chimeras. The word chimera comes from Greek mythology; the Chimera was a fire-breathing she-monster, usually depicted as a composite of a lion, a goat, and a serpent.

► Ethical Issues

Scientists disagree about both the ethics of genetic engineering and the safety risks involved.

- Dr. Maxine Frank Singer was one of the first scientists to alert the National Academy of Science to the potential hazards of genetic engineering. Due to the efforts of Dr. Singer and her colleagues, the National Institute of Health developed specific guidelines for genetic research in 1973. These guidelines regulate the production and use of genetically engineered DNA and organisms.

► Worm Work

Caenorhabditis elegans, a tiny worm used in genetic experiments, has many genes in common with humans. In fact, scientists have given these worms human antidepressants to study the genetic causes of depression.

► DNA Fingerprints

DNA fingerprints are frequently used in criminal investigations. The DNA can come from hair, skin cells, blood, or other body fluids left at the crime scene by the perpetrator. Scientists use enzymes to make many copies of the DNA and then use other enzymes to cut the DNA into fragments. The fragments are separated by size and other characteristics on a specially treated plate. A photograph of the plate is taken, showing a unique set of dark bands. This set of bands is known as a DNA fingerprint. The fingerprint is then compared with the DNA fingerprint of the suspect to help determine innocence or guilt.

For background information about teaching strategies and issues, refer to the *Professional Reference for Teachers.*

CHAPTER
4

Genes and Gene Technology

 Pre-Reading Questions

Students may not know the answers to these questions before reading the chapter, so accept any reasonable response.

Suggested Answers

1. Proteins act as chemical messengers, and they help determine how tall you will grow, what colors you can see, and whether your hair is curly or straight.

2. Genes are the inherited genetic information that code for the proteins in all living things. They are found on chromosomes.

3. Sometimes diseases are caused by problems in the DNA. Scientists are learning ways of using gene therapy to correct or replace problematic DNA.

CHAPTER
4

Genes and Gene Technology

Sections

Pre-Reading
Questions

1. How are proteins related to the way you look?
2. What are genes? Where are they found?
3. How does knowing about DNA help scientists treat diseases?

UNLOCKING LIFE'S MASTER CODES

Did you know that each one of your cells has a 2-meter-long strand of DNA? This computer-generated DNA model hints at just how complex a DNA molecule is. Like a giant puzzle, the patterns in the spiraling DNA strands contain the codes for the growth of all cells and processes in living things. Human DNA has about 3 billion individual codes, or puzzle pieces. As of the year 2000, gene scientists mapped them all. In this chapter, you will learn about the structure of DNA and the genetic information it contains.

---

internet connect

go.hrw.com
HRW On-line Resources

go.hrw.com
For worksheets and other teaching aids, visit the HRW Web site and type in the keyword: **HSTDNA**

SCILINKS. **NSTA**

www.scilinks.com
Use the sciLINKS numbers at the end of each chapter for additional resources on the **NSTA** Web site.

Smithsonian Institution

www.si.edu/hrw
Visit the Smithsonian Institution Web site for related on-line resources.

CNNfyi.com

www.cnnfyi.com
Visit the CNN Web site for current events coverage and classroom resources.

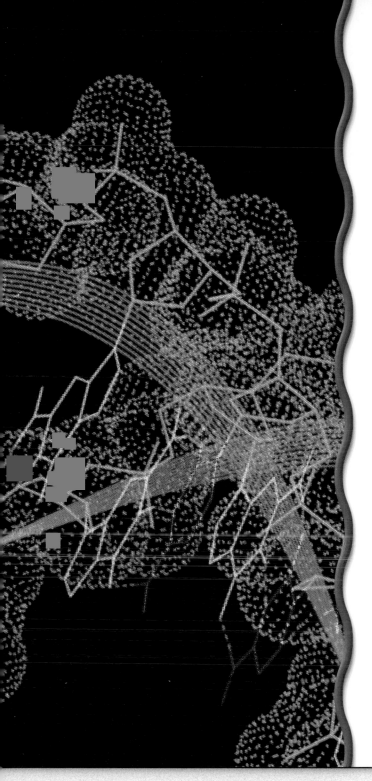

FINGERPRINT YOUR FRIENDS

One common method of identification is fingerprinting. Does it really work? Are everyone's fingerprints different? Try this activity to find out.

Procedure

1. Rub a **piece of charcoal** back and forth across a **piece of tracing paper.** Rub the tip of one of your fingers on the charcoal mark. Then place a **small piece of transparent tape** over the charcoal on your finger. Remove the tape, and stick it on a **piece of white paper.** Do the same for the rest of your fingers.

2. Observe the patterns with a **magnifying lens.** What kinds of patterns do you see? The fingerprint patterns shown below are the most common found among humans.

Analysis

3. Compare your fingerprints with those of your classmates. How many of each type do you see? Do any two people in your class have the same prints? Try to explain your findings.

Whorl   **Arch**   **Loop**

79

START-UP Activity

FINGERPRINT YOUR FRIENDS

MATERIALS
FOR EACH GROUP:
• piece of charcoal
• sheet of tracing paper
• transparent tape
• white paper
• magnifying lens

Safety Caution

Remind students to review all safety cautions and icons before beginning this lab activity. Charcoal is nontoxic, but it can stain clothes.

Teacher's Notes

The loop pattern is found in about 65 percent of the population, the whorl in about 30 percent, and the arch in about 5 percent.

Answer to START-UP Activity

3. The number of fingerprint types will vary for each class. No two students should have the same fingerprint (unless there are identical twins in the class). Any logical, reasonable explanation for this is acceptable, but students should discuss genetic variety in their explanation.

Focus

What Do Genes Look Like?

This section introduces students to the structure and function of DNA, the process of DNA replication, and the relationship of DNA to traits. The section concludes with a discussion of some exceptions to Mendelian genetics.

Bellringer

Have students unscramble the following words and use them in a sentence:

NDA (DNA)

etcutsurr (structure)

(Sample sentence: DNA has a complex structure.)

1 Motivate

ACTIVITY

Modeling Genetic Code

Create a code by pairing each letter of the alphabet with a numeral. For example, the numeral 1 could represent the letter *a*. Have students encode a brief message. Then have students exchange and decode the message. Compare the process of encoding messages with the encoding of genetic information in DNA. Explain that the genetic code is based on the sequence of the four nucleotide bases.

Directed Reading Worksheet Section 1

Terms to Learn

DNA	thymine
nucleotide	guanine
adenine	cytosine

What You'll Do

- Describe the basic structure of the DNA molecule.
- Explain how DNA molecules can be copied.
- Explain some of the exceptions to Mendel's heredity principles.

What Do Genes Look Like?

Scientists know that traits are determined by genes and that genes are passed from one generation to another. Scientists also know that genes are located on chromosomes, structures in the nucleus of most cells. Chromosomes are made of protein and **DNA,** short for deoxyribonucleic (dee AHKS ee RIE boh noo KLEE ik) acid. But which type of material makes the genes?

The Pieces of the Puzzle

The gene material must be able to do two things. First it must be able to supply instructions for cell processes and for building cell structures. Second it must be able to be copied each time a cell divides, so that each cell contains an identical set of genes. Early studies of DNA suggested that DNA was a very simple molecule. Because of this, most scientists thought protein probably carried hereditary information. After all, proteins are complex molecules.

In the 1940s, however, scientists discovered that genes of bacteria are made of DNA. How could something so simple hold the key to an organism's characteristics? To find the answer, let's take a closer look at the subunits of a DNA molecule.

Nucleotides—The Subunits of DNA DNA is made of only four subunits, which are known as **nucleotides.** Each nucleotide consists of three different types of material: a sugar, a phosphate, and a base. Nucleotides are identical except for the base. The four bases are **adenine, thymine, guanine,** and **cytosine,** and they each have a slightly different shape. The bases are usually referred to by the first letters in their names, A, T, G, and C. **Figure 1** shows diagrams of the four nucleotides.

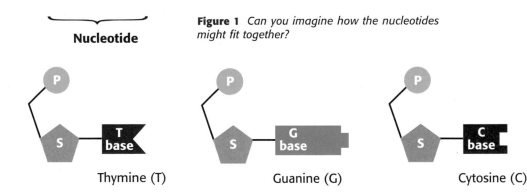

Adenine (A)

Nucleotide

Thymine (T)   Guanine (G)   Cytosine (C)

Figure 1 *Can you imagine how the nucleotides might fit together?*

Homework

Research Have students collect information on the use of amino acids to gain muscle. Suggest that they look at ads for amino acid supplements in health-food or fitness magazines or at labels of amino acid powdered drinks at the supermarket. Use these materials to discuss issues such as the expense of such supplements and how they might be used by the body. Discuss how amino acids might be acquired in a balanced diet.

Chargaff's Rules In the 1950s, a biochemist named Erwin Chargaff found that the amount of adenine in DNA always equals the amount of thymine, and the amount of guanine always equals the amount of cytosine. His findings are known as Chargaff's rules.

At the time, no one knew quite what to make of Chargaff's findings. How could Chargaff's rules help solve the mysteries of DNA's structure? Read on to find out.

A Picture of DNA

More clues came from the laboratory of British scientist Maurice Wilkins. There, chemist Rosalind Franklin, shown in **Figure 2,** was able to create images of DNA molecules. The process that she used to create these images is known as X-ray diffraction. In this process, X rays bombard the DNA molecule. When the X ray hits a particle within the molecule, the ray bounces off the particle. This creates a pattern that is captured on film. The images that Franklin created suggested that DNA has a spiral shape.

Figure 2 Rosalind Franklin, 1920–1958

Eureka!

Two other young scientists, James Watson and Francis Crick, shown in **Figure 3,** were also investigating the mystery of DNA's structure. Based on the work of others, Watson and Crick built models of DNA using simple materials, such as labeled pieces of cardboard. After seeing the X-ray images of DNA made by Rosalind Franklin, Watson and Crick concluded that DNA resembles a twisted ladder shape known as a *double helix.* Watson and Crick used their DNA model to predict how DNA is copied. Upon making the discovery, Crick is said to have exclaimed, "We have discovered the secret of life!"

Figure 3 This photo shows James Watson, on the left, and Francis Crick, on the right, with their model of DNA.

SCIENTISTS AT ODDS

In 1951, Rosalind Franklin began working with Maurice Wilkins in the lab at King's College, in London, but she and Wilkins never got along. Both Wilkins and James Watson belittled Franklin's abilities and accomplishments. Francis Crick, however, respected her work. Franklin's study suggesting the helical structure of DNA was instrumental in Watson and Crick's discovery of DNA's double-stranded shape. If Franklin had not died in 1958, she almost certainly would have shared the Nobel Prize awarded to Watson, Crick, and Wilkins in 1962 for their discovery of the structure of the DNA molecule.

READING STRATEGY

Mnemonics Have students create a mnemonic device that will remind them of the names of the bases and how they form pairs. Examples such as "**A**toms are **T**iny" or "**A**toms are **T**errific" might help remind students that **a**denine pairs with **t**hymine. "**C**athy is **G**reat" or "**C**andy is **G**ross" might remind them that **c**ytosine pairs with **g**uanine.

REAL-WORLD CONNECTION

Genes and Disease Bipolar disorder, which is characterized by extreme behavioral changes, from deep depression to mania, is being investigated for a genetic component. One 19-year study published in 1987 followed an extended family, many members of which suffered from bipolar disorder. The family members who suffered from the disorder all had the same genetic marker (an active section of DNA), and members without the marker did not exhibit the disorder. However, later studies on different populations noted that people without the disorder sometimes also have that marker. Furthermore, scientists point out that the rate of bipolar disorder among Americans has risen dramatically during the last 50 years and that the average age of onset has plummeted from 32 to 19—suggesting that inherited genes alone could not possibly be responsible for bipolar disorder. These scientists suggest that environmental causes and personal experiences are more likely causes of bipolar disorder.

Making a DNA Model

MATERIALS
FOR EACH GROUP:
• 2 licorice whips (60 cm long)
• 50–60 toothpicks
• 50–60 gumdrops in four different colors

Have students work in groups to construct a candy model of DNA. The licorice represents the sides of the DNA molecule, and the gumdrops represent the base pairs. Each group should stretch out two licorice whips parallel to each other. Tell them to slide two gumdrops onto the middle of a toothpick to resemble a complementary base pair and to then insert each end of the toothpick into the licorice whips, connecting them the way rungs connect the two sides of a ladder. After the ladder of toothpicks grows to 20–30 base pairs, have students shape the helix by spiraling it around a tube or pole.
 Sheltered English

MEETING INDIVIDUAL NEEDS

Learners Having Difficulty
To help students better understand how the term *complementary* relates to the structure of DNA, point out that the term means "completing." Using **Figure 5,** explain that complementary base pairs join together to *complete* each rung on the spiral-staircase structure of DNA. Then point out that complementary strands of DNA join together to complete one DNA molecule. Sheltered English

Teaching Transparency 19 "DNA Structure"

DNA Structure

The twisted ladder, or double helix, shape is represented in **Figure 4.** As you can see in **Figure 5,** the two sides of the ladder are made of alternating sugar molecules and phosphate molecules. The rungs of the ladder are composed of a pair of nucleotide bases. Adenine on one side always pairs up with thymine on the other side. Guanine always pairs up with cytosine in the same way. How might this structure explain Chargaff's findings?

Figure 4 *The structure of DNA can be compared to a twisted ladder.*

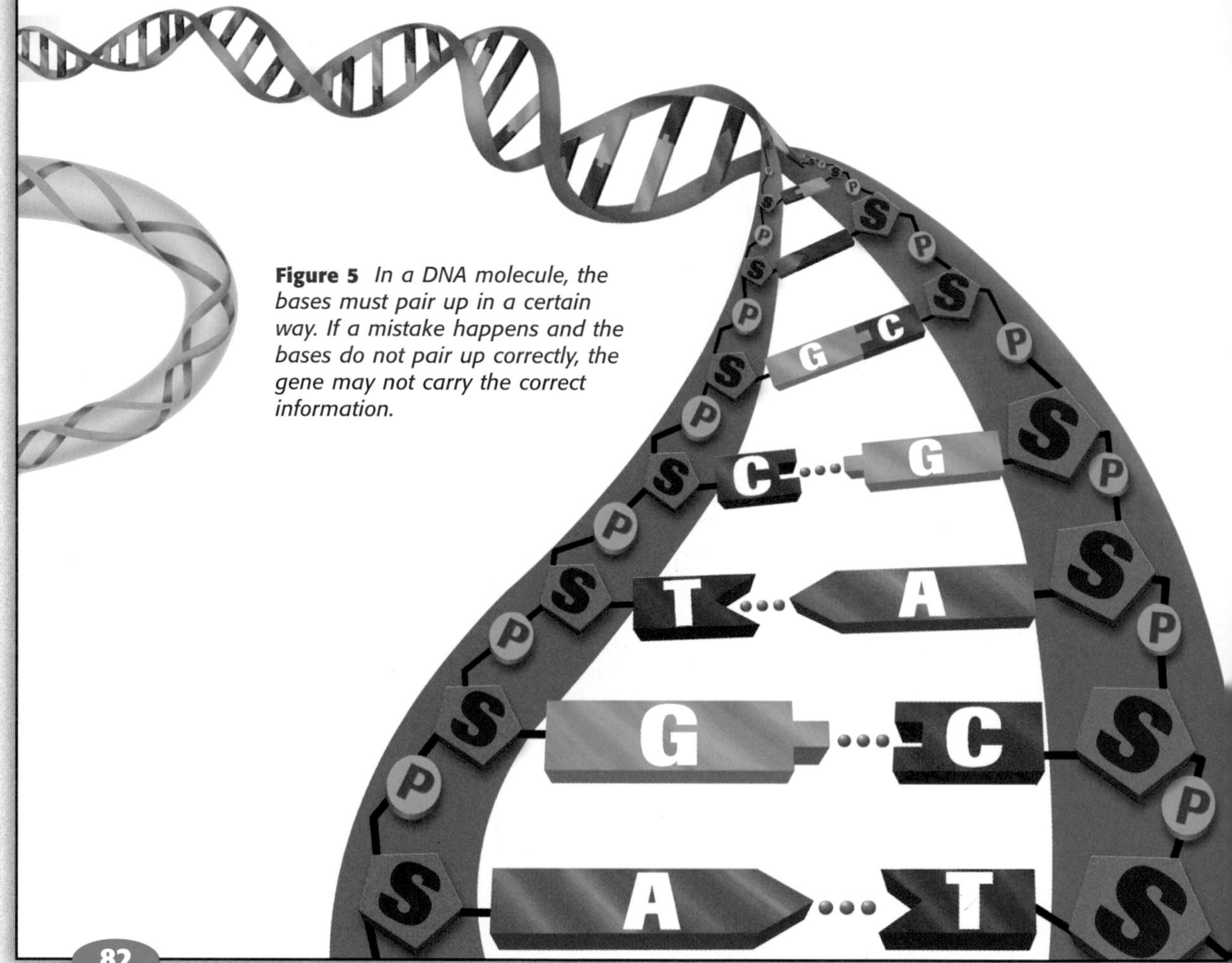

Figure 5 *In a DNA molecule, the bases must pair up in a certain way. If a mistake happens and the bases do not pair up correctly, the gene may not carry the correct information.*

WEIRD SCIENCE

Do werewolves really exist? No, but there is a gene believed to be located on the X chromosome that causes thick and abundant hair to grow on the upper body and face, including the ears, nose, cheeks, forehead, and even eyelids of affected males. This condition is sometimes called the werewolf syndrome because people with this gene resemble werewolves depicted in movies. This condition only affects people's appearance, however, not their behavior.

Making Copies of DNA

What's so great about DNA? Because adenine always bonds with thymine and guanine always bonds with cytosine, one side of a DNA molecule is *complementary* to the other. For example, a sequence such as ACCG always binds to the sequence TGGC. This allows DNA to make a copy of itself, or *replicate*.

As illustrated in **Figure 6,** a DNA molecule replicates by splitting down the middle where the two bases meet. The bases on each side of the molecule can be used as a template, or pattern, for a new complementary side. This creates two identical molecules of DNA.

Figure 6 *The illustration shows DNA separating down the middle in order to make a copy of itself. Each half of the original molecule serves as a template along which a new complementary strand forms. The photograph shows a DNA molecule that has separated. It is magnified about 1 million times.*

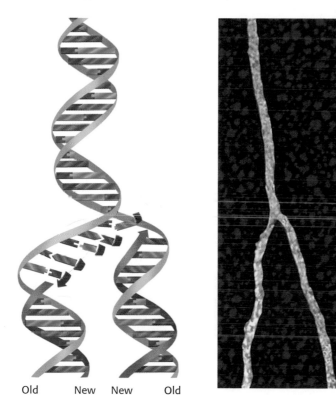

Old   New   New   Old

MATH BREAK

Genes and Bases

A human being has about 100,000 genes. If there are about 30,000 bases in each human gene, about how many bases are in all the genes?

✔ Self-Check

What would the complementary strand of DNA be for the following sequence of bases? ACCTAGTTG *(See page 216 to check your answer.)*

BRAIN FOOD

If you took all the DNA in your body from all of your cells and stretched it out end to end, it would extend about 610 million kilometers. That's long enough to stretch from Earth to the sun and back—twice!

83

MISCONCEPTION ALERT

Can ancient DNA be used to produce dinosaurs as seen in the movies *Jurassic Park* and *The Lost World*? In these movies, scientists make dinosaurs by combining fragments of ancient DNA with DNA from modern-day frogs. In reality, fragments of ancient DNA have indeed been found, but a fragment of DNA does not provide enough information to make an entire organism. Moreover, there is no way to know whether the DNA fragments are even from a dinosaur. In addition, a frog's DNA will grow a frog, which is an amphibian, not a reptile. Most scientists agree that dinosaurs were reptiles.

Answer to MATHBREAK

3,000,000,000

USING THE FIGURE

Have students compare the illustration with the photograph of DNA replication in **Figure 6.** Have them identify the fork, or upside-down V, in both images. Point out that this is the point where the two strands of DNA have separated. Ask the following question:

How many molecules of DNA will there be when the process is complete? (two)

Are the new DNA molecules complementary or identical to the original DNA molecule? (identical)

Answer to Self-Check

TGGATCAAC

MATH and MORE

By causing DNA to replicate in a test tube, scientists can make as many as a billion copies of the original DNA template in very little time. This is a chain reaction in which DNA multiplies **exponentially** with time. This process is extremely important in biotechnology and in genetic research. To help students understand the concept of exponential growth, calculate how much money you will have in 30 days if you start with a penny on day 1 and the amount of money you have doubles every day. Using a calculator, write the products of each multiplication on the board.

(In 30 days you will have $5,368,709.12!)

 Math Skills Worksheet "A Shortcut for Multiplying Large Numbers"

CROSS-DISCIPLINARY FOCUS

Music Researchers at the University of California, San Francisco, are trying to find out if a gene is responsible for "perfect pitch," the ability to immediately determine any musical note upon hearing it. It is a rare ability—possessed by perhaps only one in every 2,000 people—found most often among musicians. People with perfect pitch can easily determine the musical note of a dial tone, the hum of a refrigerator, or any sound they hear. Preliminary findings indicate that people with perfect pitch may inherit the ability, but that an early education in music may also be necessary for the trait to be fully expressed.

MISCONCEPTION ///ALERT\\\

Recessive traits are sometimes referred to in a negative way, as if having a recessive trait is a bad thing. Emphasize that some recessive traits are beautiful, such as the light blue eyes of the white tiger.

internetconnect

SCILINKS
NSTA

TOPIC: Genes and Traits
GO TO: www.scilinks.org
*sci*LINKS NUMBER: HSTL135

From Trait to Gene

The Watson-Crick model also explains how DNA can contain so much information. The bases on one side of the molecule can be put in any order, allowing for an enormous variety of genes. Each gene consists of a string of bases. The order of the bases gives the cell information about how to make each trait.

Putting It All Together DNA functions in the same way for all organisms, from bacteria to mosquitoes to whales to humans. DNA unites us all, and at the same time, it makes each of us unique. The journey from trait to DNA base is illustrated in the diagram on these two pages.

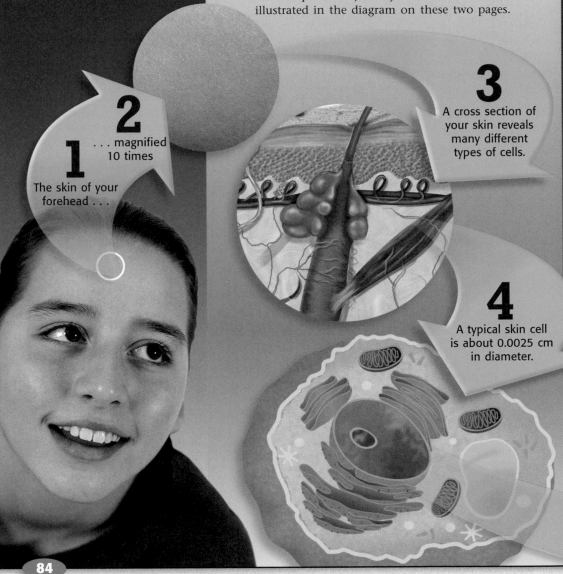

1 The skin of your forehead . . .

2 . . . magnified 10 times

3 A cross section of your skin reveals many different types of cells.

4 A typical skin cell is about 0.0025 cm in diameter.

84

Science BIOOperS

James Watson disliked Rosalind Franklin so much that at a 1951 lecture where she gave information about the size and possible shape of the DNA molecule, Watson refused to take notes. It took Watson and Crick 2 more years to discover some of the same information on their own. When they did, their great discovery of the shape of the DNA molecule came within 2 weeks!

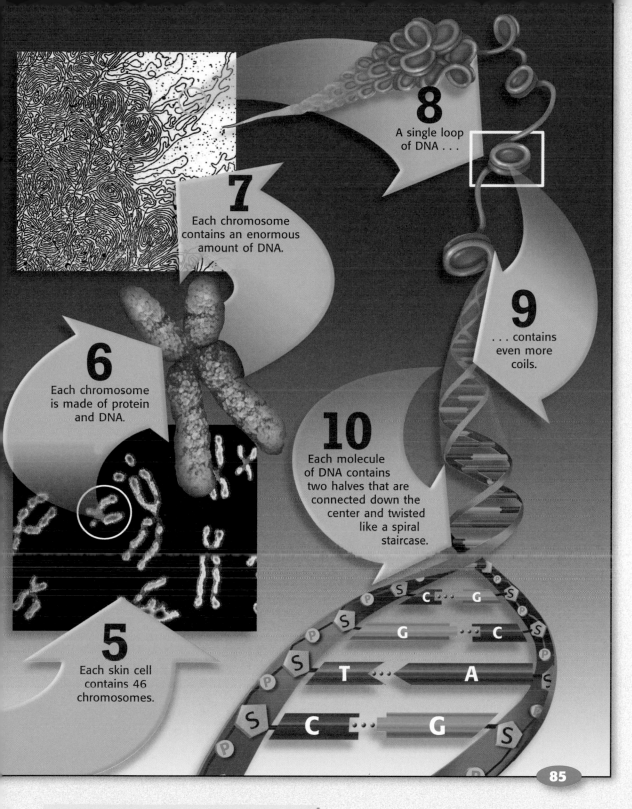

8 A single loop of DNA . . .

7 Each chromosome contains an enormous amount of DNA.

6 Each chromosome is made of protein and DNA.

9 . . . contains even more coils.

10 Each molecule of DNA contains two halves that are connected down the center and twisted like a spiral staircase.

5 Each skin cell contains 46 chromosomes.

S C···G P
S G···C S
P S
S T···A P
P S
S C···G S
P

85

IS THAT A FACT!

Genetic disorders are a serious health problem for humans. Scientists know that faulty or missing genes cause diseases such as cystic fibrosis and sickle cell anemia. Scientists hope to be able to treat genetic disorders someday by altering genes within body cells.

3 **Extend**

DEMONSTRATION

To illustrate the difficulty of fitting all of the DNA into a cell, challenge one or more students to stuff 2 m of embroidery floss into a size "O" Vegicap™. Vegicaps are available at most health-food stores. **Sheltered English**

GROUP ACTIVITY

Have students imagine that they have just discovered the structure of DNA and must present their findings to a group of scientists. Have small groups of students use a model of DNA, a poster, or another visual aid to briefly describe the structure of DNA to their classmates. **Sheltered English**

Homework

Poster Project Have students use colored pencils to draw a portion of a DNA molecule. The drawing should reflect the correct structure of DNA and should contain a legend for identifying the subunits. You may also want students to outline the steps involved in copying DNA.

Science Skills Worksheet "Science Drawing"

internet connect

SciLINKS. **NSTA**

TOPIC: DNA
GO TO: www.scilinks.org
***sci*LINKS NUMBER:** HSTL130

READING STRATEGY

Prediction Guide Before students read this page, ask them if they agree with the following three statements. Students will discover the answers as they explore Section 1.

- Tigers with white fur are likely to have blue eyes. (true)
- There are four possible shades of blue among people with blue eyes. (false)
- If a person inherits genes for tallness, that person will grow tall no matter what. (false)

USING THE FIGURE

Emphasize that not all phenotypes result from completely dominant or completely recessive genes. Ask students what the flowers in **Figure 7** would look like if the gene for red flower color were completely dominant over the gene for white flower color. (All the offspring would be red.)

RETEACHING

 Writing Have students describe three exceptions to Mendel's heredity principles in their ScienceLog.

Teaching Transparency 20
"Incomplete Dominance"

DNA
on trial?
Read all about
it on page 100.

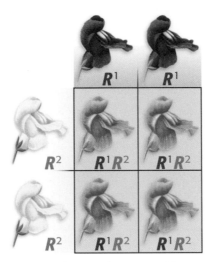

Figure 7 *The snapdragon provides a good example of incomplete dominance.*

More News About Traits

As you may have already discovered, things are often more complicated than they first appear to be. Gregor Mendel uncovered the basic principles of how genes are passed from one generation to the next. But as scientists learned more about heredity, they began to find exceptions to Mendel's principles. A few of these exceptions are explained in the following paragraphs.

Incomplete Dominance In his studies with peas, Mendel found that different traits did not blend together to produce an in-between form. Since then, researchers have found that sometimes one trait is not completely dominant over another. These traits do not blend together, but each allele has its own degree of influence. This is known as *incomplete dominance*. One example of this is the snapdragon flower. **Figure 7** shows a cross between a true-breeding red snapdragon (R^1R^1) and a true-breeding white snapdragon (R^2R^2). As you can see, all of the possible phenotypes for their offspring are pink because both alleles of the gene have some degree of influence.

One Gene Can Influence Many Traits Sometimes one gene influences more than one trait. An example of this phenomenon is shown by the white tiger at right. The white fur is caused by a single gene, but this gene influences more than just fur color. Do you see anything else unusual about the tiger? If you look closely, you'll see that the tiger has blue eyes. Here the gene that controls fur color also influences eye color.

IS THAT A FACT!

One of the many traits Mendel studied in pea plants was seed shape. He found that round seeds were dominant over wrinkled seeds. Seen under a microscope, the *RR* seeds have many starch grains that give them a full, round shape. The *rr* seeds have few starch grains, so they have a wrinkled shape. *Rr* seeds have an intermediate number of starch grains; they have enough starch to be full and round, but they have fewer starch grains than *RR* seeds. This is an example of incomplete dominance.

Many Genes Can Influence a Single Trait Some traits, such as the color of your skin, hair, and eyes, are the result of several genes acting together. That's why it's difficult to tell if a trait is the result of a dominant or recessive gene. As shown in **Figure 8,** you may have blue eyes, but they are probably a slightly different shade of blue than the blue eyes of a classmate. Different combinations of alleles result in slight differences in the amount of pigment present.

The Importance of Environment It's important to remember that genes aren't the only influences on your development. Many things in your environment also influence how you grow and develop. Consider the importance of a healthy diet, exercise, and examples set by family and friends. For example, your genes may determine that you can grow to be tall, but you must receive the proper nutrients as you grow in order to reach your full potential height. You may have inherited a special talent, but you need to practice.

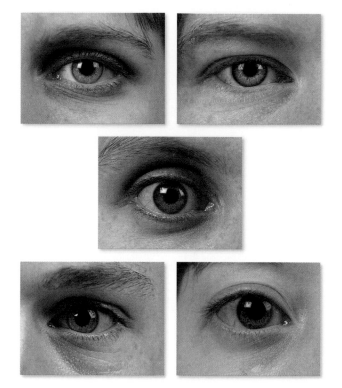

Figure 8 *At least two genes determine human eye color. That's why so many shades of a single color are possible.*

SECTION REVIEW

1. List and describe the parts of a nucleotide.

2. Which bases pair together in a DNA molecule?

3. What shape was suggested by Rosalind Franklin's X-ray images?

4. Explain what is meant by the statement, "DNA unites all organisms."

5. **Doing Calculations** If a sample of DNA were found to contain 20 percent cytosine, what percentage of guanine would be in this sample? Why?

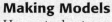

internetconnect

SC*i*LINKS.
NSTA

TOPIC: DNA, Genes and Traits
GO TO: www.scilinks.org
*sci*LINKS NUMBER: HSTL130, HSTL135

4) Close

Quiz

1. Why did scientists believe that proteins, instead of DNA, carried genetic information? (because proteins are much more complex than DNA)

2. Name the three parts of every nucleotide. (a phosphate, a sugar, and a base)

3. What is incomplete dominance? (In incomplete dominance, each of the two alleles that determine a trait has its own degree of influence.)

ALTERNATIVE ASSESSMENT

PORTFOLIO

Making Models
Have students work independently or in pairs to make a model of DNA. Provide a variety of materials, including construction paper, pipe cleaners, scissors, glue, ribbon, and paper clips. Encourage students to use their model to demonstrate base pairing and DNA replication.
Sheltered English

▼ *Answers to Section Review*

1. Phosphate and sugar combine to form a backbone. One of the four bases is attached to the backbone, forming a nucleotide.

2. Adenine pairs with thymine, and guanine pairs with cytosine.

3. Franklin's X-ray diffraction suggested a spiral or coiled shape.

4. The statement means that the genetic code contained in DNA is the same for virtually all living things.

5. Cytosine always pairs with guanine, so the percentage of guanine would also be 20 percent.

Focus

How DNA Works

This section shows how DNA is used as a template for making proteins and how errors in DNA can lead to mutations and genetic disorders. Finally, students learn about pedigrees and how they are interpreted.

Bellringer

Have students unscramble the following words and use them both in a sentence:

tpsoneir (proteins)

neesg (genes)

(Genes contain instructions for making proteins.)

1 Motivate

GROUP ACTIVITY

Ask students to work in small groups to come up with as many different three-letter codes as possible using the four different bases. Give each group four pieces of paper, with one of the following four letters printed on each piece: *A, T, C,* or *G.* Tell students that each piece of paper represents a different amino acid. (There are 64 possible three-letter codes—the number of codons in the genetic code responsible for making proteins.) Sheltered English

Directed Reading Worksheet Section 2

Terms to Learn

ribosome   mutagen
mutation   pedigree

What You'll Do

◆ Explain the relationship between genes and proteins.
◆ Outline the basic steps in making a protein.
◆ Define *mutation,* and give an example.
◆ Evaluate the information in a pedigree.

How DNA Works

Scientists knew that the order of the bases formed a code that somehow told each cell what to do. The next step in understanding DNA involved breaking this code.

Genes and Proteins

Scientists discovered that the bases in DNA read like a book, from one end to the other and in one direction only. The bases A, T, G, and C form the alphabet of the code. Groups of three bases code for a specific amino acid. For example, the three bases **CCA** code for the amino acid proline. The bases **AGC** code for the amino acid serine. As you know, proteins are made up of long strings of amino acids. The order of the bases determines the order of amino acids in a protein. Each gene is a set of instructions for making a protein. This is illustrated in **Figure 9.**

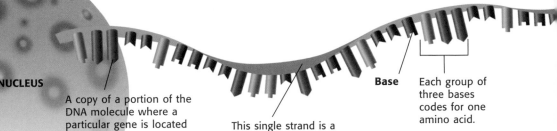

NUCLEUS

A copy of a portion of the DNA molecule where a particular gene is located is made and transferred outside of the cell nucleus.

This single strand is a copy of one strand of the original DNA.

Base

Each group of three bases codes for one amino acid.

Figure 9 *A gene is a section of DNA that contains instructions for stringing together amino acids to make a protein.*

Why Proteins? You may be wondering, "What do proteins have to do with who I am or what I look like?" Proteins are found throughout cells. They act as chemical messengers, and they help determine how tall you will grow, what colors you can see, and whether your hair is curly or straight. Human cells contain about 100,000 genes, and each gene spells out sequences of amino acids for specific proteins. Proteins exist in an almost limitless variety. The human body contains about 50,000 different kinds of proteins. Proteins are the reason for the multitude of different shapes, sizes, colors, and textures found in living things, such as antlers, claws, hair, and skin.

88

SCIENCE HUMOR

Q: Why did the mutant chromosome go to the tailor?

A: because it had a hole in its genes

The Making of a Protein

As explained in Figure 9, the first step in making a protein is to copy the section of the DNA strand containing a gene. A copy of this section is made with the help of copier enzymes. Messenger molecules take the genetic information from the sections of DNA in the nucleus out into the cytoplasm.

In the cytoplasm, the copy of DNA is fed through a kind of protein assembly line. The "factory" where this assembly line exists is known as a **ribosome.** The copy is fed through the ribosome three bases at a time. Transfer molecules act as translators of the message contained in the copy of DNA. Each transfer molecule picks up a specific amino acid from the cytoplasm. The amino acid is determined by the order of the bases the transfer molecule contains. Like pieces of a puzzle, bases on the transfer molecule then match up with bases on the copy of DNA inside the ribosome. The transfer molecules then drop off their amino acid "suitcases," which are strung together to form a protein. This process is illustrated in **Figure 10.**

Self-Check

1. How many amino acids are present in a protein that requires 3,000 bases in its code?

2. Explain how proteins influence how you look.

(See page 216 to check your answers.)

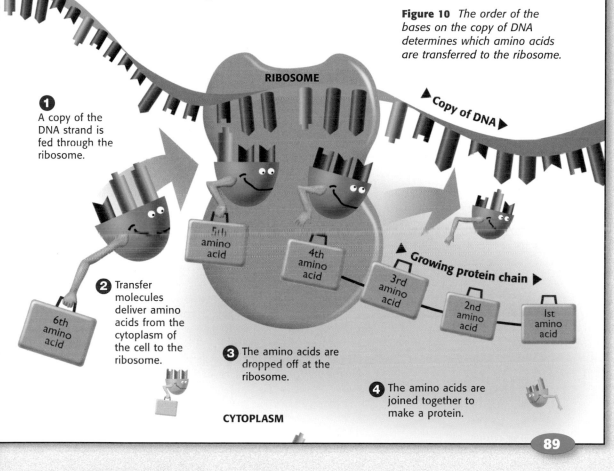

Figure 10 *The order of the bases on the copy of DNA determines which amino acids are transferred to the ribosome.*

1 A copy of the DNA strand is fed through the ribosome.

RIBOSOME

Copy of DNA ▶

5th amino acid

4th amino acid

Growing protein chain ▶

3rd amino acid

2nd amino acid

1st amino acid

6th amino acid

2 Transfer molecules deliver amino acids from the cytoplasm of the cell to the ribosome.

3 The amino acids are dropped off at the ribosome.

4 The amino acids are joined together to make a protein.

CYTOPLASM

89

SCIENCE HUMOR

Q: What happens when an amateur-tein gets paid?

A: It becomes a pro-tein.

② Teach

Answers to Self-Check

1. 1,000

2. DNA codes for proteins. Your flesh is composed of proteins, and the way those proteins are constructed and combined influences much about the way you look.

MATH and MORE

Use mathematics to discuss how DNA codes for amino acids. With four possible nucleotides in three possible positions, there are $4 \times 4 \times 4$, or 64, possible combinations. (for example, AAA, AAT, AAG, and AAC)

These combinations are called codons. DNA produces only 20 amino acids; thus, most amino acids have several corresponding codons.

COOPERATIVE LEARNING

Skit Have groups of students write and perform a short skit to demonstrate the formation of a protein. For instance, students could play the roles of a ribosome, an amino acid, a transfer enzyme, and a DNA copy.

Teaching Transparency 21 "The Making of a Protein"

GUIDED PRACTICE

Write a sequence of DNA, such as AACTACGGT, on the chalkboard. Ask students to write the sequence for a copy of the DNA using base-pairing rules. (TTGATGCCA)

Then ask students to give examples of deletion, insertion, and substitution mutations to the DNA.

MISCONCEPTION ALERT

Are mutations rare? Scientists estimate that we inherit hundreds of mutations from our parents. In addition, new mutations can happen due to environmental factors and mistakes made during DNA replication and cell division. Mistakes are made during DNA replication in approximately one out of every 1,000 base pairs. But thanks to repair enzymes and other proofing mechanisms, the final error rate is much lower—somewhere between one in a million and one in a billion.

CONNECT TO EARTH SCIENCE

Ozone is a gas made of three oxygen atoms. High in the atmosphere, ozone absorbs dangerous ultraviolet radiation (the high-energy light that can cause cancer). When produced near the surface of the Earth, however, ozone is a pollutant that affects plant growth and makes breathing more difficult. Use Teaching Transparency 167 to illustrate the process of ozone production.

Teaching Transparency 167
"The Formation of Smog"
LINK TO EARTH SCIENCE

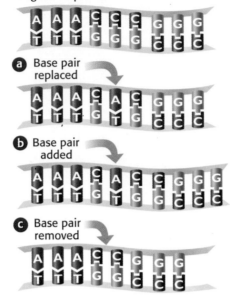

Original sequence

a Base pair replaced

b Base pair added

c Base pair removed

Figure 11 *The original base-pair sequence at the top has been changed to illustrate (a) substitution, (b) insertion, and (c) deletion.*

Meteorology
CONNECTION

The layer of ozone in the Earth's atmosphere helps shield the planet's surface from ultraviolet (UV) radiation. UV radiation can cause mutations in skin cells that can lead to cancer. Each year more than 750,000 people get skin cancer. Scientists fear that damage to the ozone layer may greatly increase the number of skin cancers each year.

Changes in Genes

Imagine that you've been invited to ride on a brand-new roller coaster at the state fair. Just before you climb into the front car, you are informed that some of the metal parts on the coaster have been replaced by parts made of a different substance. Would you still want to ride this roller coaster?

Perhaps a stronger metal was substituted. Or perhaps a material not suited to the job was used. Imagine what would happen if cardboard were used instead of metal!

Mutant Molecules Substitutions like this can occur in DNA. They are known as **mutations.** Mutations occur when there is a change in the order of bases in an organism's DNA. Sometimes a base is left out; this is known as a *deletion.* Or an extra base might be added; this is known as an *insertion.* The most common error occurs when an incorrect base replaces a correct base. This is known as a *substitution.* **Figure 11** illustrates these three types of mutations.

Mistakes Happen Fortunately, repair enzymes are continuously on the job, patrolling the DNA molecule for errors. When an error is found, it is usually repaired. But occasionally the repairs are not completely accurate, and the mistakes become part of the genetic message. There are three possible consequences to changes in DNA: an improvement, no change at all, or a harmful change. If the mutation occurs in the sex cells, it can be passed from one generation to the next.

How Can DNA Become Damaged? In addition to random errors that occur when DNA is copied, damage can be caused by physical and chemical agents known as mutagens. A **mutagen** is anything that can cause a mutation in DNA. Examples of mutagens include high-energy radiation from X rays and ultraviolet radiation. Ultraviolet radiation is the type of energy in sunlight that is responsible for suntans and sunburns. Other mutagens include asbestos and the chemicals in cigarette smoke.

WEIRD SCIENCE

A human cell contains between 50,000 and 100,000 genes. Human DNA is about 3 billion base pairs long. Only about 3 percent of those base pairs are used in making proteins; the other 97 percent are regulatory sequences and nonfunctioning genes.

An Example of a Substitution

Consider the DNA sequence containing the three bases **GAA**. GAA are the three letters that give the instructions: "Put the amino acid glutamic acid here." If a mistake occurs and the sequence is changed to **GTA**, a completely different message is sent: "Put valine here."

This simple change just described can cause the disease *sickle cell anemia*. Sickle cell anemia is a disease that affects red blood cells. When valine is substituted for glutamic acid in a blood protein, as shown in **Figure 12**, the red blood cells become distorted into a sickle shape.

The sickled cells are not as good as normal red blood cells at carrying oxygen. They are also more likely to get stuck in blood vessels, causing painful and dangerous clots.

QuickLab

Mutations

The sentence below contains all three-letter words but has experienced a mutation. Can you find the mutation?

THE IGR EDC ATA TET HEB IGB ADR AT

What kind of mutation did you find? Now what does the sentence say?

TRY at HOME

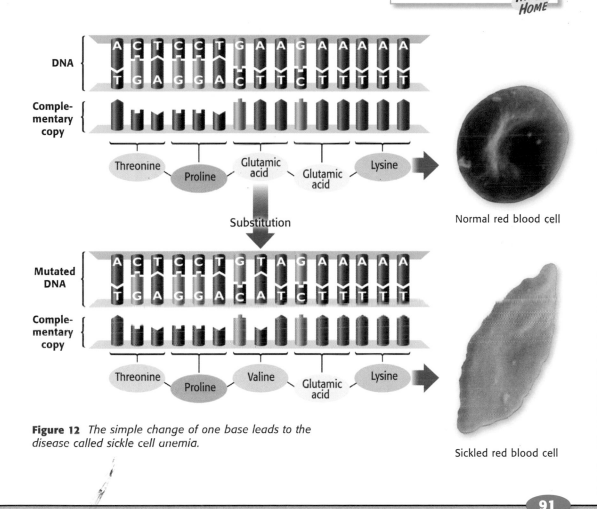

Figure 12 *The simple change of one base leads to the disease called sickle cell anemia.*

Normal red blood cell

Sickled red blood cell

91

Science Bloopers

A person who carries a single allele for sickle cell anemia is said to have *sickle cell trait*. In the past, many people did not understand that people who have sickle cell trait do not pose a risk to the community. In some areas, children with the trait were banned from public schools because people feared the condition was contagious.

3 Extend

Answers to QuickLab

The mutation is a deletion. THE BIG RED CAT ATE THE BIG BAD RAT

RETEACHING

Write a sequence of DNA on the chalkboard, and invite students to come up to the board and change the sequence. Then ask the class to discuss the possible consequences of such a mutation in DNA. (It might cause a different amino acid to be substituted. This could result in a genetic disorder, an improvement, or no change at all.)

Ask how the mutation could be corrected. (Enzymes may find and repair the error.)

Finally, ask what could have caused the mutation. (Mutations are caused by random errors in the copying of DNA, by physical and chemical damage to the DNA, or by X rays and other mutagens.)
Sheltered English

CROSS-DISCIPLINARY FOCUS

Writing **History** Have students conduct Internet or library research and write a report on the history of Queen Victoria and her descendants. The queen was a carrier of hemophilia, a recessive disorder in which a person lacks a protein needed to form blood clots. The hemophilia gene passed from Queen Victoria to her daughters and from them to the Russian, Spanish, and German families they married into.

PORTFOLIO

Teaching Transparency 22
"An Example of Substitution"

CROSS-DISCIPLINARY FOCUS

Social Studies Czar Nicholas II ruled Russia from 1894 to 1917. Nicholas, his wife, and their children were shot to death by the Bolsheviks in 1918 in the aftermath of the Russian Revolution. Their bodies were not found until 1991, when Russian anthropologists discovered their bones. To be certain of the identity of the remains, DNA samples were taken from the remains and from living members of the family. The DNA fingerprints of the deceased were similar to those of the surviving family members. The remains were determined to be Czar Nicholas II and his family.

Answer to APPLY

Individuals I$_2$ and III$_2$ are nearsighted. Both of Jane's parents are *Nn.* Jane's genotype can be either *NN* or *Nn.* It can't be *nn* because Jane is not nearsighted.

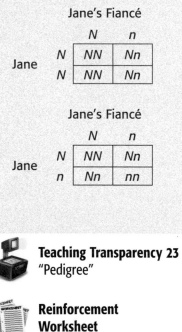

Jane's Fiancé

		N	n
Jane	N	NN	Nn
	N	NN	Nn

Jane's Fiancé

		N	n
Jane	N	NN	Nn
	n	Nn	nn

Genetic Counseling

Most hereditary disorders, such as sickle cell anemia, are recessive disorders. This means that the disease occurs only when a child inherits a defective gene from both parents. Some people, called carriers, have only one allele for the disease. Carriers of the gene may pass it along to their children without knowing that they have the mutated gene.

Genetic counseling provides information and counseling to couples who wish to have children but are worried that they might pass a disease to their children. Genetic counselors often make use of a diagram known as a **pedigree,** which is a tool for tracing a trait through generations of a family. By making a pedigree, it is often possible to predict whether a person is a carrier of a hereditary disease. In **Figure 13,** the trait for the disease cystic fibrosis is tracked through four generations. Each generation is numbered with Roman numerals, and each individual is numbered with Arabic numerals.

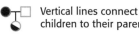
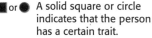

Figure 13 *Cystic fibrosis is a recessive hereditary disease that affects the respiratory system. A pedigree for cystic fibrosis is shown below.*

□ Males   ○ Females

 Vertical lines connect children to their parents.

■ or ● A solid square or circle indicates that the person has a certain trait.

◨ or ◑ A half-filled square or circle indicates that the person is a carrier of the trait.

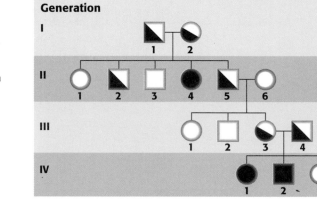

APPLY

Pedigree and Punnett Squares

The pedigree at right shows the recessive trait of nearsightedness in Jane's family. Jane, her parents, and her brother all have normal vision. Which individuals in the pedigree are nearsighted? What are the possible genotypes of Jane's parents? Jane has two possible genotypes. What are they? Jane is planning to marry a person who has normal vision but carries the trait for nearsightedness. Work two Punnett squares to show the possible genotypes of Jane's future children.

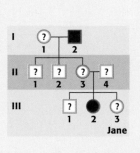

Teaching Transparency 23 "Pedigree"

Reinforcement Worksheet "DNA Mutations"

WEIRD SCIENCE

Gene therapy is an experimental field of medical research in which defective genes are replaced with healthy genes. One way to insert healthy genes involves using a delivery system called a gene gun to inject microscopic gold bullets coated with genetic material.

Designer Genes

For thousands of years, humans have been aware of the benefits of selective breeding. In *selective breeding*, organisms with certain desirable characteristics are mated to produce a new breed. You probably have enjoyed the benefits of selective breeding, although you may not have realized it. For example, you may have eaten an egg from a chicken that was bred to produce a large number of eggs. Your pet dog might even be a result of selective breeding. Some kinds of dogs, for example, have a thick coat so that they can retrieve game in icy waters.

Engineering Organisms Scientists now have the ability to produce desired characteristics in some organisms without breeding. They can manipulate individual genes using a technique known as genetic engineering. Like all types of engineering, genetic engineering puts scientific knowledge to practical use. Basically, *genetic engineering* allows scientists to transfer genes from one organism to another. Genetic engineering is already used to manufacture proteins, repair damaged genes, and identify individuals who may carry an allele for a disease. Some other uses are shown in **Figures 14** and **15.**

Figure 14 *Scientists added a gene found in fireflies to this tobacco plant. The plant now produces an enzyme that causes the plant to glow.*

Figure 15 *A sheep called Dolly was the first successfully cloned mammal.*

SECTION REVIEW

1. List the three types of mutations. How do they differ?

2. What type of mutation causes sickle cell anemia?

3. How is genetic engineering different from selective breeding?

4. **Applying Concepts** Mutations can occur in sex cells or in body cells. In which cell type might a mutation be passed from generation to generation? Explain.

internet**connect**

SCI*LINKS*
NSTA

TOPIC: Genetic Engineering
GO TO: www.scilinks.org
*sci***LINKS NUMBER:** HSTL140

93

④ Close

Quiz

1. What is the function of the ribosome? (In the ribosome, the DNA code is translated into proteins.)

2. List some causes of DNA mutations. (UV radiation, cigarette smoke, or X rays)

ALTERNATIVE ASSESSMENT

Writing Have students prepare an instruction manual for their DNA. The manual should include instructions for copying their DNA and translating it into proteins. It should also include information about protecting their DNA from mutations by avoiding mutagens and correcting any mutations that occur.

Critical Thinking Worksheet
"The Perfect Parrot"

Interactive Explorations CD-ROM "DNA Pawprints"

internet**connect**

SCI*LINKS*
NSTA

TOPIC: Genetic Engineering
GO TO: www.scilinks.org
*sci***LINKS NUMBER:** HSTL140

▼ Answers to Section Review

1. insertion: an extra base is inserted; deletion: a base is deleted; substitution: one base is substituted for another

2. substitution

3. Selective breeding involves choosing desired traits and breeding organisms that have those traits. Genetic engineering involves altering the DNA at the molecular level, thereby changing an organism's genome.

4. Mutations can only be passed from generation to generation if they occur in sex cells. This is because the genes in an individual's sex cells are used to reproduce a new individual.

Making Models Lab

Base-Pair Basics
Teacher's Notes

Time Required

One 45-minute class period

Lab Ratings

EASY ——————————→ HARD

TEACHER PREP
STUDENT SET-UP
CONCEPT LEVEL
CLEAN UP

MATERIALS

You may want to provide additional materials for the Going Further section.

Safety Caution

Remind students to review all safety cautions and icons before beginning this lab activity.

Students should always exercise care when using scissors.

Lab Notes

You may wish to enlarge the template for your students so the base pairs will be easier to cut out.

Explain to students that the white pieces and the colored pieces indicate an old side and a new side after replication.

Debra Sampson
Booker T. Washington Middle School
Elgin, Texas

Base-Pair Basics

You have learned that DNA is shaped like a twisted ladder. The side rails of the ladder are made of sugar molecules and phosphate molecules. The sides are held together by nucleotide bases. These bases join in pairs to form the rungs of the ladder. Each nucleotide base can pair with only one other nucleotide base. Each of these pairs is called a base pair. When DNA replicates, enzymes separate the base pairs. Then each half of the DNA ladder can be used as a template to complete a new half. In this activity, you will make and replicate a model of DNA.

MATERIALS

- white paper or poster board
- colored paper or poster board
- scissors
- large paper bag

Procedure

1 Trace the bases below onto white paper or poster board. Label the pieces A (for adenine), T (for thymine), C (for cytosine), and G (for guanine). Draw the pieces again on colored paper or poster board. Use a different color for each base. Draw the pieces as large as you want, and draw as many of the white pieces and as many of the colored pieces as time will allow.

2 Carefully cut out all of the pieces.

3 Gather all of the colored pieces in the classroom into a large paper bag. Spread all of the white pieces in the classroom onto a large table.

4 Withdraw nine pieces from the bag. Arrange the colored pieces in any order in a straight column so the letters A, T, C, and G are right side up. Be sure to match the sugar and phosphate tabs and notches. Draw this arrangement in your ScienceLog.

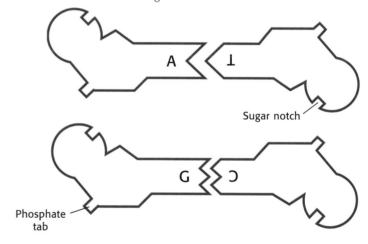

Sugar notch

Phosphate tab

94

5 Find the matching white nucleotide bases for the nine colored bases. Remember the base-pairing rules you have studied, and matching should be easy!

6 Fit the pieces together, matching all tabs and notches. You now have one piece of DNA containing nine base pairs. Draw your results in your ScienceLog.

7 Now separate the base pairs, keeping the sugar and phosphate notches and tabs together. Draw this arrangement in your ScienceLog.

8 Look at each string of bases you drew in step 7. Along each one, write the letters of the bases that should join the string to complete the base pairs.

9 Find all the bases you need to complete your replication. Find white pieces to match the bases on the left, and find colored pieces to match the bases on the right.

Be sure all the tabs and notches fit and the sides are straight. You have now replicated DNA. Are the two models identical? Draw your results in your ScienceLog.

Analysis

10 Name the correct base-pairing rules.

11 What happens when you attempt to pair thymine with guanine? Do they fit together? Are the sides straight? Do all of the tabs and notches fit? Explain.

Going Further
Construct a 3-D model of the DNA molecule, showing its twisted-ladder structure. Use your imagination and creativity to select your materials. You may want to use licorice, gum balls, and toothpicks, or pipe cleaners and paper clips! Display your model in your classroom.

Answers
10. G pairs with C, and A pairs with T.
11. The joining areas of guanine and thymine don't match up. They don't fit together.

 Datasheets for LabBook

95

Chapter Highlights

Chapter Highlights

VOCABULARY DEFINITIONS

SECTION 1

DNA deoxyribonucleic acid; hereditary material that controls all the activities of a cell, contains the information to make new cells, and provides instructions for making proteins

nucleotide a subunit of DNA consisting of a sugar, a phosphate, and one of four nitrogenous bases

adenine one of the four bases that combine with sugar and phosphate to form a nucleotide subunit of DNA; adenine pairs with thymine

thymine one of the four bases that combine with sugar and phosphate to form a nucleotide subunit of DNA; thymine pairs with adenine

guanine one of the four bases that combine with sugar and phosphate to form a nucleotide subunit of DNA; guanine pairs with cytosine

cytosine one of the four bases that combine with sugar and phosphate to form a nucleotide subunit of DNA; cytosine pairs with guanine

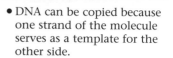

SECTION 1

Vocabulary

DNA (p. 80)
nucleotide (p. 80)
adenine (p. 80)
thymine (p. 80)
guanine (p. 80)
cytosine (p. 80)

Section Notes

- Proteins are made of long strings of amino acids.
- DNA is made of long strings of nucleotides.
- Chromosomes are made of protein and DNA.
- The DNA molecule looks like a twisted ladder. The rungs of the ladder are made of base pairs, either adenine and thymine, or cytosine and guanine.
- DNA carries genetic information in the order of the nucleotide bases.

- DNA can be copied because one strand of the molecule serves as a template for the other side.

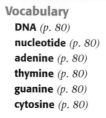

☑ Skills Check

Math Concepts

THE GENETIC CODE The MathBreak on page 83 asks you to calculate the number of bases in all of your genes. If there are about 30,000 bases in each gene and there are 100,000 genes, then multiply to find the answer.

$$30,000 \times 100,000 = 3,000,000,000$$

So, there are about 3 billion bases in all of your genes.

Visual Understanding

COPIES OF DNA Look at Figure 9 on page 88. You can see the nucleus and the pores in its membrane. The copy of DNA emerges through these pores on its way to deliver its coded message to the ribosomes. Why does DNA send a copy out of the nucleus to relay its message? The answer is that DNA is much more protected from factors that might cause a mutation if it stays inside the nucleus. The messenger copy may encounter bad luck, but the master DNA usually stays very safe!

96

Lab and Activity Highlights

Base-Pair Basics 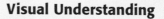 **PG 94**

 Datasheets for LabBook
(blackline masters for this lab)

SECTION 2

ribosome a small organelle in cells where proteins are made from amino acids

mutation a change in the order of the bases in an organism's DNA; deletion, insertion, or substitution

mutagen anything that can damage or cause changes in DNA

pedigree a diagram of family history used for tracing a trait through several generations

SECTION 2

Vocabulary

ribosome *(p. 89)*
mutation *(p. 90)*
mutagen *(p. 90)*
pedigree *(p. 92)*

Section Notes

• A gene is a set of instructions for assembling a protein.

• Each group of three bases in a gene codes for a particular amino acid.

• Genes can become mutated when the order of the bases is changed.

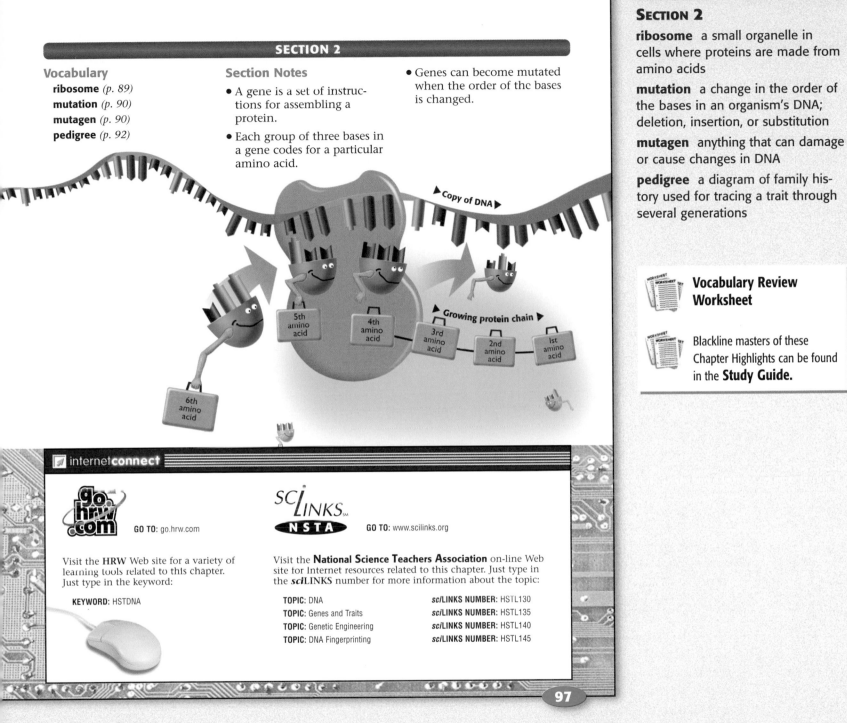

◀ Copy of DNA ▶

▶ Growing protein chain ▶

5th amino acid

4th amino acid

3rd amino acid

2nd amino acid

1st amino acid

6th amino acid

Vocabulary Review Worksheet

Blackline masters of these Chapter Highlights can be found in the **Study Guide.**

internet**connect**

GO TO: go.hrw.com

Visit the **HRW** Web site for a variety of learning tools related to this chapter. Just type in the keyword:

KEYWORD: HSTDNA

SCI LINKS SM
N S T A

GO TO: www.scilinks.org

Visit the **National Science Teachers Association** on-line Web site for Internet resources related to this chapter. Just type in the *sci*LINKS number for more information about the topic:

TOPIC: DNA   *sci*LINKS NUMBER: HSTL130
TOPIC: Genes and Traits   *sci*LINKS NUMBER: HSTL135
TOPIC: Genetic Engineering   *sci*LINKS NUMBER: HSTL140
TOPIC: DNA Fingerprinting   *sci*LINKS NUMBER: HSTL145

97

Lab and Activity Highlights

LabBank

Long-Term Projects & Research Ideas, The Antifreeze Protein

Interactive Explorations CD-ROM

 CD 3, Exploration 8, "DNA Pawprints"

Chapter Review
Answers

USING VOCABULARY
1. amino acids; nucleotides
2. recessive
3. mutation
4. mutagen

UNDERSTANDING CONCEPTS
Multiple Choice
5. b
6. d
7. b
8. c
9. c
10. b a

Short Answer
11. GAATCCGAATGGT
12. DNA molecules split down the middle, then each side of the molecule pairs up with an additional nucleotide. (Picture should resemble a zipper being zipped up.)
13. insertion

Chapter Review

USING VOCABULARY

To complete the following sentences, choose the correct term from each pair of terms listed below:

1. A protein is a long string of __?__. A strand of DNA is a long string of __?__. (*amino acids* or *nucleotides*)

2. A disorder, such as cystic fibrosis, is known as __?__ if the child must receive an allele for the disease from each parent in order to have the disease. (*dominant* or *recessive*)

3. A change in the order of bases in DNA is called a __?__. (*mutation* or *mutagen*)

4. A __?__ is a physical or chemical agent that causes damage to DNA. (*mutagen* or *pedigree*)

UNDERSTANDING CONCEPTS

Multiple Choice

5. In a DNA molecule, which of the following bases pair together?
   a. adenine and cytosine
   b. thymine and adenine
   c. thymine and guanine
   d. cytosine and thymine

6. A gene is
   a. a set of instructions for each trait.
   b. instructions on how to make a protein.
   c. a portion of a strand of DNA.
   d. All of the above

7. DNA
   a. is made up of three subunits.
   b. has a structure like a twisted ladder.
   c. cannot be repaired if it is mutated.
   d. All of the above

8. In incomplete dominance,
   a. a single gene controls many traits.
   b. genes for a trait are all recessive.
   c. each allele for a trait has its own degree of influence.
   d. the environment controls the genes.

9. Watson and Crick
   a. studied the amounts of each base in DNA.
   b. took X-ray pictures of DNA.
   c. made models to determine DNA structure.
   d. discovered that genes were located on chromosomes.

10. Which of the following is NOT a step in making a protein?
    a. Copies of DNA are taken to the cytoplasm.
    b. Transfer molecules deliver amino acids to the nucleus.
    c. Amino acids are joined together at the ribosome to make a protein.
    d. A copy of the DNA is fed through the ribosome.

Short Answer

11. What would the complementary strand of DNA be for the following sequence of bases?

    C T T A G G C T T A C C A

12. How does DNA copy itself? Draw a picture to help explain your answer.

13. If the DNA sequence TGAGCCATGA is changed to TGAGCACATGA, what kind of mutation has occurred?

Concept Mapping

14. Use the following terms to create a concept map: bases, adenine, thymine, nucleotides, guanine, DNA, cytosine.

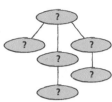

CRITICAL THINKING AND PROBLEM SOLVING

Write one or two sentences to answer the following questions:

15. If neither parent shows signs of having sickle cell anemia, does this fact guarantee that their children will not contract the disease? Explain.

16. How many amino acids does this DNA sequence code for?

    T C A G C C A C C T A T G G A

MATH IN SCIENCE

17. The goal of a project called the Human Genome Project is to discover the location and DNA sequence of all human genes. Scientists estimate that there are 100,000 human genes. In 1998, 38,000 genes had been discovered. How many more genes must the Human Genome Project discover?

18. If scientists find 6,000 genes each year, how many years will it take to finish the project?

19. Of the 38,000 genes discovered, 7,000 have been mapped to their chromosome location. What percentage of the discovered genes have been mapped?

INTERPRETING GRAPHICS

Examine the pedigree for albinism shown below, and then answer the following questions. You may need to use a Punnett square to answer some of these questions. (Albinism is a trait among individuals who produce no pigment in their skin, hair, or eyes.)

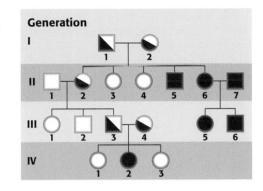

20. How many males are represented on this pedigree? How many females?

21. How many individuals in Generation II had albinism? How many were carriers of the trait?

22. Do you think albinism is a dominant trait or a recessive trait? Explain.

Reading Check-up

Take a minute to review your answers to the Pre-Reading Questions found at the bottom of page 78. Have your answers changed? If necessary, revise your answers based on what you have learned since you began this chapter.

Concept Mapping

14. An answer to this exercise can be found at the front of this book.

CRITICAL THINKING AND PROBLEM SOLVING

15. No; it does not. The trait for sickle cell anemia is recessive. Both parents could be carrying it and could transfer it to their child. If their child inherits the recessive gene from both parents, he or she will have the disease.

16. This sequence codes for five amino acids.

MATH IN SCIENCE

17. approximately 62,000
18. more than 10 years
19. about 18.4 percent

INTERPRETING GRAPHICS

20. 7 males, 11 females
21. 3, 1
22. recessive, because offspring have to inherit the albinism allele from each parent to display albinism as in III_5, III_6, and IV_2, for example

Concept Mapping Transparency 6

Blackline masters of this Chapter Review can be found in the **Study Guide.**

Background

You may wish to point out to students that the study of DNA fingerprinting brings up some interesting issues about the use of new technologies to generate evidence for use in criminal trials. In practice, most legal bodies require that a certain technique is "generally accepted" by the scientific community before it is used as evidence in court. One problem with this requirement is determining who decides whether a technique is generally accepted or not. And if a new technique is used in court, its usefulness often depends on the ability of the judge and jury to understand it. Thus, extremely complex scientific or mathematical arguments tend to be limited in their usefulness.

The FBI and state and local crime labs are starting to establish banks of DNA fingerprints from convicted criminals. When samples are taken from crime scenes, they can be compared with those fingerprints in the bank to attempt to track down possible suspects. Opponents of such practices claim this kind of system can be abused.

Discussion

Encourage students to discuss the following question: How is DNA fingerprinting similar to traditional fingerprinting? How is it different? Accept all reasonable responses.

SCIENTIFICDEBATE

DNA on Trial

The tension in the courtroom was so thick you could cut it with a knife. The prosecuting attorney presented the evidence: "DNA analysis indicates that blood found on the defendant's shoes matches the blood of the victim. The odds of this match happening by chance are one in 20 million." The jury members were stunned by these figures. Can there be any doubt that the defendant is guilty?

Next Defendant: DNA

Court battles involving DNA fingerprinting are becoming more and more common. Traditional fingerprinting has been used for more than 100 years, and it has been an extremely important identification tool. Recently, many people have claimed that DNA fingerprinting, also called DNA profiling, will replace the traditional technique. The DNA profiling technique has been used to clear thousands of wrongly accused or convicted individuals. However, the controversy begins when the evidence is used to try to prove a suspect's guilt.

Room for Reasonable Doubt

Critics claim that the DNA fingerprinting process allows too much room for human error.

▲ *This forensic scientist is gathering dead skin cells from an article of clothing in hopes of collecting samples of DNA.*

Handling samples from a crime scene can be tricky—a sample may have been removed from a small area beneath a victim's fingernail or scraped off a dirty sidewalk. Contamination by salt, chemicals, denim, or even a lab person's sneeze can affect the accuracy of the results.

Much of the controversy about DNA fingerprinting surrounds the interpretation of the results. The question becomes, "How likely is it that someone else also has that same DNA profile?" Answers can range from one in three to one in 20 million, depending on the person doing the interpreting, the sample size, and the process used.

Critics also point out that the results may be calculated without regard for certain factors. For instance, individuals belonging to certain ethnic groups are likely to share more characteristics of their DNA with others in their group than with people outside the group.

Beyond a Reasonable Doubt

Those who support DNA evidence point out that the analysis is totally objective because the labs that do the DNA analysis receive samples labeled in code. The data either clear or incriminate a suspect. Moreover, DNA evidence alone is rarely used to convict a person. It is one of several forms of evidence, including motive and access to the crime scene, used to reach a verdict.

Supporters of DNA fingerprinting say that checks and balances in laboratories help prevent human errors. In addition, recent efforts to standardize both evidence gathering and interpretation of samples have further improved results.

What Do You Think?

▶ Should DNA fingerprinting be admitted as evidence in the courtroom? Do some additional research, and decide for yourself.

100

📶 internet**connect**

SCI*LINKS*
NSTA

TOPIC: DNA Fingerprinting
GO TO: www.scilinks.org
*sci*LINKS NUMBER: HSTL145

Answer to What Do You Think?
Accept all reasonable responses.

Science Fiction

"Moby James"
by Patricia A. McKillip

Rob Trask has a problem. It's his older brother, James. Rob is convinced that James is not his real brother. Rob and his family live on a space station, and he just knows that his real brother was sent back to Earth. This person who claims to be James is really either some sort of mutant, irradiated plant life or a mutant pair of dirty sweat socks.

Now Rob has another problem—his class is reading Herman Melville's novel *Moby Dick*. At first, Rob just can't get interested in the story. But as he reads more and more, Rob becomes entranced by the story of Captain Ahab and his quest for revenge against the great white whale Moby Dick. Moby Dick had taken something from Ahab—his leg—and Ahab wants to make the whale pay!

Suddenly Rob realizes that his brother is a great white mutant whale—Moby James. As Rob follows Ahab on his search for Moby Dick, Rob begins to understand what he must do to get his real brother back again. So he watches Moby James, trying to catch James in some mistake that will reveal him for the mutant he is. Once Rob catches the fake James, he will be able to get the real James back again.

To find out if Rob is successful in his quest to find his real brother, read "Moby James" in the *Holt Anthology of Science Fiction*.

101

Further Reading If students liked this story, encourage them to read more of Patricia McKillip's stories, such as the following:

Fool's Run, Warner, 1987

Something Rich and Strange, Bantam, 1994

Winter Rose, Ace, 1996

SCIENCE FICTION
"Moby James"
by Patricia A. McKillip

Rob's brother is changing—but into what? a mutant robot? an evil irradiated skunk cabbage? a great white mutant whale? Whatever it is, it's making Rob very nervous . . .

Teaching Strategy

Reading Level This is a relatively short story that should not be difficult for students to read and comprehend.

Background

About the Author Patricia Anne McKillip (1948–) began her career not as a writer, but as a storyteller. As the second of six children, she often found herself in charge of looking after her younger brothers and sisters. She can't remember exactly when she first began telling her siblings stories. She does remember, however, her first attempt at writing. At age 14 she wrote a 30-page fairy tale.

Today McKillip is a full-time writer of science fiction and fantasy. In 1975, she won the World Fantasy Award for her novel *The Forgotten Beasts of Eld.* A few years later she was nominated for a Hugo Award for *Harpist in the Wind.* McKillip has written a number of other novels, and her short stories have appeared in various periodicals, including the *Science Fiction and Fantasy Review*, the *Los Angeles Times*, and the *New York Times Book Review*.

Chapter Organizer

CHAPTER ORGANIZATION	TIME MINUTES	OBJECTIVES	LABS, INVESTIGATIONS, AND DEMONSTRATIONS
Chapter Opener pp. 102–103	45	National Standards: UCP 2, LS 5c	**Start-Up Activity,** Making a Fossil, p. 103
Section 1 Change Over Time	90	▶ Explain how fossils provide evidence that organisms have evolved over time. ▶ Identify three ways that organisms can be compared to support the theory of evolution. UCP 2–5, SAI 2, LS 2, 3a, 3d, 5a–5c; Labs UCP 2, SAI 1, HNS 2	**Design Your Own,** Mystery Footprints, p. 122 **Datasheets for LabBook,** Mystery Footprints
Section 2 How Does Evolution Happen?	90	▶ Describe the four steps of Darwin's theory of evolution by natural selection. ▶ Explain how mutations are important to evolution. UCP 2–5, SAI 1, 2, ST 2, SPSP 2, 5, HNS 1–3, LS 2c, 3a, 3d, 5b, 5c; Labs SAI 1, HNS 2, LS 5b	**Demonstration,** Form and Function, p. 113 in ATE **QuickLab,** Could We Run Out of Food? p. 115 **Design Your Own,** Survival of the Chocolates, p. 191 **Datasheets for LabBook,** Survival of the Chocolates
Section 3 Natural Selection in Action	90	▶ Give two examples of natural selection in action. ▶ Outline the process of speciation. UCP 2, 3, LS 2c, 3d, 5b; Labs UCP 2, SAI 1, HNS 2, LS 5b, 5c	**Demonstration,** Natural Selection, p. 118 in ATE **Discovery Lab,** Out-of-Sight Marshmallows, p. 190 **Datasheets for LabBook,** Out-of-Sight Marshmallows **Whiz-Bang Demonstrations,** Adaptation Behooves You **Long-Term Projects & Research Ideas,** Evolution's Explosion

See page **T23** *for a complete correlation of this book with the*

NATIONAL SCIENCE EDUCATION STANDARDS.

TECHNOLOGY RESOURCES

Guided Reading Audio CD English or Spanish, Chapter 5

One-Stop Planner CD-ROM with Test Generator

CNN. Multicultural Connections, A Thailand Fossil Discovery, Segment 4

Science, Technology & Society, Deciphering Dog DNA, Segment 10

CLASSROOM WORKSHEETS, TRANSPARENCIES, AND RESOURCES	SCIENCE INTEGRATION AND CONNECTIONS	REVIEW AND ASSESSMENT
Directed Reading Worksheet **Science Puzzlers, Twisters & Teasers**	**Multicultural Connection,** p. 103 in ATE	
Directed Reading Worksheet, Section 1 **Transparency 24,** Changes in Life Over Earth's History **Transparency 113,** A Sedimentary Rock Cycle **Transparency 25,** Comparative Skeletal Structures **Transparency 26,** Vertebrate Embryos	**Geology Connection,** p. 106 **Multicultural Connection,** p. 106 in ATE **Connect to Earth Science,** p. 106 in ATE **Math and More,** p. 107 in ATE **Cross-Disciplinary Focus,** p. 108 in ATE	**Homework,** p. 107 in ATE **Section Review,** p. 111 **Quiz,** p. 111 in ATE **Alternative Assessment,** p. 111 in ATE
Directed Reading Worksheet, Section 2 **Math Skills for Science Worksheet,** Multiplying Whole Numbers **Transparency 27,** Natural Selection in Four Steps **Reinforcement Worksheet,** Bicentennial Celebration	**Connect to Geography,** p. 113 in ATE **Apply,** p. 117 **Eye on the Environment:** Saving at the Seed Bank, p. 128	**Homework,** p. 116 in ATE **Section Review,** p. 117 **Quiz,** p. 117 in ATE **Alternative Assessment,** p. 117 in ATE
Directed Reading Worksheet, Section 3 **Transparency 28,** Evolution of the Galápagos Finches **Critical Thinking Worksheet,** Taking the Earth's Pulse	**Real-World Connection,** p. 119 in ATE **Holt Anthology of Science Fiction,** *The Anatomy Lesson*	**Self-Check,** p. 119 **Section Review,** p. 121 **Quiz,** p. 121 in ATE **Alternative Assessment,** p. 121 in ATE

internet connect

go.hrw.com
Holt, Rinehart and Winston
On-line Resources
go.hrw.com

For worksheets and other teaching aids related to this chapter, visit the HRW Web site and type in the keyword: **HSTEVO**

sciLINKS
NSTA
National Science
Teachers Association
www.scilinks.org

Encourage students to use the *sci*LINKS numbers listed in the internet connect boxes to access information and resources on the **NSTA** Web site.

END-OF-CHAPTER REVIEW AND ASSESSMENT

Chapter Review in Study Guide
Vocabulary and Notes in Study Guide
Chapter Tests with Performance-Based Assessment, Chapter 5 Test
Chapter Tests with Performance-Based Assessment, Performance-Based Assessment 5
Concept Mapping Transparency 7

Chapter Resources & Worksheets

Visual Resources

TEACHING TRANSPARENCIES

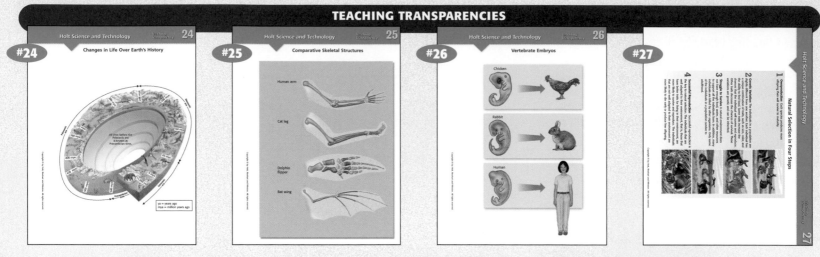

#24 — Changes in Life Over Earth's History

#25 — Comparative Skeletal Structures
- Human arm
- Cat leg
- Dolphin flipper
- Bat wing

#26 — Vertebrate Embryos
- Chicken
- Rabbit
- Human

#27 — Natural Selection in Four Steps

TEACHING TRANSPARENCIES

#28 — Evolution of the Galápagos Finches

#113 — A Sedimentary Rock Cycle
- Preexisting rock
- Weathering
- Sediment
- Erosion
- Deposition

LINK TO EARTH SCIENCE

CONCEPT MAPPING TRANSPARENCY

#7 — The Evolution of Living Things
Use the following terms to complete the concept map below: evolution, mutation, speciation, natural selection, survival

- can occur by
- which includes
- adaptation
- to ensure a species'

Meeting Individual Needs

DIRECTED READING

#5 — DIRECTED READING WORKSHEET
The Evolution of Living Things

Chapter Introduction
As you begin this chapter, answer the following.
1. Read the title of this chapter. List three things that you already know about this subject.

2. Write two questions about this subject that you would like answered by the time you finish this chapter.

Section 1: Change Over Time (p. 104)
3. Look at Figures 1–3 on this page. How does being bright red help the strawberry dart-poison frog survive?

Differences Among Organisms (p. 104)
6. Can strawberry dart-poison frogs mate with red-eyed tree frogs to produce offspring? Why or why not?

REINFORCEMENT & VOCABULARY REVIEW

#5 — REINFORCEMENT WORKSHEET
Bicentennial Celebration

Complete this worksheet after reading Chapter 8, Section 2.

Imagine that it is 2059—the 200th anniversary of the publication of Darwin's *On the Origin of Species*. You are a reporter for a science magazine that is publishing a special issue about evolutionary biology. Your assignment is to write an article about Darwin, his travels, and his scientific theory of evolution. Include details about the Galápagos finches and how Darwin first got the idea for his theory, and explain the steps in the process of natural selection. Don't forget to give your article an eye-catching headline!

#5 — VOCABULARY REVIEW WORKSHEET
Charles Darwin's Legacy

After you finish Chapter 6, give this puzzle a try!
Unscramble each of the words below, and write the word in the space provided.

1. SISEPCE — a group of organisms that mate to produce fertile offspring
2. SALAGGPAO — Darwin's tropical paradise
3. ASTRIT — passed on from parents to offspring
4. SVELETICE — _____ breeding has produced over 150 breeds of dogs.
5. TAPATIDONA — a change to survive in the existing environment
6. ALTRAUN — Successful reproduction is the fourth step of _____ selection.
7. GLEVITIAS — once-useful structures
8. SLOSFIS — solidified remains of organisms
9. MAUTONTI — a change in DNA

Now unscramble the circled letters to find Darwin's legacy.

SCIENCE PUZZLERS, TWISTERS & TEASERS

#5 — SCIENCE PUZZLERS, TWISTERS & TEASERS
The Evolution of Living Things

Double Trouble
1. Unscramble each of the words below and write it in the blanks. Then rearrange the boxed letters to solve the puzzle.
a. Charlie's canine ship — ABEEGL
b. Breeds only with its own kind — CEEISSP
c. Left over from a former life — AEGILSTV
d. Distinguishing quality — AIRTY
e. Dead, gone, and turned to stone — FILOSS
f. The cells' messenger — ADN
g. An unexpected change — AIMNOTTU
h. Selection done by nature — AALNRTU
i. Response to change — AAADINOPTT

Answer: _____
(Hint: the theory that holds modern biology together)

Word Circles
2. What is the word coiled inside each of these circles? Words can be spelled clockwise or counterclockwise.

a. _____ b. _____

Chapter 5 • The Evolution of Living Things

Review & Assessment

STUDY GUIDE

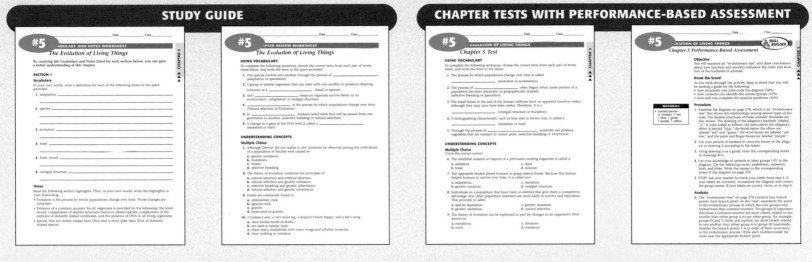

CHAPTER TESTS WITH PERFORMANCE-BASED ASSESSMENT

Lab Worksheets

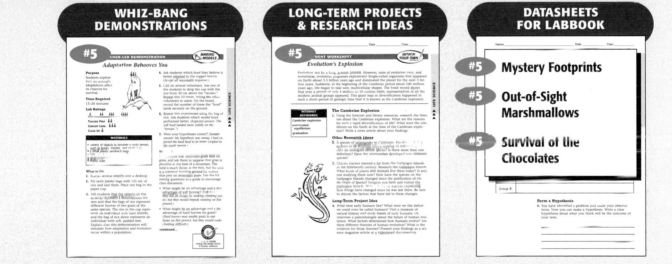

WHIZ-BANG DEMONSTRATIONS

LONG-TERM PROJECTS & RESEARCH IDEAS

DATASHEETS FOR LABBOOK

#5 **Mystery Footprints**

#5 **Out-of-Sight Marshmallows**

#5 **Survival of the Chocolates**

Applications & Extensions

CRITICAL THINKING & PROBLEM SOLVING

MULTICULTURAL CONNECTIONS

SCIENCE TECHNOLOGY

Change Over Time

▶ Homologous Versus Analogous Structures

Homologous structures have similar origins and exhibit similar anatomical patterns. Bird wings, human arms, whale flippers, and deer forelimbs, for example, are similar in skeletal structure.

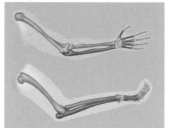

- In the early 1800s, French naturalist Etienne Geoffroy Saint-Hilaire studied embryos and recognized the importance of homologous structures for identifying evolutionary relationships among species.

- Today, scientists can study homologies among cellular components. Hemoglobin molecules from different vertebrate species have similar amino acid sequences and are therefore homologous. But hemocyanin, which transports oxygen in crabs, has a very different sequence and is analogous to hemoglobin; that is, the two molecules have a similar function but different structure.

- Bird wings and butterfly wings are another example of analogous structures.

▶ Convergent Evolution

When scientists study the fossils, skeletons, and DNA of species thought to be related, they sometimes find that the organisms are not related at all. For example, the jerboa and the kangaroo rat look almost identical, but they have different ancestors. Cases like this illustrate convergent evolution. The two species developed similar adaptations because they were subjected to the same environmental influences.

IS THAT A FACT!

- ◆ The human appendix is a vestigial organ. It's a narrow tube attached to the large intestine. It performs no function but can become infected and require surgical removal. In chimpanzees, gorillas, and orangutans the appendix is an intestinal sac that helps them digest tough plant material.

▶ Frozen Fossils

In some cases scientists can obtain DNA from ancient tissues that have not completely decomposed or fossilized. Two Japanese geneticists hope to create a mammoth-elephant hybrid by using frozen tissue from a Siberian mammoth. Critics of the project remain highly skeptical. The chances of finding intact DNA are remote, and the genetic structures of mammoths and elephants are not 100 percent compatible.

How Does Evolution Happen?

▶ Alfred Russel Wallace

Alfred Wallace (1823–1913) was born in England. He came from a poor family and had no formal scientific education. Though originally interested in botany, he began to study insects with the encouragement of British

naturalist Henry Walter Bates, whom he met when he was about 20 years old. Bates and Wallace explored the Amazon from 1848 to 1852 and found much evidence to support the theory of evolution.

- From 1854 to 1862 Wallace traveled in the Malay Archipelago to find more evidence of evolution. In 1855, he published a preliminary essay, "On the Law Which Has Regulated the Introduction of New Species."

Meanwhile, nearly 20 years after his voyage on the HMS *Beagle,* Charles Darwin was still mulling over his data. In 1858, Wallace mailed an essay to Darwin that explained Wallace's theory that natural selection pressures species to change.

- In July 1858, Wallace's essay was presented along with a paper by Darwin at a meeting of the Linnean Society in London. In the following year, after nearly two decades of delay (because of his doubts and repeated analysis of the data), Darwin published *On the Origin of Species by Means of Natural Selection*.

▶ Charles Lyell

Charles Lyell (1797–1875), the eldest of 10 children, was born in Scotland and raised in England. His father was a naturalist who traveled with him to collect butterflies and aquatic insects, informal research that Charles continued throughout college.

- Lyell's research led him to the belief that natural processes occurring over millions of years have shaped the Earth's features. This idea was known as uniformitarianism. Lyell's work influenced Darwin's formulation of his theory of natural selection. Darwin's proposed mechanism for evolution was plausible only if the Earth was ancient and if organisms had the requisite time for adaptation and change.

SECTION 3

Natural Selection in Action

▶ Adaptive Coloration

Penguins, puffins, killer whales, and blue sharks are just some of the ocean animals that have white bellies and black or dark blue dorsal surfaces. This type of coloration is called countershading. When seen from below, the white underside helps the animal blend into the lighter sky above the water. When viewed from above, the dark coloration makes the animal difficult to see against the ocean depths.

IS THAT A FACT!

- Ptarmigans (chickenlike birds), Arctic foxes, and ermines change their color twice a year! All three are white in winter to blend with the snow of their northern habitat. The ptarmigan is mottled brown in summer, the fox is grayish brown, and the ermine is white below and brown on top.

- Octopuses and squid can change their color in a second. They have special cells called chromatophores that enable them to blend in with different-colored rocks and varied light conditions.

▶ The Fruitful Fruit Fly

In the mid-1800s a fruit fly that parasitized the hawthorn tree and its fruit infested apple trees in the Hudson River Valley area of New York. During the past 150 years, the apple tree variety of these flies has spread across the United States. Biologists have observed that the flies that attack apple trees do not also infest the hawthorns. Recent DNA studies revealed that the two groups are becoming isolated genetically. Scientists have concluded that speciation is occurring in these flies.

- Since the first step in speciation is separation, how did this process begin? Scientists classify this example as sympatric speciation. The flies began specializing on new host plants without geographic isolation. Separate trees were the extent of their separation.

IS THAT A FACT!

- The largest flying bird that ever lived had a wing span of more than 7 m. It was a New World vulture, and its fossil was discovered in Argentina. These birds were known as teratorns.

For background information about teaching strategies and issues, refer to the *Professional Reference for Teachers.*

Pre-Reading Questions

Students may not know the answers to
these questions before reading the chapter, so accept any reasonable response.

Suggested Answers

1. Evolution is the process by which
   species change over time.

2. An organism's environment provides the selective pressures that
   enable some organisms to thrive
   and reproduce.

CHAPTER

5

The Evolution of Living Things

Sections

Pre-Reading
Questions

1. What is evolution?
2. What role does the
   environment play in the
   survival of an organism?

102

HIDDEN TREASURE

Can you see the fish in this picture? Look closer. The fish
are coral blennies, and they are hard to see against the
background of coral. Their coloring makes them likely to
live longer and to have more offspring than blennies that
don't blend in as well. In this chapter, you will learn how
some characteristics help organisms survive and reproduce.
You will also learn how these characteristics are passed
from parents to their offspring.

---

 internet**connect**

**HRW
On-line
Resources**

go.hrw.com

For worksheets and other
teaching aids, visit the HRW
Web site and type in the
keyword: **HSTEVO**

 **SCI LINKS**
NSTA

www.scilinks.com

Use the *sci*LINKS numbers
at the end of each chapter
for additional resources
on the **NSTA** Web site.

 **Smithsonian
Institution***

www.si.edu/hrw

Visit the Smithsonian
Institution Web site for
related on-line resources.

CNNfyi.com

www.cnnfyi.com

Visit the CNN Web site for
current events coverage
and classroom resources.

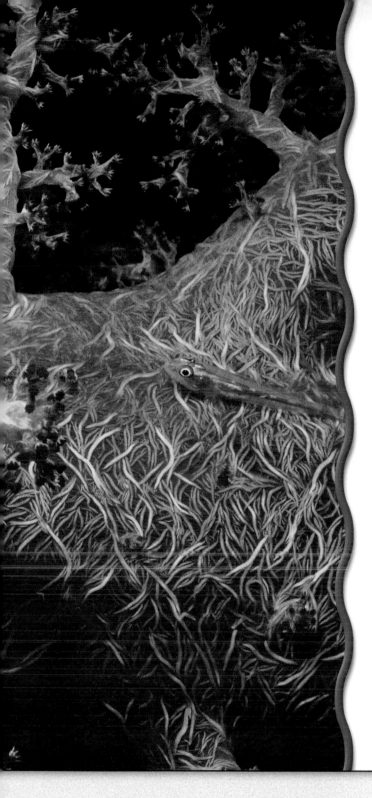

START-UP
Activity

MAKING A FOSSIL

In this activity, you will make a model of a fossil.

Procedure

1. Get a **paper plate,** some **modeling clay,** and a **leaf** or a **shell** from your teacher.

2. Flatten some of the modeling clay on the paper plate. Push the leaf or shell into the clay. Be sure that your leaf or shell has made a mark in the clay. Remove the leaf or shell carefully.

3. Ask your teacher to cover the clay completely with some **plaster of Paris.** Allow the plaster to dry overnight.

4. Carefully remove the paper plate and the clay from the plaster the next day.

Analysis

5. Which of the following do you think would make good fossils—a clam, a jellyfish, a crab, or a mushroom? Explain your answer.

6. Real fossils usually are formed when a dead organism is covered in tiny bits of sand or dirt. Oxygen cannot be present when fossils are forming. What are some limitations of your fossil model?

103

START-UP
Activity

MAKING A FOSSIL

MATERIALS
FOR EACH GROUP: • paper plate   • modeling clay   • leaf or shell   • plaster of Paris

Teacher's Notes

Some of the most famous fossilized molds are in the Laetoli region of northern Tanzania, in East Africa. In 1976, a paleontologist working with archaeologist Mary Leakey discovered thousands of animal tracks. Two years later, a team discovered human footprints. These tracks were made about 3.6 million years ago. After ash from a nearby volcano was dampened by rain, elephants, giraffes, people, and some now-extinct mammals walked across this area. Ash from another eruption of the volcano in turn covered the tracks and fossilized them.

Answers to START-UP Activity

5. The crab and clam will make the best fossils because they have hard body parts that decay slowly and leave impressions. The softer organisms—the jellyfish and mushroom—are less likely to make impressions in the sediment, and so they are less likely to make fossils.

6. This model does not show why the formation of fossils requires tiny sediment and lack of oxygen.

Focus

Change Over Time

This section introduces students to the theory of evolution. They will see how organisms change at the population level through adaptations. Students will learn about the evidence of evolution, including the fossil record and comparisons of organisms' physical structures, DNA, and embryonic structures.

Bellringer

Have the following information displayed on the chalkboard or an overhead projector when students enter:

The cockroach originated on Earth more than 250 million years ago and is thriving today all over the world. A giant deer that stood 2.1 m and had antlers up to 3.6 m evolved less than one million years ago and became extinct around 11,000 years ago.

Why do you think one animal thrived and the other perished? (Accept all reasonable answers.)

Directed Reading Worksheet Section 1

Terms to Learn

adaptation
species
evolution
fossil

fossil record
vestigial structure

What You'll Do

◆ Explain how fossils provide evidence that organisms have evolved over time.
◆ Identify three ways that organisms can be compared to support the theory of evolution.

BRAIN FOOD

Native tribes in Central America rub the poison from the strawberry dart-poison frog on their arrow tips before hunting. The poison helps to paralyze their prey.

104

Change Over Time

If someone asked you to describe a frog, you might say that a frog has long hind legs, eyes that bulge, and a habit of croaking from time to time. Then you might start to think about some of the differences among frogs—differences that set one kind of frog apart from another. Take a look at **Figures 1, 2,** and **3** on this page. These frogs look different from each other, yet they all inhabit a tropical rain forest.

Figure 1 *The red-eyed tree frog hides among a tree's leaves during the day and comes out at night.*

Figure 2 *The smoky jungle frog blends into the forest floor.*

Figure 3 *The strawberry dart-poison frog's bright coloring warns predators that it is poisonous.*

Differences Among Organisms

As you can see, these three frogs have different adaptations that enable them to survive. An **adaptation** is a characteristic that helps an organism survive and reproduce in its environment. Adaptations can include structures and behaviors for finding food, for protection, and for moving from place to place.

Living things that share the same characteristics and adaptations may be members of the same species. A **species** is a group of organisms that can mate with one another to produce fertile offspring. For example, all red-eyed tree frogs are members of the same species and can mate with one another to produce more red-eyed tree frogs.

WEIRD SCIENCE

The gastric brooding frogs of Australia, now extinct, incubated their tadpoles in their stomachs and gave birth to their young through their mouths!

Do Species Change over Time? These frogs are just a few of the millions of different species that share the Earth with us. The species on Earth today range from bacteria that lack cell nuclei to multicellular fungi, plants, and animals. Have these same species always existed on Earth?

Earth is a very old planet. Scientists estimate that it is 4.6 billion years old. The planet itself has changed a great deal during that long period of time. Fossil evidence shows that living things have changed as well. Since life first appeared on Earth, a great number of species have died out and have been replaced by newer species. **Figure 4** shows some of the different life-forms that have existed during Earth's history.

What causes species to change? Scientists think that newer species have descended from older species through the process of evolution. **Evolution** is the process by which populations accumulate inherited changes over time. Because of evolution, scientists think that all living things, from daisies to crocodiles to humans, share a common ancestor.

Figure 4 *This spiral diagram represents many changes in life on Earth since the formation of the planet 4.6 billion years ago.*

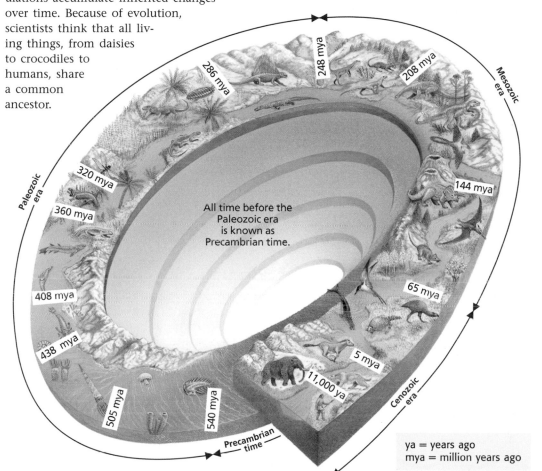

All time before the Paleozoic era is known as Precambrian time.

Paleozoic era
286 mya
320 mya
360 mya
408 mya
438 mya
505 mya
540 mya
Precambrian time

248 mya
208 mya
Mesozoic era
144 mya
65 mya
5 mya
11,000 ya
Cenozoic era

ya = years ago
mya = million years ago

IS THAT A FACT!

There are more than 100,000 living mollusk species, and at least 35,000 extinct forms are known from the fossil record. As a group, mollusks are very successful—there have been mollusks on Earth for nearly 600 million years.

1 Motivate

DISCUSSION

Adaptation Ask students if a polar bear could live comfortably in Hawaii. Ask if a fish could survive in a forest. Why or why not? Help students understand that each animal has characteristics that make it well-suited for its home environment. The polar bear has a thick layer of fat and dense fur to keep it warm. The fish's gills allow it to obtain oxygen from water. These are physical adaptations to specific environments.

2 Teach

USING THE FIGURE

Direct students to review **Figure 4** and explain why there are more fossils from the Cenozoic era than the earlier eras. (Sample answer: Fossils from earlier eras are usually deeper in the Earth and harder to find.)

Ask students how they think changes in the planet could have affected the appearance and disappearance of various life-forms over time. (Sample answer: Temperature fluctuations due to ice ages and other climactic changes would have affected which plants and animals could survive. Climate changes caused changes in the vegetation and in the availability of food for animals. Until the planet was able to support a lot of vegetation, there wouldn't have been much food for animals to eat.)

 Teaching Transparency 24 "Changes in Life over Earth's History"

Multicultural CONNECTION

Mary Anning (1799–1847) made some of the most important fossil discoveries of her time. She was born in Lyme Regis, in southern Great Britain, an area with many fossils. Her father, a cabinetmaker and amateur fossil collector, died when Mary was 11 years old, leaving the family in debt. Mary's fossil-finding skills provided the family with needed income. Even before she reached her teens, Mary had discovered part of the first *Ichthyosaurus* to be recognized by scientists in London. In the early 1820s, a professional fossil collector sold his private collection and gave the proceeds to the Anning family. He recognized that they had contributed many specimens for scientific investigation. Soon after, Mary took charge of the family fossil business. She later discovered the first plesiosaur. However, many of Mary Anning's finds ended up uncredited. Many scientists could not accept that a person of her financial and educational background could have acquired such expertise.

CONNECT TO EARTH SCIENCE

Using sedimentary layers as reference points, scientists can find the relative age of a fossil. Use Teaching Transparency 113, "A Sedimentary Rock Cycle," to illustrate the sedimentary rock cycle.

Teaching Transparency 113 "A Sedimentary Rock Cycle"
LINK TO EARTH SCIENCE

BRAIN FOOD

To date, scientists have described and named about 300,000 fossil species.

Geology CONNECTION

Fossils are usually found in layered rock called sedimentary rock. Sedimentary rock usually forms when rock is broken into sediment by wind, water, and other means. The wind and water move the sediment around and deposit it. Over time, layers of sediment pile up. Lower layers are compressed and changed into rock.

Evidence of Evolution: The Fossil Record

Evidence that living things evolve comes from many different sources. This evidence includes fossils as well as comparisons among different groups of organisms.

Fossils The Earth's crust is arranged in layers, with different kinds of rock and soil stacked on top of one another. These layers are formed when sediments, particles of sand, dust, or soil are carried by wind and water and are deposited in an orderly fashion. Older layers are deposited before newer layers and are buried deeper within the Earth. **Fossils,** the solidified remains or imprints of once-living organisms, are found in these layers. Fossils, like those pictured in **Figure 5,** can be of complete organisms, parts of organisms, or just a set of footprints.

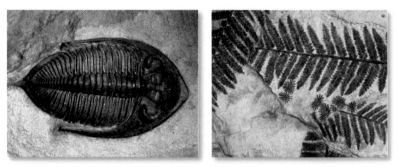

Figure 5 *The fossil on the left is of a trilobite, an ancient aquatic animal. The fossils on the right are of seed ferns.*

Fossils are usually formed when a dead organism is covered by a layer of sediment. Over time, more sediment settles on top of the organism. Minerals in the sediment may seep into the organism, gradually replacing the organism with stone. Or the organism may rot away completely after being covered, leaving a hole in the rock called a *mold*.

Reading the Fossil Record Fossils provide a historical sequence of life known as the **fossil record.** The fossil record supplies evidence about the order in which evolutionary changes have occurred. Fossils found in the upper, or newer, layers of the Earth's crust tend to resemble present-day organisms. This similarity indicates that the fossilized organisms were close relatives of present-day organisms. The deeper in the Earth's crust fossils are found, the less they tend to look like present-day organisms. These fossils are of earlier forms of life that may now be extinct.

106

internet connect

SCI LINKS
NSTA

TOPIC: The Fossil Record
GO TO: www.scilinks.org
*sci*LINKS NUMBER: HSTL160

Gaps in the Fossil Record If every organism that lived left an imprint behind, the fossil record would resemble a very large evolutionary family tree. **Figure 6** shows a hypothetical fossil record in which all relationships between organisms are clearly mapped.

Although scientists have collected thousands of fossils, gaps remain in the current fossil record, as shown in **Figure 7.** This is because specific conditions are necessary for fossils to form. The organism must be buried in very fine sediment. Also, oxygen—which promotes decay—cannot be present. However, very few places are free of oxygen. Because the conditions needed for fossils to form are rare, fossils are often difficult to find. Nevertheless, scientists have identified some fossils that complete sections of the fossil record.

Vestigial Structures Whales are similar in shape to fish. Yet whales are *mammals*—animals that breathe air, give birth to live young, and produce milk. Although modern whales do not have hind limbs, there are remnants of hind-limb bones inside their bodies, as shown in **Figure 8.** These remnants of once-useful structures are known as **vestigial** (ves TIJ ee uhl) **structures.** Scientists think that over millions of years, whales evolved from doglike land dwellers into sea-dwelling organisms. But scientists have not had the fossil evidence to support their ideas—until now. Read the following case study to learn the story of whale evolution.

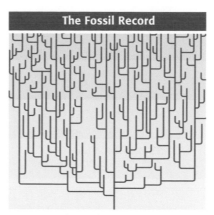

The Fossil Record

Figure 6 *This is the way the fossil record might appear if fossils from every species had been found.*

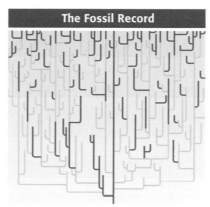

The Fossil Record

Figure 7 *This diagram illustrates the many gaps in the existing fossil record.*

Figure 8 *Remnants of hind-limb bones are embedded deep inside the whale's body.*

107

IS THAT A FACT!

Indricotherium, a giant land mammal that was about 4 m tall and was up to 6 m long, lived in Asia between 18 million and 32 million years ago.

MATH and MORE

Say to students: Imagine that you are a scientific time traveler assigned to count the life-forms in what will become your home state 1 million years from now. You know that at present your home state contains 1,200 insect species, 550 animal species, and 600 plant species. Only 24 percent of these species are expected to survive the next million years. How many species existing now should you expect to find in 1 million years?
(insects: $1{,}200 \times 0.24 = 288$
animals: $550 \times 0.24 = 132$
plants: $600 \times 0.24 = 144$)

Homework

Writing **Research the Horse** Have students check additional resources to find the four main ancestors of the horse as revealed through the fossil record. (*Eohippus, Mesohippus, Merychippus, Pliohippus*)

Ask students to make a poster that shows each ancestral horse in order of appearance and to write a paragraph about each one explaining its unique physical characteristics. Students should conclude their reports by answering the following question:

Are the wild horses in North America direct descendants of fossil horses found on this continent? (No; the fossil record shows that horses native to North America disappeared. Today's wild horses are descendants of horses introduced to this continent by Spanish explorers in the early 1500s.)

CROSS-DISCIPLINARY FOCUS

Art The role of a scientific illustrator is to make accurate pictures of organisms and things that scientists study. In the case of long-extinct species, such as dinosaurs, artists must sometimes fill in where science leaves off. Have students look for examples of illustrations of extinct animals and compare them with other illustrations of the same animal. Have students try to identify areas where artistic interpretation is used. You may wish to provide students with examples of similar illustrations from hundreds of years ago, when much less was known about these animals.
Sheltered English

ACTIVITY

Making Posters
Have students create pictures of their own imaginary animal that is evolving from an ocean-dwelling species into a terrestrial one. Tell them to draw at least three stages of the progression and to label each significant body part with a description of how the animals of that species use that part. Sheltered English

---

internetconnect

SCiLINKS
NSTA

TOPIC: Species and Adaptation
GO TO: www.scilinks.org
*sci*LINKS **NUMBER:** HSTL155

Case Study: Evolution of the Whale

Scientists hypothesize that whales evolved from land-dwelling mammals like *Mesonychid* (muh ZOH ni kid), shown below, which returned to the ocean about 55 million years ago. During the 1980s and 1990s, several fossils of whale ancestors were discovered. These discoveries support a theory of whale evolution.

55 million years ago
Mesonychid

Ambulocetus (AM byoo loh SEE tuhs), pictured below, lived in coastal waters. *Ambulocetus* had shorter legs than *Mesonychid*, but it still had feet and toes that could support its weight on land. Although *Ambulocetus* had a tail, scientists think it kicked its legs like an otter in order to swim and used its tail for balance.

50 million years ago
Ambulocetus

108

WEIRD SCIENCE

In 1938, some fishermen caught a live coelacanth, a primitive type of fish that was thought to have been extinct for about 65 million years.

46 million years ago
Rodhocetus

Forty-six million years ago, *Rodhocetus* (roh doh SEE tuhs) appeared in the fossil record. This animal more closely resembled modern whales, but it had hind limbs and feet that it retained from its land-dwelling ancestor. Because of its short legs, *Rodhocetus* was restricted to a crocodile-like waddle while on land. Unlike the legs of *Ambulocetus*, these legs were not necessary for swimming. Instead, *Rodhocetus* depended on its massive tail to propel it through the water. While *Ambulocetus* probably pulled itself onto land every night, *Rodhocetus* probably spent most of its time in the water.

Prozeuglodon (pro ZOO gloh dahn), which appeared in the fossil record 6 million years after *Rodhocetus*, was well adapted for life at sea. Although it still had a pair of very small legs, *Prozeuglodon* lived only in the water.

BRAIN FOOD

During their early development, modern whale embryos have four limbs. The rear limbs disappear before birth, and the front limbs develop into flippers.

40 million years ago
Prozeuglodon

109

IS THAT A FACT!
Baby blue whales can weigh 9,000 kg (about 20,000 lb) at birth.

DISCUSSION

Inland Whales Explain to students that in 1849 workers constructing a railroad near the town of Charlotte, Vermont, discovered bones that were later identified as those of a beluga whale. Ask students to locate Charlotte on a map and explain why this discovery is so unusual. (It is more than 150 miles from the nearest ocean.)

Ask students what these bones tell us about the history of the land around Charlotte. (It used to be part of an ocean.)

Explain that the Champlain Sea, an extension of the ocean, existed for 2,500 years after the last glaciers retreated 12,500 years ago.

MISCONCEPTION ALERT

It is easy for students to confuse adaptation with acclimation or intentional change or adjustment. For example, a student might write that over many years, a species learned to adapt to its new environment. Explain to students that adaptation is something that happens to a species over many generations and not an activity that a species learns or chooses to do.

Acclimation is an adjustment to a condition that is within an organism's range of tolerance, such as seasonal adjustment to climate changes. This, too, is a part of an organism's evolutionary adaptations and is not something it learns to do.

3 Extend

Over the years, some bacteria have become resistant to antibiotics that doctors use to treat or prevent diseases. Some scientists suggest that as bacteria become more and more resistant, people will be increasingly susceptible to microbes that cannot be stopped. Scientists are concerned that by using antibiotics, we are creating a larger problem for the future.

RESEARCH

Writing Scientists study animal skeletons and DNA to determine evolutionary relationships and development because merely looking at the outward appearance of a species can be misleading. The giant panda and red panda illustrate this problem. Their common names indicate that the two pandas seem closely related, but scientists now believe that the red panda is the only member of the subfamily Ailurinae of the raccoon family Procyonidae, which is quite separate from the giant panda. Have students investigate and write a report based on recent studies on the classification of these two pandas.

Teaching Transparency 25 "Comparative Skeletal Structures"

Evidence of Evolution: Comparing Organisms

Evidence that life has evolved also comes from comparisons of different groups of organisms. On the following pages, the different kinds of evidence that support the theory of evolution are discussed in greater detail.

Human arm

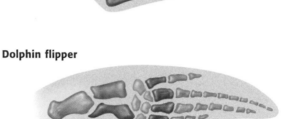

Cat leg

Dolphin flipper

Bat wing

Figure 9 *The bones in the front limbs of these animals are similar, even though the limbs are used in different ways. Similar bones are shown in the same color.*

110

Comparing Skeletal Structures What does your arm have in common with the front leg of a cat, the front flipper of a dolphin, or the wing of a bat? At first glance, you might think that they have little in common. After all, these structures don't look very much alike and are not used in the same way. If you look under the surface, however, the structure and order of the bones in the front limbs of these different animals, shown in **Figure 9,** are actually similar to the structure and order of the bones found in your arm.

The similarities indicate that animals as different as a cat, a dolphin, a bat, and a human are all related by a common ancestor. The evolutionary process has modified these bones over millions of years to perform specific functions.

Comparing DNA from Different Species Scientists hypothesize that if all organisms living today evolved from a common ancestor, they should all have the same kind of genetic material. And in fact they do. From microscopic bacteria to giant polar bears, all organisms share the same genetic material—DNA.

In addition, scientists hypothesize that species appearing to be close relatives should have greater similarities in their DNA than species appearing to be distant relatives. For example, chimpanzees and gorillas appear to be close relatives. Chimpanzees and toucans appear to be distant relatives. The DNA of chimpanzees is, in fact, more similar to the DNA of gorillas than to the DNA of toucans.

WEIRD SCIENCE

It seems as though the knee joints of birds bend backward, but they bend just like a human's knees. Birds walk on their toes. The long bone just above the toes is the foot! The first big joint above that (the one people often think is the knee) is actually a bird's ankle.

Comparing Embryonic Structures Can you tell the difference between a chicken, a rabbit, and a human? It's pretty easy when you compare adults from each species. But what about comparing members of these species before they are born? Look at the left side of **Figure 10,** which depicts the very early embryos of a chicken, a rabbit, and a human.

All the organisms shown in the figure are *vertebrates*, or animals that have a backbone. Early in development, human embryos and the embryos of all other vertebrates are similar. These early similarities are evidence that all vertebrates share a common ancestor. Although the embryos look similar to each other in very early stages, none of them look like their adult forms. Embryo development has evolved over millions of years, causing the embryonic structures to grow into many different species of vertebrates. The changes in the process of embryo development therefore produce animals as different as a chicken and a human.

Chicken

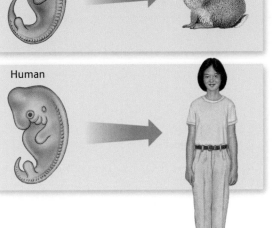
Rabbit

Human

Figure 10 *The embryos of different vertebrates are very similar during the earliest stages of development.*

SECTION REVIEW

1. How does the fossil record suggest that species have changed over time?

2. How do the similarities in the fore-limb bones of humans, cats, dolphins, and bats support the theory of evolution?

3. **Interpreting Graphics** The photograph at right shows the layers of sedimentary rock exposed during the construction of a road. Imagine that a species which lived 200 million years ago is found in the layer designated as **b.** Its ancestor, which lived 250 million years ago, would most likely be found in which layer, **a** or **c**? Explain your answer.

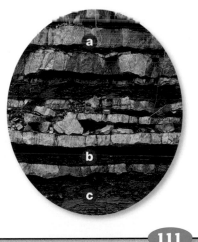

111

Quiz

1. Use the words *adaptations, population,* and *evolution* together in a sentence. (Sample answer: Evolution is the process by which a population accumulates inherited adaptations over time.)

2. List two reasons why gaps exist in the fossil record. (Fossilization requires precise and sometimes rare conditions, including the absence of oxygen and burial in very fine sediment.)

ALTERNATIVE ASSESSMENT

Writing | Charles Darwin's journals contain notes and records from his travels. Ask students to imagine that they are traveling with Darwin and keeping their own journals. Their notes and drawings should reflect what they see, the questions that arise from their observations, and the hypotheses that they form. Encourage students to write journal entries about other animals on the Galápagos Islands besides the finches, such as the Galápagos tortoise and marine iguanas.

MISCONCEPTION //ALERT

Explain to students that the embryonic figures shown in **Figure 10** are not all at the same stage of development. The similarities are fleeting, but they are shown here to indicate that the vertebrate body plan is evident in early development.

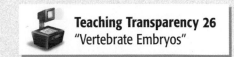
Teaching Transparency 26 "Vertebrate Embryos"

Answers to Section Review

1. Fossils provide a historical sequence of life. The fossils found in the upper, or newer, layers of the Earth's crust tend to resemble present-day organisms. The deeper in the Earth's crust fossils are found, the less they look like present-day organisms; these are fossils of earlier forms of life that are now extinct.

2. The similarities indicate that animals as different as a cat, a dolphin, a bat, and a human are all descendants of a common ancestor. They have been modified over millions of years to perform different functions.

3. c

Focus

How Does Evolution Happen?

This section introduces students to Charles Darwin and his voyage to the Galápagos Islands. Students will learn how artificial selection, geology, and the writings of Thomas Malthus and Charles Lyell helped Darwin formulate his theory of natural selection. Finally, students will learn that twentieth-century biologists used their knowledge of genetics to explain that species change through genetic mutation.

Bellringer

On the board or on an overhead projector write the following list:

upright walking, hair, fingerprints, binocular vision, speech

These are traits that almost all humans have in common. Ask students to list the advantages and disadvantages of each trait.

1 Motivate

DISCUSSION

Dinosaurs Ask students to describe a dinosaur. Ask them to explain why there are no dinosaurs alive today. Ask them, finally, if they think dinosaurs became extinct because they were not "evolved" enough to survive until the present. (Explain that dinosaurs were well adapted to their environment and lived over 150 million years on Earth. But a catastrophic event changed the environment faster than the dinosaurs could adapt, and they became extinct.)

Terms to Learn

trait
selective breeding
natural selection
mutation

What You'll Do

◆ Describe the four steps of Darwin's theory of evolution by natural selection.
◆ Explain how mutations are important to evolution.

How Does Evolution Happen?

The early 1800s was a time of great scientific discovery. Geologists realized that the Earth is much older than anyone had previously thought. Evidence showed that gradual processes had shaped the Earth's surface over millions of years. Fossilized remains of bizarre organisms were found. Fossils of familiar things were also found, but some of them were in unusual places. For example, fish fossils and shells were found on the tops of mountains. The Earth suddenly seemed to be a place where great change was possible. Many people thought that evolution occurs, but no one had been able to determine *how* it happens—until Charles Darwin.

Charles Darwin

In 1831, 21-year-old Charles Darwin, shown in **Figure 11,** had just graduated from college. Like many young people just out of college, Darwin didn't know what he wanted to do with his life. His father wanted him to become a doctor. However, Darwin was sickened by watching surgery. Although he eventually earned a degree in theology, he was *really* interested in the study of plants and animals.

Darwin was able to talk his father into letting him sign on for a 5-year voyage around the world. He served as the naturalist (a scientist who studies nature) on a British naval ship, the HMS *Beagle*. During this voyage, Darwin made observations that later became the foundation for his theory of evolution by natural selection.

Figure 11 *Charles Darwin, shown at far left, sailed around the world on a ship very similar to this one.*

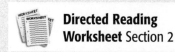
Directed Reading Worksheet Section 2

internetconnect

SCiLINKS
NSTA
TOPIC: The Galápagos Islands
GO TO: www.scilinks.org
*sci*LINKS NUMBER: HSTL165

WEIRD SCIENCE

The tailbone in humans is a vestigial structure that is a remnant of the tails of ancestor species.

Darwin's Excellent Adventure

As the HMS *Beagle* made its way around the world, Darwin collected thousands of plant and animal samples and kept detailed notes of his observations. The *Beagle*'s journey is charted in **Figure 12.** During the journey, the ship visited the Galápagos Islands, shown below, which are 965 km (600 mi) west of Ecuador, a country in South America.

Darwin's Finches

Darwin observed that the animals and plants on the Galápagos Islands were very similar, yet not identical, to the animals and plants on the nearby South American mainland. For example, he noted that the finches living on the Galápagos Islands differed slightly from the finches in Ecuador. The finches on the islands were different not only from the mainland finches but also from each other. As you can see in **Figure 13,** the birds differed from each other mainly in the shape of their beaks and in the food they ate.

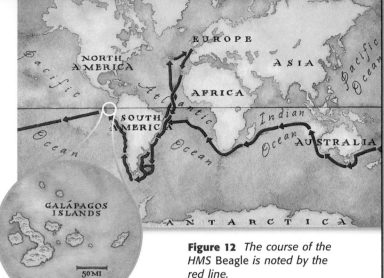

Figure 12 *The course of the HMS* Beagle *is noted by the red line.*

Figure 13 *The beaks of these three species of finches are adapted to the different ways the finches obtain food.*

The **large ground finch** has a heavy, strong beak adapted for cracking big, hard seeds. This finch's beak works like a nutcracker.

The **cactus finch** has a tough beak that is good for eating cactus and its nectar. It works like a pair of needle-nosed pliers.

The **warbler finch's** small, pointed beak is adapted for probing into cracks and crevices to obtain small insects. This beak works like a pair of tweezers.

113

IS THAT A FACT!

The giant tortoises of the Galápagos Islands weigh up to 270 kg and can live for over 150 years.

LabBook **PG 191**
Survival of the Chocolates

2 Teach

DEMONSTRATION

Form and Function Present and identify to students the following pieces of clothing:

> sneaker, dress pump, loafer, necktie, scarf, anklet, knee sock

Explain that all these items are pieces of clothing but some are more closely related than others. Within each group (shoes, neckwear, socks), every item is best suited for one particular function. This relationship of similarities and differences is what Charles Darwin observed in many animal and plant species.

MEETING INDIVIDUAL NEEDS

Writing **Advanced Learners** Encourage interested students to investigate Darwin's voyage and similar long-distance travel by explorers in the 1800s in greater detail. Topics for reports include the types of ships used for travel in that era, the kinds of food eaten by the explorers, and the sophistication and thoroughness of maps in the 1800s.

CONNECT TO GEOGRAPHY

The Galápagos Islands are administratively part of the country of Equador, though they are 1,000 km west of the mainland. They are a group of 19 volcanically formed islands. Though they have a land area of only 8,000 km², they are dispersed over almost 60,000 km² of the Pacific Ocean. It is easy to imagine how new species could arise in such a place.

2 Teach, continued

READING 📖 STRATEGY

Prediction Guide Before reading this page, have students answer the following questions:

- Why did the finches Darwin saw on the Galápagos Islands look similar to those he saw in South America?

- Why did they look a little different?

Have students evaluate their answers after they read the page.

MEETING INDIVIDUAL NEEDS

Writing **Advanced Learners**
Biogeography is the study of where animals and plants are found and how they came to live in their particular location. It uses information from the fossil record and integrates ideas from biology, geology, paleontology, and chemistry. Encourage interested students to write a report about island biogeography. Have them include information about how it is used to design and manage terrestrial wildlife refuges.

RETEACHING

Writing To help students understand the process of speciation, have them write a brief paragraph about each new term in this chapter. Each paragraph should begin with a definition. Then have students write sample sentences using the term.

Have you ever heard of a bank that has no money, only seeds? Read about it on page 128.

Darwin Does Some Thinking

Darwin's observations raised questions that he couldn't easily answer, such as, "Why are the finches on the islands similar but not identical to the finches on the mainland?" and "Why do the finches from different islands differ from one another?" Darwin thought that perhaps all the finches on the Galápagos Islands descended from finches on the South American mainland. The original population of finches may have been blown from South America to the Galápagos Islands by a storm. Over many generations, the finches that survived may have adapted to various ways of living on the Galápagos Islands.

After Darwin returned to England, he spent many years working on his theory of how evolution happens. During this period, he gathered many ideas from a variety of sources.

Darwin Learned from Farmers and Animal and Plant Breeders

In Darwin's time, many varieties of farm animals and plants had been selectively produced. Farmers chose certain **traits,** distinguishing qualities such as plump corn kernels, and bred only the individuals that had the desired traits. This procedure is called **selective breeding** because humans, not nature, select which traits will be passed along to the next generation. Selective breeding in dogs, shown in **Figure 14,** has exaggerated certain traits to produce more than 150 different breeds.

In your studies of genetics and heredity, you learned that a great variety of traits exists among individuals in a species. Darwin was impressed that farmers and breeders could direct and shape these traits and make such dramatic changes in animals and plants in just a few short generations. He thought that wild animals and plants could change in a similar way but that the process would take much longer because variations would be due to chance.

Ancestral Dog

Figure 14 *Dogs are a good example of how selective breeding works. Over the past 12,000 years, dogs have been selectively bred to produce more than 150 different breeds.*

114

IS THAT A FACT!

As a result of selective breeding, the smallest horse is the Falabella, which is only about 76 cm tall. The largest is the Shire, originally bred in England. It can grow more than 1.73 m high at the shoulder and weigh as much as 910 kg.

Darwin Learned from Geologists

Geologists told Darwin that they had evidence that the Earth was much older than anyone had imagined. He learned from reading *Principles of Geology*, by Charles Lyell, that Earth had been formed by natural processes over a long period of time. Lyell's data were important because Darwin thought that populations of organisms changed very slowly, requiring a lot of time.

Darwin Learned from the Work of Thomas Malthus In his *Essay on the Principle of Population*, Malthus proposed that humans have the potential to reproduce beyond the capacity of their food supplies. However, he also recognized that death caused by starvation, disease, and war affects the size of human populations. Malthus's thoughts are represented in **Figure 15.**

Darwin realized that other animal species are also capable of producing too many offspring. For these animal species, starvation, disease, and predators affect the size of their populations. Only a limited number survive to reproduce. Thus, there must be something special about the survivors. What traits make them better equipped to survive and reproduce? Darwin reasoned that the offspring of the survivors inherit traits that help them survive in their environment.

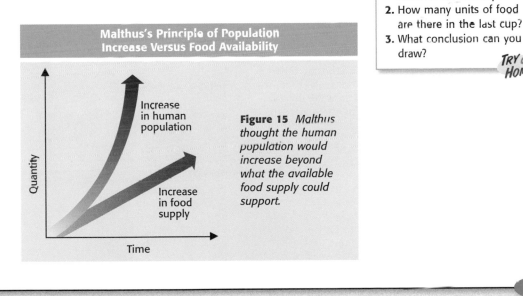

Malthus's Principle of Population Increase Versus Food Availability

Increase in human population

Increase in food supply

Quantity

Time

Figure 15 Malthus thought the human population would increase beyond what the available food supply could support.

QuickLab

Could We Run out of Food?

Malthus thought we could. Do the following activity to better understand Malthus's hypothesis. Get **2 empty egg cartons** and a **bag of rice.** Label one carton "Food supply" and the second carton "Population growth." In the food supply carton, place one grain of rice in the first cup. Increase the amount by one in each subsequent cup. Each grain represents a unit of food. In the population growth carton, place one grain of rice in the first cup, and double the number of grains of rice in each subsequent cup. This rice represents people.

1. How many "people" are there in the last cup?
2. How many units of food are there in the last cup?
3. What conclusion can you draw?

TRY at HOME

QuickLab

MATERIALS

FOR EACH STUDENT:
- 2 empty 12-egg cartons
- bag of rice

In a balanced system organisms interact so that there is maximum diversity, and population increase equals population decrease. The QuickLab demonstrates an unbalanced system. There is nothing to slow the rapid increase of the rice grain population.

Answers to QuickLab

1. There are 2,048 "people."
2. There are 12 grains of rice.
3. There is not enough food to support the population.

Students should work this out mathematically before each step. They should also divide the task of counting after the first 6 cups.

SCIENTISTS AT ODDS

Not all scientists who study evolution agree on how the process takes place. Gradualism, the theory that Darwin supported, is based on the principle that changes in species occur slowly and steadily over thousands of years. In the 1970s, Stephen Jay Gould and others proposed the theory of punctuated equilibrium, which holds that species can remain unchanged for millions of years and then, due to dramatic environmental changes, undergo relatively rapid changes. The fossil record provides evidence that supports both sides of this debate.

115

SCIENCE HUMOR

Q: How did the dinosaurs listen to music?

A: on their fossil records

Math Skills Worksheet "Multiplying Whole Numbers"

INDEPENDENT PRACTICE

Concept Mapping Have students make a concept map in their ScienceLog that outlines the process of change for a population of squirrels (each of which is black, red, grey, or white) marooned on a treeless island of black sand that is also home to squirrel-eating foxes.
Sheltered English

Homework

Poster Project Have students research the natural history and current status of sea turtles (or a specific sea turtle species) to find examples for each of the four steps of natural selection. Have them construct a display to present their findings. For example, cotton balls glued to the poster board can represent eggs, and a dark plastic bag can symbolize a polluted ocean. Present the following questions as guides for their research:

1. On average, how many offspring does a sea turtle produce each year?

2. What physical adaptations have helped sea turtles survive in their environment?

3. What specific environmental factors affect their ability to survive?

4. What natural and man-made factors may be affecting their ability to survive long enough to reproduce successfully?

Teaching Transparency 27
"Natural Selection in Four Steps"

Natural Selection

In 1858, about 20 years after he returned from his voyage on the HMS *Beagle*, Darwin received a letter from a naturalist named Alfred Russel Wallace. Wallace had independently arrived at the same theory of evolution that Darwin had been working on for so many years. Darwin and Wallace discussed their research and made plans to present their findings at a meeting later in the year. Then, in 1859, Darwin published his own results in his book called *On the Origin of Species by Means of Natural Selection.* Darwin theorized that evolution occurs through a process he called **natural selection.** This process, examined below, is divided into four parts.

Natural Selection in Four Steps

1 **Overproduction** Each species produces more offspring than will survive to maturity.

2 **Genetic Variation** The individuals in a population are slightly different from one another. Each individual has a unique combination of traits, such as size, color, and the ability to find food. Some traits increase the chances that the individual will survive and reproduce. Other traits decrease the chances of survival. These variations are genetic and can be inherited.

3 **Struggle to Survive** A natural environment does not have enough food, water, and other resources to support all the individuals born. In addition, many individuals are killed by other organisms. Only some of the individuals in a population survive to adulthood.

4 **Successful Reproduction** Successful reproduction is the key to natural selection. The individuals that are well adapted to their environment, that is, those that have better traits for living in their environment, are more likely to survive and reproduce. The individuals that are not well adapted to their environment are more likely to die early or produce few offspring.

116

IS THAT A FACT!

In 1809 French naturalist Jean Baptiste Lamarck's theory of evolution stated that if an animal changed a body part through use or nonuse, that change would be inherited by its offspring. For example, larger or stronger leg muscles as a result of extensive running would be passed on to the next generation. Genetic studies in the 1930s and 1940s, however, disproved Lamarck's mechanism for inherited traits.

APPLY

A Breed All Their Own

Imagine that your grandfather has owned a kennel for more than 50 years but has never sold a dog. He cares for the dogs and keeps them in one large pen. Originally there were six labs, six terriers, and six pointers. There are now 76 dogs, and you are surprised that only a few look like pointers, labs, and terriers. The other dogs look similar to each other but not

to any of the specific breeds. Your grandfather says that over the past 50 years each generation has looked less like the generation that preceded it.

By the time you visited the kennel, what may have happened to make most of the dogs look similar to each other but not to any specific original breed? Base your answer on what you've learned about selective breeding in this section.

More Evidence of Evolution

One of the observations on which Darwin based his theory of evolution by natural selection is that parents pass traits to their offspring. But Darwin did not know *how* inheritance occurs or *why* individuals vary within a population.

During the 1930s and 1940s, biologists combined the principles of genetic inheritance with Darwin's theory of evolution by natural selection. This combination of principles explained that the variations Darwin observed within a species are caused by **mutation,** or changes in a gene.

Since Darwin's time, new evidence has been collected from many fields of science. Although scientists recognize that other mechanisms may also play a part in the evolution of a species, the theory of evolution by natural selection provides the most thorough explanation for the diversity of life on Earth.

SECTION REVIEW

1. Why are some animals more likely to survive to adulthood than other animals?

2. **Summarizing Data** What did Darwin think happened to the first small population of finches that reached the Galápagos Islands from South America?

3. **Doing Calculations** A female cockroach can produce 80 offspring at a time. If half of the offspring were female, and each female produced 80 offspring, how many cockroaches would there be in 3 generations?

internet connect

SCILINKS
NSTA

TOPIC: The Galápagos Islands, Darwin and Natural Selection
GO TO: www.scilinks.org
*sci***LINKS NUMBER:** HSTL165, HSTL170

▼ **Answers to Section Review**

1. Sample answer: Some animals are more likely to survive because they inherit traits that enable them to find food, escape predators, or resist disease more effectively than other animals.

2. Darwin thought that the first population of finches on the Galápagos Islands

gave rise to all the different species of finches living there today.

3. The first generation = 80; 40 are female that produce 80 each. The second generation = 3,200; 1,600 are female that produce 80 each. There are 128,000 in the third generation.

---

4 Close

Answer to APPLY

The dogs were no longer being selectively bred for specific traits, so dogs with different traits were breeding together. After several generations, the dogs looked similar as the genetic mixing grew more complete.

Quiz

1. Who was Charles Lyell? (He was a British geologist.)

2. What did Darwin learn from Lyell's data about the age of Earth? (Darwin learned from Lyell that Earth was old enough for slow changes to happen in a population.)

ALTERNATIVE ASSESSMENT

Writing Locate the Rocky Mountains on a map. Explain to students that bird identification guides for North America usually classify birds into those that are east of the Rocky Mountains and those that are west of the Rocky Mountains. Have them write an explanation for why ornithologists use this system. Then tell students to research the differences and similarities of eastern and mountain bluebirds, or of blue jays and piñon jays.

Reinforcement Worksheet
"Bicentennial Celebration"

internet connect

SCILINKS
NSTA

TOPIC: Darwin and Natural Selection
GO TO: www.scilinks.org
*sci***LINKS NUMBER:** HSTL170

SECTION 3
READING WARM-UP

Focus

Natural Selection in Action

In this section students will learn that natural selection is occurring constantly and is not just a historical relic. They will learn how a species' generation time affects its ability to adapt. Finally, students will learn the three steps of speciation: separation, adaptation, and division.

Bellringer

Display on the board or the overhead projector these instructions to students:

Write the four steps of natural selection, and create a mnemonic device to remember each step by using the first letter of each step.

1 Motivate

DEMONSTRATION

Natural Selection Place 20 black jellybeans and 20 red jellybeans on a piece of black paper, and call the display *Generation 1.* Tell students to pretend the candies are fish and ask which would most likely be eaten first by the jellybean shark. Then add 5 black jellybeans and take away 5 red ones. Call this group *Generation 2.* Ask students how many fish in this generation might survive the jellybean shark. Have students offer explanations for what happened between *Generation 1* and *Generation 2.*

PG 190

Out-of-Sight Marshmallows

Directed Reading Worksheet Section 3

Terms to Learn

generation time
speciation

What You'll Do

◆ Give two examples of natural selection in action.
◆ Outline the process of speciation.

Natural Selection in Action

The theory of natural selection explains how a population changes over many generations in response to its environment. In fact, members of a population tend to be well adapted to their environment because natural selection is continuously taking place.

Insecticide Resistance To keep crops safe from certain insects, some farmers use a wide variety of chemical insecticides. However, some insecticides that worked well in the past are no longer as effective. In the 50 years that insecticides have been widely used, more than 500 species of insects have developed resistance to certain insecticides.

Insects quickly develop resistance to insecticides because they produce many offspring and usually have short generation times. A **generation time** is the period between the birth of one generation and the birth of the next generation. Look at **Figure 16** to see how a common household pest, the cockroach, has adapted to become resistant to certain insecticides.

1 An insecticide will kill most insects, but a few may survive. These survivors have genes that make them resistant to the insecticide.

2 The survivors then reproduce, passing the insecticide-resistance genes to their offspring.

3 In time, the replacement population of insects is made up mostly of individuals that have the insecticide-resistance genes.

4 When the same kind of insecticide is used on the insects, only a few are killed because most of them are resistant to that insecticide.

Figure 16 *Variety in a population's characteristics helps ensure that some individuals will be able to survive a change in the environment.*

We're off to hunt the marshmallows! Look on page 190 to find out why.

SCIENCE HUMOR

Q: What do you get when you cross a crocodile with an abalone?

A: a crocabaloney

Adaptation to Pollution There are two color variations among European peppered moths, as shown in **Figure 17.** Before 1850, the dark peppered moth was considered rare. The pale peppered moth was much more common. After the 1850s, however, dark peppered moths became more abundant in heavily industrialized areas.

Figure 17 *Against a dark tree trunk (above), the pale peppered moth stands out. Against a light tree trunk (right), the dark peppered moth stands out.*

What caused this change in the peppered moth population? Several species of birds eat peppered moths that rest on tree trunks. Before the 1850s, the trees had a gray appearance, and pale peppered moths blended into their surroundings. Dark peppered moths were easier for the birds to see and were eaten more frequently. After the 1850s, soot and smoke from newly developing industrial areas blackened nearby trees. The dark peppered moths became less visible on the dark tree trunks. The pale peppered moths stood out against the dark background and became easy prey for the birds. More dark moths survived and produced more dark offspring. Thus, the population changed from mostly light-colored moths to mostly dark-colored moths.

 **Self-Check**

If the air pollution in Europe were cleaned up, what do you think would happen to the population of light-colored peppered moths? *(See page 216 to check your answers.)*

119

2 Teach

READING 📖 STRATEGY

Activity After students read this page, have them draw pictures of hypothetical intermediate color variations for peppered moths in their ScienceLog. Tell them to write a caption for each picture that explains why that particular variation would have a better or worse chance for survival before 1850 and after 1850.
Sheltered English

REAL-WORLD CONNECTION

Natural Pest Control The use of natural predators against insect pests provides a safe alternative to insecticides. Ladybugs, for example, which are actually beetles, are purchased in large numbers and released on crops. They are used to combat infestations of aphids, whiteflies, fruit-worms, mites, the broccoli worm, and the tomato hornworm.

MAKING MODELS

Bat Houses One way to control mosquitoes is to encourage insect-eating bats to take up residence in your yard by hanging bat houses. Encourage students to research the design of a bat house and to construct one from cardboard. Interested students could use the model to build a bat house out of wood, hang it up outside, and see if bats move in.
Sheltered English

Answer to Self-Check

The population of light-colored moths would increase.

IS THAT A FACT!

The cecropia moth can measure over 15 cm (over 6 in) from wing tip to wing tip.

GOING FURTHER

Ask students if they can define *subspecies*. (A subspecies is a population within a species that is different enough to be given its own name.)

Because subspecies can breed with one another, all are still members of the same species. Then tell them that all seven subspecies of a particular salamander can be found in California. Each one gradually integrates into the next subspecies. But in two locations, two of the subspecies interbreed rarely if at all. Ask students if they should be considered different species. Why or why not? (They are not yet different species because they can still interbreed.)

Ask how they would research this question. Then tell them that early DNA studies indicate that the single salamander species is becoming two different species, possibly more.

SCIENTISTS AT ODDS

Scientists at the American Ornithologists' Union are responsible for the official list of scientific bird names used in the United States. They used to recognize the Eastern towhee and the spotted towhee. Then they decided to make them one species, the rufous-sided towhee. Then they changed their minds (based on further study) and "split" the classification again. Stay tuned.

Formation of New Species

The process of natural selection can explain how a species can evolve into a new species. A portion of a species' population can become separated from the original population. Over time, the two populations can become so different that they can no longer interbreed. This process is called **speciation.** One way that speciation can occur is shown in the following three steps:

1. Separation   The process of speciation often begins when a portion of a population becomes isolated. **Figure 18** shows some of the ways this can happen. A newly formed canyon, mountain range, and lake are a few of the ways that populations can be divided.

Figure 18 *Populations can become separated in a variety of ways.*

2. Adaptation   If a population has been divided by one of the changes illustrated above, the environment may also change. This is where natural selection comes in. As the environment changes, so may the population that lives there. Over many generations, the separated groups may adapt to better fit their environment, as shown in **Figure 19**. If the environmental conditions are different for each of the groups, the adaptations in the groups may also be different.

Figure 19 *When a single population becomes divided, the groups may evolve separately and may form separate species.*

120

IS THAT A FACT!

Some species that have adapted to live in total darkness no longer even have eyes! Just as whales have evolved into legless forms, these species have completely adapted to life without light, and some have evolved forms lacking eyes altogether. There are blind cave fish, eels, salamanders, worms, shrimp, crayfish, spiders, beetles, and crickets.

3. Division Over many hundreds, thousands, or even millions of generations, the two groups of a population may become so different that they can no longer interbreed, even if the geographical barrier is removed. At this point, the two groups are no longer the same species. Scientists think that the finches on the Galápagos Islands evolved by these three basic steps. **Figure 20** illustrates how this might have happened.

Figure 20 *The finches on the Galápagos Islands might have evolved into different species by the process depicted below.*

1 Some finches left the mainland and reached one of the islands (separation).

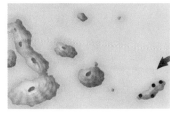

2 The finches reproduced and adapted to the environment (adaptation).

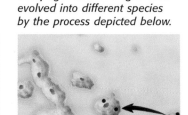

3 Some finches flew to a second island (separation).

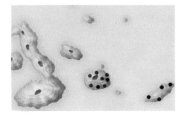

4 The finches reproduced and adapted to the different environment (adaptation).

5 Some finches flew back to the first island but could no longer interbreed with the finches there (division)

6 This process may have occurred over and over again as the finches flew to the other islands.

SECTION REVIEW

1. Why did the number of dark peppered moths increase after the 1850s?

2. What factor indicates that a population has evolved into two separate species?

3. **Applying Concepts** Most cactuses have spines, which are leaves modified to protect the plant. The spines cover a juicy stem that stores water. Explain how cactus leaves and stems might have changed through the process of natural selection.

internet**connect**

sciLINKS.
NSTA

TOPIC: Species and Adaptation
GO TO: www.scilinks.org
*sci***LINKS NUMBER:** HSTL155

DEBATE

People and Nature During the past several hundred years, a rapidly expanding human population has caused some species to become extinct either from habitat destruction or overhunting. Ask:

> If people are as much a part of the environment as trees and birds, are their actions just another natural process?

4 **Close**

Quiz

Concept Mapping Construct a concept map that shows how a population of mosquitoes can develop resistance to a pesticide.

ALTERNATIVE ASSESSMENT

Have each student research and give an oral presentation on how the three steps of speciation (separation, adaptation, and division) worked in providing a particular animal with a distinctive feature. For example, a student interested in giraffes might investigate how it came to have a long neck.

Teaching Transparency 28 "Evolution of the Galápagos Finches"

Critical Thinking Worksheet "Taking the Earth's Pulse"

▼ *Answers to Section Review*

1. After the 1850s, soot and smoke from industrial areas blackened nearby trees. The dark peppered moths became less visible than the pale peppered moths on the dark tree trunks. More dark moths survived predation on the dark tree trunks and produced more dark offspring.

2. Over time, two groups of a population may become so different that they can no longer interbreed. At this point, they are no longer the same species.

3. The changes in a cactus's leaves help protect the plant and conserve water, and the stem stores water. In each generation, as plants with sharper leaves and larger stems thrived in the harsh climate, these features became more prevalent and defined in their offspring, which survived and reproduced.

Mystery Footprints
Teacher's Notes

Time Required

Two 45-minute class periods

Lab Ratings

EASY ——————→ HARD

TEACHER PREP 🧪🧪🧪
STUDENT SET-UP 🧪🧪
CONCEPT LEVEL 🧪🧪
CLEAN UP 🧪

Preparation Notes

To set up this lab, you will need to either construct a long, shallow sandbox out of wood or cardboard for use indoors or find (or build) a sandy area outside. Ask a boy and a girl (preferably students who are not in your science class) or two adults, one male and one female, to walk through the sand with their bare feet. The sand should be about 16 cm deep, and the area they walk through should be long enough that three or four footprints can be seen in the sand. Of course, you may want to make the footprints more permanent by using plaster-of-Paris. If you do not have access to sand, soil that will hold a footprint will substitute for sand nicely.

Maurine Marchani
Raymond Park Middle School
Indianapolis, Indiana

Design Your Own Lab

USING SCIENTIFIC
METHODS

Mystery Footprints

Sometimes scientists find evidence of past life in clues preserved in rocks. Evidence such as preserved footprints can give important information about an organism. Imagine that your class has been asked by a group of scientists to help study some footprints. These footprints were found in rocks just outside of town.

MATERIALS

- large box of damp sand, at least 1 m² (large enough to hold three or four footprints)
- metric ruler or meterstick

Form a Hypothesis

1. Your teacher will give you some mystery footprints in sand. Study the footprints. Brainstorm ideas about what you might learn about the people who walked on this patch of sand. As a class, formulate as many testable hypotheses as possible about the people who left the footprints.

2. Form groups of three people, and choose one hypothesis for your group to investigate.

Test the Hypothesis

3. Use a computer or graph paper to construct a table for organizing your data. If your hypothesis is that the footprints were made by two adult males who were walking in a hurry, your table might look like the one below.

Mystery Footprints		
	Footprint set 1	**Footprint set 2**
Length		
Width		
Depth of toe		
Depth of heel		
Length of stride		

DO NOT WRITE IN BOOK

122

4 You may first want to look at your own footprints to help you draw conclusions about the mystery footprints. For example, with the help of your group, use a meterstick to measure your stride when you are running. How long is it when you are walking? Does your weight affect the depth of the footprint? What part of your foot touches the ground first when you are running? What part touches the ground first when you are walking? When you are running, which part of your footprint is deeper? Make a list of the kind of footprint each activity makes. For example, you might write, "When I am running, my footprints are deep near the toe. These footprints are 110 cm apart."

Analyze the Results

5 Compare the data from your footprints with the data from the mystery footprints. How are the footprints alike? How are they different?

6 Were the footprints made by one person or more than one person? Explain your interpretation.

7 Can you tell if the footprints were made by men, women, children, or a combination? Explain your interpretation.

Draw Conclusions

8 Based on your analysis of your own footprints, would you conclude that the people who made the mystery footprints were standing still, walking, or running?

9 Do your data support your hypothesis? Explain.

10 How could you improve your experiment?

Communicate Results

11 Outline your group's conclusions in a letter addressed to the scientists who asked for your help. Begin by stating your hypothesis. Then tell the scientists how you gathered information from the study of your own footprints. Include the comparisons you made between your footprints and the mystery footprints. Before stating your conclusions, offer some suggestions about how you could improve your investigation.

12 Make a poster or chart, or use a computer if one is available, to present your findings to the class.

Lab Notes

Tell the students to imagine that a scientist wishes to analyze footprints found in the rocks near fossilized remains, and he has contacted the class, seeking help in the investigation. The scientist wants to know how the students intend to gather information to make inferences about the humans who left the prints. Explain that a scientist should be able to make the same type of inferences about an organism from fresh tracks as from preserved tracks. Use the mystery footprints in the sand to help students design investigations for gathering data. From that data, students can learn to draw inferences.

Much research in evolution is dependent on scientific inferences. To conclude the laboratory experience, lead the students in a discussion of the importance of large sets of data in helping scientists make inferences.

Datasheets for LabBook

123

Answers

The answers for this activity will depend on the footprints your students observe. They should be able to compare their own activities with variations in the footprints they leave. Then they should be able to apply what they've learned to the mystery footprints.

Chapter Highlights

VOCABULARY DEFINITIONS

SECTION 1

adaptation a hereditary characteristic that helps an organism survive and reproduce in its environment

species the most specific of the seven levels of classification; characterized by a group of organisms that can mate with one another to produce fertile offspring

evolution the process by which populations accumulate inherited changes over time

fossil the solidified remains or imprints of once-living organisms

fossil record a historical sequence of life indicated by fossils found in layers of the Earth's crust

vestigial structure the remnant of a once-useful anatomical structure

SECTION 2

trait distinguishing qualities that can be passed from one generation to another

selective breeding breeding of organisms that have a certain desired trait

natural selection the process by which organisms with favorable traits survive and reproduce at a higher rate than organisms without the favorable trait

mutation a change in the order of the bases in an organism's DNA; deletion, insertion, or substitution

Chapter Highlights

SECTION 1

Vocabulary
  adaptation *(p. 104)*
  species *(p. 104)*
  evolution *(p. 105)*
  fossil *(p. 106)*
  fossil record *(p. 106)*
  vestigial structure *(p. 107)*

Section Notes

- Evolution is the process by which populations change over time. Those changes are inherited.

- Evidence of a common ancestor for all organisms is provided by the following: the fossil record, comparisons of skeletal structures found in related species, comparisons of the embryos of distantly related vertebrates, and the presence of DNA in all living organisms.

- Species that are closely related have DNA that is more alike than DNA of distantly related species.

SECTION 2

Vocabulary
  trait *(p. 114)*
  selective breeding *(p. 114)*
  natural selection *(p. 116)*
  mutation *(p. 117)*

Section Notes

- Charles Darwin developed an explanation for evolution after years of studying the organisms he observed on the voyage of the *Beagle*.

- Darwin's study was influenced by the concepts of selective breeding, the age of the Earth, and the idea that some organisms are better equipped to survive than others.

☑ Skills Check

Math Concepts

MALTHUS'S PRINCIPLE The graph on page 115 shows two types of growth. The straight line represents an increase in which the same number is added to the previous number, as in 3, 4, 5, 6, . . . , where 1 is added to each number.

The curved line represents an increase in which each number is multiplied by the same factor, as in 2, 4, 8, 16, . . . , where each number is multiplied by 2. As you can see on the graph, the curved line increases at a much faster rate than the straight line.

Visual Understanding

SKELETAL STRUCTURE Figure 9 on page 110 illustrates skeletal evidence for evolution. By looking at the same-colored bones, you can see how the early mammalian skeletal structure has evolved in certain species to help with specialized tasks such as flying and swimming.

124

Lab and Activity Highlights

Mystery Footprints PG 122

Out-of-Sight Marshmallows PG 190

Survival of the Chocolates PG 191

 Datasheets for LabBook
(blackline masters for these labs)

SECTION 3

generation time the period between the birth of one generation and the birth of the next generation

speciation the process by which two populations of the same species become so different that they can no longer interbreed

SECTION 2

• Darwin explained that evolution occurs through natural selection. Natural selection can be divided into four parts:

(1) Each species produces more offspring than will survive to reproduce.

(2) Individuals within a population are slightly different from one another.

(3) Individuals within a population compete with one another for limited resources.

(4) Individuals that are better equipped to live in an environment are more likely to survive and reproduce.

• Evolution is explained today by combining the principles of natural selection with the principles of genetic inheritance.

Labs

Survival of the Chocolates (p. 191)

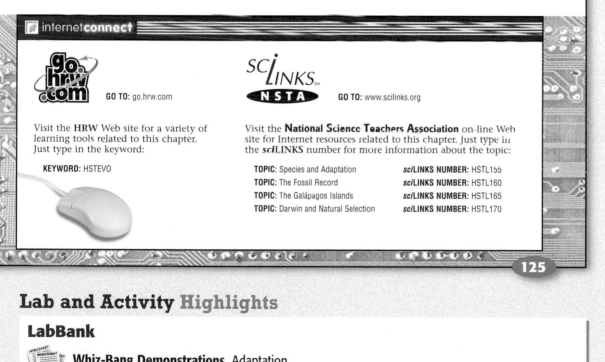

SECTION 3

Vocabulary

generation time (p. 118)
speciation (p. 120)

Section Notes

• Natural selection allows a population to adapt to changes in environmental conditions.

• Evidence of natural selection can be seen by studying generations of organisms that have developed resistance to an insecticide or antibiotic.

• Natural selection also explains how one species may evolve into another through the process of speciation.

Labs

Out-of-Sight Marshmallows (p. 190)

Vocabulary Review Worksheet

Blackline masters of these Chapter Highlights can be found in the **Study Guide**.

---

internet**connect**

GO TO: go.hrw.com

Visit the **HRW** Web site for a variety of learning tools related to this chapter. Just type in the keyword:

KEYWORD: HSTEVO

SC*LINKS*sm

NSTA

GO TO: www.scilinks.org

Visit the **National Science Teachers Association** on-line Web site for Internet resources related to this chapter. Just type in the *sci*LINKS number for more information about the topic:

TOPIC: Species and Adaptation   *sci*LINKS NUMBER: HSTL155
TOPIC: The Fossil Record   *sci*LINKS NUMBER: HSTL160
TOPIC: The Galápagos Islands   *sci*LINKS NUMBER: HSTL165
TOPIC: Darwin and Natural Selection   *sci*LINKS NUMBER: HSTL170

125

Lab and Activity Highlights

LabBank

Whiz-Bang Demonstrations, Adaptation Behooves You

Long-Term Projects & Research Ideas, Evolution's Explosion

Chapter Review
Answers

USING VOCABULARY

1. speciation
2. species
3. adaptation
4. Evolution
5. selective breeding
6. mutation

UNDERSTANDING CONCEPTS

Multiple Choice

7. b
8. d
9. a
10. a
11. b
12. b

Short Answer

13. a. overproduction: Each species produces more offspring than will survive.
    b. genetic variation: Each individual has a unique combination of traits. Some traits increase the chances that the individual will survive and reproduce.
    c. struggle to survive: Individuals compete for limited resources. Some will not compete successfully and will not survive to adulthood.
    d. successful reproduction: Those individuals that are well-adapted and have traits that help them survive in their environment are more likely to survive and reproduce.
14. Fossils of the stages of whale evolution have been discovered that clearly indicate their sequence of change from land-dwelling carnivores to sea-dwelling mammals.
15. The required conditions for fossil formation are rare. The shell or bones must be completely covered in sediment in an anaerobic environment.

Chapter Review

USING VOCABULARY

To complete the following sentences, choose the correct term from each pair of terms listed below:

1. One species evolves into another through the process of __?__ . *(adaptation* or *speciation)*

2. A group of similar organisms that can mate with one another to produce offspring is known as a __?__ . *(fossil* or *species)*

3. A(n) __?__ helps an organism survive better in its environment. *(adaptation* or *vestigial structure)*

4. __?__ is the process by which populations change over time. *(Natural selection* or *Evolution)*

5. In __?__ , humans select traits that will be passed from one generation to another. *(selective breeding* or *natural selection)*

6. A change in a gene at the DNA level is called a __?__ . *(mutation* or *trait)*

UNDERSTANDING CONCEPTS

Multiple Choice

7. Although Darwin did not realize it, the variations he observed among the individuals of a population of finches were caused by
   a. genetic resistance.   c. fossils.
   b. mutations.   d. selective breeding.

8. The theory of evolution combines the principles of
   a. natural selection and artificial selection.
   b. natural selection and genetic resistance.
   c. selective breeding and genetic inheritance.
   d. natural selection and genetic inheritance.

9. Fossils are commonly found in
   a. sedimentary rock.
   b. igneous rock.
   c. granite.
   d. loose sand or granite.

10. A human's arm, a cat's front leg, a dolphin's front flipper, and a bat's wing
    a. have similar kinds of bones.
    b. are used in similar ways.
    c. share many similarities with insect wings and jellyfish tentacles.
    d. have nothing in common.

11. The fact that all organisms have DNA as their genetic material is evidence that
    a. natural selection occurred.
    b. all organisms descended from a common ancestor.
    c. selective breeding takes place every day.
    d. genetic resistance rarely occurs.

12. What body part of the Galápagos finches appears to have been most modified by natural selection?
    a. their webbed feet
    b. their beaks
    c. the bone structure of their wings
    d. the color of their eyes

Short Answer

13. Describe the four parts of Darwin's theory of evolution by natural selection.

14. How do the fossils of whales provide evidence that whales have evolved over millions of years?

15. What might account for gaps in the fossil record?

126

Concept Mapping

16. An answer to this exercise can be found at the front of this book.

**Concept Mapping
Transparency 7**

Concept Mapping

16. Use the following terms to create a concept map: struggle to survive, genetic variation, Darwin, overpopulation, natural selection, successful reproduction.

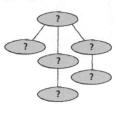

CRITICAL THINKING AND PROBLEM SOLVING

Write one or two sentences to answer the following questions:

17. In selective breeding, humans influence the course of evolution. What determines the course of evolution in natural selection?

18. Many forms of bacteria evolve resistance to antibiotics, drugs that kill bacteria. Based on what you know about how insects evolve to resist insecticides, suggest how bacteria might evolve to resist antibiotics.

19. The two species of squirrels shown below live on opposite sides of the Grand Canyon, in Arizona. The two squirrels look very similar, but they cannot interbreed to produce fertile offspring. Explain how a single species of squirrel might have become two species.

INTERPRETING GRAPHICS

Use the following graphs to answer questions 20, 21, and 22:

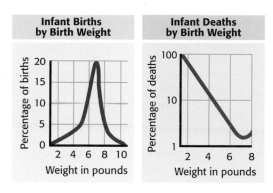

Infant Births by Birth Weight

Percentage of births / Weight in pounds

Infant Deaths by Birth Weight

Percentage of deaths / Weight in pounds

20. What is the most common birth weight?

21. What birth weight has the highest survival rate?

22. How do the principles of natural selection help explain why there are more deaths among babies with low birth weights than among babies of average birth weights?

Reading Check-up

Take a minute to review your answers to the Pre-Reading Questions found at the bottom of page 102. Have your answers changed? If necessary, revise your answers based on what you have learned since you began this chapter.

CRITICAL THINKING AND PROBLEM SOLVING

17. Conditions in the environment to which organisms must be adapted are part of the selection process in nature. Natural selection is the process of adaptation over time to changes in environmental conditions. The genetic changes that bring about adaptations in a species are thought to determine the course of evolution through natural selection.

18. A course of antibiotics may leave behind bacteria that have traits that help them survive. The survivors may reproduce, producing more individuals that have the survival trait. In this way, a strain of bacteria may become immune to an antibiotic.

19. Individual organisms in a population have their own unique set of traits. When a population becomes separated over time, each separate group may evolve in a different direction. Eventually, the groups may become different genetically and they are no longer able to interbreed. Even though they may retain a similar appearance, they have become separate species.

INTERPRETING GRAPHICS

20. 7 lb
21. 7 lb
22. Human babies are best adapted to survive at a birth weight of about 7 lb.

Blackline masters of this Chapter Review can be found in the **Study Guide.**

Teaching Strategy

In order to help students understand the changes in agriculture, you may wish to create a table that contrasts "traditional" and "industrial" farming practices. Under the heading *Traditional*, list words or phrases that describe traditional farming practices, such as *smaller scale, few machines or manual labor, more plant varieties*, and *mainly for sustenance*. Under the heading *Industrial*, list words or phrases that describe industrial farming practices, such as *larger scale, more mechanized, fewer plant varieties*, and *primarily for profit*. Encourage students to add their own words or phrases to contrast the types of farming practices.

In addition, point out to students that farmers in some areas, including many developing countries, practice some form of traditional agriculture. Consequently, scientists at seed banks try to visit those areas as often as necessary to obtain samples of those seeds.

EYE ON THE ENVIRONMENT

Saving at the Seed Bank

A very unusual laboratory can be found in Fort Collins, Colorado. There, sealed in test tubes, locked in specialized drawers, and even frozen in liquid nitrogen at −196°C, are hundreds of thousands of seeds and plants. Although in storage for now, these organisms may hold the keys to preventing worldwide famine or medicine shortage in the future. Sound serious? Well, it is.

This laboratory is called the National Seed Storage Lab, and it is the largest of a worldwide network of seed banks. The seeds and plant cuttings stored within these seed banks represent almost every plant grown for food, clothing, and medicine.

▲ *To protect tomorrow's wheat fields, we need the genetic diversity of crops stored in seed banks.*

No More Pizza!

Imagine heading out for pizza only to discover a sign on the door that says, "Closed today due to flour shortage." Flour shortage? How can that be? What about burritos? When you get to the burrito stand, the sign is the same, "Closed due to flour shortage." Think this sounds far-fetched? Well, it really isn't.

If wheat crops around the world are ruined by a disease, we could have a flour shortage. And the best way to fight such devastation, and even prevent it, is by breeding new varieties. Through the process of selective breeding, many plants have been improved to increase their yields and their resistance to disease and insects. But to breed new crops, plant breeders need lots of different genetic material. Where do they get this genetic material? At the seed bank, of course!

Why We'll Never Know

But what if some plants never make it to the seed bank? We have the new and improved varieties, so why does it matter if we keep the old ones? It matters because these lost varieties often have important traits, like resistance to disease and drought, that might come in handy in the future. Once a variety of plant is improved, demand for the old variety can dwindle to nothing. If an old variety is no longer grown, it may become extinct if it is not placed in the seed bank. In fact, many varieties of plants have already been lost forever. We'll never know if one of those lost varieties was capable of resisting a severe drought.

It's All in the Bank

Fortunately, seed banks have collected seeds and plants for more than a century. They preserve the genetic diversity of crop plants while allowing farmers to grow the most productive varieties in their fields. As long as there are seed banks across the globe, it is unlikely that there will be a flour shortage. Let's go out for pizza!

Going Further

▶ Many seed banks are in jeopardy. Why? Find out by doing research to learn more about the complicated and costly process of operating a seed bank.

128

Answer to Going Further
Answers will vary.

Science Fiction

SCIENCE FICTION

"The Anatomy Lesson"
by Scott Sanders

While studying for an exam, a medical student attempts to assemble a very unusual skeleton that may drastically change the student's future.

"The Anatomy Lesson"

by Scott Sanders

You know what it's like. You have an important test tomorrow, or your semester project is due, and you've forgotten your book or just run out of clay. Suddenly things seem very serious.

That's the situation a certain medical student faces in Scott Sanders's "The Anatomy Lesson." The student needs to learn the bones of the human body for an anatomy exam the next day. After arriving at the anatomy library to check out a skeleton-in-a-box, the student finds that all the skeletons have been checked out. Without bones to assemble as practice, the student knows passing the exam will be impossible. So the student asks the librarian to look again. Sure enough, the librarian finds one last box. And that's when things start to get strange.

There are too many bones. They are the wrong shape. They don't fit together just right. Somebody must be playing a joke! The bones fit together, sort of—but not in any way that helps the medical student get ready for the exam. When the student complains to the librarian, the librarian isn't very sympathetic. It seems she has other things on her mind. Now the student is really worried.

Find out what this medical student and a quiet librarian have in common. And find out how they will never be the same after "The Anatomy Lesson." You can read it in the *Holt Anthology of Science Fiction.*

129

Teaching Strategy

Reading Level This is a relatively short story and should not be difficult for the average student to read and comprehend.

Background

About the Author Scott Sanders (1945–) writes many different kinds of stories—from folktales to science fiction. Early in life, he chose to become a writer rather than a scientist, though he has a keen interest in both writing and science. Sanders has written about a range of subjects, including folklore, physics, the naturalist John James Audubon, and settlers of Indiana. Much of his work is nonfiction. His writing has been published in many different newspapers and magazines, including the *Chicago Sun-Times, Harper's,* and *Omni.* Currently, Sanders lives and teaches in Indiana, where he belongs to writers' groups and to groups such as the Sierra Club and Friends of the Earth.

Further Reading If students enjoy this story, you may wish to recommend some of Sanders's other works, such as the following:

Terrarium, Indiana University Press, 1996

The Engineer of Beasts, Orchard Books, 1988

Hear the Wind Blow: American Folksongs Retold, Simon & Shuster Children's, 1985

Chapter Organizer

CHAPTER ORGANIZATION	TIME MINUTES	OBJECTIVES	LABS, INVESTIGATIONS, AND DEMONSTRATIONS
Chapter Opener pp. 130–131	45	National Standards: UCP 2, HNS 3	**Start-Up Activity,** Earth's Timeline, p. 131
Section 1 Evidence of the Past	90	▶ Explain how fossils are dated. ▶ Describe the geologic time scale and the information it provides scientists. ▶ Describe the possible causes of mass extinctions. ▶ Explain the theory of plate tectonics. UCP 1–4, SAI 1, 2, SPSP 3, HNS 1–3, LS 3a, 5c; Labs UCP 1, 3, SAI 1, LS 5c	**Skill Builder,** The Half-life of Pennies, p. 150 **Datasheets for LabBook,** The Half-life of Pennies
Section 2 Eras of the Geologic Time Scale	90	▶ Outline the major developments that allowed for the existence of life on Earth. ▶ Describe the different types of organisms that arose during the four eras of the geologic time scale. UCP 1, 3, SPSP 3, LS 1b, 3a, 5c	**Interactive Explorations CD-ROM,** Rock On! *A **Worksheet** is also available in the **Interactive Explorations Teacher's Guide.***
Section 3 Human Evolution	90	▶ Discuss the shared characteristics of primates. ▶ Describe what is known about the differences between hominids. UCP 2, 5, SAI 2, HNS 2, 3, LS 1a, 5a	**QuickLab,** Thumb Through This, p. 145 **Long-Term Projects & Research Ideas,** A Horse Is a Horse

*See page **T23** for a complete correlation of this book with the*

NATIONAL SCIENCE EDUCATION STANDARDS.

TECHNOLOGY RESOURCES

Guided Reading Audio CD English or Spanish, Chapter 6

One-Stop Planner CD-ROM with Test Generator

Science Discovery Videodiscs Image and Activity Bank with Lesson Plans: The Time Machine

Science Sleuths: The Misplaced Fossil

CNN. Multicultural Connections, Protecting New Mexico's Petroglyphs, Segment 6

Scientists in Action, Creating Digital Dinos, Segment 12 Ice Age Discoveries, Segment 23

Interactive Explorations CD-ROM CD 2, Exploration 6, Rock On!

CLASSROOM WORKSHEETS, TRANSPARENCIES, AND RESOURCES	SCIENCE INTEGRATION AND CONNECTIONS	REVIEW AND ASSESSMENT
Directed Reading Worksheet **Science Puzzlers, Twisters & Teasers**		
Directed Reading Worksheet, Section 1 **Transparency 110,** The Rock Cycle **Transparency 29,** Unstable Atoms and the Half-life **Math Skills for Science Worksheet,** Radioactive Decay and the Half-life **Transparency 30,** The Geologic Time Scale and Representative Organisms **Critical Thinking Worksheet,** Fossil Revelations **Math Skills for Science Worksheet,** Geologic Time Scale **Transparency 31,** Formation of the Modern Continents **Transparency 32,** The Tectonic Plates **Reinforcement Worksheet,** Earth Timeline	**Connect to Earth Science,** p. 133 in ATE **Connect to Earth Science,** p. 136 in ATE **Multicultural Connection,** p. 136 in ATE **Careers:** Paleobotanist—Bonnie Jacobs, p. 157	**Homework,** p. 133 in ATE **Self-Check,** p. 135 **Section Review,** p. 137 **Quiz,** p. 137 in ATE **Alternative Assessment,** p. 137 in ATE
Directed Reading Worksheet, Section 2 **Math Skills for Science Worksheet,** Subtraction Review **Reinforcement Worksheet,** Condensed History	**Connect to Earth Science,** p. 139 in ATE **Environment Connection,** p. 140 **Math and More,** p. 141 in ATE **Real-World Connection,** p. 141 in ATE **Multicultural Connection,** p. 142 in ATE **Across the Sciences:** Windows into the Past, p. 156	**Self-Check,** p. 141 **Homework,** p. 141 in ATE **Section Review,** p. 143 **Quiz,** p. 143 in ATE **Alternative Assessment,** p. 143 in ATE
Transparency 33, Primate Skeletal Structures **Directed Reading Worksheet,** Section 3	**Cross-Disciplinary Focus,** p. 145 in ATE **Cross-Disciplinary Focus,** p. 146 in ATE **Cross-Disciplinary Focus,** p. 147 in ATE	**Section Review,** p. 149 **Quiz,** p. 149 in ATE **Alternative Assessment,** p. 149 in ATE

END-OF-CHAPTER REVIEW AND ASSESSMENT

Chapter Review in Study Guide
Vocabulary and Notes in Study Guide
Chapter Tests with Performance-Based Assessment, Chapter 6 Test
Chapter Tests with Performance-Based Assessment, Performance-Based Assessment 6
Concept Mapping Transparency 8

internet connect

go. hrw .com **Holt, Rinehart and Winston On-line Resources** **go.hrw.com**

For worksheets and other teaching aids related to this chapter, visit the HRW Web site and type in the keyword: **HSTHIS**

sciLINKS **National Science Teachers Association** **www.scilinks.org**

Encourage students to use the *sci*LINKS numbers listed in the internet connect boxes to access information and resources on the **NSTA** Web site.

Chapter Resources & Worksheets

Visual Resources

TEACHING TRANSPARENCIES

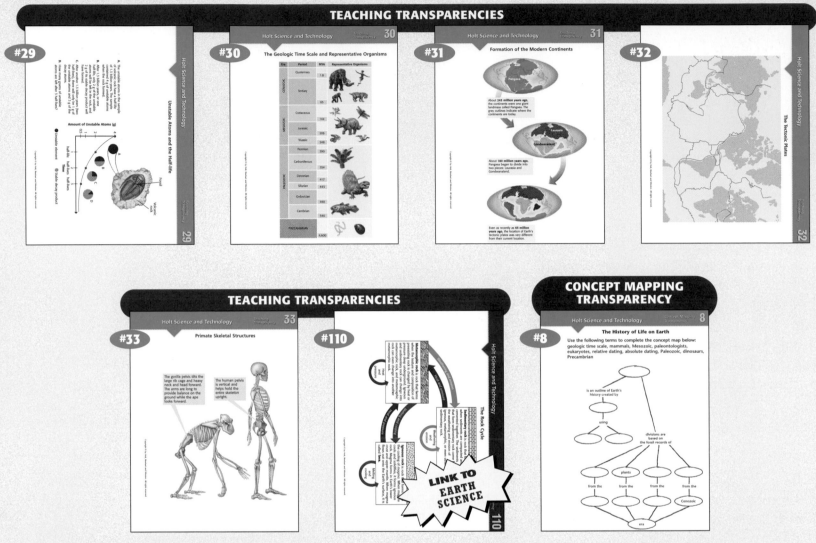

#29 — Holt Science and Technology — Unstable Atoms and the Half-Life — 29

#30 — Holt Science and Technology — The Geologic Time Scale and Representative Organisms — 30

#31 — Holt Science and Technology — Formation of the Modern Continents — 31

#32 — Holt Science and Technology — The Tectonic Plates — 32

TEACHING TRANSPARENCIES

#33 — Holt Science and Technology — Primate Skeletal Structures — 33

#110 — Holt Science and Technology — The Rock Cycle — 110 — LINK TO EARTH SCIENCE

CONCEPT MAPPING TRANSPARENCY

#8 — Holt Science and Technology — The History of Life on Earth — 8

Use the following terms to complete the concept map below: geologic time scale, mammals, Mesozoic, paleontologists, eukaryotes, relative dating, absolute dating, Paleozoic, dinosaurs, Precambrian

Meeting Individual Needs

DIRECTED READING

#6 — DIRECTED READING WORKSHEET — The History of Life on Earth

Chapter Introduction

As you begin this chapter, answer the following.
1. Read the title of the chapter. List three things that you already know about this subject.

2. Write two questions about this subject that you would like answered by the time you finish this chapter.

3. How does the title of the Start-Up Activity relate to the subject of the chapter?

Section 1: Evidence of the Past (p. 130)
4. Which of the following are true of Paul Sereno? (Circle all that apply.)
   a. He looks for fossils.   c. He is a police detective.
   b. He studies human history.   d. He is a paleontologist.

Fossils (p. 130)
5. Using Figure 2, place the following steps of fossil formation in the correct order by writing the appropriate number in the space provided.
   ___ The organism dissolves.
   ___ The organism is covered with sediment.
   ___ The hollow impression is filled with sediment.

REINFORCEMENT & VOCABULARY REVIEW

#6 — REINFORCEMENT WORKSHEET — Condensed History

Complete this worksheet after you finish reading Section 1.
Scientists use four major divisions to tell about the Earth's history: Precambrian time, the Paleozoic era, the Mesozoic era, and the Cenozoic era. Precambrian time lasted for about 88 percent of the 4.6 billion years of Earth's history. The Paleozoic era was about 6.3 percent of Earth's history. The Mesozoic era was 4.0 percent of Earth's history. The Cenozoic era has lasted for about 1.4 percent of Earth's history.

It is difficult to imagine the Earth's history because it is so long. But what if the entire history of the Earth could fit into a single human life span of 90 years? Fill in the timeline to show how old the person would be when each era begins. How old would he or she be when the first single-celled organism appears on Earth? How old would he or she be when the first primate evolves?

Age in years
0
5
10
15
20
25
30
35
40
45
50
55
60
65
70
75
80
85
90

#6 — VOCABULARY REVIEW WORKSHEET — Mary Leakey's Search

Complete this worksheet after you finish reading Section 2.
Many important events that have occurred since the Earth was formed are listed below. Fill in the diagram below, listing the events in chronological order.

Prokaryotes form.
Cells with nuclei form.
First birds appear.
Large mammals appear.
The ozone layer develops.
Dinosaurs dominate the Earth.
Plants become established on land.
Homo habilis scrapes meat out of a carcass.
Crawling insects appear on land.
Many reptile species evolve.
Marine animals suffer mass extinction.
Small mammals survive mass extinction.
Cro-Magnon does cave art.
Photosynthesis comes into being.
Mary Leakey discovers footprints in Tanzania.
Winged insects appear.

SCIENCE PUZZLERS, TWISTERS & TEASERS

#6 — SCIENCE PUZZLERS, TWISTERS & TEASERS — The History of Life on Earth

Scientific Sleuthing
1. Each of the statements below was made by an organism during the era in which it evolved. Write the correct era in the space provided. The organisms evolved during the following eras: Precambrian, Paleozoic, Mesozoic, or Cenozoic.
   a. I've seen the greatest swimmers of my generation destroyed.
   b. People often accuse me of monkeying around.
   c. Oxygen? What is that?
   d. Smoke and flames have frightened me ever since the day a large meteorite came crashing into my backyard.
   e. My mother had to settle for a potted plant instead of flowers for her birthday.
   f. I couldn't find clams on the menu anywhere.

Consonant Tectonics
2. The following sentences about plate tectonics were put through a "word filter" in which all their spaces and vowels were filtered out. What did the sentences say before they were filtered?
   bt24vtsllngthctcntnwvsgrtndtmscldPng.bt180mllnyrsg.Pnghgvndvdntwpcs.WcllHtdwcntntsLrsndGndwndlnd.rpssndy-cmmtnwtttslnvng.

Review & Assessment

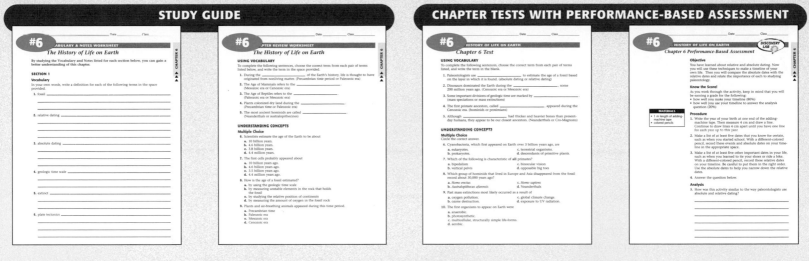

STUDY GUIDE

#6 VOCABULARY & NOTES WORKSHEET
The History of Life on Earth

By studying the Vocabulary and Notes listed for each section below, you can gain a better understanding of this chapter.

SECTION 1
Vocabulary
In your own words, write a definition for each of the following terms in the space provided.

1. fossil

2. relative dating

3. absolute dating

4. geologic time scale

5. extinct

6. plate tectonics

#6 CHAPTER REVIEW WORKSHEET
The History of Life on Earth

USING VOCABULARY
To complete the following sentences, choose the correct term from each pair of terms listed below, and write the term in the space provided.

1. During the _____ of the Earth's history, life is thought to have originated from nonliving matter. (absolute dating or relative dating)

2. The Age of Mammals refers to the _____. (Mesozoic era or Cenozoic era)

3. The Age of Reptiles refers to the _____. (Paleozoic era or Mesozoic era)

4. Plants colonized dry land during the _____. (Precambrian time or Paleozoic era)

5. The most ancient hominids are called _____. (Neanderthals or australopithecines)

UNDERSTANDING CONCEPTS
Multiple Choice
6. Scientists estimate the age of the Earth to be about
   a. 10 billion years.
   b. 4.6 billion years.
   c. 3.8 billion years.
   d. 4.4 million years.

7. The first cells probably appeared about
   a. 10 billion years ago.
   b. 4.6 billion years ago.
   c. 3.5 billion years ago.
   d. 4.4 million years ago.

8. How is the age of a fossil estimated?
   a. by using the geologic time scale
   b. by measuring unstable elements in the rock that holds the fossil
   c. by studying the relative position of continents
   d. by measuring the amount of oxygen in the fossil rock

9. Plants and air-breathing animals appeared during this time period.
   a. Precambrian time
   b. Paleozoic era
   c. Mesozoic era
   d. Cenozoic era

CHAPTER TESTS WITH PERFORMANCE-BASED ASSESSMENT

#6 HISTORY OF LIFE ON EARTH
Chapter 6 Test

USING VOCABULARY
To complete the following sentences, choose the correct term from each pair of terms listed, and write the term in the blank.

1. Paleontologists use _____ to estimate the age of a fossil based on the layer in which it is found. (absolute dating or relative dating)

2. Dinosaurs dominated the Earth during the _____, some 200 million years ago. (Cenozoic era or Mesozoic era)

3. Some important divisions of geologic time are marked by _____. (mass speciations or mass extinctions)

4. The first primate ancestors, called _____, appeared during the Cenozoic era. (hominids or prosimians)

5. Although _____ had thicker and heavier bones than present-day humans, they appear to be our closest ancestors. (Neanderthals or Cro-Magnons)

UNDERSTANDING CONCEPTS
Multiple Choice
6. Cyanobacteria, which first appeared on Earth over 3 billion years ago, are
   a. eukaryotes.
   b. prokaryotes.
   c. terrestrial organisms.
   d. descendants of primitive plants.

7. Which of the following is characteristic of all primates?
   a. bipedalism
   b. vertical pelvis
   c. binocular vision
   d. opposable big toes

8. Which group of hominids that lived in Europe and Asia disappeared from the fossil record about 30,000 years ago?
   a. *Homo erectus*
   b. *Australopithecus afarensis*
   c. *Homo sapiens*
   d. Neanderthals

9. Past mass extinctions most likely occurred as a result of
   a. oxygen pollution.
   b. ozone destruction.
   c. global climate change.
   d. exposure to UV radiation.

10. The first organisms to appear on Earth were
    a. anaerobic.
    b. photosynthetic.
    c. multicellular, structurally simple life-forms.
    d. aerobic.

#6 HISTORY OF LIFE ON EARTH
Chapter 6 Performance-Based Assessment

Objective
You have learned about relative and absolute dating. Now you will use these techniques to make a timeline of your own life. Then you will compare the absolute dates with the relative dates and relate the importance of each to studying paleontology.

Know the Score!
As you work through the activity, keep in mind that you will be earning a grade for the following:
• how well you make your timeline (80%)
• how well you use your timeline to answer the analysis question (20%)

MATERIALS
• 1 m length of adding-machine tape
• colored pencils

Procedure
1. Write the year of your birth at one end of the adding-machine tape. Then measure 4 cm and draw a line. Continue to draw lines 4 cm apart until you have one line for each year up to this year.

2. Make a list of at least five dates that you know for certain, such as when you started school. With a different-colored pencil, record these events and absolute dates on your time-line in the appropriate space.

3. Make a list of at least five other important dates in your life, such as when you learned to tie your shoes or ride a bike. With a different-colored pencil, record these relative dates on your timeline. Be careful to put them in the right order. Use the absolute dates to help you narrow down the relative dates.

4. Answer the question below.

Analysis
5. How was this activity similar to the way paleontologists use absolute and relative dating?

Lab Worksheets

LONG-TERM PROJECTS & RESEARCH IDEAS

#6 STUDENT WORKSHEET
DESIGN YOUR OWN
A Horse Is a Horse

Horses haven't always had hooves. In the tropical forests of the Eocene epoch, a many-toed creature about the size of a dog fed on soft tree leaves. Scientists call it *Hyracotherium*, but we also know it as *Eohippus*, the dawn horse. *Hyracotherium* was an ancient ancestor of the modern horse.

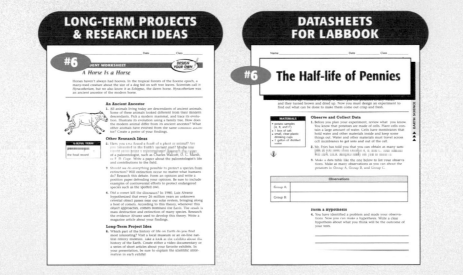

An Ancient Ancestor
1. All animals living today are descendants of ancient animals. Some of these animals looked different from their modern descendants. Pick a modern mammal, and trace its evolution. Illustrate its evolution using a family tree. How does the modern animal differ from its ancient ancestor? What other animals have evolved from the same common ancestor? Create a poster of your findings.

USEFUL TERM
the fossil record

Other Research Ideas
2. Have you ever found a fossil of a plant or animal? Are you interested in the Earth's ancient past? Maybe you would enjoy being a paleontologist! Research the career of a paleontologist, such as Charles Walcott, O. C. Marsh, or E. D. Cope. Write a paper about the paleontologist's life and contributions to the field.

3. Should we do everything possible to protect a species from extinction? Will extinction occur no matter what humans do? Research this debate, form an opinion and write a position paper defending your opinion. Be sure to include examples of controversial efforts to protect endangered species such as the spotted owl.

4. Find a comet kill the dinosaurs? In 1980, Luis Alvarez hypothesized that every 26 million years an unknown celestial object passes near our solar system, bringing along a host of comets. According to this theory, whenever this object approaches, comets dominate the Earth. The result is mass destruction and extinction of many species. Research the evidence Alvarez used to develop this theory. Write a magazine article about your findings.

Long-Term Project Idea
5. Which part of the history of life on Earth do you find most interesting? Visit a local museum or an on-line natural history museum. Take a look at an exhibit about the history of the Earth. Create either a video documentary or a series of short articles about your favorite exhibits. In your presentation, be sure to explain the scientific information in each exhibit.

DATASHEETS FOR LABBOOK

Name _____ Date _____ Class _____

#6 **The Half-life of Pennies**

... to the top button of your pennies. Now you must design an experiment to find out what can be done to make them come out of crisp and fresh.

MATERIALS
• potato samples (A, B, and C)
• 1 box of salt
• small, clear-plastic drinking cups
• 1 gallon of distilled water

Observe and Collect Data
1. Before you plan your experiment, review what you know. You know that potatoes are made of cells. Plant cells contain a large amount of water. Cells have membranes that hold water and other materials inside and keep some things out. Water and other materials must travel across cell membranes to get into and out of the cell.

2. Mr. Frias has told you that you can obtain as many samples as you need. With careful, mix a box of salt into the water with thick, thick, samples ready for you to observe.

3. Make a data table like the one below to list your observations. Make as many observations as you can about the potatoes in Group A, Group B, and Group C.

Observations		
Group A:		
Group B:		

Form a Hypothesis
4. You have identified a problem and made your observations. Now you can make a hypothesis. Write a clear hypothesis about what you think will be the outcome of your tests.

Applications & Extensions

CRITICAL THINKING & PROBLEM SOLVING

#6 CRITICAL THINKING WORKSHEET
Fossil Revelations

From the Foreign Space Materials Logbook:

Date: 3-9-18050
Agent: Rusty Steele
A foreign space material was found. The message there says the following:

S.O.S. FROM EARTH! WE ARE IN THE MIDST OF AN EMERGENCY. OUR TIMES AND OUR AIR ARE DETERIORATING! PLEASE SEND HELP! FEBRUARY 6, 5080

I have permission from my commander to investigate. Even though the message is very old, I may still be able to help. I will depart for Earth tomorrow.

Date: 4-22-18050
Agent: Rusty Steele
When I landed on Earth, all human life was gone. I suspect there was a mass extinction. I have begun to gather fossil evidence.

Analyzing Observations
1. Help Agent Steele analyze the evidence of the mass extinction of humans on Earth. The left column of the chart contains his observations. Fill in the right side with your interpretations of the evidence. The first one is done for you.

Earth's Evidence

Evidence found	What the evidence indicates
A large number of plant fossils are found in the "extinction layer" of the geologic record.	*Many plants must have been buried at the same time.*
Numerous full landfills are found.	
A layer of ash is found worldwide directly beneath the extinction layer.	
A crater with a diameter of 50 km is found.	
Fossils of underdeveloped, withered plants are found worldwide. Dating methods indicate that a large number of plants died at the same time.	
Some areas contain many ancient buildings in a small space.	

MULTICULTURAL CONNECTIONS

#6 *Science in the News:* **Critical Thinking Worksheets**

Segment 6
Protecting New Mexico's Petroglyphs

1. Why do you think the ancient people living in New Mexico made the petroglyphs?

2. Do you think that community growth in Albuquerque should be halted to save the petroglyphs? Why or why not?

3. Why do park officials worry that construction of the highway would lead to development in protected areas in other places in the United States?

4. What do you think would be the economic impact of the highway?

SCIENTISTS IN ACTION

#12 *Science in the News:* **Critical Thinking Worksheets**

Segment 12
Creating Digital Dinos

#23

1. ... information paleontologists use to make educated guesses about a dinosaur's ...

2. What are some of the barriers paleontologists face when hypothesizing about dinosaurs' makeup?

3. What is the importance of having strong evidence to support a hypothesis?

4. What other scientific technology besides that described is used by paleontologists in their research? Explain.

INTERACTIVE EXPLORATIONS

#2-6

Exploration 6
Worksheet

Rock On!

1. Claudia Stone is supervising the development of an information kiosk at a new state park. What does she need to know to complete the project?

2. What kinds of things are available in the lab to help you provide Ms. Stone with the information she needs?

3. Briefly describe the differences between igneous, sedimentary, and metamorphic rocks. Use the CD-ROM articles to help you.

CD-ROM

Chapter Background

SECTION 1

Evidence of the Past

▶ Fossils

Fossils are not only preserved plants and animals but also traces of plants and animals. Preserved footprints, feces, gnaw marks, and root holes can all be considered fossils.

- Despite what many people think, fossils are not particularly difficult to find. Nearly every state in the United States contains an abundance of fossils. However, scientists think that only a tiny fraction of the countless organisms that lived on Earth have been preserved as fossils. Many organisms have lived and died without leaving evidence of their existence in the fossil record.

IS THAT A FACT!

- ➤ The oldest fossils are of prokaryotes that are more than 3 billion years old.

▶ Law of Superposition

The law of superposition states that in a series of sedimentary rock layers, each layer is older than the one above it and younger than the one below it. This law is based on an observation made by Nicolaus Steno, a Danish physician, in 1669.

▶ Methods of Absolute Dating

Absolute dating determines a fossil's age in years. Radioisotope dating is the most widely used method for dating a fossil. This method gives only a range of probable ages. A newly developed method uses a particle accelerator and can date fossils up to 60,000 years old.

▶ Modern Mass Extinction

Many scientists believe that our planet has entered another era of mass extinction and that human activities are mainly responsible for these extinctions. Urban sprawl and pollution threaten many species. During the last 200 years, more than 50 species of birds, more than 75 species of mammals, and perhaps hundreds of other species of animals and plants have become extinct.

IS THAT A FACT!

- ➤ Dinosaurs are not the biggest animals ever to live on Earth. Blue whales are bigger than the largest known dinosaur.

SECTION 2

Eras of the Geologic Time Scale

▶ Probing into Earth's Past and Beyond

In an effort to gain insights into Earth's past, a huge machine called an *ion microprobe* is closely examining tiny clusters of atoms in ancient rocks. When a flake of rock is placed in the machine, isotopes of certain elements in the flake can be sorted and counted. Using this technique to study the apatite from an island off Greenland, scientists were able to learn that the first signs of life on Earth came 400 million years earlier than previously thought. There weren't any fossils in the apatite, but there was chemical evidence that the 3.85-billion-year-old apatite had an organic origin.

▶ Experiment About the Origin of Life

In 1953, American scientist Stanley Miller devised an experiment to simulate life-forming conditions in the early environment. He mixed together hydrogen, ammonia, and methane (to represent the early air) and water (to represent the early oceans) in a flask. Then he applied electricity to the mixture and produced amino acids. His experiment demonstrated that the building blocks of life could be created on Earth chemically. Scientists have since found amino acids in meteorites, confirming that conditions favorable for their formation exist elsewhere and not just on primeval Earth.

IS THAT A FACT!

☛ Bristlecone pines are the oldest living trees. Some Colorado bristlecones have lived over 2,500 years. But they're young compared with the Sierra bristlecones, which have been dated as old as 4,765 years!

SECTION 3

Human Evolution

▶ Clues to Migration Route

Scientists believe that people passed through the Nile Valley of Egypt when they migrated from Africa, beginning about 100,000 years ago. Up until recently, no evidence supporting this idea existed. Now Pierre Vermeersch, an archaeologist from the Catholic University of Louvain, in Belgium, and some colleagues have found the skeleton of a child at Taramsa Hill, in the Nile Valley of southern Egypt. The skeleton of the child may be 80,000 years old

and is clearly that of a modern human. Similarities between its skull and teeth and those of equally old human remains found in East Africa and the Middle East suggest a relationship between the two populations.

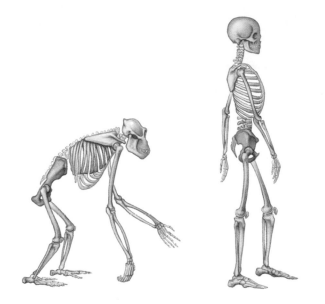

▶ Dawn of Language

Scientists Matt Cartmill and Richard Kay examined fossil hominid skulls and measured the hole through which the hypoglossal nerve passes in its course from the brain to the tongue. The hypoglossal nerve enables precise control over the tongue movements needed for speech. A large hole suggests a larger nerve. Chimpanzees have much smaller holes in their skulls than do modern humans. Because australopithecine skulls have small holes, like the skulls of chimpanzees, Cartmill and Kay think that australopithecines were unable to form words, as modern humans do.

For background information about teaching strategies and issues, refer to the *Professional Reference for Teachers.*

CHAPTER 6

The History of Life on Earth

Pre-Reading Questions

Students may not know the answers to these questions before reading the chapter, so accept any reasonable response.

Suggested Answers

1. by finding out where it was in relation to other fossils and by measuring the percentage of radioactive atoms in the sample

2. 150 million years

CHAPTER 6

The History of Life on Earth

Sections

Pre-Reading Questions

1. How can you tell how old a fossil is?

2. How long did dinosaurs roam the Earth?

130

MAMMOTH DISCOVERY

What is 23,000 years old, nine feet tall, and nicknamed "Zharkov"? Give up? It is the partial remains of a woolly mammoth—including huge tusks, bones, skin, and hair—dug up from the frozen ground in Siberia in late 1999. Its gigantic tusks appear in the photo. Scientists have determined that woolly mammoths roamed the frozen arctic until about 3,000 years ago. In this chapter, you will learn how scientists determine the age of fossils and about the history of life on Earth.

---

internet connect

go.hrw.com HRW On-line Resources	**sci LINKS** NSTA	**Smithsonian Institution**	**CNN fyi.com**
go.hrw.com For worksheets and other teaching aids, visit the HRW Web site and type in the keyword: **HSTHIS**	**www.scilinks.com** Use the sciLINKS numbers at the end of each chapter for additional resources on the **NSTA** Web site.	**www.si.edu/hrw** Visit the Smithsonian Institution Web site for related on-line resources.	**www.cnnfyi.com** Visit the CNN Web site for current events coverage and classroom resources.

EARTH'S TIMELINE

To help you understand Earth's history, make a timeline.

Procedure

1. Mark off 10 cm sections on a **strip of adding machine paper** that is 46 cm long. Divide each 10 cm section into ten 1 cm sections. (Each 1 cm represents 100 million years.)

2. Label each 10 cm section in order from top to bottom as follows: 1 bya (billion years ago), 2 bya, 3 bya, and 4 bya. The timeline begins at 4.6 bya.

3. At the appropriate place on your timeline, mark these important events of Earth's history:

   a. Earth began about 4.6 billion years ago.

   b. The earliest cells appeared about 3.5 billion years ago.

   c. Dinosaurs first appeared on Earth about 215 million years ago. Then about 65 million years ago, they became extinct.

   d. About 100,000 years ago, humans with modern features appeared.

4. Continue to mark events on your timeline as you learn about them in this chapter.

Analysis

5. Compare the length of time dinosaurs roamed the Earth with the length of time humans have existed.

131

START-UP
Activity

EARTH'S TIMELINE

MATERIALS

FOR EACH GROUP:
- pencil
- metric ruler
- strip of adding machine paper, 46 cm long

Teacher's Notes

Suggest that students tape the full length of the strip of paper securely to a flat surface before they begin to record measurements.

Make sure students can relate distance to a time scale.

Answer to START-UP Activity

5. Dinosaurs roamed for approximately 150 million years, and humans have existed for about 5 million years. Dinosaurs existed 30 times longer than humans have so far.

Focus

Evidence of the Past

This section introduces students to fossils and how they provide clues to Earth's past. Students learn how fossils form in sedimentary rock. They explore the methods scientists use to determine the age of fossils. Finally, students learn how scientists place events in the Earth's history in the correct order and what they think might have caused mass extinctions.

 Bellringer

Ask students to imagine that they didn't clean their room for 30 years. After 30 years, they finally decide to sort through the 2 m pile of stuff on their floor. Ask:

What might you find on the top of the pile? in the middle? on the bottom?

1) Motivate

ACTIVITY

Photo Analysis Have students bring in copies (*not* originals, since they may be irreplaceable) of old photos of themselves, and tack the copies on the bulletin board. Ask students to describe how they have changed during the years since the pictures were taken. Point out that scientists use traces or imprints of living things preserved in rock in a similar way to observe how life on Earth has changed over time.
Sheltered English

**Directed Reading
Worksheet Section 1**

Terms to Learn

fossil
relative dating
absolute dating
geologic time
  scale

extinct
plate tectonics

What You'll Do

◆ Explain how fossils are dated.
◆ Describe the geologic time scale and the information it provides scientists.
◆ Describe the possible causes of mass extinctions.
◆ Explain the theory of plate tectonics.

Evidence of the Past

Some scientists look for clues to help them reconstruct what happened in the past. These scientists are called paleontologists. *Paleontologists,* like the man in **Figure 1,** use fossils to reconstruct the history of life millions of years before humans existed. Fossils show us that life on Earth has changed a great deal. They also provide us with clues to how those changes occurred.

Figure 1 *In 1995, Paul Sereno found this dinosaur fossil in the Sahara Desert. The dinosaur may have been the largest land predator that has ever existed!*

Fossils

Fossils are traces or imprints of living things—such as animals, plants, bacteria, and fungi—that are preserved in rock. Fossils are usually formed when a dead organism is covered by a layer of sediment. These sediments may later be pressed together to form sedimentary rock. **Figure 2** shows one way fossils can be formed in this type of rock.

Figure 2 *The pictures below show one way fossils can form.*

❶ An organism dies and becomes buried in sediment.

❷ The organism gradually dissolves, leaving a hollow impression, or mold, in the sediment.

❸ Over time, the mold fills with sediment that forms a cast of the original organism.

SCIENTISTS AT ODDS

In the 1870s, two American scientists, Edward Drinker Cope and Othniel Charles Marsh, studied dinosaur fossils. They became bitter rivals and often argued. In 1878, Marsh and Cope were both excavating fossils near Como Bluff, Wyoming.

They had separate excavations and didn't want to share their findings. Both groups found more fossils than they could carry. To prevent the other group from taking their fossils, each group smashed all the fossils that couldn't be carried away.

The Age of Fossils

When paleontologists find a fossil, how do they determine its age? They can use one of two methods: relative dating or absolute dating.

Relative Dating A cross section of sedimentary rock shows many layers. The oldest layers are on the bottom, and the newer layers are on the top. If fossils are found in the rock, a scientist could start at the bottom and work upward to examine a sequence of fossils in the order that the organisms existed. This method of ordering fossils to estimate their age is known as **relative dating.**

Absolute Dating How can scientists determine the age of a fossil? The answer lies in particles called *atoms* that make up all matter. Atoms, in turn, are made of smaller particles. These particles are held together by strong forces. If there isn't enough force to hold them together, the atom is said to be unstable. Unstable atoms decay by releasing either energy or particles or both. That way, the atom becomes stable, but it also becomes a different kind of atom.

Each kind of unstable atom decays at its own rate. As shown in **Figure 3,** the time it takes for half of the unstable atoms in a sample to decay is its *half-life*. Half-lives range from fractions of a second to billions of years. By measuring the ratio of unstable atoms to stable atoms, scientists can determine the approximate age of a rock sample and the fossil it contains. This method is called **absolute dating.**

Figure 3 *Sometimes volcanic rock will cover a dead organism. By finding the age of the rock, scientists can get a good idea about the age of the fossil.*

Half-lives

A. The unstable atoms in the sample of volcanic rock have a half-life of 1.3 billion years. The sample contained 4 mg of unstable atoms when the rock formed.

B. After 1.3 billion years, or one half-life, only 2 mg of the unstable atoms will be left in the rock, and 2 mg of its stable decay product will have formed.

C. After another 1.3 billion years (two half-lives), there will only be 1 mg of the unstable atoms and 3 mg of the decay atoms.

D. How many milligrams of unstable atoms are left after 3 half-lives?

● Unstable element   ● Stable decay product

133

2 Teach

RETEACHING

Obtain a stack of old daily newspapers. Tell students that the dailies represent layers of sedimentary rock and that the pictures on the front pages represent fossils. Scramble the newspapers to make sure that they are not ordered according to date. Then have students stack the newspapers from oldest to newest, to simulate the layering of fossils over time. **Sheltered English**

CONNECT TO EARTH SCIENCE

The relative age of a fossil can be estimated by determining which layer of sedimentary rock the fossil is found in. You can illustrate the formation of sedimentary rock using Teaching Transparency 110.

Teaching Transparency 110
"The Rock Cycle"
LINK TO EARTH SCIENCE

Teaching Transparency 29
"Unstable Atoms and the Half-life"

Math Skills Worksheet
"Radioactive Decay and the Half-life"

Homework

Calculating To help students grasp the concept of half-life, have them solve these problems.

1. Thorium-232 has a half-life of 14.1 billion years. How much of an 8 mg sample will be unchanged after one half-life? (4 mg) two half-lives? (2 mg) three half-lives? (1 mg) four half-lives? (0.5 mg)

2. Carbon-14 has a half-life of 5,730 years. How much of the original sample will be left after 11,560 years? (one-fourth of the original sample) after 17,190 years? (one-eighth of the original sample)

internet connect

SCiLINKS   NSTA
TOPIC: Evidence of the Past
GO TO: www.scilinks.org
*sci*LINKS NUMBER: HSTL180

MEETING INDIVIDUAL NEEDS

Advanced Learners Geologic time is the period of time that Earth has been in existence. Geologic time is divided into eras. Eras are broken into smaller divisions called periods. Periods can be divided into epochs. Challenge students to construct a geologic time line that identifies all of these divisions. Tell them they can research in the library or on the Internet for information.

RESEARCH

Students could research plant and animal species that have become extinct within the last 200 years. Many of the extinctions were caused by human activities. Extinct birds include the dodo, great auk, Labrador duck, moa, and passenger pigeon. Extinct mammals include the Steller's sea cow and the quagga.

DISCUSSION

Explain to students that *mya* means "million years ago." Likewise, *my* means "million years" and *bya* means "billion years ago." Ask students why they think geologists use this form of dating.

Teaching Transparency 30 "The Geologic Time Scale and Representative Organisms"

The Geologic Time Scale

When you consider important events that have happened during your lifetime, you usually recall each event in terms of the day, month, or year in which it occurred. These divisions of time make it easier to recall when you were born, when you kicked the winning soccer goal, or when you started the fifth grade. Because the span of time is so great from the formation of the Earth to now, scientists also use a type of calendar to divide the Earth's long history into very long units of time.

The calendar scientists use to outline the history of life on Earth is called the **geologic time scale,** shown in the table at left. After a fossil is dated using relative and absolute dating techniques, a paleontologist can place the fossil in chronological order with other fossils. This forms a picture of the past that shows how organisms have changed over time.

Divisions in the Geologic Time Scale Paleontologists have divided the time scale into large blocks of time called *eras*. Each era has been subdivided into smaller blocks of time as paleontologists have continued to find more fossil information.

Eras are characterized by the type of animal that dominated the Earth at the time. For instance, the Mesozoic era—dominated by dinosaurs and other reptiles—is referred to as the Age of Reptiles. The end of each era is marked by the extinction of certain organisms. The next section analyzes the different eras of the geologic time scale in greater detail.

The Geologic Time Scale

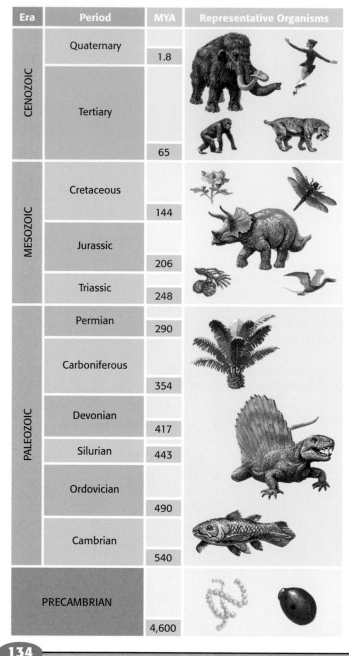

Era	Period	MYA	Representative Organisms
CENOZOIC	Quaternary	1.8	
	Tertiary	65	
MESOZOIC	Cretaceous	144	
	Jurassic	206	
	Triassic	248	
PALEOZOIC	Permian	290	
	Carboniferous	354	
	Devonian	417	
	Silurian	443	
	Ordovician	490	
	Cambrian	540	
PRECAMBRIAN		4,600	

134

In 1997, the most complete skeleton of a *Tyrannosaurus rex* ever found was auctioned. The winning bid was $8.36 million, made by the Field Museum of Natural History in Chicago. Scientists were relieved that a museum-led consortium was the highest bidder; their fear was that a private collector would buy the skeleton fossil, and scientists and the public would not be allowed to view it. Ask students how they feel about nonscientists owning and controlling access to fossils.

Mass Extinctions Some of the important divisions in the geologic time scale are marked by events that caused many animal and plant species to die out completely, or become **extinct.** Once a species is extinct, it does not reappear. There have been several periods in the Earth's history when a large number of species died out at the same time. These periods of large-scale extinction are called *mass extinctions.*

Scientists are not sure what causes mass extinctions. Mass extinctions may result from major changes in the Earth's climate or atmosphere. Some scientists think the mass extinction of the dinosaurs occurred when a meteorite collided with Earth and caused catastrophic climate changes. An artist's depiction of this event is shown in **Figure 4.** Changes in the climate may have also been caused by the movement of continents. Read on to find out how this is possible.

Figure 4 *A meteorite hit Earth about 65 million years ago, perhaps leading to major climatic changes.*

Scientists estimate that only a small fraction ($1/20$ of 1 percent) of all the species that have ever existed on Earth are living today. All the other species existed in the past and then became extinct.

Self-Check

Ten grams of an unstable atom were present in a rock when the rock solidified. In grams, how much of these atoms will be present after one half-life? What amount of the unstable atoms will be present after two half-lives? *(See page 216 to check your answers.)*

135

GOING FURTHER

Poster Project Have students research what their area was like millions of years ago. They can develop a written report and a poster describing the climate, living things, and landforms at different points in time.

INDEPENDENT PRACTICE

If any students have rock collections, ask them to share these collections with the class. Allow students time to observe the different collections and to ask questions about them.
 Sheltered English

Answer to Self-Check

5 g, 2.5 g

Critical Thinking Worksheet 8
"Fossil Revelations"

Math Skills Worksheet 45
"Geologic Time Scale"

 internet**connect**

SciLINKS
NSTA
TOPIC: Mass Extinctions
GO TO: www.scilinks.org
*sci*LINKS NUMBER: HSTL185

TOPIC: The Geologic Time Scale
GO TO: www.scilinks.org
*sci*LINKS NUMBER: HSTL190

 **SCIENCE**

One species that became extinct during the time of the dinosaurs was the insect having the largest wingspan on record. The insect belonged to the order Protodonata, and it measured an astonishing 76 cm (30 in.) from wingtip to wingtip. Its body was 46 cm (18 in.) long. It died out about 200 million years ago. Fossils of this insect have been found in Kansas.

RETEACHING

Ask students to draw a picture in their ScienceLog illustrating how future plate movements might change the geography of the world. (Some predictions might include a wider Atlantic Ocean and a shift northward of Africa, Australia, and South America.)

MEETING INDIVIDUAL NEEDS

Advanced Learners Ask students: What might have happened to the animals inhabiting Pangea as it broke up? How might the changing landscape influence the evolution of living things? Have students explain how the breakup might have affected the distribution of animal species. Encourage students to use diagrams or other visual effects when sharing their ideas with the class. (Student responses should demonstrate an understanding that changes within the environment affect the ability of certain organisms to survive.)

CONNECT TO EARTH SCIENCE

The Great Rift Valley of Africa marks a spreading center that is found on a continent. Have students identify the rift valley on a map. Ask: What kind of features mark this location? (deep valleys and lakes)

What do you think will become of this rift valley in a few million years? (It will probably continue to widen and eventually become an inland sea.)

Teaching Transparency 31 "Formation of the Modern Continents"

The Changing Earth

Do you know that dinosaur fossils have been found on Antarctica? Antarctica, now frozen, must have once had a warm climate to support these large reptiles. How could this be? Antarctica and the other continents have not always been in their present position. Antarctica was once located nearer the equator!

About **245 million years ago,** the continents were one giant landmass called Pangaea. The grey outlines indicate where the continents are today.

About **180 million years ago,** Pangaea began to divide into two pieces: Laurasia and Gondwanaland.

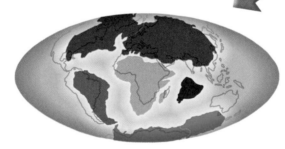

Even as recently as **65 million years ago,** the location of Earth's continents was very different from their current location.

Pangaea If you take a look at a map of the world, you might notice that the shapes of the continents seem to resemble pieces of a puzzle. If you could move the pieces around, you might find that some of them almost fit together. A similar thought occurred to the German scientist Alfred Wegener in the early 1900s. He proposed that long ago the continents were part of one great landmass surrounded by a single gigantic ocean. Wegener called that single landmass *Pangaea* (pan JEE uh), meaning "all Earth."

Wegener thought our present continents were once part of one great supercontinent for three reasons. First, the shapes of the continents seemed to "fit" together. Second, fossils of plants and animals discovered on either side of the Atlantic Ocean were very similar. Third, Wegener noticed that glaciers had existed in places that now have very warm climates. **Figure 5** shows how the continents may have formed from Pangaea.

Figure 5 *Because the continents are moving 1–10 cm per year, the continents will be arranged very differently in 150 million years.*

Multicultural CONNECTION

Tell the class that the Mid-Atlantic Ridge rises above water at only one place, Iceland. Point to Iceland on a map, and indicate the Arctic Circle, which includes the northern part of the island. Tell students that these two features suggest that Iceland is a place of both extreme cold and extreme heat. Ask students to do some research on what life is like in Iceland. Have them focus on how geologic processes, such as glaciers, geysers, and volcanic activity, affect the lifestyle of the people who live there.

Do the Continents Move? In the mid-1960s, J. Tuzo Wilson of Canada came up with the idea that it wasn't the continents that were moving. Wilson thought that huge pieces of the Earth's crust are driven back and forth by forces within the planet. Each huge piece of crust is called a *tectonic plate*. Wilson's theory of how these huge pieces of crust move around the globe is called **plate tectonics.**

According to Wilson, the outer crust of the Earth is broken into seven large, rigid plates and several smaller ones, shown in **Figure 6.** The continents and oceans ride on top of these plates. It is the motion of the plates that causes continents to move.

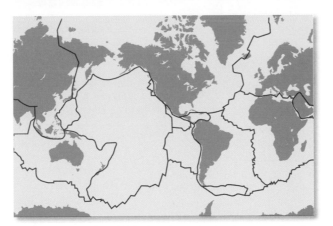

Figure 6 *Scientists think that the tectonic plates, outlined above, have been slowly rearranging the continents since the crust cooled billions of years ago.*

Adaptation in Slow Motion Although tectonic plates move very slowly, the motion of continents affects living organisms. Living things usually have time to adapt, through evolution, to the changes brought about by moving continents. That is why you are able to see living things that are well adapted to the environment they live in. In the same location, however, you may find fossil evidence of very different organisms that could not survive the changes.

SECTION REVIEW

1. What information does the geologic time scale provide, and what are the major divisions of time?

2. What is one possible cause of mass extinctions?

3. Explain one way that geological changes in the Earth can cause plants and animals to change.

4. What is the difference between relative dating and absolute dating of fossils?

5. **Understanding Concepts** Fossils of *Mesosaurus,* a small aquatic lizard, shown at right, have been found only in Africa and South America. Using what you know about plate tectonics, how would you explain this finding?

137

▼ *Answers to Section Review*

1. The geologic time scale provides classification of geologic time; Precambrian time, Paleozoic, Mesozoic, Cenozoic

2. perhaps a drastic change in the environment

3. Geologic changes cause animals of a single species to become separated and new species to form.

4. Relative dating is determining when a fossil was formed by examining where the fossil appears in the layers of rock. Absolute dating is measuring the percentage of radioactive material left in the rock surrounding a fossil.

5. Perhaps *Mesosaurus* evolved after Laurasia and Gondwanaland separated but before South America and Africa separated.

4) Close

Quiz

1. What is a fossil? How are fossils usually formed? (Fossils are traces or imprints of living things that are preserved in rock. Fossils are usually formed when an organism is buried in sediments that harden into rock.)

2. What can scientists learn about Earth's past from fossils? (Fossils provide evidence that life on Earth has changed and show how those changes occurred.)

3. Why would fossils found in rock layers near Earth's surface probably be younger than those found in rock layers at the bottom of a deep canyon? (The upper layers were deposited more recently than the lower layers.)

ALTERNATIVE ASSESSMENT

Each student in a group receives three blank cards. The group looks at the geologic time scale on page 134 and thinks of questions that could be answered using information presented on the time scale. Students write a question on one side of a card. They stack the cards with the blank sides up. In turn, each student draws a card, reads the question on it, and attempts to answer the question. Group members determine if the answer is correct by consulting the geologic time scale.

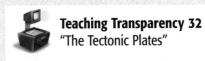

Teaching Transparency 32 "The Tectonic Plates"

Reinforcement Worksheet "Earth Timeline"

Focus

Eras of the Geologic Time Scale

This section discusses current theories regarding the origin of life. Students are introduced to the four eras of geological time in chronological order:

the Precambrian, the Paleozoic, the Mesozoic, and the Cenozoic. They learn about the life-forms that characterize each era.

Bellringer

Write the following supposition on the board or on an overhead projector for students to address in their ScienceLog:

Suppose that electric energy was never developed. How would your life differ from what it is like now?

Discuss with students the consequences of great changes over time.

1 Motivate

DISCUSSION

Historical Perspective Have students pretend that they are in a time-travel machine. What scientifically significant events would they witness as they travel back in time to Earth's origin? List the events on the board in the order that they are suggested. Ask students how they can determine whether the events are in chronological order. (They can consult the geologic time scale or other scientific materials.)

Directed Reading Worksheet Section 2

Terms to Learn

Precambrian time
Paleozoic era
Mesozoic era
Cenozoic era

What You'll Do

◆ Outline the major developments that allowed for the existence of life on Earth.
◆ Describe the different types of organisms that arose during the four eras of the geologic time scale.

Eras of the Geologic Time Scale

Look at the photograph of the Grand Canyon shown in **Figure 7**. If you look closely, you will notice that the walls of the canyon are layered with different kinds and colors of rocks. The deeper you go down into the canyon, the older the layer of rocks. It may surprise you to learn that each layer of the Grand Canyon was once the top layer. Billions of years ago the bottom layer was on top!

Each layer tells a story about what was happening on Earth when that layer was on top. The story is told mainly by the types of rocks and fossils found in the layer. In studying these different rocks and fossils, scientists have divided geologic history into four eras: Precambrian time, the Paleozoic era, the Mesozoic era, and the Cenozoic era.

Precambrian Time

If you journey to the bottom of the Grand Canyon, you can see layers of Earth that are over 1 billion years old. These layers are from Precambrian time. **Precambrian time** began when the Earth originated 4.6 billion years ago, and continued until about 540 million years ago. During this time life began and transformed the planet.

Figure 7 Each rock layer of the Grand Canyon is like a page in the "history book of the Earth."

138

IS THAT A FACT!

Throughout Earth's history, the forces of erosion have been altering the planet's surface, making it almost impossible to find rocks older than 3.5 billion years. However, a number of rocks dating from about 3.5 to 3.9 billion years ago have been found in Canada and Greenland. The oldest of the rocks was found in the Northwest Territories of Canada in 1989.

The Early Earth Scientists hypothesize that life began when conditions were quite different from Earth's current environment. These conditions included an atmosphere that lacked oxygen but was rich in other gases, such as carbon monoxide, carbon dioxide, hydrogen, and nitrogen. Also, the early Earth, as illustrated in **Figure 8,** was a place of great turmoil. Meteorites crashed into the Earth's surface. Violent thunderstorms and volcanic eruptions were constant on the young planet. Intense radiation, including ultraviolet radiation from the sun, bombarded Earth's surface.

Figure 8 *The early Earth was a violent place.*

How Did Life Begin? Scientists hypothesize that under these conditions, life developed from nonliving matter. In other words, life started from the chemicals that already existed in the environment. These chemicals included water, clay, dissolved minerals in the oceans, and the gases present in the atmosphere. The energy present in the early Earth caused these chemicals to react with one another, forming the complex molecules that made life possible.

Some scientists further hypothesize that for millions of years these small, complex molecules floated in the ancient oceans and joined together to form larger molecules. These larger molecules combined into more-complicated structures. As time passed, complicated structures developed into cell-like structures that eventually became the first true cells, called prokaryotes. *Prokaryotes* are cells that lack a nucleus. Early prokaryotic cells, like the one shown in **Figure 9,** were *anaerobic,* which means they did not require oxygen to survive. Many varieties of anaerobic organisms still live on Earth today. Organisms that need oxygen could not have survived on early Earth because there was no free oxygen in the atmosphere.

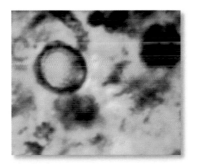

Figure 9 *Fossilized prokaryotes (such as the circular structure in the photograph) suggest that life first appeared on Earth more than 3.5 billion years ago.*

2 Teach

ACTIVITY

Using Maps Have students locate the three earthquake and volcano zones on a world map. One zone extends nearly all the way around the edge of the Pacific Ocean. A second zone is located near the Mediterranean Sea and extends across Asia into India. The third zone extends through Iceland to the middle of the Atlantic Ocean. Sheltered English

GUIDED PRACTICE

Concept Mapping Have students construct a concept map that shows how life on Earth developed from nonliving matter. They should base their map on information presented in the last two paragraphs on this page. The primary subject headings should refer to the chemicals that already exist in the environment. The final part of the concept map should identify prokaryotes as the first life-forms to appear on Earth.

USING THE FIGURE

Tell students that fossils can indicate how the Earth's surface has evolved. Ask them what they think scientists could infer if they found a fossil, such as the one shown in **Figure 9,** in rocks high above sea level. (The area was once covered by water.)

139

CONNECT TO
EARTH SCIENCE

Have students research mountain ranges that formed during the different geologic eras and locate them on a world map. Paleozoic era: Caledonian Mountains of Scandinavia, Acadian Mountains of New York, Appalachian Mountains of North America, and the Ural Mountains of Russia; Mesozoic era: Palisades Mountains of New Jersey and the Rocky Mountains of North America; Cenozoic era: Andes Mountains of South America, Alps of Central Europe, and the Himalayas of Central Asia.

DISCUSSION

Ask students how they think the emergence of cyanobacteria and their ability to photosynthesize affected the evolution of organisms on Earth. (Organisms that use oxygen were able to evolve.)

USING THE FIGURE

The organisms in **Figure 10** are cyanobacteria. These organisms can photosynthesize, making their own food from sunlight and carbon dioxide. Unlike plants, however, many species also can take in nitrogen from the atmosphere and convert it to a form that plants can use. Plants rely on other organisms to "fix" nitrogen gas into a form plants can use. Ask students: How might this ability to fix nitrogen make cyanobacteria useful to rice farmers? (Rice is grown in "paddies," which are wet, warm areas. The plants actually grow in the shallow water of the paddies. Cyanobacteria in the water make nitrogen compounds and excrete them, fertilizing the rice plants.)

MEETING INDIVIDUAL NEEDS

Learners Having Difficulty

Help students understand the importance of photosynthesis in the evolution of life on Earth. Ask them what kind of organisms were living before the development of photosynthesis. (anaerobic prokaryotes)

Then ask them how life on Earth changed after photosynthesis. (Many aerobic organisms evolved.)

Have students write answers to the questions and accompany their answers with illustrations.

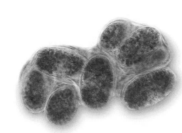

Figure 10 *Cyanobacteria are the simplest living organisms that photosynthesize.*

Environment
CONNECTION

Ozone depletion in the upper atmosphere is a serious problem. Chemicals, such as those used in refrigerators and air conditioners, are slowly destroying the ozone layer in the Earth's atmosphere. Because of ozone depletion, all living things are exposed to higher levels of radiation, which can cause skin cancer. Some countries have outlawed ozone-depleting chemicals.

140

Most of us think of Earth as an oxygen-rich planet. In actuality, only about 20 percent of Earth's present atmosphere is oxygen. The rest is made up mostly of nitrogen.

The Earth's First Pollution—Oxygen! As indicated by the fossil record, prokaryotic organisms called cyanobacteria appeared more than 3 billion years ago. Cyanobacteria, pictured in **Figure 10,** are photosynthetic organisms, which means that they use sunlight to produce food. One of the byproducts of this process is oxygen. As cyanobacteria carried out photosynthesis, they released oxygen gas into the oceans. The oxygen then escaped out into the air, changing Earth's atmosphere forever. Over the next several million years, more and more oxygen was added to the atmosphere.

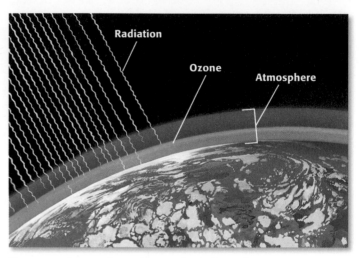

Figure 11 *Oxygen from photosynthesis formed ozone, which helps to absorb ultraviolet radiation.*

Radiation Shield As the atmosphere filled with oxygen, some of the oxygen formed a layer of ozone in the upper atmosphere, as shown in **Figure 11.** *Ozone* is a gas that absorbs ultraviolet (UV) radiation from the sun. UV radiation damages DNA but is absorbed by water. Before ozone formed, therefore, life was restricted to the oceans and underground. But the new ozone blocked out most of the UV radiation. This brought radiation on Earth's surface down to a level that allowed life to move onto dry land.

Life's So Complex The fossil record tells us that after a long period of time, about 1 billion years, more-complex life-forms appeared. These organisms, known as *eukaryotes,* are much larger than prokaryotes. They contain a central nucleus and a complicated internal structure. Scientists think that over the past 2.5 billion years, eukaryotic cells have evolved together to form organisms that are composed of many cells.

The Paleozoic Era

The **Paleozoic era** began about 540 million years ago and ended about 248 million years ago. *Paleozoic* comes from the Greek words meaning "ancient life." Considering how long Precambrian time lasted, the Paleozoic era was relatively recent. Rocks from the Paleozoic era are rich in fossils of animals such as sponges, corals, snails, clams, squids, and trilobites. Fishes, the earliest animals with backbones, also appeared during this era, and ancient sharks became abundant. Some Paleozoic organisms are shown in **Figure 12.**

The Greening of the Earth During the Paleozoic era, plants, fungi, and air-breathing animals colonized dry land over a period of 30 million years. Plants provided the first land animals with food and shelter. By the end of the Paleozoic era, forests of giant ferns, club mosses, horsetails, and conifers covered much of the Earth. All major plant groups except for flowering plants appeared during this era.

Creepers Crawl onto Land Fossils indicate that crawling insects were some of the first animals to appear on land. They were followed by large salamanderlike animals. Near the end of the Paleozoic era, reptiles, winged insects, cockroaches, and dragonflies appeared.

The largest mass extinction known occurred at the end of the Paleozoic era, about 248 million years ago. As many as 90 percent of all marine species died out.

Self-Check

Place the following events in chronological order:

a. The ozone layer formed, and living things moved onto dry land.

b. Gases in the atmosphere and minerals in the oceans combined to form small molecules.

c. The first prokaryotic, anaerobic cells appeared.

d. Cyanobacteria appeared.

(See page 216 to check your answer.)

Figure 12 *Organisms that appeared in the Paleozoic era include the first reptiles, amphibians, fishes, worms, and ferns.*

141

Homework

Comparing Organisms Have students compare the characteristics of each of the Paleozoic organisms pictured on this page with those of a descendant living today. Students can organize the information in the form of a chart.

READING STRATEGY

Have students read the text on this page. Have them write in their ScienceLog new headings for the first three paragraphs. For example, the heading for the first paragraph might be *Life Is Abundant in the Seas;* the heading for the second paragraph might be *Huge Forests of Ferns and Other Plants Develop;* and the heading for the third paragraph might be *Animals That Live on Land All the Time Appear.*

MATH and MORE

Using the premise that the Earth is 4.6 billion years old, have students calculate the length of the Earth's Precambrian and Paleozoic eras. They should use the information presented in the first paragraph on this page to determine the length of each of the eras (in millions of years). (Precambrian: 4,600−540 = 4,060, Paleozoic: 540−248 = 292.)

Math Skills Worksheet "Subtraction Review"

Answer to Self-Check

b, c, d, a

REAL-WORLD CONNECTION

The huge plants that grew in forests during the Paleozoic era later became coal. Ask students to research the locations of the world's coal deposits and mark them on a world map. (Most of the known coal reserves are in Australia, China, Germany, Poland, Great Britain, India, Russia, South Africa, the United States, and Canada.)

READING 📖 STRATEGY

Prediction Guide Before students read the text on these pages, ask them whether the following events occurred in the Mesozoic era, which began about 248 million years ago, or in the Cenozoic era, which began about 65 million years ago and continues today:

- Dinosaurs dominated Earth and then died out by the end of this era. (Mesozoic)
- Mammals appeared. (Mesozoic)
- Rock layers close to Earth's surface contain fossils from this era. (Cenozoic)
- The first birds appeared. (Mesozoic)
- Humans appeared. (Cenozoic)

RESEARCH

Writing Have students research reptiles and list their distinctive characteristics. (Reptiles are ectothermic; they have a distinctive type of heart; most reptiles have scales; many reptiles have claws; and most reptiles lay their eggs on land.)

Tell students that all living reptiles fall into four orders—turtles, lizards and snakes, crocodiles and related forms, and the tuatara. Have students investigate these orders and list examples of each.

internet**connect**

SCI**LINKS**
NSTA

TOPIC: Birds and Dinosaurs
GO TO: www.scilinks.org
sciLINKS NUMBER: HSTL200

The Mesozoic Era

The **Mesozoic era** began about 248 million years ago and lasted about 183 million years. *Mesozoic* comes from the Greek words meaning "middle life." Scientists think that, after the extinctions of the Paleozoic era, a burst of evolution occurred among the surviving reptiles, resulting in many different species. Therefore, the Mesozoic era is commonly referred to as the Age of Reptiles.

Life in the Mesozoic Era Dinosaurs are the most well known of the reptiles that evolved during the Mesozoic era. Dinosaurs dominated the Earth for about 150 million years. (Consider that humans and their ancestors have been around for only about 4 million years.) Dinosaurs had a great variety of physical characteristics, such as duck bills and projecting spines. In addition to dinosaurs, there were giant marine lizards that swam in the ocean. The first birds also appeared during the Mesozoic era. The most important plants during the early part of the Mesozoic era were cone-bearing seed plants, which formed large forests. Flowering plants appeared later in the Mesozoic era. Some of the organisms that appeared during the Mesozoic era are shown in **Figure 13.**

A Bad Time for Dinosaurs At the end of the Mesozoic era, 65 million years ago, dinosaurs and many other animal and plant species became extinct. What happened to the dinosaurs? According to one hypothesis, a large meteorite hit the Earth and generated giant dust clouds and enough heat to cause worldwide fires. The dust and smoke from these fires blocked out much of the sunlight, causing many plants to die out. Without enough plants to eat, the plant-eating dinosaurs died out. As a result, the meat-eating dinosaurs that fed on the plant-eating dinosaurs died. Global temperatures may have dropped for many years. Only a few organisms, including some small mammals, were able to survive.

Figure 13 *The Mesozoic era ended with the mass extinction of most of the large animals. Survivors included small mammals and* Archaeopteryx.

142

🌐 **Multicultural CONNECTION**

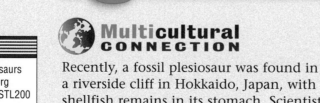

Recently, a fossil plesiosaur was found in a riverside cliff in Hokkaido, Japan, with shellfish remains in its stomach. Scientists had long suspected that plesiosaurs were predators, but they had no proof. Geologist Tamaki Sato thinks that the plesiosaur swallowed its tiny prey whole because its long, sharp teeth were unsuitable for crushing hard outer shells.

The Cenozoic Era

The **Cenozoic era** began about 65 million years ago and continues today. *Cenozoic* comes from the Greek words meaning "recent life." Scientists have more information about the Cenozoic era than about any of the previous eras because fossils from the Cenozoic era are embedded in rock layers that are close to the Earth's surface. This makes them easier to find. During the Cenozoic era, many kinds of mammals, birds, insects, and flowering plants appeared. Some organisms that appeared in the Cenozoic era are shown in **Figure 14.**

A Good Time for Large Mammals The Cenozoic era is sometimes referred to as the Age of Mammals. Mammals came to dominate the Cenozoic era much as reptiles dominated the Mesozoic era. Early Cenozoic mammals were small forest dwellers. Larger mammals appeared later. Some of these larger mammals had long legs for running, teeth that were specialized for eating different kinds of food, and large brains. Cenozoic mammals include mastodons, saber-toothed cats, camels, giant ground sloths, and small horses.

Figure 14 *Many types of mammals evolved during the Cenozoic era.*

SECTION REVIEW

1. What is the main difference between the atmosphere 3.5 billion years ago and the atmosphere today?
2. How do prokaryotic cells and eukaryotic cells differ?
3. Explain why cyanobacteria are so important to the development of new life-forms.
4. **Identifying Relationships** Match the organisms to the time period in which they first appeared.

1. eukaryotes	a. Precambrian time
2. dinosaurs	b. Paleozoic era
3. fishes	c. Mesozoic era
4. flowering plants	d. Cenozoic era
5. birds	

internetconnect

SCI LINKS. NSTA

TOPIC: Mass Extinctions, The Geologic Time Scale

GO TO: www.scilinks.org

***sci*LINKS NUMBER:** HSTL185, HSTL190

4 Close

Quiz

On index cards write the names of the organisms mentioned in the four geologic eras. Then on paper strips write the names of the geologic eras, and place the strips on a tabletop. Direct students to classify each organism named on a card by placing the card under the paper strip with the name of the appropriate geologic era.

Alternative Assessment

Divide students into groups of four. Groups should use boxes with covers and art materials to make a diorama of each of the four geologic eras. Each group member should be responsible for a designated era. Sheltered English

Going Further

Making Models Dinosaurs varied greatly in size and appearance. Have groups of students consult reference books to find information about the many kinds of dinosaurs. Then have them use art materials to make models of different dinosaurs. Models should include flying and marine reptiles as well as land-dwelling reptiles. Sheltered English

Answers to Section Review

1. Now we have enough atmospheric oxygen for life as we know it to exist.
2. Eukaryotes are usually much bigger, have a nucleus, and have a more complicated structure than do prokaryotes.
3. Cyanobacteria were the first significant source of atmospheric oxygen on the planet.
4. 1. a; 2. c; 3. b; 4. c ; 5. c

Reinforcement Worksheet "Condensed History"

Interactive Explorations CD-ROM "Rock On!"

Focus

Human Evolution

In this section, students will learn that scientists think humans share a common ancestor and common characteristics with other primates, such as apes and monkeys. This section describes the characteristics of hominids and explains how trends in their evolution gave rise to modern humans.

🔊 Bellringer

On the board or an overhead projector, pose the following question to your students at the beginning of class:

What makes you unique among your family members? Please write the answer in your Science-Log. (Responses might include references to food preferences, physical appearances, and talents.)

Point out that understanding evolution requires recognizing similarities and differences, like those seen in families.

1 Motivate

DISCUSSION

Comparing Primates Display a picture of an ape and a picture of a human for students to compare. Have students identify characteristics that the two animals have in common. (Most likely answers will include references to common physical characteristics.)

Then ask students how the two animals are different from each other. (Most likely answers will include references to differences in intellectual ability.)

Terms to Learn

primate	australopithecine
hominid	Neanderthal

What You'll Do

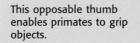

- ◆ Discuss the shared characteristics of primates.
- ◆ Describe what is known about the differences between hominids.

Human Evolution

After studying thousands of fossilized skeletons and other evidence, scientists theorize that humans evolved over millions of years from a distant ancestor that is also common to apes and monkeys. This common ancestor is thought to have lived more than 30 million years ago. How did we get from that distant ancestor to who we are today? This section presents some of the evidence that has been gathered so far.

Primates

To understand human evolution, we must first understand the characteristics that make us human beings. Humans are classified as primates. **Primates** are a group of mammals that includes humans, apes, monkeys, and prosimians. Primates have the characteristics illustrated below and in **Figure 15.**

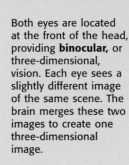

Figure 15 *The gorilla (left) and these orangutans (right) have characteristics that make them nonhuman primates, including opposable big toes!*

Characteristics of Primates

Most primates have five flexible fingers—four fingers plus an opposable thumb.

This opposable thumb enables primates to grip objects.

Both eyes are located at the front of the head, providing **binocular,** or three-dimensional, vision. Each eye sees a slightly different image of the same scene. The brain merges these two images to create one three-dimensional image.

144

BRAIN FOOD

Although the skulls of a human and a chimpanzee appear to be very similar, there are significant differences. The cranium of a human skull is domed, whereas the chimpanzee's cranium is flatter. Also, the canine teeth in the human skull do not overlap, as they do in the chimpanzee skull. Ask students what conclusions they might make about the brain and the chewing ability of a human and of a chimpanzee based on these differences. (A human brain is larger than a chimp's brain. A chimp can't easily move its jaws from side to side when chewing.)

Based on physical and genetic similarities, the closest living relative of humans is thought to be the chimpanzee. This conclusion does not mean that humans descended from chimpanzees. Rather, it means that humans and chimpanzees share a common ancestor. The ancestor of humans is thought to have diverged from the ancestor of the chimpanzee about 7 million years ago. Since then, humans and chimpanzees have evolved along different paths.

Hominids Humans are assigned to a family separate from other primates, called **hominids.** The word *hominid* refers specifically to humans and their human-like ancestors. The main characteristic that distinguishes hominids from other primates is walking upright on two legs as their main way of moving around. Walking on two legs is called *bipedalism*. Examine **Figure 16** to see some skeletal similarities and differences between a hominid and an ape. Except for present-day humans, all hominid species are now extinct.

Figure 16 *The bones of a gorilla and a human are basically the same in form, but the human pelvis is suited for walking upright.*

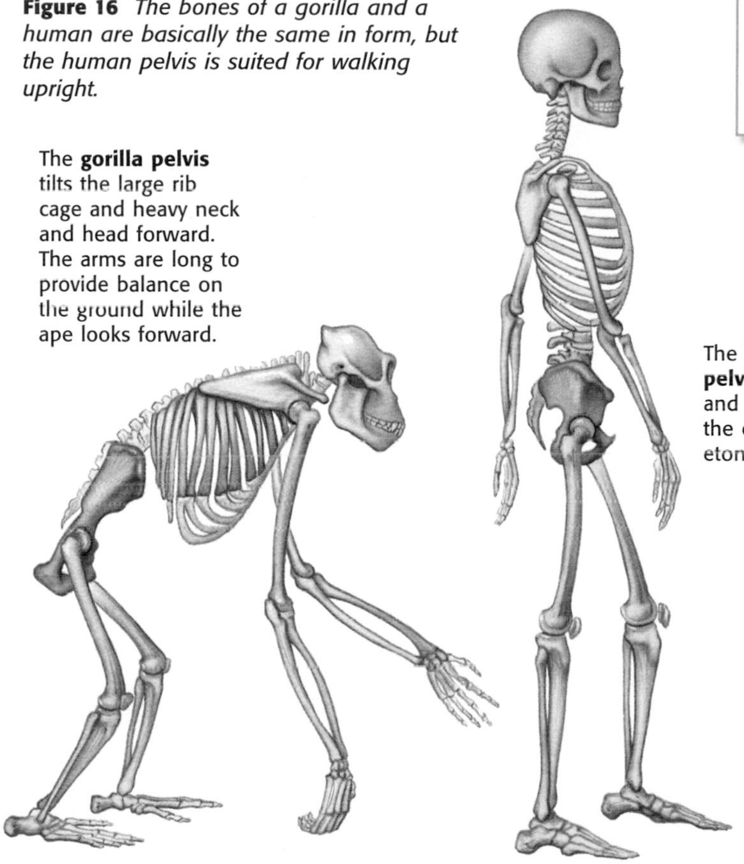

The **gorilla pelvis** tilts the large rib cage and heavy neck and head forward. The arms are long to provide balance on the ground while the ape looks forward.

The **human pelvis** is vertical and helps hold the entire skeleton upright.

QuickLab

Thumb Through This

Tape your thumbs to the side of your hands so they cannot be used. Attempt each of the tasks listed below.

- Sharpen a pencil.
- Cut a circle out of a piece of paper using scissors.
- Tie your shoelaces.
- Button several buttons.

After each attempt, answer the following questions:

1. Is the task more difficult with or without an opposable thumb?
2. Without an opposable thumb, do you think you would carry out this task on a regular basis?

TRY at HOME

145

CROSS-DISCIPLINARY FOCUS

Anthropology The ability to walk fully upright distinguishes us from the apes. So do our large rear ends. But are they a prerequisite or a consequence of upright posture? Thomas Greiner, a physical anthropologist, believes the latter is true. Greiner developed a computer model that shows how muscle action changes in response to changes in bone shape. By means of his model, Greiner concluded that having both a smaller gluteus maximus and a larger ilium than a human hinders an ape's ability to walk upright.

2) Teach

ACTIVITY

Exploring Vision Students can explore the utility of binocular vision by making a dot on a sheet of paper and placing the paper on a desktop. Have them stand about half a meter away from the desk and close their right eye. Then have them try to touch the dot on the paper with the tip of a pencil. Have them repeat the action with their left eye closed and then with both eyes open. (Students should find that it is easier to touch the dot with a pencil when they have both eyes open than when they have one eye closed.) Sheltered English

Answers to QuickLab

1. without
2. Probably not; it would be too difficult.

USING THE FIGURE

Discuss with students how binocular vision, illustrated at the bottom of page 144, is important. How is it useful to humans? (Answers should reflect an understanding that binocular vision enables humans to perceive depth and to judge distances, to hunt, use tools, drive vehicles, and play sports.)

Teaching Transparency 33 "Primate Skeletal Structures"

Directed Reading Worksheet Section 3

CROSS-DISCIPLINARY FOCUS

History Many cartoons in the nineteenth century satirized humans' relationship to apes. In one such cartoon, Henry Bergh, the founder of the Society for the Prevention of Cruelty to Animals, chides Charles Darwin for insulting apes by suggesting that they are related to humans.

USING THE FIGURE

Discuss the characteristics of the lemur shown in **Figure 17,** How might each characteristic help the lemur survive in its environment? (Students might suggest that the lemur's fur helps keep it warm, that its tail aids in balance, and so on.) Sheltered English

MEETING INDIVIDUAL NEEDS

Learners Having Difficulty Help students identify the characteristics that distinguish primates from other mammal groups. Show them pictures of primate and nonprimate mammals. Ask how the primates are different from the other animals. Help students determine that primates generally have flatter faces than nonprimates. Their eyes are located at the front of the head rather than at the sides, their snouts are small, and their fingers are flexible.

Figure 17 *Prosimians, such as this lemur, hunt in trees for insects and small animals.*

Hominid Evolution

The first primate ancestors appeared during the Cenozoic era, 55 million years ago, and evolved in several directions. These ancestors are thought to have been mouse-like mammals that were active during the night, lived in trees, and ate insects. When the dinosaurs died out, these mammals survived and gave rise to the first primates called *prosimians,* which means "before monkeys." Only a few species, such as the one pictured in **Figure 17,** survive today. How long after prosimians appeared did the first hominid appear? No one has been able to answer that question, but scientists have discovered fossil bones of hominids that date back to 4.4 million years ago.

Australopithecines Scientists think hominid evolution began in Africa. Among the oldest hominids are **australopithecines** (ah STRA loh PITH uh seens). The word *Australopithecus* means "southern man ape." These early hominids had long arms, short legs, and small brains. Fossil evidence shows that the australopithecines differed from apes in several important ways. For example, they were bipedal. Also, australopithecine brains were generally larger than ape brains, although they were still much smaller than the brains of present-day humans.

In 1976, paleoanthropologist Mary Leakey discovered a series of footprints in Tanzania. Mary Leakey and the footprints are pictured in **Figure 18.** By determining the age of the rock containing the prints, she learned that the footprints were more than 3.6 million years old. The footprints indicated that a group of three hominids had walked in an upright position across the wet volcanic ash-covered plain.

Figure 18 *Mary Leakey is shown here with the 3.6-million-year-old footprints.*

146

SCIENTISTS AT ODDS

In 1975, fossils of 13 hominids were found in Ethiopia. These fossils differed in body size and jaw shape. Some anthropologists think that the larger fossils represent the males and the smaller fossils represent the females of a particular species. Other anthropologists, including Mary Leakey, believe that the differences indicate that the fossils are of two distinct species.

Lucy In 1979, a group of fossils was discovered in Ethiopia. Included in this group was the most complete skeleton of an australopithecine ever found. Nicknamed Lucy, this australopithecine lived about 2 million years ago. Lucy had a sturdy body and stood upright, but her brain was about the size of a chimpanzee's. Fossil discoveries like this one demonstrate that upright posture evolved long before the brain enlarged.

A Face Like Ours Hominids with more humanlike facial features appeared approximately 2.3 million years ago, probably evolving from australopithecine ancestors. This species is known as *Homo habilis*. Its skull is shown in **Figure 19.** Fossils of *Homo habilis* have been found along with crude stone tools. About 2 million years ago, *Homo habilis* was replaced by its larger-brained descendant, *Homo erectus,* pictured in **Figure 20.** *Homo erectus* was larger than *Homo habilis* and had a smaller jaw.

Figure 19 Homo habilis *is called handy man because this group of hominids made stone tools.*

Hominids Go Global Fossil evidence shows that *Homo erectus* may have lived in caves, built fires, and wore clothing. They successfully hunted large animals and butchered them using tools made of flint and bone. The appearance of *Homo erectus* marks the beginning of the expansion of human populations across the globe. *Homo erectus* survived for more than 1 million years, which is longer than any other species of hominid has lived. *Homo erectus* disappeared about 200,000 years ago. This is about the time present-day humans, called *Homo sapiens*, first appear in the fossil record.

Although *Homo erectus* migrated across the globe, it is thought that *Homo sapiens* evolved in Africa and then migrated to Asia and Europe.

Figure 20 Homo erectus *lived about 2 million years ago and may have looked like the sculpture above.*

IS THAT A FACT!

Lucy's nickname came from the Beatles's hit song "Lucy in the Sky with Diamonds."

RETEACHING

Help students complete an outline describing the most important characteristics of *Australopithecus, Homo habilis,* and *Homo erectus.* Then have students identify characteristics common to two or more of the hominid species; for example, all of the species walked in an upright position, and both *Homo habilis* and *Homo erectus* made and used tools. Students could also identify characteristics unique to a species, such as that *Homo erectus* built fires.
 Sheltered English

DISCUSSION

Analyzing Tools *Homo habilis* is thought to have made one of the oldest recognizable stone tools. The tool was a pebble with some sharp edges. Ask students how they think the tool was made. (Answers should express the idea that flakes were chipped off the pebble to sharpen it.)

CROSS-DISCIPLINARY FOCUS

Art Sculptors probably helped paleoanthropologists determine the physical appearance of the hominid shown in **Figure 20.** Sculptors can apply their knowledge of anatomy to reconstruct body features. Have students use clay to sculpt a model of the head of *Homo erectus.*

internetconnect

TOPIC: Human Evolution
GO TO: www.scilinks.org
***sci*LINKS NUMBER:** HSTL195

3 Extend

GOING FURTHER

Have students use the description of Cro-Magnons on this page as a guide for drawing the head of a Cro-Magnon with facial features. **Sheltered English**

GROUP ACTIVITY

Writing Small groups of students can work together to write a play about hunting and killing a mammoth. Tell students that Cro-Magnons hunted together and that a mammoth kill was a group endeavor. How did they do it? What weapons might they have used? How did they carve the meat? What did they do with the skin, tusks, and bones? Did the hunt include women? Have each group present its play to the class.

INDEPENDENT PRACTICE

Poster Project
Provide students with markers and poster board. Have them construct evolutionary trees of humans with whole-body sketches.

Answer to Activity

Answers should include spearpoints, arrowheads, choppers, skinners, or scrapers.

Figure 21 *Neanderthals had heavy brow ridges, like* Homo erectus, *but a larger brain than modern humans.*

Activity

Neanderthals made sophisticated spear points and other stone tools. Examine the Neanderthal tools below. Each of these tools was specialized for a particular task. Can you suggest what each stone tool was used for?

TRY at HOME

148

Neanderthals In the Neander Valley, in Germany, fossils were discovered that belonged to a group of hominids referred to as **Neanderthals** (nee AN duhr TAHLS). They lived in Europe and western Asia beginning about 230,000 years ago.

Neanderthals hunted large animals, made fires, and wore clothing. There is evidence that they also cared for the sick and elderly and buried their dead, sometimes placing food, weapons, and even flowers with the dead bodies. Pictured in **Figure 21** is an artist's idea of how a Neanderthal might have looked. About 30,000 years ago, Neanderthals disappeared; nobody knows what caused their extinction.

Some scientists think the Neanderthals are a separate species, *Homo neanderthalensis*, from present-day humans, *Homo sapiens*. Other scientists think Neanderthals are a race of *Homo sapiens*. There is not yet enough evidence to fully answer this question.

Cro-Magnons In 1868, fossil skulls were found in caves in southwestern France. The skulls were about 35,000 years old, and they belonged to a group of *Homo sapiens* with modern features, called *Cro-Magnons*. Cro-Magnons may have existed in Africa 100,000 years ago and migrated from Africa about 40,000 years ago, coexisting with Neanderthals. Compared with Neanderthals, Cro-Magnons had a smaller and flatter face, and their skulls were higher and more rounded, like an artist has modeled in **Figure 22**. The only significant physical difference between Cro-Magnons and present-day humans is that Cro-Magnons had thicker and heavier bones.

Figure 22 *This is an artist's idea of how a Cro-Magnon woman may have looked.*

Science BlOOpers

A skull of a *Homo sapiens* who had bad teeth was found in Zambia. There was a hole in one side and signs of a partially healed abscess. This skull was made famous by a writer who imagined the hole was caused by a bullet shot from an interplanetary visitor's gun 120,000 years ago.

Some Cro-Magnon people made beautiful cave paintings. These paintings are the earliest known examples of human art. In fact, Cro-Magnon culture is marked by an amazing diversity of artistic efforts, including cave paintings, sculptures, and carvings, like the one shown in **Figure 23.** The preserved villages and burial grounds of Cro-Magnon groups also show that they had a complex social organization.

Figure 23 *Cro-Magnons left many kinds of paintings, sculptures, and carvings, such as this carving of a bull.*

New Evidence of Human Evolution Although we know a great deal about our hominid ancestors, much remains to be understood. Each fossil discovery causes great excitement and raises new questions, such as, "Where did *Homo sapiens* evolve?" Current evidence suggests that *Homo sapiens* evolved in Africa. "Which australopithecine gave rise to humans?" Some scientists think *Australopithecus afarensis* is the ancestor of all hominids, including present-day humans. But recent fossil discoveries indicate another australopithecine species gave rise to human ancestors. There is still much to be learned about the evolution of humans.

SECTION REVIEW

1. Identify three characteristics of primates.

2. Compare *Homo habilis* with *Homo erectus*. What made the two species different from one another?

3. What evidence suggests Neanderthals were like present-day humans?

4. **Inferring Conclusions** Imagine you are a scientist excavating an ancient campsite. What might you conclude about the people who used the site if you found the charred bones of large animals and various stone blades among human fossils?

internetconnect

SC*LINKS*
NSTA

TOPIC: Human Evolution
GO TO: www.scilinks.org
*sci*LINKS **NUMBER:** HSTL195

149

▼ **Answers to Section Review**

1. mammals, opposable thumbs, binocular vision

2. *Homo erectus* was larger, had a larger brain, and was a hunter.

3. They lived in social groups, buried their dead, made tools, hunted large animals, and wore clothing.

4. This group hunted, made and used tools, cooked with fire, and perhaps had a social organization.

4) Close

Quiz

1. What evidence do scientists have that Neanderthals are not a race of *Homo sapiens*? (DNA evidence from a Neanderthal tooth fossil suggests that they are a unique species.)

2. Among primates, what is distinctive about hominids? (The main characteristic that distinguishes hominids from other primates is walking upright on two legs as their main way of moving around.)

ALTERNATIVE ASSESSMENT

Concept Mapping Have students construct a chronological concept map of the following stages in human evolution:

human ancestors, *Homo erectus, Australopithecus*, Cro-Magnon, prosimian, *Homo habilis,* and Neanderthal

Tell students to then expand the concept map with at least three characteristics of each group.

ACTIVITY

Writing Have students provide written answers to the Review. (Answers are provided at the bottom of the page.)

Then have them write in their ScienceLog the conclusions that they think anthropologists 100,000 years in the future might make about us when they find the remains of food we ate and tools we used at an archaeological site.

The Half-life of Pennies
Teacher's Notes

Time Required

One 45-minute class period

Lab Ratings

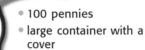

EASY ———————→ HARD

TEACHER PREP 🧪
STUDENT SET-UP 🧪🧪
CONCEPT LEVEL 🧪🧪
CLEAN UP 🧪

Lab Notes

It is useful to use coin tosses to explain half-life because approximately half the coins will land heads and half will land tails. Therefore, about half the entire quantity of coins tossed will be eliminated with each successive toss.

Skill Builder Lab

The Half-life of Pennies

Carbon-14 is an unstable element that is used in the absolute dating of material that was once alive, such as fossil bones. Every 5,730 years, half of the carbon-14 in a fossil specimen decays or breaks down into a more stable element. In the following activity, you will see how pennies can show the same kind of "decay."

MATERIALS

- 100 pennies
- large container with a cover

Procedure

1 Place 100 pennies in a large, covered container. Shake the container several times.

2 Remove the cover from the container. Carefully empty the contents of the container on a flat surface, making sure the pennies don't roll away.

3 Remove all the pennies that have the "head" side turned upward. In a data table similar to the one below, record the number of pennies removed and the number of pennies remaining.

4 Repeat the process until no pennies are left in the container. Remember to remove only the coins showing "heads."

Shake number	Number of coins remaining	Number of coins removed
1		
2	DO NOT WRITE	
3	IN BOOK	
4		
5		

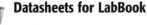
Datasheets for LabBook

CLASSROOM TESTED & APPROVED

Karma Houston-Hughes
Kyrene Middle School
Tempe, Arizona

5 In your ScienceLog, draw a graph similar to the one at right. Label the x-axis "Number of shakes," and label the y-axis "Pennies remaining." Use data from your data table to plot on your graph the number of coins remaining at each shake.

Analysis

6 Examine the "Half-life of Carbon-14" graph at right. Compare the graph you have made for the pennies with the one for carbon-14. Explain any similarities that you see.

7 The probability of landing "heads" in a coin toss is $\frac{1}{2}$. Use this information to explain why the remaining number of pennies is reduced by about half each time they are shaken and tossed.

8 Assume that each flip equals 5,000 years. How long did it take to remove all the pennies from the container?

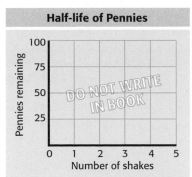

Half-life of Pennies

DO NOT WRITE IN BOOK

(y-axis: Pennies remaining — 25, 50, 75, 100; x-axis: Number of shakes — 0, 1, 2, 3, 4, 5)

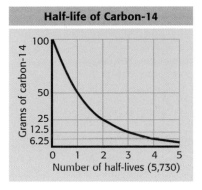

Half-life of Carbon-14

(y-axis: Grams of carbon-14 — 6.25, 12.5, 25, 50, 100; x-axis: Number of half-lives (5,730) — 0, 1, 2, 3, 4, 5)

Answers

6. The graphs should be very similar in shape. With each half-life and each shake, the number remaining will be reduced by half.

7. The remaining number of pennies is reduced by about half each time the pennies are shaken and tossed because there are only two faces on each coin. The rules of probability suggest that half will land heads and half will land tails, and therefore the amount will be reduced by about half with each shake.

8. Theoretically it would take 40,000 years to remove all of the pennies. Student answers may range from 40,000 to 55,000 years.

Chapter Highlights

Chapter Highlights

VOCABULARY DEFINITIONS

SECTION 1

fossil the solidified remains or imprints of once living organisms

relative dating determining whether an event or object, such as a fossil, is older or younger than other events or objects

absolute dating estimating the age of a sample or event in years, usually by measuring the ratio of unstable atoms to stable atoms in the sample

geologic time scale the division of Earth's 4.6-billion-year history into distinct intervals of time

extinct a species of organism that has died out completely

plate tectonics the study of the forces that drive the movement of pieces of the Earth's crust around the surface of the planet

SECTION 2

Precambrian time the period in the geologic time scale beginning when the Earth originated 4.6 billion years ago and continuing until complex organisms appear about 540 million years ago

SECTION 1

Vocabulary

fossil (p. 132)
relative dating (p. 133)
absolute dating (p. 133)
geologic time scale (p. 134)
extinct (p. 135)
plate tectonics (p. 137)

Section Notes

- Paleontologists are scientists who study fossils.

- The age of a fossil can be determined using relative dating and absolute dating. Relative dating is an estimate based on the known age of the sediment layer in which the fossil is found. Absolute dating usually involves the measurement of the rate of decay of the unstable atoms found in the rock surrounding the fossil.

- The geologic time scale is a calendar scientists use to outline the history of Earth and life on Earth.

- Many species existed for a few million years and then became extinct. Mass extinctions have occurred several times in Earth's history.

SECTION 2

Vocabulary

Precambrian time (p. 138)
Paleozoic era (p. 141)
Mesozoic era (p. 142)
Cenozoic era (p. 143)

Section Notes

- Precambrian time includes the formation of the Earth, the beginning of life, and the evolution of simple multi-cellular organisms.

☑ Skills Check

Math Concepts

HALF-LIFE To understand half-life better, imagine that you have $10.00 in your pocket. You determine that you are going to spend half of all the money you have in your possession every 30 minutes. How much will you have after 30 minutes? ($5.00) How much will you have after another 30 minutes? ($2.50) How much will you have after 3 hours? (a little more than 15¢)

Visual Understanding

THE GEOLOGIC TIME SCALE You have probably seen old movies or cartoons that show humans and dinosaurs inhabiting the same environment. Can this be possible? Dinosaurs and humans did not exist at the same time. Dinosaurs became extinct 65 million years ago. Humans and their ancestors have been around for less than 4 million years. Review the Geologic Time Scale on page 134.

152

Lab and Activity Highlights

The Half-life of Pennies PG 150

Datasheets for LabBook
(blackline masters for these labs)

SECTION 2

- The Earth is about 4.6 billion years old. Life formed from nonliving matter on the turbulent early Earth.

- The first cells, prokaryotes, were anaerobic. Later, photosynthetic cyanobacteria evolved and caused oxygen to enter the atmosphere.

- During the Paleozoic era, animals appeared in the oceans, and plants and animals colonized the land.

- Dinosaurs and other reptiles roamed the Earth during the Mesozoic era. Flowering plants, birds, and primitive mammals also appeared.

- Primates evolved during the Cenozoic era, which extends to the present day.

SECTION 3

Vocabulary

primate *(p. 144)*

hominid *(p. 145)*

australopithecine *(p. 146)*

Neanderthal *(p. 148)*

Section Notes

- Humans, apes, and monkeys are primates. Primates are distinguished from other mammals by their opposable thumbs and binocular vision.

- Hominids, a subgroup of primates, include humans and their human-like ancestors. The oldest known hominids are australopithecines.

- Neanderthals were a species of humans that disappeared about 30,000 years ago.

- Cro-Magnons did not differ very much from present-day humans.

VOCABULARY DEFINITIONS, *continued*

Paleozoic era the period in the geologic time scale beginning about 570 million years ago and ending about 248 million years ago

Mesozoic era the period in the geologic time scale beginning about 248 million years ago and ending about 65 million years ago

Cenozoic era the period in the geologic time scale beginning about 65 million years ago and continuing until the present day

SECTION 3

primate a group of mammals that includes humans, apes, and monkeys; distinguished by opposable thumbs and binocular vision

hominid a family of humans and several extinct humanlike species, some of which were human ancestors

australopithecine an early hominid that evolved more than 3.6 million years ago

Neanderthal a species of hominid that lived in Europe and western Asia from 230,000 years ago to about 30,000 years ago, when they mysteriously went extinct

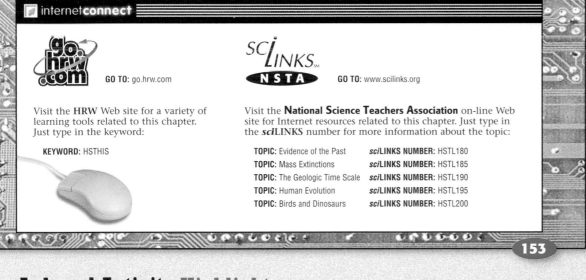

internetconnect

GO TO: go.hrw.com

Visit the **HRW** Web site for a variety of learning tools related to this chapter. Just type in the keyword:

KEYWORD: HSTHIS

SCi LINKS
N S T A

GO TO: www.scilinks.org

Visit the **National Science Teachers Association** on-line Web site for Internet resources related to this chapter. Just type in the *sci*LINKS number for more information about the topic:

TOPIC: Evidence of the Past   *sci*LINKS NUMBER: HSTL180
TOPIC: Mass Extinctions   *sci*LINKS NUMBER: HSTL185
TOPIC: The Geologic Time Scale   *sci*LINKS NUMBER: HSTL190
TOPIC: Human Evolution   *sci*LINKS NUMBER: HSTL195
TOPIC: Birds and Dinosaurs   *sci*LINKS NUMBER: HSTL200

153

Vocabulary Review Worksheet

Blackline masters of these Chapter Highlights can be found in the **Study Guide**.

Lab and Activity Highlights

LabBank

Long-Term Projects & Research Ideas, A Horse Is a Horse

Interactive Explorations CD-ROM

 CD 2, Exploration 6, "Rock On!"

Chapter Review
Answers

USING VOCABULARY
1. Precambrian time period
2. Cenozoic era
3. Mesozoic era
4. Paleozoic era
5. australopithecines

UNDERSTANDING CONCEPTS
Multiple Choice
6. b
7. c
8. b
9. b
10. c

Short Answer
11. Fossils tell us about the kinds of organisms that existed and how they changed over time.
12. Precambrian: life begins, prokaryotes and eukaryotes appear; Paleozoic: multicellular organisms, plants, insects, and amphibians appear; Mesozoic: dinosaurs and other reptiles, birds, and small mammals appear; Cenozoic: large mammals, including humans, and more-diverse birds and insects appear
13. Fossils in the Cenozoic era are closer to the surface of Earth and thus are easier to find.

Chapter Review

USING VOCABULARY

To complete the following sentences, choose the correct term from each pair of terms listed below:

1. During the ___?___ of the Earth's history, life is thought to have originated from nonliving matter. (*Precambrian time period* or *Paleozoic era*)

2. The Age of Mammals refers to the ___?___. (*Mesozoic era* or *Cenozoic era*)

3. The Age of Reptiles refers to the ___?___. (*Paleozoic era* or *Mesozoic era*)

4. Plants colonized dry land during the ___?___. (*Precambrian time* or *Paleozoic era*)

5. The most ancient hominids are called ___?___. (*Neanderthals* or *australopithecines*)

UNDERSTANDING CONCEPTS

Multiple Choice

6. Scientists estimate the age of the Earth to be about
   a. 10 billion years.
   b. 4.6 billion years.
   c. 3.8 billion years.
   d. 4.4 million years.

7. The first cells probably appeared about
   a. 10 billion years ago.
   b. 4.6 billion years ago.
   c. 3.5 billion years ago.
   d. 4.4 million years ago.

8. How is the age of a fossil estimated?
   a. by using the geologic time scale
   b. by measuring unstable elements in the rock that holds the fossil
   c. by studying the relative position of continents
   d. by measuring the amount of oxygen in the fossil rock

9. Plants and air-breathing animals appeared during this time period.
   a. Precambrian time
   b. Paleozoic era
   c. Mesozoic era
   d. Cenozoic era

10. These hominids made sophisticated tools, hunted large animals, wore clothing, and cared for the sick and elderly. Their extinction is a mystery.
    a. australopithecines
    b. hominids in the genus *Homo*
    c. Neanderthals
    d. Cro-Magnons

Short Answer

11. What kinds of information do fossils provide about the evolutionary history of life?

12. Name at least one important biological event that occurred during each of the following geologic eras: Precambrian time, Paleozoic era, Mesozoic era, and Cenozoic era.

13. Why are there usually more fossils from the Cenozoic era than from other geologic eras?

Concept Mapping

14. Use the following terms to create a concept map: Earth's history, humans, Paleozoic era, dinosaurs, Precambrian time, cyanobacteria, Mesozoic era, land plants, Cenozoic era.

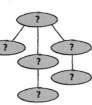

Concept Mapping

14. 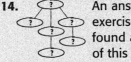 An answer to this exercise can be found at the front of this book.

CRITICAL THINKING AND PROBLEM SOLVING

Write one or two sentences to answer the following questions:

15. Why do scientists think the first cells were anaerobic?

16. List three evolutionary changes in early hominids that led to the rise of modern humans.

MATH IN SCIENCE

17. A rock containing a newly discovered fossil is found to contain 5 mg of an unstable form of potassium and 5 mg of the stable element formed from its decay. If the half-life of the unstable form of potassium is 1.3 billion years, how old is the rock? What can you infer about the age of the fossil?

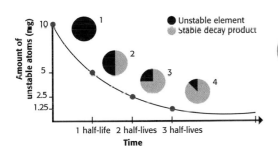

● Unstable element
● Stable decay product

1 half-life 2 half-lives 3 half-lives

Time

Amount of unstable atoms (mg)

INTERPRETING GRAPHICS

The figure below illustrates the evolutionary relationships between some primates. Examine the figure, and answer the questions.

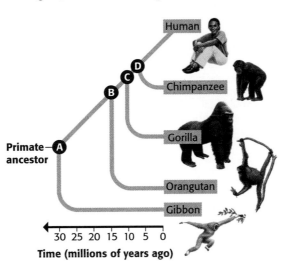

Human
Chimpanzee
Gorilla
Orangutan
Gibbon

Primate ancestor — A

30 25 20 15 10 5 0

Time (millions of years ago)

18. Which letter represents when gorillas took a different evolutionary path?

19. About how long ago did orangutan diverge from the human evolutionary line?

20. Which group has been separated from the human line of evolution the longest?

Reading Check-up

Take a minute to review your answers to the Pre-Reading Questions found at the bottom of page 130. Have your answers changed? If necessary, revise your answers based on what you have learned since you began this chapter.

Concept Mapping

14. An answer to this exercise can be found at the front of this book.

CRITICAL THINKING AND PROBLEM SOLVING

15. There was no oxygen available when they developed.

16. larger brains, longer legs, shorter arms

MATH IN SCIENCE

17. 1.3 billion years old; the fossil is also about 1.3 billion years old.

INTERPRETING GRAPHICS

18. point C
19. 15 million years ago
20. the gibbons

Concept Mapping Transparency 8

Blackline masters of this Chapter Review can be found in the **Study Guide**.

Background

Unlike the sun and the giant gas planets of the outer solar system, Earth and its three nearest planetary neighbors, Mercury, Venus, and Mars, are solid bodies with surfaces of rock. For this reason they are known as terrestrial planets. But even though the Earth has a solid, durable surface, it is constantly changing because of forces acting at and below its surface.

Rock is any naturally occurring solid mixture of minerals and other materials. Minerals, in turn, are any naturally occurring, inorganic chemical compound found in the Earth. Because there are so many minerals in the Earth's crust, there are also many types of rock. Rocks are broadly classified according to how they are formed.

Although all three rock types are found on the Earth's surface, most of the Earth's crust consists of igneous rock. We don't often see these igneous rocks because most of the continents are covered by a relatively thin layer of sedimentary rock. Only in a few places have natural processes brought the "basement rocks" to the Earth's surface, where we can see them.

LIFE SCIENCE • EARTH SCIENCE

Windows into the Past

When you think about the history of life on Earth, you may not think of rocks. After all, rocks are nonliving! What can they tell you about life? It may surprise you to learn that a great deal of what we know about life on Earth has been provided by rocks. How? It just so happens that life-forms have been fossilized between layers of rock for million of years—maybe even since life first appeared on Earth. And finding these fossils is like finding an old snapshot of ancient life-forms.

Layers of Rock

Fossils are most likely to be found in sedimentary rock. This is a type of rock that forms as exposed rock surfaces are worn away by wind, rain, and ice. The particles from these rock surfaces then collect in low-lying areas. As these layers build up, their combined weight compacts the particles, and chemical reactions cement them together. After thousands of years, the layers of particles become solid rock— and so do parts of any organism that has been trapped in the layers.

The Rock Cycle

The illustration at right shows how sedimentary rock forms. It also shows how igneous rock and metamorphic rock form. Notice that sedimentary and

metamorphic rock can melt and become igneous rock; this happens deep underground. Can you see why fossils would not normally be found in igneous rock?

The rock cycle is a continuous process. All three kinds of rock eventually become another type of rock. Fortunately for life scientists, this process can take millions of years. If this process happened more quickly—and sedimentary rock became either metamorphic or igneous rock at a faster pace—our fossil record would be much shorter. We may not have found out about the dinosaurs!

Cycle This!

▶ Suppose you found several fossils of the same organism. You found some fossils in very deep layers of sedimentary rock and some fossils in very shallow layers of sedimentary rock. What does this say about the organism?

▼ *The Rock Cycle*

Answer to Cycle This!

If fossils of the same type of organism are found in both deep and shallow layers of sedimentary rock, this probably indicates that the organism existed for the time span that the sedimentary rock containing the fossils was forming.

CAREERS

PALEOBOTANIST

In school **Bonnie Jacobs** was fascinated by fossils, ancient cultures, and geology. "I have always had an interest in ancient things," she says. To pursue her interests, Jacobs became a paleobotanist. "A paleobotanist is someone who studies fossil plants," she explains. "That means you study fossilized leaves, wood, pollen, flower parts, or anything else that comes from a plant."

Bonnie Jacobs teaches and does research at Southern Methodist University, in Dallas, Texas. As a paleobotanist, she uses special "snapshots" that let her "see" back in time. If you look at these snapshots, you might see an ancient grassland, desert, or rain forest. Jacobs's snapshots might even give you a glimpse of the place where our human family may have started.

Fossil Plants and Ancient Climates

Jacobs and other paleobotanists study present-day plant species and how they grow in different climates. Plants that grow in warm, wet climates today probably grew in the same kind of climate millions of years ago. So when Jacobs finds ancient plant fossils that are similar to plants that exist today, she can determine what the ancient climate was like. But her fossils give more than just a climate report.

Plants and . . . Ancient Bones

Because some of these same plant fossils are found in rocks that also contain bits of bone—some from human ancestors—they may hold clues to human history. "Ideas about the causes of human evolution have a lot to do with changes in the landscape," Jacobs explains. "For instance, many scientists who study human evolution assumed that there was a big change from forested to more-open environments just before the origin of the human family. That assumption needs to be tested. The best way to do that is to go back to the plants themselves."

It's an Adventure!

In doing her research, Jacobs has traveled to many different places and worked with a wide variety of people. "Kiptalam Chepboi, a colleague we worked with in Kenya, grew up in the area where we do fieldwork. He took me to a sweat-bee hive. Sweat bees don't sting. You can take a honeycomb out from under a rock ledge, pop the whole thing in your mouth, and suck out the honey without worrying about getting stung. That was one of the neatest things I did out there."

Making a Modern Record

▶ Make your own plant fossil. Press a leaf part into a piece of clay. Fill the depression with plaster of Paris. Then write a report describing what the fossil tells you about the environment it came from.

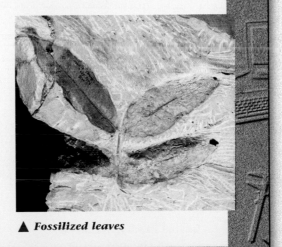

▲ *Fossilized leaves*

157

Background

Paleobotanists study the fossils of plants not only to learn about the plants themselves but also to search for clues about ancient climates, ecosystems, and the evolution of species.

Jacobs is one of a group of experts from all over the world who have studied in the Lake Baringo region of Kenya. Researchers studying the evolution of humans and of a wide variety of plants, mammals, fish, and microorganisms have joined forces with specialists in geology and dating techniques to gather information from the area. Human fossils from this area are among the oldest human remains ever found.

Answer to Making a Modern Record

The fossils that the students make will be representative of the environment in which the students live. Their descriptions should reflect that.

Chapter Organizer

CHAPTER ORGANIZATION	TIME MINUTES	OBJECTIVES	LABS, INVESTIGATIONS, AND DEMONSTRATIONS
Chapter Opener pp. 158–159	45	National Standards: UCP 1	**Start-Up Activity,** Classifying Shoes, p. 159
Section 1 **Classification: Sorting It All Out**	90	▶ List the seven levels of classification. ▶ Explain the importance of having scientific names for species. ▶ Explain how scientific names are written. ▶ Describe how dichotomous keys help in identifying organisms. UCP 1, SAI 2, HNS 1–3, LS 5a; Labs UCP 1, SAI 1	**Demonstration,** Classifying Objects, p. 160 in ATE **QuickLab,** Evolutionary Diagrams, p. 163 **Skill Builder,** Shape Island, p. 172 **Datasheets for LabBook,** Shape Island **Discovery Lab,** Voyage of the USS *Adventure,* p. 192 **Datasheets for LabBook,** Voyage of the USS *Adventure* **EcoLabs & Field Activities,** Water Wigglers
Section 2 **The Six Kingdoms**	90	▶ Explain how classification schemes for kingdoms developed as greater numbers of different organisms became known. ▶ List the six kingdoms, and provide two characteristics of each. UCP 5, SAI 1, HNS 1, 2, LS 1b, 1f, 2a, 2c, 4b, 4c, 5b	**Long-Term Projects & Research Ideas,** The Panda Mystery

See page **T23** *for a complete correlation of this book with the*

NATIONAL SCIENCE EDUCATION STANDARDS.

TECHNOLOGY RESOURCES

Guided Reading Audio CD English or Spanish, Chapter 7

One-Stop Planner CD-ROM with Test Generator

CLASSROOM WORKSHEETS, TRANSPARENCIES, AND RESOURCES	SCIENCE INTEGRATION AND CONNECTIONS	REVIEW AND ASSESSMENT
Directed Reading Worksheet **Science Puzzlers, Twisters & Teasers**		
Directed Reading Worksheet, Section 1 **Transparency 34,** Levels of Classification **Science Skills Worksheet,** Boosting Your Memory **Math Skills for Science Worksheet,** A Shortcut for Multiplying Large Numbers **Transparency 35,** Evolutionary Relationships Among Four Mammals **Transparency 35,** Evolutionary Relationships Among Four Plants **Transparency 36,** Dichotomous Key to 10 Common Mammals in the Eastern United States **Problem Solving Worksheet,** A Breach on Planet Biome	**Connect to Environmental Science,** p. 160 in ATE **Math and More,** p. 162 in ATE **Multicultural Connection,** p. 164 in ATE **Scientific Debate:** It's a Bird, It's a Plane, It's a *Dinosaur*? p. 178	**Section Review,** p. 165 **Quiz,** p. 165 in ATE **Alternative Assessment,** p. 165 in ATE
Transparency 112, Intrusive Igneous Rock Formations **Directed Reading Worksheet,** Section 2 **Math Skills for Science Worksheet,** Arithmetic with Decimals **Reinforcement Worksheet,** Keys to the Kingdoms	**Connect to Environmental Science,** p. 166 in ATE **Connect to Earth Science,** p. 167 in ATE **Real-World Connection,** p. 168 in ATE **MathBreak,** Building a Human Chain Around a Giant Sequoia, p. 169 **Environment Connection,** p. 169 **Multicultural Connection,** p. 169 in ATE **Apply,** p. 170 **Weird Science:** Lobster-Lip Life-Form, p. 179	**Homework,** pp. 167, 168 in ATE **Self-Check,** p. 168 **Section Review,** p. 171 **Quiz,** p. 171 in ATE **Alternative Assessment,** p. 171 in ATE

 internetconnect

 Holt, Rinehart and Winston On-line Resources
go.hrw.com

For worksheets and other teaching aids related to this chapter, visit the HRW Web site and type in the keyword: **HSTCLS**

SCiLINKS NSTA **National Science Teachers Association**
www.scilinks.org

Encourage students to use the *sci*LINKS numbers listed in the internet connect boxes to access information and resources on the **NSTA** Web site.

END-OF-CHAPTER REVIEW AND ASSESSMENT

Chapter Review in Study Guide
Vocabulary and Notes in Study Guide
Chapter Tests with Performance-Based Assessment, Chapter 7 Test
Chapter Tests with Performance-Based Assessment, Performance-Based Assessment 7
Concept Mapping Transparency 9

Chapter Resources & Worksheets

Visual Resources

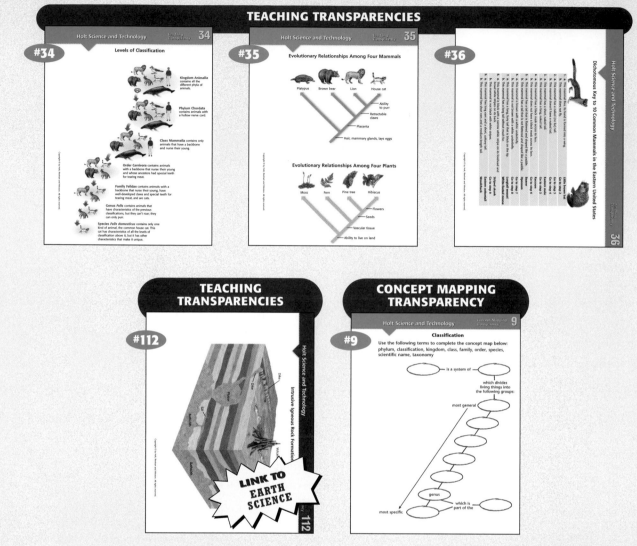

TEACHING TRANSPARENCIES

#34 — Levels of Classification

#35 — Evolutionary Relationships Among Four Mammals / Evolutionary Relationships Among Four Plants

#36 — Dichotomous Key to 10 Common Mammals in the Eastern United States

TEACHING TRANSPARENCIES

#112 — Intrusive Igneous Rock Formation — LINK TO EARTH SCIENCE

CONCEPT MAPPING TRANSPARENCY

#9 — Classification
Use the following terms to complete the concept map below: phylum, classification, kingdom, class, family, order, species, scientific name, taxonomy

Meeting Individual Needs

DIRECTED READING

#7 — DIRECTED READING WORKSHEET

Classification

Chapter Introduction
As you begin this chapter, answer the following.
1. Read the title of the chapter. List three things that you already know about this subject.

2. Write two questions about this subject that you would like answered by the time you finish this chapter.

Section 1: Classification: Sorting It All Out (p. 160)
3. Organizing plants based on whether they are poisonous or not is an example of classification. True or False? (Circle one.)

Why Classify? (p. 160)
4. Why do biologists classify organisms? (Circle all that apply.)
   a. to make sense of the sheer number of living things
   b. to discover how many known species there are
   c. to help study the characteristics of known species
   d. to study the relationships between species
5. What are the seven levels of classification?

REINFORCEMENT & VOCABULARY REVIEW

#7 — REINFORCEMENT WORKSHEET

Keys to the Kingdoms

Complete this worksheet after you have finished reading Chapter 10, Section 2.
Patty dropped her notes while she was studying the six kingdoms of living things, and now she isn't sure which facts belong to which kingdom. Each of the six boxes on the next page is labeled with the name of one of the kingdoms. Help Patty out by listing the facts, descriptions, and examples from Patty's notes below in the appropriate boxes.

• Possess nervous systems
• Break down material outside their bodies and then absorb the nutrients
• *Escherichia coli*
• Most are single-celled organisms
• Usually green
• Have existed for at least 3 billion years
• All eukaryotes that are not plants, animals, or fungi
• *Felis domesticus*
• May be found in hot springs where the temperature is 90°C
• Cells lack cell walls
• Prokaryotes that may be found in the human body
• Algae
• Use the sun's energy to make food
• Yeasts
• Evolved from bacteria about 2 billion years ago
• Ferns
• Mushrooms

#7 — VOCABULARY REVIEW WORKSHEET

Classification Clues

Complete this puzzle after you have finished Chapter 10.
Solve the clues to see what words are hidden in the puzzle. Words in the puzzle are hidden vertically, horizontally, and diagonally.
1. List the seven levels used by scientists to classify organisms:
   a. _____
   b. _____
   c. _____
   d. _____
   e. _____
   f. _____
   g. _____
2. List the six kingdoms of living things:
   a. _____
   b. _____
   c. _____
   d. _____
   e. _____
   f. _____
3. Linnaeus founded _____, the science of naming and classifying living things.
4. A _____ key is a special guide used to identify unknown organisms.

SCIENCE PUZZLERS, TWISTERS & TEASERS

#7 — SCIENCE PUZZLERS, TWISTERS & TEASERS

Classification

Classification Riddles
1. You have learned that living things are classified into groups based on genetic similarity. Try to solve the following riddles about real organisms that aren't so easy to classify.

   a. I have a beak like a bird,
   And my arms are like snakes.
   I have more ink than a pen,
   But I write to confuse.
   What am I?

   b. I have a bill like a duck,
   But the hair of a mammal.
   I lay eggs like a bird,
   But I nurse my young.
   What am I?

   c. Some take me for a plant,
   But I don't like the sun.
   I'm sure not an animal
   For I'm not on the run.
   I make bread
   And I make bread rise.
   Try to guess my kingdom—
   It's quite a surprise.
   What am I?

Review & Assessment

STUDY GUIDE

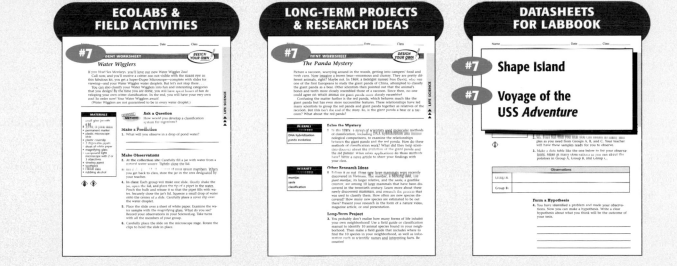

#7 VOCABULARY AND NOTES WORKSHEET
Classification

By studying the Vocabulary and Notes listed for each section below, you can gain a better understanding of this chapter.

SECTION 1
Vocabulary
In your own words, write a definition for each of the following terms in the space provided.

1. classification
2. kingdom
3. phylum
4. class
5. order
6. family
7. genus
8. species
9. taxonomy

#7 CHAPTER REVIEW WORKSHEET
Classification

USING VOCABULARY
To complete the following sentences, choose the correct term from each pair of terms listed below, and write the term in the space provided.

1. Linnaeus founded the science of _____ (DNA analysis or taxonomy)
2. All of the organisms classified into a single kingdom are then divided into one of several _____ (phyla or classes)
3. The narrowest level of classification is the _____ (genus or species)
4. Linnaeus began naming organisms using _____ (two-part scientific names or evolutionary relationships)
5. Archaebacteria and eubacteria are _____ (prokaryotes or eukaryotes)

UNDERSTANDING CONCEPTS
Multiple Choice
6. When scientists classify organisms, they
  a. arrange them in orderly groups.
  b. give them many common names.
  c. decide whether they are useful.
  d. ignore evolutionary relationships.
7. When the seven levels of classification are listed from broadest to narrowest, which level is in the fifth position?
  a. class
  b. order
  c. genus
  d. family
8. The scientific name for the European white water lily is *Nymphaea alba*. What is the genus to which this plant belongs?
  a. *Nymphaea*
  b. *alba*
  c. water lily
  d. alba lily
9. "Kings Play Chess On Fine-Grained Sand" is a mnemonic device that helps one remember
  a. the scientific names of different organisms.
  b. the six kingdoms.
  c. the seven levels of classification.
  d. the difference between prokaryotic and eukaryotic cells.

CHAPTER TESTS WITH PERFORMANCE-BASED ASSESSMENT

#7 CLASSIFICATION
Chapter 7 Test

USING VOCABULARY
To complete the following sentences, choose the correct term from each pair of terms listed, and write the term in the blank.

1. Members of the kingdom _____ include such organisms as the mold that grows on bread. (Fungi or Plantae)
2. _____ have existed on Earth at least 3 billion years. (Archaebacteria or Eubacteria)
3. Orders of organisms are further broken down into _____ (classes or families)
4. Two organisms that are in the same class will also be in the same _____ (phylum or order)
5. Some organisms in the kingdom _____ are able to live inside the human body. (Eubacteria or Plantae)

UNDERSTANDING CONCEPTS
Multiple Choice
Circle the correct answer.
6. A pine tree is a member of the kingdom
  a. Animalia.
  b. Protista.
  c. Fungi.
  d. Plantae.
7. Some members of the kingdom Protista
  a. have flagella.
  b. are bacterial organisms.
  c. are mushrooms.
  d. have no nucleus.
8. The seven levels of classification, from general to specific, are:
  a. kingdom, class, order, phylum, family, genus, species.
  b. kingdom, phylum, class, family, order, genus, species.
  c. kingdom, phylum, class, order, family, genus, species.
  d. kingdom, class, phylum, order, family, genus, species.
9. Linnaeus is known for
  a. founding the science of taxonomy.
  b. proposing the theory of evolution by natural selection.
  c. identifying the characteristics of rare species.
  d. creating a mnemonic device for recalling the levels of classification.
10. Organisms in the kingdom _____ usually move by themselves and have advanced nervous systems that allow them to respond to their environment.
  a. Fungi
  b. Plantae
  c. Animalia
  d. Protista

#7 CLASSIFICATION
Chapter 7 Performance-Based Assessment

DISCOVERY LAB

Objective
You've read about how scientists classify living things. Now you will have a chance to create and use your own classification system to divide buttons into groups. Scientists had to make important choices when they designed the classification system used for living things that is in place today. You will make similar choices in this activity.

Know the Score!
As you work through the activity, keep in mind that you will be earning a grade for the following:
• how well you work with the materials and equipment (20%)
• how accurately you perform the instructions to create your own system of classification (40%)
• how well you complete the analysis questions (40%)

MATERIALS
• selection of buttons
• containers, such as jars, boxes, or less lids
• labels

Procedure
1. Look at your selection of buttons. Choose some interesting features by which you can divide them into "classes." Separate the buttons and give each class a descriptive name.
2. Label each container with the class of button it will hold and put the buttons in the correct containers.
3. Now that you have your buttons divided into classes, decide how you can divide your buttons further, into families. Separate the buttons and give each family a descriptive name.

Analysis
4. How many classes of buttons do you have?
5. List the classes here and describe the major characteristic of each class.

Lab Worksheets

ECOLABS & FIELD ACTIVITIES

#7 STUDENT WORKSHEET
Water Wigglers

DESIGN YOUR OWN

If you liked Sea Monkeys, you'll love our new Water Wiggler Zoo! Call now, and you'll receive a critter zoo not visible with the naked eye in this fabulous kit, you get a Super-Duper Microscope—complete with slides for viewing—and your Water Wiggler water droplets. But let's not stop there.

You can also classify your Water Wigglers into fun and interesting categories that you design! By the time you are done, you will have spent hours of fun developing your own critter classification system. In the end, you will have your very own zoo! So order now! Your Water Wigglers await!
(Water Wigglers are not guaranteed to be in every water droplet.)

MATERIALS
• small glass jar with lid
• 250 mL of pond water
• permanent marker
• plastic microscope slide
• plastic coverslip
• 3 disposable pipets
• sheet of white paper
• magnifying glass
• compound light microscope with 2 or 3 objectives
• stewing water
• toothpick
• rubbing alcohol

SCIENTIFIC METHOD
Ask a Question
How would you develop a classification system for organisms?

Make a Prediction
1. What will you observe in a drop of pond water?

Make Observations
2. At the collection site: Carefully fill a jar with water from a natural water source. Tightly close the lid.
3. As soon as you get back to class, store the jar in the area designated by your teacher.
4. In class: Each group will make one slide. Gently shake the jar, open the lid, and place the tip of a pipet in the water. Pinch the bulb and release it so that the pipet fills with water. Securely close the jar's lid. Squeeze a small drop of water onto the center of a slide. Carefully place a cover slip over the water droplet.
5. Place the slide over a sheet of white paper. Examine the water sample with the magnifying glass. What do you see? Record your observations in your ScienceLog. Take turns with all the members of your group.
6. Carefully place the slide on the microscope stage. Rotate the clips to hold the slide in place.

LONG-TERM PROJECTS & RESEARCH IDEAS

#7 STUDENT WORKSHEET
The Panda Mystery

DESIGN YOUR OWN

Picture a raccoon, scurrying around in the woods, getting into campers' food and trash cans. Now imagine a brown bear—enormous and clumsy. They are pretty different animals, right? Maybe not. In 1869, a biologist named Père David, who was one of the first Europeans to study the giant panda of China, attempted to classify the giant panda as a bear. Other scientists then pointed out that the animal's bones and teeth more closely resembled those of a raccoon. Since then, no one could agree on which animal the giant panda most closely resembled.

Confusing the matter further is the red panda, which behaves much like the giant panda but has even more raccoonlike features. These relationships have led many scientists to group the red panda and giant panda together as relatives of the raccoon. But this isn't the end of the story. Is, is the giant panda a bear or a raccoon? What about the red panda?

Solve the Mystery
1. In the 1990s, a group of scientists used molecular methods of classification, including DNA testing and biochemical comparisons, to examine the relationships between the giant panda and the red panda. How do these methods of classification work? What did they help scientists discover about the evolution of the giant panda and the red panda? What other applications do these methods have? Write a news article to share your findings with your class.

Other Research Ideas
2. Believe it or not, three new large mammals were recently discovered in Vietnam. The muntjac, a barking deer, the giant muntjac, its larger relative, and the saola, a goatlike creature, are among 10 large mammals that have been discovered in the twentieth century. Learn more about these newly discovered mammals, and research the process that was used to classify them. How often are new species discovered? How many new species are estimated to be out there? Present your research in the form of a nature video, magazine article, or oral presentation.

INTERNET
DNA hybridization
panda evolution

INTERNET
muntjac
saola
classification

Long-Term Project
3. You probably don't realize how many forms of life inhabit your own neighborhood! Use a field guide or classification manual to identify 10 animal species found in your neighborhood. Then make a field guide that includes where to find the 10 species in your neighborhood, as well as information such as scientific names and interesting facts. Be creative!

DATASHEETS FOR LABBOOK

#7 Shape Island

#7 Voyage of the USS *Adventure*

2. Place as many samples as you need from Groups A, B, and C. Your teacher will have these samples ready for you to observe.
3. Make a data table like the one below to list your observations. Make as many observations as you can about the potatoes in Group A, Group B, and Group C.

Observations	
Group A:	
Group B:	

Form a Hypothesis
4. You have identified a problem and made your observations. Now you can make a hypothesis. Write a clear hypothesis about what you think will be the outcome of your tests.

Applications & Extensions

CRITICAL THINKING & PROBLEM SOLVING

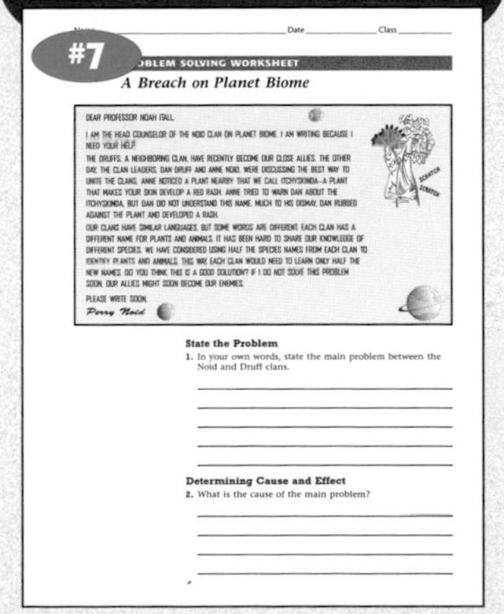

#7 PROBLEM SOLVING WORKSHEET
A Breach on Planet Biome

DEAR PROFESSOR NOAH FALL,
I AM THE HEAD COUNSELOR OF THE NOID CLAN ON PLANET BIOME. I AM WRITING BECAUSE I NEED YOUR HELP.
THE DRUFFS, A NEIGHBORING CLAN, HAVE RECENTLY BECOME OUR CLOSE ALLIES. THE OTHER DAY THE CLAN LEADERS, DAN GRUFF AND AMY WISE, DISCOVERED THE BEST WAY TO UNITE THE CLANS. ANNIE NOTICED A PLANT NEARBY THAT WE CALL YICHIYONGA. A PLANT THAT MAKES YOUR SKIN DEVELOP A RED RASH. ANNIE TRIED TO WARN DAN ABOUT THE YICHIYONGA, BUT DAN DID NOT UNDERSTAND THE NAME, MUCH TO HIS DISMAY, DAN RUBBED AGAINST THE PLANT AND DEVELOPED A RASH.
OUR CLANS HAVE SIMILAR LANGUAGES, BUT SOME WORDS ARE DIFFERENT. EACH CLAN HAS A DIFFERENT NAME FOR PLANTS AND ANIMALS. IT WAS BEEN HARD TO SHARE OUR KNOWLEDGE OF DIFFERENT PLANTS AND ANIMALS USING HALF THE SPECIES NAMES FROM EACH CLAN TO IDENTIFY PLANTS AND ANIMALS. THEY MAY EACH CLAN WOULD NEED TO LEARN ONLY HALF THE NEW NAMES. DO YOU THINK THIS IS A GOOD SOLUTION? IF I DO NOT SOLVE THIS PROBLEM SOON, OUR ALLIES MIGHT SOON BECOME OUR ENEMIES.
PLEASE WRITE SOON.
Perry Noid

State the Problem
1. In your own words, state the main problem between the Noid and Druff clans.

Determining Cause and Effect
2. What is the cause of the main problem?

Chapter Background

SECTION 1

Classification: Sorting It All Out

▶ Aristotle's Classification System

The great Greek philosopher and scientist Aristotle (384–322 B.C.) began classifying animals into logical groupings more than 2,000 years ago. Although Aristotle did not view different kinds of organisms as being related by descent, he arranged all living things in an ascending ladder with humans at the top.

- Animals were separated into two major groups—those with red blood and those without red blood—which correspond very closely with our modern classification of vertebrates and invertebrates.

- Animals were further classified according to their way of life, their actions, and their body parts.

- Aristotle grouped plants as herbs, shrubs, or trees, based on their size and appearance.

▶ Species in Classification

In the late 1600s, the English scientist John Ray established the species as the basic unit of classification.

▶ Basis for Modern Classification System

Our modern system of classification was introduced by Swedish scientist Carolus Linnaeus. He published a book on plant classification in 1753 and a book on animal classification in 1758.

- Organisms were classified according to their structure.

- Plants and animals were arranged into genus and species, and the categories of class and order were introduced.

- Species were given distinctive two-word names. Linnaeus's system is still in use today, although with many changes.

- Carolus Linnaeus is the Latin translation of the Swedish scientist's given name, Carl von Linné.

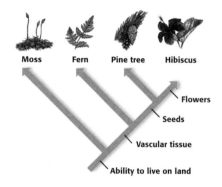

Moss   Fern   Pine tree   Hibiscus

Flowers
Seeds
Vascular tissue
Ability to live on land

▶ Subgroups in the Animal Kingdom

Baron Cuvier Georges first divided the animal kingdom into subgroups, such as Vertebrata, Mollusca, Articulata, and Radiata, in 1817.

IS THAT A FACT!

- The legs of birds are covered in scales very similar to the scales that cover many reptiles.

SECTION 2

The Six Kingdoms

▶ Variations of the Classification System

Variations of the five-kingdom system introduced by R. H. Whittaker in 1969 are used by some modern scientists. Whittaker's system classifies organisms according to whether they are prokaryotic or eukaryotic, whether they are unicellular or multicellular, and whether they obtain food by photosynthesis, ingestion, or absorption of nutrients from their environment.

- Because studies of DNA indicate that there are significant differences between archaebacteria and eubacteria, many scientists place archaebacteria in a sixth kingdom.

▶ Different Classification Methods

Branches of biology use different methods of classification.

- The classification method microbiologists use is organized by volume, section, family, and genus.

- Botanists used to use the term *division* instead of *phylum* for plants and fungi.

▶ The Planet Within

When we organize life on Earth into categories, it is important to remember that organisms are not equally distributed throughout our classification system. Even though we often think of the Earth's living things in terms of plants and animals—organisms living above the Earth's surface—the largest kingdoms in terms of the number of species, number of individuals,

and total biomass are bacteria. And their most common home may be deep within the Earth's crust.

- Scientists have known for some time that bacteria exist all around us and that some have the ability to live in extreme environments. Some live in hot geysers, others in water with salt concentrations so high no other organisms can survive in it. Scientists have also known that many archaebacteria can thrive in anaerobic and high-pressure environments, such as those found underground. But only recently have scientists learned just how far underground they are and just how many bacteria live there.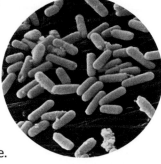

- In 1987, scientists were drilling in the rock beneath the Savannah River in South Carolina, investigating the safety of the drinking water. The cores of the rock they investigated at a depth of 500 m harbored bacteria. Other scientists found bacteria in the ocean at 750 m. A South African gold mine, as far down as 5 km, yielded other bacteria.

- Once scientists knew to look deep in the Earth for life-forms, they began looking in the sediment under the ocean and found more organisms. That sediment is 15 km deep in places, and some speculate that organisms could inhabit the sediment even to that depth. If that is the case, then the total biomass of these astonishing organisms beneath the surface of the Earth may exceed the total biomass of all the living things on the Earth's surface.

- No one knows exactly how these creatures tolerate the tremendous pressures and temperatures of their environment, but scientists have learned that these organisms are meeting their nutritional needs in a variety of ways. Some live on oxidized forms of sulfur; others on bits of organic matter found in the sediment. Some bacteria have even been found in igneous rocks, apparently subsisting on the carbon dioxide and hydrogen gas trapped in the rock.

For background information about teaching strategies and issues, refer to the *Professional Reference for Teachers.*

Classification

 Pre-Reading Questions

Students may not know the answers to these questions before reading the chapter, so accept any reasonable response.

Suggested Answers

1. Classification is systematically organizing things or ideas.

2. People classify many things that are important in their everyday lives, such as food, addresses, and clothing.

3. Scientists classify things in order to find similarities that help us understand our world.

Classification

Sections

 Pre-Reading Questions

1. What is classification?
2. How do people use classification in their everyday lives?
3. Why do scientists classify living things?

158

ALL SORTS OF INSECTS!

Look at the katydids, grasshoppers, and other insects on this page. Every insect has a label that bears the insect's name and other information. Suppose you discovered a new insect. How would you name, sort, and identify— or classify—the new insect? Where would you start? In this chapter, you will learn how scientists classify living things. You will also learn about the six kingdoms into which all living things are classified.

internet connect

HRW On-line Resources

go.hrw.com
For worksheets and other teaching aids, visit the HRW Web site and type in the keyword: **HSTCLS**

sciLINKS **NSTA**

www.scilinks.com
Use the *sci*LINKS numbers at the end of each chapter for additional resources on the **NSTA** Web site.

Smithsonian Institution

www.si.edu/hrw
Visit the Smithsonian Institution Web site for related on-line resources.

CNNfyi.com

www.cnnfyi.com
Visit the CNN Web site for current events coverage and classroom resources.

START-UP Activity

CLASSIFYING SHOES

In this activity, you will develop a system of classification for shoes.

Procedure

1. Gather **10 different shoes.** Use **masking tape** to label each sole with a number (1–10).

2. Make a list of shoe features, such as left or right, color, size, and laces or no laces. In your ScienceLog, make a table with a column for each feature. Complete the table by describing each shoe.

3. Use the data in the table to make a shoe identification key. The key should be a list of steps. Each step should have two statements about the shoes. The statements will lead you to two more statements. For example, step 1 might be:
   1a. This is a red sandal.
       Shoe 4
   1b. This isn't a red sandal.
       Go to step 2.

4. Each step should eliminate more shoes until only one shoe fits the description, such as in 1a, above. Check the number on the sole of the shoe to see if you are correct.

5. Trade keys with another group. How did their key help you to identify the shoes?

Analysis

6. How helpful was it to list the shoe features before making the key?

7. Could you identify the shoes using another group's key? Explain.

159

START-UP Activity

CLASSIFYING SHOES

MATERIALS

FOR EACH GROUP:
• 10 different shoes (from class members, a second-hand store, or a garage sale)
• masking tape

Teacher's Notes

Make certain students understand that the list of shoe characteristics should be unique to a particular set of 10 shoes.

Characteristics of shoes listed should be those that can easily be observed. For example, whether a shoe belongs to a boy or to a girl is not always obvious to an observer.

Answers to START-UP Activity

6. Making a list of characteristics is important to help you decide on the series of descriptive statements.

7. Each group may describe the shoes differently, but their descriptions should be clear enough to lead the other groups to the same conclusion.

Focus

Classification: Sorting It All Out

In this section, students learn about the modern biological classification system. The section explains how organisms are classified based on their evolutionary relationships and how their scientific names are determined. Finally, students learn how to identify animals using a dichotomous key.

Bellringer

Ask students to think about the different ways humans classify things. Ask them to list in their ScienceLog at least five groups of things that humans classify. You may want to give them examples, such as library books, department-store merchandise, and addresses.

1) Motivate

DEMONSTRATION

Classifying Objects Display a variety of small solid objects. Ask students for their ideas on ways to put the objects into groups. For each grouping, record the defining characteristic and the objects that belong in the group. Identify objects that fit in more than one grouping. Discuss how putting objects into groups can be helpful.

Directed Reading Worksheet Section 1

Terms to Learn

classification	family
kingdom	genus
phylum	species
class	taxonomy
order	dichotomous key

What You'll Do

- ◆ List the seven levels of classification.
- ◆ Explain the importance of having scientific names for species.
- ◆ Explain how scientific names are written.
- ◆ Describe how dichotomous keys help in identifying organisms.

Classification: Sorting It All Out

Imagine that you live in a tropical rain forest and are responsible for getting your own food, shelter, and clothing from the forest. If you are going to survive, you will need to know which plants you can eat and which are poisonous. You will need to know which animals to eat and which may eat you. You will need to organize the living things around you into categories, or classify them. **Classification** is the arrangement of organisms into orderly groups based on their similarities.

Why Classify?

For thousands of years, humans have classified different kinds of organisms based on their usefulness. For example, the Chácabo people of Bolivia, like the family shown in **Figure 1,** know of 360 species of plants in the forest where they live, and they have uses for 305 of those plants. How many plants can you name that are useful in your life?

Biologists also classify organisms—both living and extinct. Why? There are millions of different living things in the world. Making sense of the sheer number and diversity of living things requires classification. Classifying living things makes it easier for biologists to find the answers to many important questions, including the following:

- How many known species are there?

- What are the characteristics of each?

- What are the relationships between these species?

In order to classify an organism, a biologist must use a system that groups organisms according to shared characteristics and their relationships between one another. There are seven levels of classification used by biologists—kingdom, phylum, class, order, family, genus, and species.

Figure 1 *The Chácabo people have a great amount of knowledge about their environment.*

CONNECT TO
ENVIRONMENTAL SCIENCE

Some tropical rain forests are being cut down and converted into farms to feed native populations. Scientists suspect that the forests we are losing may be pharmaceutical treasure troves. One-fifth of all the world's known plant species live in tropical rain forests. Only a small percentage of the species have been studied. These plants might be sources of medicines that can be used to treat diseases. Ask students what they think could be done to ensure that rain-forest species are preserved while food needs are also met.

Levels of Classification

Each organism is classified into one of several **kingdoms,** which are the largest, most general groups. All the organisms in a kingdom are then sorted into several *phyla* (singular, **phylum**). The members of one phylum are more like each other than they are like members of another phylum. Then all the organisms in a given phylum are further sorted into **classes.** Each class is subdivided into one or more **orders,** orders are separated into **families,** families are sorted into *genera* (singular, **genus**), and genera are sorted into **species.**

Examine **Figure 2** to follow the classification of the ordinary house cat from kingdom Animalia to species *Felis domesticus.*

Figure 2 *Kingdom Animalia contains all species of animals, while species Felis domesticus contains only one.*

Kingdom Animalia contains all the different phyla of animals.

Phylum Chordata contains animals with a hollow nerve cord.

Class Mammalia contains only animals that have a backbone and nurse their young.

Order Carnivora contains animals with a backbone that nurse their young and whose ancestors had special teeth for tearing meat.

Family Felidae contains animals with a backbone that nurse their young, have well-developed claws and special teeth for tearing meat, and are cats.

Genus *Felis* contains animals that have characteristics of the previous classifications, but they can't roar; they can only purr.

Species *Felis domesticus* contains only one kind of animal, the common house cat. It has characteristics of all the levels above it, but it has other unique characteristics.

Activity

A mnemonic device is a tool to help you remember something. One way to remember the levels of classification is to use a mnemonic device like this sentence:
King **P**hillip **C**ame **O**ver **F**or **G**rape **S**oda.

Invent your own mnemonic device for the levels of classification using words that are meaningful to you.

TRY at HOME

161

IS THAT A FACT!

The term *dinosaur* wasn't coined until the nineteenth century. Until then, as dinosaur bones were uncovered all over the world, the most widely accepted view was that they belonged to dragons.

Teaching Transparency 34 "Levels of Classification"

Science Skills Worksheet "Boosting Your Memory"

MEETING INDIVIDUAL NEEDS

Learners Having Difficulty To help students understand what constitutes a species, genus, family, order, class, phylum, and kingdom, ask them the following questions:

What does a species contain? (organisms that have the same characteristics)

What does a genus contain? (similar species)

What does a family contain? (similar genera)

What does an order contain? (similar families)

What does a class contain? (similar orders)

What does a phylum contain? (similar classes)

What does a kingdom contain? (similar phyla) Sheltered English

USING THE FIGURE

Concept Mapping Refer students to **Figure 2.** Have them answer these questions to enhance their understanding of the sorting process used to classify the common house cat. What animals are pictured at the kingdom level? (lion, bird, human, bear, lynx, house cat, worm, whale)

Which of these pictured animals do not fit the description of a chordate? (the worm)

Which of the animals pictured at the chordate level do not fit the description of a mammal? (the bird)

Continue this questioning pattern for the remaining levels of classification. Have students put the information expressed in the diagram into a concept map.

ACTIVITY

Evolutionary Diagrams Fossils show that one difference between ancestral genera of the modern horse, *Equus*, is the number of toes:

Eohippus (55 mya*) 4 toes
Mesohippus (35 mya) 3 toes
Merychippus (26 mya) 1 large toe, 2 small toes
Pliohippus (3 mya) 1 large toe surrounded by a hoof
Equus (modern) 1 large toe, more broad and flat, surrounded by a hoof

(*mya = million years ago)

Have students use this information to construct their own evolutionary diagram. Use the diagram on this page as a model.

MATH and MORE

Give students the following information:

There are more than 700,000 known species of insects in the world. The number of insect species accounts for about half of all known species. Have students calculate the approximate total number of Earth's known species. (over 1.4 million)

Math Skills Worksheet "A Shortcut for Multiplying Large Numbers"

Teaching Transparency 35 "Evolutionary Relationships Among Four Mammals"

What Is the Basis for Classification?

Carolus Linnaeus (lin AY uhs), pictured in **Figure 3,** was a Swedish physician and botanist who lived in the 1700s. Linnaeus founded **taxonomy,** the science of identifying, classifying, and naming living things.

Linnaeus attempted to classify all known organisms only by their shared characteristics. Later, scientists began to recognize that evolutionary changes form a line of descent from a common ancestor. Taxonomy changed to include these new ideas about evolutionary relationships.

Modern Classification Today's taxonomists still classify organisms based on presumed evolutionary relationships. Species with a recent common ancestor can be classified together. For example, the platypus, brown bear, lion, and house cat are related because they are thought to have an ancestor in common—an ancient mammal. Because of this relationship, all four animals are grouped into the same class—Mammalia.

A brown bear, lion, and house cat are more closely related to each other than to the platypus. They are all mammals, but only the platypus lays eggs. Brown bears, lions, and house cats share a different common ancestor—an ancient carnivore. Thus, they are classified into the same order—Carnivora.

Figure 3 *Carolus Linnaeus classified more than 7,000 species of plants.*

Branching Diagrams The close evolutionary relationship between lions and house cats is shown by the branching diagram in **Figure 4.** The characteristics listed on the arrow pointing to the right are the characteristics that make the next animal unique. The house cat and the platypus share the characteristics of hair and mammary glands. But they are different in many ways. The branch that leads to lions is closest to the branch that leads to house cats. The lion and the house cat are closely related because they share the most recent common ancestor—an ancient cat.

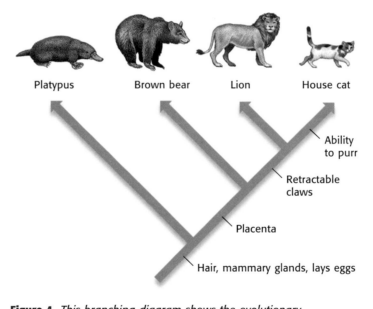

Figure 4 *This branching diagram shows the evolutionary relationships between four mammals.*

SCIENTISTS AT ODDS

Chinese paleontologists have found a 121-million-year-old fossil of a dinosaur that appeared to have feathers. This, say some scientists, is further proof that birds evolved directly from dinosaurs. Other scientists refute that hypothesis because of the lack of a relationship between dinosaurs' fossilized "finger" bones and the corresponding bones in bird embryos. Additional studies by zoologists dispute the bird-dinosaur connection with comparisons of the respiratory structures of modern birds, mammals, and crocodiles and those of early bird fossils and theropod dinosaurs.

Naming Names

By classifying organisms, biologists are also able to give them scientific names. A scientific name is always the same for a specific organism no matter how many common names it might have.

Before Linnaeus's time, scholars used Latin names up to 12 words long to identify species. Linnaeus simplified the naming of organisms by giving each species a two-part scientific name. The first part of the name identifies the genus, and the second part identifies the species. The scientific name for the Indian elephant, for example, is *Elephas maximus*. No other species has this name, and all scientists know that *Elephas maximus* refers to the Indian elephant.

It's All Greek (or Latin) to Me Scientific names might seem difficult to understand because they are in Latin or Greek. Most scientific names, however, are actually full of meaning. Take a look at **Figure 5.** You probably already know this animal's scientific name. It's *Tyrannosaurus rex*! The first word is a combination of two Greek words meaning "tyrant lizard," and the second word is Latin for "king." The genus name always begins with a capital letter, and the species name begins with a lowercase letter. Both words are underlined or italicized. You may have heard *Tyrannosaurus rex* called *T. rex*. This is acceptable in science as long as the genus name is spelled out the first time it is used. The species name is incomplete without the genus name or its abbreviation.

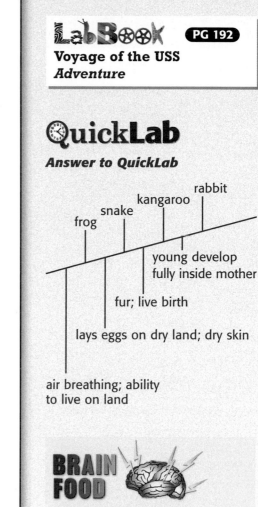

Lab Book

Come aboard the starship USS *Adventure*! Turn to page 192 in your LabBook.

QuickLab

Evolutionary Diagrams

A branching evolutionary diagram can be used to show evolutionary relationships between different organisms.

Construct a diagram similar to the one on page 162. Use a frog, a snake, a kangaroo, and a rabbit. What do you think is one major evolutionary change between one organism and the next? Write them on your diagram.

TRY at HOME

Figure 5
You would never call
Tyrannosaurus rex *just* rex!

163

Lab Book PG 192
Voyage of the USS *Adventure*

QuickLab
Answer to QuickLab

rabbit

kangaroo

snake

frog

young develop fully inside mother

fur; live birth

lays eggs on dry land; dry skin

air breathing; ability to live on land

BRAIN FOOD

Have students consider the importance of classification to human thought. Ask students to try to think of something that cannot be classified in some way. Suggest that they test any item or concept they come up with by placing it in the following sentence:

(A) _____ is a type of _____.

For example, if the word is *speech*, the sentence could be filled in as follows:

Speech is a type of communication.

You may wish to hold a contest or have students share their examples in class.

IS THAT A FACT!

If you put all the insects in the world together, they would weigh more than all the people and the rest of the animals combined.

 internet**connect**

SCi**LINKS**
NSTA

TOPIC: The Basis for Classification
GO TO: www.scilinks.org
*sci*LINKS NUMBER: HSTL205

Have small groups of students work together to create an identification key that would identify common mammals in your area.

Multicultural CONNECTION

Point out to students that some of the common names we have for animals came from other languages. For example, *burro* came from Spanish, *grebe* came from French, *macaw* came from Portuguese, and *orangutan* came from Malay. Encourage interested students to look in a dictionary for the language source of other common animal names.

RETEACHING

Display a picture of a bird whose common name is not well-known to your students. Without providing any additional information about the bird, ask them to give the bird a name. Then list all the given names on the chalkboard. Help students understand that scientists around the world would have difficulty sharing information about the bird if they used more than one name for it.   Sheltered English

internet connect

SCiLINKS
NSTA

TOPIC: Levels of Classification
GO TO: www.scilinks.org
*sci*LINKS NUMBER: HSTL210

TOPIC: Dichotomous Keys
GO TO: www.scilinks.org
*sci*LINKS NUMBER: HSTL215

Why Are Scientific Names So Important? Examine the cartoon in **Figure 6**. What name do you have for the small black and white and sometimes smelly animal pictured? The skunk is called by several common names in English and has even more names—at least one name in every language! All of these common names can cause quite a bit of confusion for biologists who want to discuss the skunk. Biologists from different parts of the world who are interested in skunks need to know that they are all talking about the same animal, so they use its scientific name, *Mephitis mephitis*. All known living things have a two-part scientific name.

Figure 6 *Using an organism's two-part scientific name is a sure way for scientists to know they are discussing the same organism.*

When and where did the first bird live? Find out about the debate on page 178.

Dichotomous Keys

Taxonomists have developed special guides known as **dichotomous keys** to aid in identifying unknown organisms. A dichotomous key consists of several pairs of descriptive statements that have only two alternative responses. From each pair of statements, the person trying to identify the unknown organism chooses the appropriate statement. From there, the person is directed to another pair of statements. By working through the statements in the key, the person can eventually identify the organism. Using the simple dichotomous key on the next page, try to identify the two animals shown.

WEIRD SCIENCE

It's exciting when scientists find new species of plants or insects that have gone unnoticed, but it is rare when scientists find a new mammal. Between 1992 and 1998, scientists in Vietnam discovered three new species of deerlike mammals. The most recent was discovered in August 1997. This newly discovered mammal, the Truong Son muntjac, is about one-third of a meter (14 in.) tall, weighs 15.5 kg (34 lb), has a black coat and very short antlers, and barks like a dog. These mammals stay well hidden in the thick Vietnamese forest. The two other mammal species discovered recently are the Vu Quang ox and the giant muntjac.

Dichotomous Key to 10 Common Mammals in the Eastern United States

1. a. This mammal flies. Its hand is formed into a wing.	**Little brown bat**
b. This mammal does not fly.	**Go to step 2**
2. a. This mammal has a naked (no fur) tail.	**Go to step 3**
b. This mammal doesn't have a naked tail.	**Go to step 4**
3. a. This mammal has a short, naked tail.	**Eastern mole**
b. This mammal has a long, naked tail.	**Go to step 5**
4. a. This mammal has a black mask across its face.	**Raccoon**
b. This mammal does not have a black mask across its face.	**Go to step 6**
5. a. This mammal has a tail that is flattened and shaped like a paddle.	**Beaver**
b. This mammal has a tail that is not flattened or shaped like a paddle.	**Opossum**
6. a. This mammal is brown with a white underbelly.	**Go to step 7**
b. This mammal is not brown with a white underbelly.	**Go to step 8**
7. a. This mammal has a long, furry tail that is black on the tip.	**Longtail weasel**
b. This mammal has a long tail without much fur.	**White-footed mouse**
8. a. This mammal is black with a narrow white stripe on its forehead and broad white stripes on its back.	**Striped skunk**
b. This mammal is not black with white stripes.	**Go to step 9**
9. a. This mammal has long ears and a short, cottony tail.	**Eastern cottontail**
b. This mammal has short ears and a medium-length tail.	**Woodchuck**

SECTION REVIEW

1. Why do scientists use scientific names for organisms?

2. Explain the two parts of a scientific name.

3. List the seven levels of classification.

4. Describe how a dichotomous key helps to identify unknown organisms.

5. **Interpreting Illustrations** Study the figure at right. Which plant is the closest relative of the hibiscus? Which plant is most distantly related to the hibiscus? Which plants have seeds?

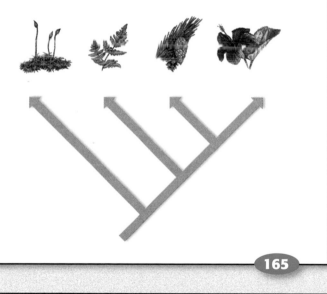

Quiz

1. Why do scientists classify animals? (to facilitate studying them)

2. What was the basis for classification systems in the past? (shared characteristics)

3. What is the basis of modern classification systems? (evolutionary relationships)

ALTERNATIVE ASSESSMENT

Have students create a cartoon that shows how using different common names for an animal instead of its scientific name creates confusion. Students must include authentic common names and scientific names in their cartoon. **Sheltered English**

Answer to Dichotomous Key

Mammal on the top left:
1b, 2b, 4b, 6a, 7a, longtail weasel

Mammal on the top right:
1b, 2b, 4b, 6b, 8b, 9b, woodchuck

Teaching Transparency 35 "Evolutionary Relationships Among Four Plants"

Teaching Transparency 36 "Dichotomous Key to 10 Common Mammals in the Eastern United States"

Problem Solving Worksheet "A Breach on Planet Biome"

▼ Answers to Section Review

1. Scientists use scientific names for organisms to be clear and precise.

2. genus and species; The genus is a broader classification, and the species name is more specific and is often given by the species' discoverer.

3. Kingdom, Phylum, Class, Order, Family, Genus, Species

4. A dichotomous key is organized into a series of pairs of questions. By working through the statements in the key, unknown organisms can be identified.

5. pine tree; moss; pine tree and hibiscus

Focus

The Six Kingdoms

This section explains how improved understanding of organisms leads to revisions in our system of biological classification. Students are introduced to the six kingdoms: Archaebacteria, Eubacteria, Protista, Plantae, Fungi, and Animalia. They learn how organisms belonging in each kingdom are distinguished.

🔔 Bellringer

Have students list seven musical artists, bands, or acts. Have them categorize the names on their lists by style of music. Ask them to describe in their ScienceLog the categories they chose and also explain which bands might fit into more than one category.

1 Motivate

DISCUSSION

Grouping Animals Ask students how zoos group animals. (Answers may include by type, by climate preferences, and by natural habitats.)

Encourage knowledgeable students to describe the layout of zoos with which they are familiar.

Have students write letters to zoos all around the country requesting a copy of the map they issue to visitors. Students could then compare the layouts of many zoos. Be sure to have students include a stamped, self-addressed envelope with their letter describing the project.

Terms to Learn

Archaebacteria	Plantae
Eubacteria	Fungi
Protista	Animalia

What You'll Do

◆ Explain how classification schemes for kingdoms developed as greater numbers of different organisms became known.

◆ List the six kingdoms, and provide two characteristics of each.

Figure 7 *How would you classify this organism?* Euglena, *shown here magnified 1,000 times, has characteristics of both plants and animals.*

BRAIN FOOD

If *Euglena*'s chloroplasts are shaded from light or removed, it will begin to hunt for food like an animal. If the chloroplasts are shaded long enough, the chloroplasts degenerate and never come back.

166

The Six Kingdoms

For hundreds of years, all living things were classified as either plants or animals. These two kingdoms, Plantae and Animalia, worked just fine until organisms like the species *Euglena*, shown in **Figure 7,** were discovered. If you were a taxonomist, how would you classify such an organism?

What Is It?

As you know, organisms are classified by their characteristics. Being the excellent taxonomist that you are, you decide to list the characteristics of *Euglena*:

- *Euglena* are a species of single-celled organisms that live in pond water.

- *Euglena* are green and, like most plants, can make their own food through photosynthesis.

"This is easy!" you think to yourself. "*Euglena* are plants." Not so fast! There are other important characteristics to consider:

- *Euglena* can move about from place to place by whipping their "tails," called flagella.

- Sometimes *Euglena* use food obtained from other organisms.

Plants don't move around and usually do not eat other organisms. Does this mean that *Euglena* are animals? As you can see, neither category seems to fit. Scientists ran into the same problem, so they decided to add another kingdom for classifying organisms such as *Euglena*. This kingdom is known as Protista.

More Kingdoms As scientists continued to learn more about living things, they added kingdoms in order to account for the differences and similarities between organisms. Currently, most scientists agree that the six-kingdom classification system works best. There is still some disagreement, however, and still more to be learned. In the following pages, you will learn more about each of the kingdoms.

CONNECT TO ENVIRONMENTAL SCIENCE

Recently, signs of salmonella infection were found in the droppings of an Antarctic gentoo penguin. The bacteria were most likely introduced from outside the Antarctic. The bacterium, *Salmonella enteritidis,* is not endemic to penguins. Scientists think that sewage dumped from passing ships or visiting albatrosses that feed on waste-contaminated squid in the oceans surrounding South America might be the sources of the bacteria. The bacteria could become infectious and pathogenic and kill the penguin chicks.

The Two Kingdoms of Bacteria

Bacteria are extremely small single-celled organisms. Bacteria are different from all other living things in that they are *prokaryotes*, organisms that do not have nuclei. Many biologists divide bacteria into two kingdoms, **Archaebacteria** (AHR kee bak TEER ee uh) and **Eubacteria** (YOO bak TEER ee uh).

Archaebacteria have been on Earth at least 3 billion years. The prefix *archae* comes from a Greek word meaning "ancient." Today you can find archaebacteria living in places where most organisms could not survive. **Figure 8** shows a hot spring in Yellowstone National Park. The yellow and orange rings around the edge of the hot spring are formed by the billions of archaebacteria that live there.

Most of the other thousands of kinds of bacteria are eubacteria. These microscopic organisms live in the soil, in water, and even on and inside the human body! For example, the eubacterium *Escherichia coli*, pictured in **Figure 9,** is present in great numbers in human intestines, where it produces vitamin K. Another kind of eubacterium converts milk to yogurt, and yet another species causes ear and sinus infections and pneumonia.

Figure 8 *The Grand Prismatic Spring, in Yellowstone National Park, contains water that is about 90°C (194°F). The spring is home to archaebacteria that thrive in its hot water.*

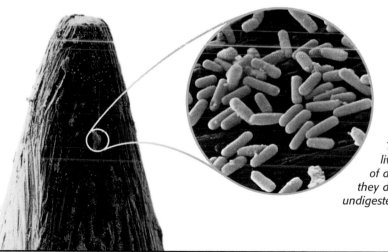

Figure 9 E. coli, *shown on the point of a pin, are seen with a scanning electron microscope. These eubacteria live in the intestines of animals, where they decompose undigested food.*

167

Homework

Writing **Researching Sanitation** Have students research and write reports on measures that protect against harmful bacteria. How can bacteria be killed? How can bacteria be prevented from growing on living tissues? When harmful bacteria get inside the body, how does the body defend itself?

internet**connect**

SC**LINKS**
NSTA

TOPIC: The Six Kingdoms
GO TO: www.scilinks.org
*sci*LINKS NUMBER: HSTL220

2 Teach

READING STRATEGY

Prediction Guide Before students read this page, ask them whether the following statements are true or false. Students will discover the answers as they explore Section 2.

- All living things were once classified into either kingdom Plantae or kingdom Animalia. (true)
- Members of the kingdom Protista are prokaryotes. (false)
- Kingdom Fungi contains multicellular photosynthetic organisms. (false)
- Kingdom Animalia contains multicellular organisms that do not photosynthesize. (true)

CONNECT TO
EARTH SCIENCE

Bacteria have even been found living in igneous rocks deep in the Earth's crust. The rocks contain little water and no organic matter. The bacteria subsist on carbon dioxide and hydrogen gas dissolved in the rock, slowly making their own organic compounds. These organisms may divide only once every couple of hundred years. Use the following Teaching Transparency to illustrate what igneous rocks are, and discuss with students the amazing range of bacterial environments.

Teaching Transparency 112 "Intrusive Igneous Rock Formations" LINK TO EARTH SCIENCE

Directed Reading Worksheet Section 2

REAL-WORLD CONNECTION

People in China, Japan, and other Asian countries have been practicing mariculture for thousands of years. Seaweed, shrimp, and mussels are commonly grown and harvested for food. In western countries, mariculture has experienced steady growth since the 1960s. Farmers grow kelp, fish, and shellfish for food in special farms near ocean shores or in ponds.

Answers to Self-Check

1. The two kingdoms of bacteria are different from all other kingdoms because bacteria are prokaryotes—single-celled organisms that have no nucleus.

2. The organisms in the kingdom Protista are all eukaryotes.

Homework

Writing **Researching Protists** Have students research the protists shown in the pictures in **Figures 10, 11,** and **12** (*Paramecium*, slime mold, and giant kelp, respectively). Have them write descriptions about each of the protists, including information about its size, form, method of obtaining nutrients, method of reproduction, and in the case of the giant kelp, its commercial uses.

Figure 10 Paramecium *usually moves about rapidly.*

Figure 11 *A slime mold spreads over a fallen log on the forest floor.*

Figure 12 *This giant kelp is a multicellular protist.*

168

Kingdom Protista

Members of the kingdom **Protista,** commonly called protists, are single-celled or simple multicellular organisms. Unlike bacteria, protists are *eukaryotes,* organisms that have cells with a nucleus and membrane-bound organelles. Kingdom Protista contains all eukaryotes that are not plants, animals, or fungi. Scientists think the first protists evolved from ancient bacteria about 2 billion years ago. Much later, protists gave rise to plants, fungi, and animals as well as to modern protists.

As you can see, kingdom Protista contains many different kinds of organisms. Protists include protozoa, which are animal-like protists; algae, which are plantlike protists; and slime molds and water molds, which are funguslike protists. *Euglena,* which were discussed earlier, are also members of kingdom Protista, as are the *Paramecium* and the slime mold pictured in **Figures 10** and **11.** Most protists are single-celled organisms, but some are multicellular, such as the giant kelp shown in **Figure 12.**

✓ Self-Check

1. How are the two kingdoms of bacteria different from all other kingdoms?
2. How would you distinguish Protista from the two kingdoms of bacteria?

(See page 216 to check your answers.)

SCIENTISTS AT ODDS

Is a slime mold a fungus? They were traditionally classified as Fungi because despite other differences they exhibit a similar life cycle, including the formation of spores on sporangia. But critics point out that some bacteria (myxobacteria) do this also, and those organisms are not reclassified as Fungi.

IS THAT A FACT!

Farmers on the Orkney Islands of Scotland have historically used seaweed as fertilizer and food for their sheep.

Kingdom Plantae

Although plants vary remarkably in size and form, most people easily recognize the members of kingdom **Plantae.** Plants are complex multicellular organisms that are usually green and use the sun's energy to make sugar by a process called *photosynthesis.* The giant sequoias and flowering plants shown in **Figures 13** and **14** are examples of the different organisms classified in the kingdom Plantae.

Figure 13 *A giant sequoia can measure 30 m around its base and can grow to more than 91.5 m tall.*

Figure 14 *Plants such as these are common in the rain forest.*

MATH BREAK

Building a Human Chain Around a Giant Sequoia

How many students would it take to join hands and form a human chain around a giant sequoia that is 30 m in circumference? Assume for this calculation that the average student can extend his or her arms about 1.3 m. NOTE: You can't have a fraction of a student, so be sure to round up your answer to the nearest whole number.

Environment
CONNECTION

Giant sequoia trees are very rare. They grow only in California and are a protected species. Some of them are over 3,000 years old.

Multicultural
CONNECTION

The name sequoia comes from *Sequoya,* the name of a Cherokee who is credited with developing the Cherokee written language during the 1820s.

DISCUSSION

Compare Structures Ask students what structures are common to the plants in **Figures 13** and **14**. (stems, leaves, and so on)

Ask them to assess differences and similarities between features on various kinds of plants, such as maple leaves and pine needles, tomato stems and tree trunks.

Answer to MATHBREAK

It would take 23 students to join hands and make a human chain around a 30 m sequoia.

MEETING INDIVIDUAL NEEDS

Learners Having Difficulty
Have students work together in small groups to find pictures in magazines of ferns and flowering plants that grow in North America. Provide resource books for the students to use to identify the plants. Then have students mount the plant pictures on poster board and label them. Sheltered English

MISCONCEPTION ALERT

Physical similarities are not always the best indicator of the relatedness of two organisms. For example, a small lizard, such as a skink, may look more like a salamander than a turtle, but it is more closely related to the turtle. Both the lizard and turtle are reptiles, and the salamander is an amphibian.

 Math Skills Worksheet "Arithmetic with Decimals"

169

GOING FURTHER

Writing Tell students that Pennsylvania, which has many caves, is one of the major mushroom-growing regions of the United States. Caves are ideal places in which to grow some kinds of mushrooms. Ask students to research and write a report on mushroom farming in the United States. What kinds of mushrooms are grown commercially, and what special conditions does each species require? Inexpensive kits are available for growing mushrooms, and interested students might enjoy the experience of raising their own.

RESEARCH

Students can research members of the six kingdoms that are prevalent in your immediate area. They can draw pictures of the organisms accompanied by descriptive paragraphs.

Answers to APPLY

Students are likely to think this plant is a fungus related to mushrooms because of its color and texture, but it is a plant. They will probably suggest that they need to know how it makes food because it obviously is not a green plant with leaves. Indian pipe, or *Monotropa uniflora*, is actually a wildflower member of the wintergreen family. It is a saprophyte living on the decayed roots of other plants. It gets all of its nutrients from other plants and needs neither leaves nor chlorophyll.

Kingdom Fungi

Molds and mushrooms are examples of the complex multi-cellular members of the kingdom **Fungi.** Fungi (singular, *fungus*) were originally classified as plants, but fungi do not obtain nutrients by photosynthesis. Moreover, fungi do not have many animal characteristics. Because of their unusual combination of characteristics, fungi are classified in a separate kingdom.

Fungi do not perform photosynthesis, as plants do, and they do not eat food, as animals do. Instead, fungi absorb nutrients from their surroundings after breaking them down with digestive juices. **Figure 15** shows a pretty but deadly mushroom, and **Figure 16** shows black bread mold (a fungus) growing on a piece of bread. Have you ever seen this type of mold on bread?

Figure 15 *This beautiful mushroom of the genus* Amanita *is poisonous.*

Figure 16 *This black bread mold can be dangerous if you inhale the spores. Some molds are dangerous, and others produce life-saving antibiotics.*

APPLY

Classify This!

You and a friend are walking through the forest and you come upon the organism shown at right. You think it is a plant, but you are not sure. It has a flower and seeds, very small leaves, and roots that are growing into a rotting log. But this organism is white from its roots to its petals. To which kingdom do you think this organism belongs? What characteristic is your answer based on? What additional information would you need in order to give a more accurate answer?

170

IS THAT A FACT!

About 3,000 mushroom species grow in North America. Worldwide, about 70–80 species are poisonous.

Kingdom Animalia

Animals are complex multicellular organisms that belong to the kingdom **Animalia.** Most animals can move about from place to place and have nervous systems that help them sense and react to their surroundings. At the microscopic level, animal cells differ from those of fungi, plants, most protists, and bacteria because animal cells lack cell walls. **Figure 17** shows some members of the kingdom Animalia.

Figure 17 *The kingdom Animalia contains many different organisms, such as eagles, tortoises, beetles, and dolphins.*

SECTION REVIEW

1. Name the six kingdoms.

2. Which of the six kingdoms include prokaryotes, and which include eukaryotes?

3. Explain the different ways plants, fungi, and animals obtain nutrients.

4. Why are protists placed in their own kingdom?

5. **Applying Concepts** To which kingdom do humans belong? What characteristics place humans in this kingdom?

internetconnect

SCI**LINKS**

NSTA

TOPIC: The Basis for Classification, The Six Kingdoms
GO TO: www.scilinks.org
*sci***LINKS NUMBER:** HLST205, HSTL220

④ Close

Quiz

1. What causes increases in the number of kingdoms in the modern classification system? (discovery that some organisms do not fit in established kingdoms)

2. Which of the six kingdoms have single-celled organisms and which have multicellular organisms? (single-celled: Archaebacteria, Eubacteria, Protista; multicellular: Protista, Plantae, Fungi, Animalia)

ALTERNATIVE ASSESSMENT

Have students construct a chart of the six kingdoms. They should list the major characteristics of each kingdom on the chart, with a representative organism for each.

ACTIVITY

Writing Have students provide written answers to the Review. (Answers are provided at the bottom of the page.)

Then have students describe and illustrate an animal in their ScienceLog that might require the formation of a seventh kingdom.

Reinforcement Worksheet
"Keys to the Kingdoms"

▼ Answers to Section Review

1. Plantae, Animalia, Protista, Eubacteria, Archaebacteria, Fungi

2. Eubacteria and Archaebacteria contain the prokaryotes. Plantae, Animalia, Protista, and Fungi are all eukaryotes.

3. Plants make food in their tissues from CO_2, water, and the energy in sunlight. Fungi absorb nutrients from their surroundings after breaking them down with digestive juices. Animals eat plants and other animals to obtain food.

4. Protists are organisms that don't fit in the other kingdoms.

5. Animalia; we move, have a nervous system, and lack cell walls.

Shape Island
Teacher's Notes

Time Required

One 45-minute class period

Lab Ratings

EASY ————————→ HARD

TEACHER PREP
STUDENT SET-UP
CONCEPT LEVEL
CLEAN UP

Lab Notes

This lab will help students demonstrate an understanding of binomial nomenclature by using a key to assign scientific names to fictional organisms. After completing the lab, students should be able to explain the function of the scientific name system.

In the chapter on classification, the vocabulary "two-part scientific name" has been used instead of "binomial nomenclature." You may wish to introduce the latter here.

This activity may be more successful if you review prefixes, suffixes, and root words briefly before beginning. Tell students that the genus name is capitalized but the species name is not and that both words are underlined or italicized.

Skill Builder Lab

Shape Island

You are a biologist looking for new animal species. You sailed for days across the ocean and finally found an uncharted island hundreds of miles south of Hawaii. You decided to call it "Shape Island." This island has some very unusual organisms. Each of them has some variation of a geometric shape. You have spent over a year collecting specimens and classifying them according to Linnaeus's system. You have given a scientific name to most species you have collected. You must give names to the last 12 specimens before you sail for home.

Procedure

1 In your ScienceLog, draw each of the organisms shown below. Beside each organism, draw a line for its name, as shown on the following page. The first organism has been named for you, but you have 12 more to name. Use the glossary of Greek and Latin prefixes, suffixes, and root words on page 173 to help you name the organisms.

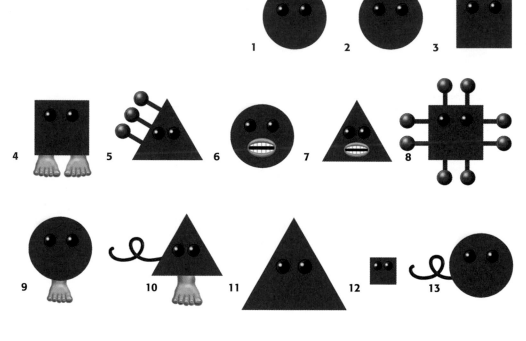

172

Datasheets for LabBook

Maurine Marchani
Raymond Park Middle School
Indianapolis, Indiana

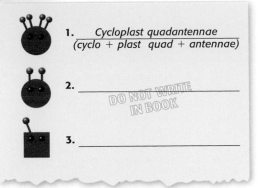

1. *Cycloplast quadantennae*
   (cyclo + plast quad + antennae)

2. _____

3. _____

DO NOT WRITE IN BOOK

② One more organism lives on Shape Island, but you have not been able to capture it. Unfortunately, your supplies are running out, and soon you must sail home. You have had a good look at the unusual animal and can draw it in detail. In your ScienceLog, draw an animal that is different from all the others. Then use the glossary at right to help you give the animal a two-part scientific name.

Analysis

③ If you gave Species 1 a common name, such as round-face-no-nose, would other scientists know which new organism you were referring to? Explain.

④ Describe two characteristics shared by all your specimens from Shape Island.

Glossary	
Greek and Latin roots, prefixes and suffixes	Meaning
ankylos	angle
antennae	external sense organs
tri-	three
bi-	two
cyclo-	circle
macro-	large
micro-	small
mono-	one
peri-	all around
-plast	body
-pod	foot
quad-	four
stoma	mouth
uro-	tail

DO NOT WRITE IN BOOK

Going Further

Look up the scientific names listed below. You can use the library, the Internet, a taxonomy index, or field guides.
- *Mertensia virginica*
- *Porcellio scaber*

For each organism answer the following questions: Is it a plant or an animal? How many common names does it have? How many scientific names does it have?

Think of the name of your favorite fruit or vegetable. Find out if it has other common names, and find out its two-part scientific name.

Answers

1. Below are sample answers. Student answers may vary, but they should demonstrate an understanding of the key provided. Each name should consist of two words: the first describes the organism generally, and the second describes it more specifically.

   1. *Cycloplast quadantennae*
   2. *Cycloplast biantennae*
   3. *Quadankylosplast monoantennae*
   4. *Quadankylosplast bipod*
   5. *Triankylosplast triantennae*
   6. *Cycloplast stoma*
   7. *Triankylosplast stoma*
   8. *Quadankylosplast periantennae*
   9. *Cycloplast monopod*
   10. *Triankylosplast uromonopod*
   11. *Triankylos macroplast*
   12. *Quadankylos microplast*
   13. *Cycloplast uro*

2. Answers will vary according to student drawings.

3. No. There are five species that have round faces and lack noses.

4. Answers will vary but should indicate that they all have geometric shapes and two eyes. They are all the same color, all animals, and all living.

173

Going Further

Mertensia virginica, Virginia bluebells, are common wildflowers found in April and May in shady areas, mostly in moist spots near streams. Flower buds are pink, turning blue when the flower is fully opened. This plant is quite plentiful in some places and is very common in western Kentucky.

Porcellio scaber is a species of wood louse. Wood lice are crustaceans, related to shrimps, crabs, and lobsters, and they belong to a class of arthropods called Isopoda. They are the only crustaceans that have been able to invade land without needing to return to water, although they tend to be restricted to fairly damp places.

Chapter Highlights

Chapter Highlights

VOCABULARY DEFINITIONS

SECTION 1

classification the arrangement of organisms into orderly groups based on their similarities and presumed evolutionary relationships

kingdom the most general of the seven levels of classification

phylum the level of classification after kingdom; the organisms from all the kingdoms are sorted into several phyla

class the level of classification after phylum; the organisms in all phyla are sorted into classes

order the level of classification after class; the organisms in all the classes are sorted into orders

family the level of classification after order; the organisms in all orders are sorted into families

genus the level of classification after family; the organisms in all families are sorted into genera

species the most specific of the seven levels of classification; characterized by a group of organisms that can mate with one another to produce fertile offspring

taxonomy the science of identifying, classifying, and naming living things

dichotomous key an aid to identifying unknown organisms that consists of several pairs of descriptive statements; of each pair of statements, only one will apply to the unknown organism, and that will lead to another set of statements, and so on, until the unknown organism can be identified

SECTION 1

Vocabulary

classification (p. 160)

kingdom (p. 161)

phylum (p. 161)

class (p. 161)

order (p. 161)

family (p. 161)

genus (p. 161)

species (p. 161)

taxonomy (p. 162)

dichotomous key (p. 164)

Section Notes

• Classification refers to the arrangement of organisms into orderly groups based on their similarities and evolutionary relationships.

• Biologists classify organisms in order to organize the number and diversity of living things and to give them scientific names.

• The classification scheme used today is based on the work of Carolus Linnaeus. Linnaeus founded the science of taxonomy, in which organisms are described, named, and classified.

• Modern classification schemes include evolutionary relationships.

• Today organisms are classified using a seven-level system of organization. The seven levels are kingdom, phylum, class, order, family, genus, and species. The genus and species of an organism compose its two-part scientific name.

• A scientific name is always the same for a specific organism, no matter how many common names it has.

• Dichotomous keys help to identify organisms.

Labs

Voyage of the USS Adventure (p. 192)

☑ Skills Check

Math Concepts

LARGE ORGANISMS The rounding-off rule states: If the number you wish to round is greater than or equal to the midpoint, round the number to the next greater number.

Sometimes when you are working with objects instead of numbers, you have to use a different rule! The MathBreak on page 169 asks you to round up your answer even though the answer includes a fraction that is less than halfway to the next number. Why is that? The answer is that if you don't round up, you won't have enough students to encircle the tree.

Visual Understanding

LEVELS OF CLASSIFICATION If you are still a little unsure about how organisms are grouped into levels of classification, turn back to page 161. Review Figure 2. Notice that the broadest, most inclusive level is kingdom. For example, all animals are grouped into kingdom Animalia. From there, the groups become more and more specific until only one animal is included under the level of species. Working from species up, notice that more and more animals are included in the group as you move toward the level of kingdom.

Lab and Activity Highlights

Shape Island PG 172

Voyage of the USS Adventure PG 192

 Datasheets for LabBook (blackline masters for these labs)

SECTION 2

Archaebacteria a classification kingdom that contains ancient bacteria that thrive in extreme environments

Eubacteria a classification kingdom containing mostly free-living bacteria found in many varied environments

Protista a kingdom of eukaryotic single-celled or simple, multicellular organisms; kingdom Protista contains all eukaryotes that are not plants, animals, or fungi

Plantae the kingdom that contains plants—complex, multicellular organisms that are usually green and use the sun's energy to make sugar by photosynthesis

Fungi a kingdom of complex organisms that obtain food by breaking down other substances in their surroundings and absorbing the nutrients

Animalia the classification kingdom containing complex, multicellular organisms that lack cell walls, are usually able to move about, and possess nervous systems that help them be aware of and react to their surroundings

---

SECTION 2

Vocabulary

Archaebacteria *(p. 167)*
Eubacteria *(p. 167)*
Protista *(p. 168)*
Plantae *(p. 169)*
Fungi *(p. 170)*
Animalia *(p. 171)*

Section Notes

- At first, living things were classified as either plants or animals. As scientists discovered more about living things and discovered more organisms, new kingdoms were added that were more descriptive than the old two-kingdom system.

- Most biologists recognize six kingdoms—Archaebacteria, Eubacteria, Protista, Plantae, Fungi, and Animalia.

- Bacteria are prokaryotes, single-celled organisms that do not contain nuclei. The organisms of all other kingdoms are eukaryotes, organisms that have cells with nuclei.

- Archaebacteria have been on Earth for about 3 billion years and can live where most other organisms cannot survive.

- Most bacteria are eubacteria and live almost everywhere. Some are harmful, and some are beneficial.

- Plants, most fungi, and animals are complex multicellular organisms. Plants perform photosynthesis. Fungi break down material outside their body and then absorb the nutrients. Animals eat food, which is digested inside their body.

---

internetconnect

GO TO: go.hrw.com

Visit the **HRW** Web site for a variety of learning tools related to this chapter. Just type in the keyword:

KEYWORD: HSTCLS

SCiLINKS **NSTA**

GO TO: www.scilinks.org

Visit the **National Science Teachers Association** on-line Web site for Internet resources related to this chapter. Just type in the *sci*LINKS number for more information about the topic:

TOPIC: The Basis for Classification	*sci*LINKS NUMBER: HSTL205
TOPIC: Levels of Classification	*sci*LINKS NUMBER: HSTL210
TOPIC: Dichotomous Keys	*sci*LINKS NUMBER: HSTL215
TOPIC: The Six Kingdoms	*sci*LINKS NUMBER: HSTL220

175

Vocabulary Review Worksheet

Blackline masters of these Chapter Highlights can be found in the **Study Guide.**

Lab and Activity Highlights

LabBank

EcoLabs & Field Activities, Water Wigglers

Long-Term Projects & Research Ideas,
The Panda Mystery

USING VOCABULARY

1. taxonomy
2. phyla
3. species
4. two-part scientific names
5. prokaryotes

UNDERSTANDING CONCEPTS

Multiple Choice

6. a
7. d
8. a
9. c
10. b
11. a

Short Answer

12. More than one million species have scientific names. Each of them is unique, and all scientists know specifically which organism is being discussed without the confusion of common names.

13. Two kinds of evidence of evolutionary relationships are thought to be species that have shared characteristics and species that have common ancestors.

14. A eubacterium is a prokaryote because it is always single-celled and has no nucleus or other membrane-bound organelles.

Chapter Review

USING VOCABULARY

To complete the following sentences, choose the correct term from each pair of terms listed below:

1. Linnaeus founded the science of ___?___. (*DNA analysis* or *taxonomy*)

2. All of the organisms classified into a single kingdom are then divided into one of several ___?___. (*phyla* or *classes*)

3. The narrowest level of classification is the ___?___. (*genus* or *species*)

4. Linnaeus began naming organisms using ___?___. (*two-part scientific names* or *evolutionary relationships*)

5. Archaebacteria and eubacteria are ___?___. (*prokaryotes* or *eukaryotes*)

UNDERSTANDING CONCEPTS

Multiple Choice

6. When scientists classify organisms, they
   a. arrange them in orderly groups.
   b. give them many common names.
   c. decide whether they are useful.
   d. ignore evolutionary relationships.

7. When the seven levels of classification are listed from broadest to narrowest, which level is in the fifth position?
   a. class
   b. order
   c. genus
   d. family

8. The scientific name for the European white water lily is *Nymphaea alba*. What is the genus to which this plant belongs?
   a. *Nymphaea*   c. water lily
   b. *alba*   d. alba lily

9. "Kings Play Chess On Fine-Grained Sand" is a mnemonic device that helps one remember
   a. the scientific names of different organisms.
   b. the six kingdoms.
   c. the seven levels of classification.
   d. the difference between prokaryotic and eukaryotic cells.

10. Most bacteria are classified in which kingdom?
    a. Archaebacteria   c. Protista
    b. Eubacteria   d. Fungi

11. What kind of organism thrives in hot springs and other extreme environments?
    a. archaebacteria   c. protists
    b. eubacteria   d. fungi

Short Answer

12. Why is the use of scientific names so important in biology?

13. List two kinds of evidence used by modern taxonomists to classify organisms based on evolutionary relationships.

14. Is a eubacterium a type of eukaryote? Explain your answer.

Concept Map

15. Use the following terms to create a concept map: kingdom, fern, lizard, Animalia, Fungi, algae, Protista, Plantae, mushroom.

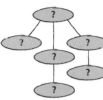

CRITICAL THINKING AND PROBLEM SOLVING

Write one or two sentences to answer the following questions:

16. How are the levels of classification related to evolutionary relationships among organisms?

17. Explain why two species that belong to the same genus, such as white oak *(Quercus alba)* and cork oak *(Quercus suber),* also belong to the same family.

18. What characteristic do the members of all six kingdoms have in common?

MATH IN SCIENCE

19. Scientists estimate that millions of species are yet to be discovered and classified. If only 1.5 million, or 10 percent, of species have been discovered and classified, how many species do scientists think exist on Earth?

20. Sequoia trees can grow to more than 90 m in height. There are 3.28 ft per meter. How many feet are in 90 m?

INTERPRETING GRAPHICS

The diagram below illustrates the evolutionary relationships among several primates.

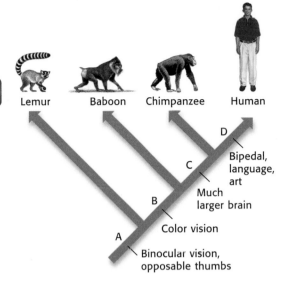

Lemur   Baboon   Chimpanzee   Human

D — Bipedal, language, art

C — Much larger brain

B — Color vision

A — Binocular vision, opposable thumbs

21. Which primate is the closest relative to the common ancestor of all primates?

22. Which primate shares the most traits with humans?

23. Do lemurs share the characteristics listed at point D with humans? Explain your answer.

24. What characteristic do baboons have that lemurs do not have? Explain your answer.

Reading Check-up
Take a minute to review your answers to the Pre-Reading Questions found at the bottom of page 158. Have your answers changed? If necessary, revise your answers based on what you have learned since you began this chapter.

177

Concept Mapping

15. An answer to this exercise can be found at the front of this book.

CRITICAL THINKING AND PROBLEM SOLVING

16. Each level of classification groups organisms according to characteristics they share. Starting at the kingdom level, each level contains fewer organisms with characteristics in common until there is only one species at the species level.

17. The family level of classification contains genuses and all the species in those genuses. All of the *Quercus* genera are in the same family because of shared characteristics.

18. All members of all six kingdoms are or once were living organisms. All living things share a common ancestor. They also have the genetic code in common, which means they all have DNA.

MATH IN SCIENCE

19. 15 million; Some scientists think that there may be as many as 15 million species on Earth today, most of which are undiscovered and unnamed.

20. 295.2 ft

INTERPRETING GRAPHICS

21. lemur
22. chimpanzee
23. No; lemurs branched off between points A and B.
24. Color vision; color vision appears on the diagram after lemurs have branched off.

Concept Mapping Transparency 9

Blackline masters of this Chapter Review can be found in the **Study Guide.**

It's a Bird, It's a Plane, It's a *Dinosaur*?

Background

Scientists have identified many physical traits of birds that appear similar to those of dinosaurs. For example, some dinosaur skeletons contain a birdlike wishbone. Also, the two-legged upright stance of certain dinosaurs suggests that they were endothermic (birds are endothermic). All ectothermic animals are "sprawlers," meaning that they move around on all four feet.

The *Sinosauropteryx* found in northern China was first thought to support the birds-from-dinosaurs hypothesis because the fossil has featherlike features. But other paleontologists contend that rather than feathers, the structures are bristly fibers of collagen. Still other scientists believe these "feathers" are made of the same material as modern feathers but lack the organization of true feathers.

A 1997 find in Argentina gives some support to the proponents of the birds-from-dinosaurs hypothesis. A 6 ft long fossil found in Argentina shows the most birdlike dinosaur ever discovered. Its skeletal structure indicates it had arms that could flap and fold like wings. It had a birdlike pelvis as well. The sediments the dinosaur was found in suggest it is 90 million years old. But this fossil, too, has fueled the debate. Some experts say the dinosaur existed long after the development of modern birds. Birds, they argue, evolved from another line of reptiles.

It's a Bird, It's a Plane, It's a *Dinosaur*?

Think about birds. Parrots, pigeons, buzzards, emus . . . they're everywhere! But once there were no birds. So where did they come from? When did birds evolve? Was it 225 million years ago, just 115 million years ago, or somewhere in between? No one really knows for sure, but the topic has fueled a long-standing debate among scientists.

The debate began when the fossil remains of a 150-million-year-old dinosaur with wings and feathers—*Archaeopteryx*—were found in Germany in 1860 and 1861.

▲ Archaeopteryx *was the first true bird.*

Birds Are Dinosaurs!

Some scientists think that birds evolved from small, carnivorous dinosaurs like *Velociraptor* about 115 million to 150 million years ago. Their idea relies on similarities between modern birds and these small dinosaurs. Particularly impor-

tant are the size, shape, and number of toes and "fingers"; the location and shape of the breastbone and shoulder; the presence of a hollow bone structure; and the development of wrist bones that "flap" for flight. To many scientists, all this evidence is overwhelming. It can lead to only one conclusion: Modern birds are descendants of dinosaurs.

No They Aren't!

"Not so fast!" say a smaller but equally determined group of scientists who think that birds developed 100 million years before *Velociraptor* and its relatives. They point out that all these dinosaurs were ground dwellers and were the wrong shape and size for flying. They would never get off the ground! Further, these dinosaurs lacked at least one of the bones necessary for flight in today's birds.

This "birds came before dinosaurs" idea rests on fossils of *thecodonts,* small tree-dwelling reptiles that lived about 225 million years ago. One thecodont, a small, four-legged tree dweller called *Megalancosaurus,* had the right bones and body shape—and the right center of gravity—for flight. The evidence is clear, say these scientists, that birds flew long before dinosaurs even existed!

▲ *This small tree-dwelling reptile,* Megalancosaurus, *may have evolved into the birds we know today.*

So Who Is Right?

Both sides are debating fossils 65 million years to 225 million years old. Some species left many fossils, while some left just a few. In the last few years, new fossils discovered in China, Mongolia, and Argentina have just added fuel to the fire. So scientists will continue to study the available evidence and provide their educated guesses. Meanwhile, the debate rages on!

Compare for Yourself

▶ Find photographs of *Sinosauropteryx* and *Archaeopteryx* fossils, and compare them. How are they similar? How are they different? Do you think birds could be modern dinosaurs? Debate your idea with someone who holds the opposite view.

178

Answer to Compare for Yourself

All reasonable answers should be accepted. These are some possible responses. Similarities between *Sinosauropteryx* and *Archeopteryx* include: a reptilian skeleton, a long tail, sharp teeth, and claws of approximately the same size. The most noticeable difference between *Archeopteryx* and *Sinosauropteryx* is that *Archeopteryx* had wings and feathers and *Sinosauropteryx* had short front limbs without feathers.

LOBSTER-LIP LIFE-FORM

Have you ever stopped to think about lobsters' lips? Did you even know that lobsters have lips? Oddly enough, they do. And even stranger, scientists have found a tiny animal living on lobsters' lips. Surprised? Although scientists noticed this little critter about 30 years ago, they had never studied it closely. When they finally did, they were astounded! This tiny organism is different from anything else in the world. Meet *Symbion pandora.*

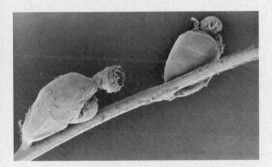

▲ *Although scientists knew of* Symbion pandora's *existence for 30 years, they did not realize how unusual it was.*

A Little Weird

What makes *Symbion pandora* so unusual? As if spending most of its life on lobster lips isn't strange enough, *S. pandora* also seems to combine the traits of very different animals. Here are some of its strange characteristics:

- **Life stages:** *S. pandora*'s life cycle involves many different *stages,* or body forms. The stages are very different from each other. For instance, at certain times in its life, *S. pandora* can swim around, while at other times, it can exist only by attaching to a lobster's mouth.
- **Dwarf males:** Male *S. pandora* are much smaller than the females. Thus, they are called *dwarf males.*

- **Feeding habits:** Dwarf males don't eat; they can only find a female, reproduce, and then die!
- **Budding:** Many individuals are neither male nor female. These animals reproduce through a process called *budding.* In budding, a new, complete animal can sprout out of the adult. In turn, the new offspring can reproduce in the same way.
- **Disappearing guts:** When an adult starts to form a new bud, its digestive and nervous systems disappear! Part of these guts help make the new bud. Then the adult forms new digestive and nervous systems to replace the old ones.

How Unusual Is It?

When scientists discover a new plant or animal, they may conclude that it represents a new species within an existing genus. In that case scientists make up a name for the new species. Usually, the person who finds the new organism gets to name it. If the new organism is *very* unusual, scientists may place it not only in a new species but also in a new genus.

S. pandora is so unusual that it was placed not only in a new species and a new genus, but also in a new family, a new order, a new class, and even a new phylum! Such a scientific discovery is extremely rare. In fact, when this discovery was made, in 1995, it was announced in newspapers all over the world!

Where Would You Look?

▶ *S. pandora* was first noticed more than 30 years ago, but no one realized how unusual it was until scientists studied it. Scientists estimate that we've identified less than 10 percent of Earth's organisms. Find out about other new animal species that have been discovered within the last 10 years. Where are some places you would look for new species?

179

Answer to Where Would You Look?
Answers will vary.

WEIRD SCIENCE
Lobster-Lip Life-Form

Background

When *Symbion pandora* was proposed as a new species, the scientists who described it decided that it didn't fit into any existing phyla. Thus, they made up a new phylum, Cycliophora.

When someone proposes a new phylum, it usually takes some time before other scientists decide whether they agree that a new phylum designation is warranted. Even after debate, scientists often disagree. As a result, there are between 30 and 40 existing animal phyla, depending on whom you ask. Most biologists agree that there are at least 34 living phyla of animals. Before Cycliophora, no new phyla had been proposed since 1983.

The name *Symbion pandora* was deliberately chosen. *Symbion* refers to the organism's close association with lobsters. (The relationship is an example of commensalism, because *S. pandora* benefits and the lobster is largely unaffected.) *Pandora* was chosen because the bud-within-bud structure of the animal reminded the researchers of the Greek myth of Pandora's box. You may wish to have a group of students learn about this myth and share their results with the class.

SAFETY FIRST!

Exploring, inventing, and investigating are essential to the study of science. However, these activities can also be dangerous. To make sure that your experiments and explorations are safe, you must be aware of a variety of safety guidelines.

You have probably heard of the saying, "It is better to be safe than sorry." This is particularly true in a science classroom where experiments and explorations are being performed. Being uninformed and careless can result in serious injuries. Don't take chances with your own safety or with anyone else's.

Following are important guidelines for staying safe in the science classroom. Your teacher may also have safety guidelines and tips that are specific to your classroom and laboratory. Take the time to be safe.

Safety Rules!

Start Out Right

Always get your teacher's permission before attempting any laboratory exploration. Read the procedures carefully, and pay particular attention to safety information and caution statements. If you are unsure about what a safety symbol means, look it up or ask your teacher. You cannot be too careful when it comes to safety. If an accident does occur, inform your teacher immediately, regardless of how minor you think the accident is.

Safety Symbols

All of the experiments and investigations in this book and their related worksheets include important safety symbols to alert you to particular safety concerns. Become familiar with these symbols so that when you see them, you will know what they mean and what to do. It is important that you read this entire safety section to learn about specific dangers in the laboratory.

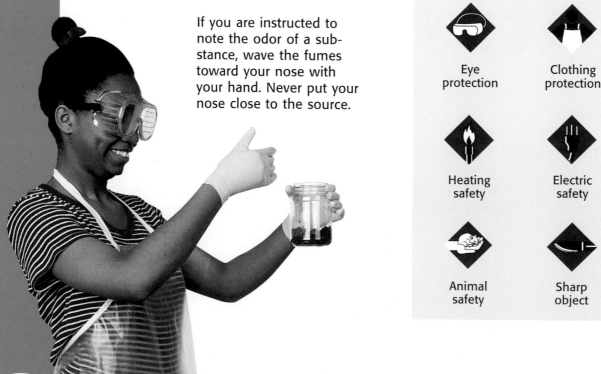

If you are instructed to note the odor of a substance, wave the fumes toward your nose with your hand. Never put your nose close to the source.

Eye protection	Clothing protection	Hand safety
Heating safety	Electric safety	Chemical safety
Animal safety	Sharp object	Plant safety

Eye Safety

Wear safety goggles when working around chemicals, acids, bases, or any type of flame or heating device. Wear safety goggles any time there is even the slightest chance that harm could come to your eyes. If any substance gets into your eyes, notify your teacher immediately, and flush your eyes with running water for at least 15 minutes. Treat any unknown chemical as if it were a dangerous chemical. Never look directly into the sun. Doing so could cause permanent blindness.

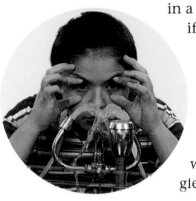

Avoid wearing contact lenses in a laboratory situation. Even if you are wearing safety goggles, chemicals can get between the contact lenses and your eyes. If your doctor requires that you wear contact lenses instead of glasses, wear eye-cup safety goggles in the lab.

Safety Equipment

Know the locations of the nearest fire alarms and any other safety equipment, such as fire blankets and eyewash fountains, as identified by your teacher, and know the procedures for using them.

Be extra careful when using any glassware. When adding a heavy object to a graduated cylinder, tilt the cylinder so the object slides slowly to the bottom.

Neatness

Keep your work area free of all unnecessary books and papers. Tie back long hair, and secure loose sleeves or other loose articles of clothing, such as ties and bows. Remove dangling jewelry. Don't wear open-toed shoes or sandals in the laboratory. Never eat, drink, or apply cosmetics in a laboratory setting. Food, drink, and cosmetics can easily become contaminated with dangerous materials.

Certain hair products (such as aerosol hair spray) are flammable and should not be worn while working near an open flame. Avoid wearing hair spray or hair gel on lab days.

Sharp/Pointed Objects

Use knives and other sharp instruments with extreme care. Never cut objects while holding them in your hands. Place objects on a suitable work surface for cutting.

Heat

Wear safety goggles when using a heating device or a flame. Whenever possible, use an electric hot plate as a heat source instead of an open flame. When heating materials in a test tube, always angle the test tube away from yourself and others. In order to avoid burns, wear heat-resistant gloves whenever instructed to do so.

Electricity

Be careful with electrical cords. When using a microscope with a lamp, do not place the cord where it could trip someone. Do not let cords hang over a table edge in a way that could cause equipment to fall if the cord is accidentally pulled. Do not use equipment with damaged cords. Be sure your hands are dry and that the electrical equipment is in the "off" position before plugging it in. Turn off and unplug electrical equipment when you are finished.

Chemicals

Wear safety goggles when handling any potentially dangerous chemicals, acids, or bases. If a chemical is unknown, handle it as you would a dangerous chemical. Wear an apron and safety gloves when working with acids or bases or whenever you are told to do so. If a spill gets on your skin or clothing, rinse it off immediately with water for at least 5 minutes while calling to your teacher.

Never mix chemicals unless your teacher tells you to do so. Never taste, touch, or smell chemicals unless you are specifically directed to do so. Before working with a flammable liquid or gas, check for the presence of any source of flame, spark, or heat.

Animal Safety

Always obtain your teacher's permission before bringing any animal into the school building. Handle animals only as your teacher directs. Always treat animals carefully and with respect. Wash your hands thoroughly after handling any animal.

Plant Safety

Do not eat any part of a plant or plant seed used in the laboratory. Wash hands thoroughly after handling any part of a plant. When in nature, do not pick any wild plants unless your teacher instructs you to do so.

Glassware

Examine all glassware before use. Be sure that glassware is clean and free of chips and cracks. Report damaged glassware to your teacher. Glass containers used for heating should be made of heat-resistant glass.

Time Required

Two 45-minute class periods

Lab Ratings

EASY ———————————————→ HARD

TEACHER PREP 🍼🍼
STUDENT SET-UP 🍼🍼
CONCEPT LEVEL 🍼🍼🍼
CLEAN UP 🍼

Safety Caution

Remind students to review all safety cautions and icons before beginning this lab activity.

Preparation Notes

Some students may find it difficult to work with a nonspecific unit of measurement. If so, the cube models easily convert to centimeters. You may want to add some small items, such as peas, beans, popcorn, or peppercorns, to the sand to represent organelles floating in the cytoplasm. Some students may need to review what a ratio is and how ratios are used.

Terry Rakes
Elmwood Junior High School
Rogers, Arkansas

Elephant-Sized Amoebas?

MAKING MODELS

Why can't amoebas grow to be as large as elephants? An amoeba is a single-celled organism. Amoebas, like most cells, are microscopic. If an amoeba could grow to the size of a quarter, it would starve to death. To understand how this can be true, build a model of a cell and see for yourself.

Materials

- cubic cell patterns
- pieces of heavy paper or poster board
- scissors
- transparent tape
- scale or balance
- fine sand

Procedure

1. Use heavy paper to make four cube-shaped cell models from the patterns supplied by your teacher. Cut out each cell model, fold the sides to make a cube, and tape the tabs on the sides. The smallest cell model has sides that are one unit long. The next larger cell has sides of two units. The next cell has sides of three units, and the largest cell has sides of four units. These paper models represent the cell membrane, the part of a cell's exterior through which food and waste pass.

Two-unit cell model

2. In your ScienceLog, copy the data table at right. Use each formula to calculate the data about your cell models. A key to the formula symbols can be found on the next page. Record your calculations in the table. Calculations for the smallest cell have been done for you.

Data Table for Measurements

Length of side	Area of one side (A = S×S)	Total surface area of cube cell (TA = S×S×6)	Volume of cube cell (V = S×S×S)	Mass of cube cell
1	1 unit²	6 unit²	1 unit³	
2				
3		DO NOT WRITE IN BOOK		
4				

Data Table for Measurements

Length of side S	Area of one side (square unit)	Total surface area of cube cell (square units)	Volume of cube cell (cubic units)	Mass of cube cell (approximate, in grams)
1	1	6	1	4.5
2	4	24	8	30
3	9	54	27	105
4	16	96	64	230

3. Carefully fill each model with fine sand until the sand is level with the top edge. Find the mass of the filled models using a scale or a balance. What does the sand in your model represent?

4. Record the mass of each cell model in the table. (Always remember to use the appropriate mass unit.)

5. In your ScienceLog, make a data table like the one below.

Data Table for Ratios		
Length of side	Ratio of total surface area to volume	Ratio of total surface area to mass
1		
2	DO NOT WRITE IN BOOK	
3		
4		

6. Use the data from your Data Table for Measurements to find the ratios for each of your cell models. Fill in the Data Table for Ratios for each of the cell models.

Analysis

7. As a cell grows larger, does the ratio of total surface area to volume increase, decrease, or stay the same?

8. Which is better able to supply food to all the cytoplasm of the cell—the cell membrane of a small cell or that of a large cell? Explain your answer.

9. As a cell grows larger, does the total surface area to mass ratio increase, decrease, or stay the same?

10. Is the cell membrane of a cell with high mass or the cell membrane of a cell with low mass better able to feed all the cytoplasm of the cell? You may explain your answer in a verbal presentation to the class or you may choose to write a report and illustrate it with drawings of your models.

Key to Formula Symbols
S = the length of one side
A = area
V = volume
TA = total area

Cell Model Template

Using the template above, prepare four patterns for students to use to make their cubes. Make one cube 1 unit wide, one cube 2 units wide, one cube 3 units wide, and one cube 4 units wide. The unit can be the size of your choosing.

Answers

3. The sand represents cytoplasm.

4. Masses will vary.

6. See the tables below.

7. decrease

8. A small cell has a higher surface-area-to-volume ratio than a large cell has, allowing more nutrients per cubic unit of volume to enter.

9. decrease

10. low mass

185

Data Table for Ratios

Length of side S	Total surface area/volume ratio	Total surface area/mass ratio
1	$\frac{6}{1} = 6$	$\frac{6}{4.5} = 1.33$
2	$\frac{24}{8} = 3$	$\frac{24}{30} = 0.80$
3	$\frac{54}{27} = 2$	$\frac{54}{105} = 0.51$
4	$\frac{96}{64} = 1.5$	$\frac{96}{230} = 0.42$

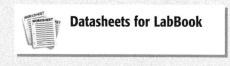

Datasheets for LabBook

The Perfect Taters Mystery

Teacher's Notes

Time Required

Two 45-minute class periods

Lab Ratings

EASY	HARD

TEACHER PREP ⚗️⚗️

STUDENT SET-UP ⚗️⚗️

CONCEPT LEVEL ⚗️⚗️⚗️

CLEAN UP ⚗️

MATERIALS

The materials listed on the student page are enough for 1 class of students. You will need 1 or 2 small potatoes per class. Do not allow students to cut or peel potatoes. You will need to do this ahead of time. Allow students to choose the number of containers they will need for the experiment. They may wish to test several salt concentrations.

Safety Caution

Remind students to review all safety cautions and icons before beginning this lab activity.

Avoid including green or discolored parts of the potato in the pieces students work with. These could cause illness.

Susan Gorman
North Ridge Middle School
North Richland Hills, Texas

DESIGN YOUR OWN

The Perfect Taters Mystery

You are the chief food detective at Perfect Taters Food Company. The boss, Mr. Fries, wants you to find a way to keep his potatoes fresh and crisp while they are waiting to be cooked. His workers have tried several methods already, but nothing has worked. Workers in Group A put the potatoes in very salty water, and the potatoes did something unexpected. Workers in Group B put the potatoes in water with no salt, and the potatoes did something else! Workers in Group C didn't put the potatoes in any water, and that didn't work either. Now you must design an experiment to find out what can be done to make the potatoes come out crisp and fresh.

Materials

- potato samples (A, B, and C)
- freshly cut potato pieces
- salt
- 6 small, clear plastic drinking cups
- 4 L of distilled water

1. Before you plan your experiment, review what you know. You know that potatoes are made of cells. Plant cells contain a large amount of water. Cells have membranes that hold water and other materials inside and keep some things out. Water and other materials must travel across cell membranes to get into and out of the cell.

2. Mr. Fries has told you that you can obtain as many samples as you need from the workers in Groups A, B, and C. Your teacher will have these samples ready for you to observe.

3. Make a data table like the one below in your ScienceLog to list your observations. Make as many observations as you can about the potatoes tested by workers in Group A, Group B, and Group C.

Observations	
Group A:	
Group B:	DO NOT WRITE IN BOOK
Group C:	

Ask a Question

4. Now that you have made your observations, state Mr. Fries's problem in the form of a question that can be answered by your experiment.

Lab Notes

Osmosis is often a confusing and misunderstood concept in life science. Quite often, students can repeat the definition of the process but are unable to apply the concept to explain the movement of water in different osmotic environments. In this lab, students will have an opportunity to observe osmosis in a model and obtain measurable results. This lab can be done as a class demonstration if materials and space are limited. The purpose of this lab is to reinforce comprehension of osmosis and to practice the scientific method.

Form a Hypothesis

5. Form a hypothesis based on your observations and your questions. The hypothesis should be a statement about what causes the potatoes to shrivel or swell. Based on your hypothesis, make a prediction about the outcome of your experiments. State your prediction in an "if-then" format.

Test the Hypothesis

6. Once you have made a prediction, design your investigation. Check your experimental design with your teacher before you begin. Mr. Fries will give you potato pieces, water, salt, and no more than six containers.

7. Keep very accurate records. Write out your plan and procedure. Make data tables. To be sure of your data, measure all materials carefully and make drawings of the potato pieces before and after the experiment.

Draw Conclusions

8. Explain what happened to the potato cells in Groups A, B, and C in your experiment. Include a discussion of the cell membrane and the process of osmosis.

Communicate Results

9. Write a letter to Mr. Fries that explains your experimental method, your results, and your conclusion. Then make a recommendation about how he should handle the potatoes so they will stay fresh and crisp.

187

Datasheets for LabBook

Science Skills Worksheet
"Designing an Experiment"

Answers

8. The potato cells in group A were placed in very salty water. The potatoes shriveled up because water moved out of the cell and into the salty water (from an area of high concentration of water to an area of low concentration of water). This may be confusing to some students, who may think that because the concentration of salt is high outside the potato, the salt should move to the area of lower concentration. Explain that although water can move through a cell membrane by osmosis, salt must be moved across a cell membrane by a process that requires energy.

The potato cells in group B were placed in water with no salt. The potatoes swelled because the concentration of water was lower inside the cell. (The concentration of salt and other molecules was higher inside the potato cell.)

The potato cells in group C turned brown and dried up because the water concentration outside the cell was low. In fact, there wasn't any water at all. The water evaporated as soon as it left the cell membrane. The potato cells turned brown because of chemical reactions with the air.

9. Letters to Mr. Fries will vary according to each student's results. However, all students should explain that through trial and error they found one salt concentration that was closest to the concentration of salt and other molecules inside the potato. This is the concentration that should be used to maintain an osmotic balance in the potato. Furthermore, some students will realize that the potatoes must be kept in water to prevent them from turning brown.

Tracing Traits
Teacher's Notes

Time Required

Two 45-minute class periods, separated by several days so students have time to complete their surveys

Lab Ratings

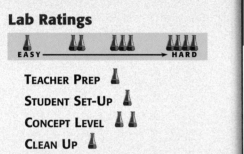

EASY ——————→ HARD

TEACHER PREP   ♦
STUDENT SET-UP   ♦
CONCEPT LEVEL   ♦♦
CLEAN UP   ♦

Lab Notes

Family histories will vary. Encourage students to include at least three generations in their histories.

Survey results will vary. Make sure that students actually surveyed each family member who was available. Responses will vary. You may check family members with shaded symbols against the survey results for accuracy.

Percentages will vary. A family member may receive a recessive allele from the father and a recessive allele from the mother. In such a case, this family member will exhibit the recessive form of the trait rather than the dominant form.

Because so many children are adopted or live in foster homes or group homes, please emphasize to your students that they may choose any family to study.

Tracing Traits

DESIGN YOUR OWN

Have you ever wondered about the traits you inherited from your parents? Do you have a trait that neither of your parents has? In this project, you will develop a family tree, or pedigree, similar to the one shown in the diagram below. You will trace an inherited trait through a family to determine how it has passed from generation to generation.

Procedure   TRY at HOME

1. The diagram at right shows a family history. On a separate piece of paper, draw a similar diagram of the family you have chosen. Include as many family members as possible, such as grandparents, parents, children, and grandchildren. Use circles to represent females and squares to represent males. You may include other information, such as the family member's name, birthdate, or picture.

2. Draw a chart similar to the one on the next page. Survey each of the family members shown in your family tree. Ask them if they have hair on the middle segment of their fingers. Write each person's name in the appropriate square. Explain to each person that it is normal to have either trait. The presence of hair on the middle segment is the dominant form of this trait.

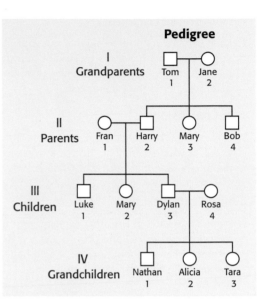

Pedigree

I Grandparents — Tom 1, Jane 2

II Parents — Fran 1, Harry 2, Mary 3, Bob 4

III Children — Luke 1, Mary 2, Dylan 3, Rosa 4

IV Grandchildren — Nathan 1, Alicia 2, Tara 3

CLASSROOM TESTED & APPROVED

Kerry Johnson
Isbell Middle School
Santa Paula, California

Dominant trait	Recessive trait	Family members with the dominant trait	Family members with the recessive trait
Hair present on the middle segment of fingers (H)	Hair absent on the middle segment of fingers (h)	*DO NOT WRITE IN BOOK*	

3. Trace this trait throughout the family tree you diagrammed in step 1. Shade or color the symbols of the family members who demonstrate the dominant form of this trait.

Analysis

4. What percentage of the family members demonstrate the dominant form of the trait? Calculate this by counting the number of people who have the dominant trait and dividing this number by the total number of people you surveyed. Multiply your answer by 100. An example has been done at right.

5. What percentage of the family members demonstrates the recessive form of the trait? Why doesn't every family member have the dominant form of the trait?

6. Choose one of the family members who demonstrates the recessive form of the chosen trait. What is this person's genotype? What are the possible genotypes for the parents of this individual? Does this person have any brothers or sisters? Do they show the dominant or recessive trait?

7. Draw a Punnett square like the one at right. Use this to determine the genotypes of the parents of the person you chose in step 7. Write this person's genotype in the bottom right-hand corner of your Punnett square. **Hint:** There may be more than one possible genotype for the parents. Don't forget to consider the genotypes of the person's brothers and sisters.

Example: Calculating percentage

$$\frac{10 \text{ people with trait}}{20 \text{ people surveyed}} = \frac{1}{2}$$

$$\frac{1}{2} = 0.50 \times 100 = 50\%$$

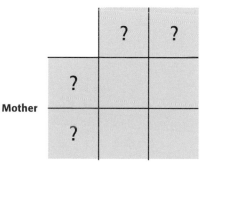

Father

Mother

189

Answers

4. Answers will vary.

5. Answers will vary.

6. The genotype of the recessive form of the characteristic must be *hh* (homozygous recessive). Each allele came from one of the individual's parents. Possible genotypes for the parents of the individual expressing the recessive form are *Hh* and *hh*. Does the student know whether either of the parents expresses the recessive form of the trait? Does the student know if the individual chosen has brothers or sisters? Are their genotypes known? If so, have the student decide if each of them has a dominant or recessive genotype. If a dominant genotype is found among the siblings and one of the parents is known to have the recessive form, ask the student what the genotype of the other parent must be *(Hh)*.

7. The Punnett square should show *hh* in the bottom right-hand corner. One of the parents must have the genotype *hh*. The other parent must have either *hh* or *Hh*. If any sibling has the dominant trait, the genotype of the other parent must be *Hh*.

Datasheets for LabBook

Time Required

One 45-minute class period

Lab Ratings

EASY ———————————→ HARD

TEACHER PREP
STUDENT SET-UP
CONCEPT LEVEL
CLEAN UP

Safety Cautions

Tell students not to eat the marshmallows after the lab. The marshmallows will have been handled thoroughly.

Preparation Notes

Choose several colors of mini-marshmallows and a piece of cloth or a napkin that will make the marshmallows hard to see at first glance.

Datasheets for LabBook

Georgiann Delgadillo
East Valley School District
Continuous Curriculum School
Spokane, Washington

DISCOVERY LAB

Out-of-Sight Marshmallows

An adaptation is a trait that helps an organism survive in its environment. In nature, camouflage is a form of coloration that enables an organism to blend into its immediate surroundings.

Materials

- 50 white mini-marshmallows
- 50 colored mini-marshmallows (all one color is preferable)
- 50 cm² of colored cloth, matching one of the marshmallow colors
- watch or clock with a second hand

Hypothesis

Organisms that are camouflaged have a better chance of escaping from predators and therefore a better chance of survival.

Test the Hypothesis

1. Working in pairs, count out 50 white marshmallows and 50 colored marshmallows. Your marshmallows will represent the prey (food) in this experiment.

2. Place the white and colored marshmallows randomly on the piece of colored cloth.

3. One student per pair should be the hungry hunter (predator). The other student should record the results of each trial. The predator should look at the food for a few seconds, pick up the first marshmallow he or she sees, and then look away.

4. Continue this process without stopping for 2 minutes or until your teacher signals to stop.

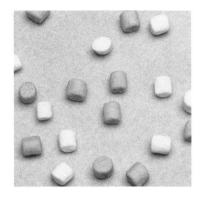

Analyze the Results

5. How many white marshmallows did the hungry hunter choose?

6. How many colored marshmallows did the hungry hunter choose?

Draw Conclusions

7. What did the cloth represent in your investigation?

8. Did the color of the cloth affect the color of marshmallows chosen? Explain your answer.

9. Which marshmallow color represented camouflage?

10. Describe an organism that has a camouflage adaptation.

190

Answers

5. Answers will vary according to the students' experiments.

6. Answers will vary, but the marshmallow that most closely resembles the background cloth is expected to be chosen less often.

7. The cloth represents the organism's background, environment, or surroundings.

8. The marshmallow with the color that does not blend in with the color of the cloth will probably be chosen most often because it is easier to see. So the color of the cloth is important to the "organism's" protection.

9. Answers will vary according to the colors used in the lab.

10. Answers will vary, but students should describe an organism that is difficult to see in its natural surroundings.

Survival of the Chocolates

Imagine a world populated with candy, and hold that delicious thought for just a moment. Try to apply the idea of natural selection to a population of candy-coated chocolates. According to the theory of natural selection, individuals who have favorable adaptations are more likely to survive. In the "species" of candy you will study in this experiment, shell strength is an adaptive advantage. Plan an experiment to find out which candy characteristics correspond to shell (candy coating) strength.

Materials

- small candy-coated chocolates in a variety of colors
- other materials as needed, according to the design of your experiment

Form a Hypothesis

1. Form a hypothesis and make a prediction. For example, if you chose to study candy color, your prediction might look like this: If the _____?_____ colored shell is the strongest, then fewer of the candies with this color of shell will _____?_____ when _____?_____.

Test Your Hypothesis

2. Design a procedure to determine which candy is best suited to survive by not "cracking under pressure." In your plan, be sure to include materials and tools you may need to complete this procedure. Check your experimental design with your teacher before you begin. Your teacher will supply the candy and assist you in gathering materials and tools.

3. Record your results in a data table you have designed in your ScienceLog. Be sure to organize your data in a clear and understandable way.

Analyze the Results

4. Write a report that describes your experiment. Explain how your data either support or do not support your hypothesis. Include possible errors and ways to improve your procedure.

Going Further

Can you think of another characteristic of these candies that can be tested to determine which candy is best adapted to survive? Explain your choice.

191

Karma Houston-Hughes
Kyrene Middle School
Tempe, Arizona

Datasheets for LabBook

Survival of the Chocolates
Teacher's Notes

Time Required

One or two 45-minute class periods

Lab Ratings

EASY			HARD

TEACHER PREP 🧪
STUDENT SET-UP 🧪🧪
CONCEPT LEVEL 🧪🧪
CLEAN UP 🧪

Safety Caution

Safety concerns will vary with each design.

Preparation Notes

You will need to be prepared for different experimental designs. Some students may wish to find out if the different colored candy shells differ in hardness by testing which one will crack easiest under physical stress. Others may want to test the colors to see which one will dissolve more readily in water (cold or warm). Encourage different ways of testing. Part of the purpose of this lab is to help students learn how to design an experiment.

Answers

1. The statement made for the student here is for example only. Students may not wish to test for hardness or cracking. Help them make a prediction about their own experiment.

2. Again, students should conduct their own experiment.

Voyage of the USS *Adventure*
Teacher's Notes

Time Required

One 45-minute class period

Lab Ratings

EASY ———————————————→ HARD

TEACHER PREP ▲
STUDENT SET-UP ▲
CONCEPT LEVEL ▲▲
CLEAN UP ▲

Preparation Notes

Some students will find it easier to make the charts on graph paper, so you may wish to add graph paper to the list of materials needed.

Lab Notes

Students should know that we are not yet able to travel outside our solar system. This activity should help students categorize organisms or objects by noticing subtle differences. It is a good activity to begin a study of classification of animals, rocks, or plants. This lab may be useful before introducing dichotomous keys, for example.

DISCOVERY LAB

Voyage of the USS *Adventure*

You are a crew member on the USS *Adventure*. The *Adventure* has been on a 5-year mission to collect life-forms from outside the solar system. On the voyage back to Earth, your ship went through a meteor shower, which ruined several of the compartments containing the extraterrestrial life-forms. Now it is necessary to put more than one life-form in the same compartment.

You have only three undamaged compartments in your starship. You and your crewmates must stay in one compartment, and that compartment should be used for extraterrestrial life-forms only if absolutely necessary. You and your crewmates must decide which of the life-forms could be placed together. It is thought that similar life-forms will have similar needs. You can use only observable characteristics to group the life-forms.

Life-form 1

Life-form 2

Life-form 3

Procedure *TRY at HOME*

1. Make a data table similar to the one below. Label each column with as many characteristics of the various life-forms as possible. Leave enough space in each square to write your observations. The life-forms are pictured on this page.

Life-form 4

Life-form Characteristics				
	Color	Shape	Legs	Eyes
Life-form 1				
Life-form 2				
Life-form 3				
Life-form 4				

DO NOT WRITE IN BOOK

Life-form 5

2. Describe each characteristic as completely as you can. Based on your observations, determine which of the life-forms are most alike.

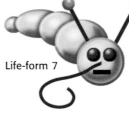
Life-form 7

Life-form 6

192

Datasheets for LabBook

CLASSROOM TESTED & APPROVED

Georgiann Delgadillo
East Valley School District
Continuous Curriculum School
Spokane, Washington

3. Make a data table like the one below. Fill in the table according to the decisions you made in step 2. State your reasons for the way you have grouped your life-forms.

Life-form Room Assignments		
Compartment	Life-forms	Reasons
1		
2		
3		

DO NOT WRITE IN BOOK

4. The USS *Adventure* has to make one more stop before returning home. On planet X437 you discover the most interesting life-form ever found outside of Earth—the CC9, shown at right. Make a decision, based on your previous grouping of life-forms, about whether you can safely include CC9 in one of the compartments for the trip to Earth.

CC9

Analysis

5. Describe the life-forms in compartment 1. How are they similar? How are they different?

6. Describe the life-forms in compartment 2. How are they similar? How do they differ from the life-forms in compartment 1?

7. Are there any life-forms in compartment 3? If so, describe their similarities. In which compartment will you and your crewmates remain for the journey home?

8. Are you able to safely transport life-form CC9 back to Earth? Why or why not? If you are able to include CC9, in which compartment will it be placed? How did you decide?

Going Further

In 1831, Charles Darwin sailed from England on a ship called the HMS *Beagle*. You have studied the finches that Darwin observed on the Galápagos Islands. What were some of the other unusual organisms he found there? For example, find out about the Galápagos tortoise.

193

Answers

There are no right or wrong answers in this activity. The objective is to allow students an opportunity to recognize subtle differences and to recognize that organisms may be more alike than they are different. However, you should make sure the students provide good reasons why they grouped certain life-forms together. There are several ways these seven organisms are similar. For example, four of them are segmented and have no legs. Three of them are geometrically shaped, and three others have mouths. Have students examine them for less observable characteristics, such as what kind of body plan or symmetry they have, how they might obtain food, or whether they might be land dwelling or aquatic.

Going Further

The Galápagos tortoise can have a shell length of 1.3 m, a mass of 180 kg, and live to be 150 years old.

Concept Mapping: A Way to Bring Ideas Together

What Is a Concept Map?

Have you ever tried to tell someone about a book or a chapter you've just read and found that you can remember only a few isolated words and ideas? Or maybe you've memorized facts for a test and then weeks later discovered you're not even sure what topics those facts covered.

In both cases, you may have understood the ideas or concepts by themselves but not in relation to one another. If you could somehow link the ideas together, you would probably understand them better and remember them longer. This is something a concept map can help you do. A concept map is a way to see how ideas or concepts fit together. It can help you see the "big picture."

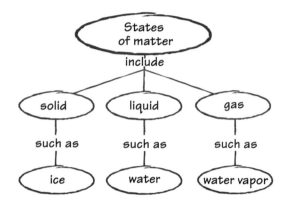

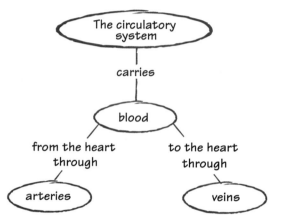

How to Make a Concept Map

❶ Make a list of the main ideas or concepts.

It might help to write each concept on its own slip of paper. This will make it easier to rearrange the concepts as many times as necessary to make sense of how the concepts are connected. After you've made a few concept maps this way, you can go directly from writing your list to actually making the map.

❷ Arrange the concepts in order from the most general to the most specific.

Put the most general concept at the top and circle it. Ask yourself, "How does this concept relate to the remaining concepts?" As you see the relationships, arrange the concepts in order from general to specific.

❸ Connect the related concepts with lines.

❹ On each line, write an action word or short phrase that shows how the concepts are related.

Look at the concept maps on this page, and then see if you can make one for the following terms:

plants, water, photosynthesis, carbon dioxide, sun's energy

One possible answer is provided at right, but don't look at it until you try the concept map yourself.

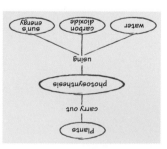

194 Appendix

SI Measurement

The International System of Units, or SI, is the standard system of measurement used by many scientists. Using the same standards of measurement makes it easier for scientists to communicate with one another.

SI works by combining prefixes and base units. Each base unit can be used with different prefixes to define smaller and larger quantities. The table below lists common SI prefixes.

SI Prefixes			
Prefix	**Abbreviation**	**Factor**	**Example**
kilo-	k	1,000	kilogram, 1 kg = 1,000 g
hecto-	h	100	hectoliter, 1 hL = 100 L
deka-	da	10	dekameter, 1 dam = 10 m
		1	meter, liter
deci-	d	0.1	decigram, 1 dg = 0.1 g
centi-	c	0.01	centimeter, 1 cm = 0.01 m
milli-	m	0.001	milliliter, 1 mL = 0.001 L
micro-	μ	0.000 001	micrometer, 1 μm = 0.000 001 m

SI Conversion Table		
SI units	**From SI to English**	**From English to SI**
Length		
kilometer (km) = 1,000 m	1 km = 0.621 mi	1 mi = 1.609 km
meter (m) = 100 cm	1 m = 3.281 ft	1 ft = 0.305 m
centimeter (cm) = 0.01 m	1 cm = 0.394 in.	1 in. = 2.540 cm
millimeter (mm) = 0.001 m	1 mm = 0.039 in.	
micrometer (μm) = 0.000 001 m		
nanometer (nm) = 0.000 000 001 m		
Area		
square kilometer (km^2) = 100 hectares	1 km^2 = 0.386 mi^2	1 mi^2 = 2.590 km^2
hectare (ha) = 10,000 m^2	1 ha = 2.471 acres	1 acre = 0.405 ha
square meter (m^2) = 10,000 cm^2	1 m^2 = 10.765 ft^2	1 ft^2 = 0.093 m^2
square centimeter (cm^2) = 100 mm^2	1 cm^2 = 0.155 in.^{2}	1 in.^{2} = 6.452 cm^2
Volume		
liter (L) = 1,000 mL = 1 dm^3	1 L = 1.057 fl qt	1 fl qt = 0.946 L
milliliter (mL) = 0.001 L = 1 cm^3	1 mL = 0.034 fl oz	1 fl oz = 29.575 mL
microliter (μL) = 0.000 001 L		
Mass		
kilogram (kg) = 1,000 g	1 kg = 2.205 lb	1 lb = 0.454 kg
gram (g) = 1,000 mg	1 g = 0.035 oz	1 oz = 28.349 g
milligram (mg) = 0.001 g		
microgram (μg) = 0.000 001 g		

Temperature Scales

Temperature can be expressed using three different scales: Fahrenheit, Celsius, and Kelvin. The SI unit for temperature is the kelvin (K).

Although 0 K is much colder than 0°C, a change of 1 K is equal to a change of 1°C.

Three Temperature Scales

	Fahrenheit	Celsius	Kelvin
Water boils	212°	100°	373
Body temperature	98.6°	37°	310
Room temperature	68°	20°	293
Water freezes	32°	0°	273

Temperature Conversions Table

To convert	Use this equation:	Example
Celsius to Fahrenheit °C ⟶ °F	$°F = \left(\dfrac{9}{5} \times °C\right) + 32$	Convert 45°C to °F. $°F = \left(\dfrac{9}{5} \times 45°C\right) + 32 = 113°F$
Fahrenheit to Celsius °F ⟶ °C	$°C = \dfrac{5}{9} \times (°F - 32)$	Convert 68°F to °C. $°C = \dfrac{5}{9} \times (68°F - 32) = 20°C$
Celsius to Kelvin °C ⟶ K	$K = °C + 273$	Convert 45°C to K. $K = 45°C + 273 = 318\ K$
Kelvin to Celsius K ⟶ °C	$°C = K - 273$	Convert 32 K to °C. $°C = 32\ K - 273 = -241°C$

Measuring Skills

Using a Graduated Cylinder

When using a graduated cylinder to measure volume, keep the following procedures in mind:

1 Make sure the cylinder is on a flat, level surface.

2 Move your head so that your eye is level with the surface of the liquid.

3 Read the mark closest to the liquid level. On glass graduated cylinders, read the mark closest to the center of the curve in the liquid's surface.

Using a Meterstick or Metric Ruler

When using a meterstick or metric ruler to measure length, keep the following procedures in mind:

1 Place the ruler firmly against the object you are measuring.

2 Align one edge of the object exactly with the zero end of the ruler.

3 Look at the other edge of the object to see which of the marks on the ruler is closest to that edge. **Note:** Each small slash between the centimeters represents a millimeter, which is one-tenth of a centimeter.

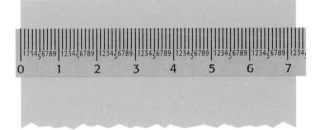

Using a Triple-Beam Balance

When using a triple-beam balance to measure mass, keep the following procedures in mind:

1 Make sure the balance is on a level surface.

2 Place all of the countermasses at zero. Adjust the balancing knob until the pointer rests at zero.

3 Place the object you wish to measure on the pan. **Caution:** Do not place hot objects or chemicals directly on the balance pan.

4 Move the largest countermass along the beam to the right until it is at the last notch that does not tip the balance. Follow the same procedure with the next-largest countermass. Then move the smallest countermass until the pointer rests at zero.

5 Add the readings from the three beams together to determine the mass of the object.

6 When determining the mass of crystals or powders, use a piece of filter paper. First find the mass of the paper. Then add the crystals or powder to the paper and re-measure. The actual mass of the crystals or powder is the total mass minus the mass of the paper. When finding the mass of liquids, first find the mass of the empty container. Then find the mass of the liquid and container together. The mass of the liquid is the total mass minus the mass of the container.

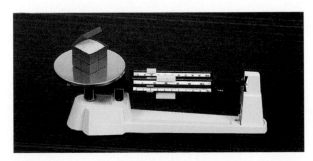

Scientific Method

The series of steps that scientists use to answer questions and solve problems is often called the **scientific method.** The scientific method is not a rigid procedure. Scientists may use all of the steps or just some of the steps of the scientific method. They may even repeat some of the steps. The goal of the scientific method is to come up with reliable answers and solutions.

Six Steps of the Scientific Method

1 **Ask a Question** Good questions come from careful **observations.** You make observations by using your senses to gather information. Sometimes you may use instruments, such as microscopes and telescopes, to extend the range of your senses. As you observe the natural world, you will discover that you have many more questions than answers. These questions drive the scientific method.

Questions beginning with *what, why, how,* and *when* are very important in focusing an investigation, and they often lead to a hypothesis. (You will learn what a hypothesis is in the next step.) Here is an example of a question that could lead to further investigation.

Question: How does acid rain affect plant growth?

Ask a Question

2 **Form a Hypothesis** After you come up with a question, you need to turn the question into a **hypothesis.** A hypothesis is a clear statement of what you expect the answer to your question to be. Your hypothesis will represent your best "educated guess" based on your observations and what you already know. A good hypothesis is testable. If observations and information cannot be gathered or if an experiment cannot be designed to test your hypothesis, it is untestable, and the investigation can go no further.

Here is a hypothesis that could be formed from the question, "How does acid rain affect plant growth?"

Form a Hypothesis

Hypothesis: Acid rain causes plants to grow more slowly.

Notice that the hypothesis provides some specifics that lead to methods of testing. The hypothesis can also lead to predictions. A **prediction** is what you think will be the outcome of your experiment or data collection. Predictions are usually stated in an "if . . . then" format. For example, **if** meat is kept at room temperature, **then** it will spoil faster than meat kept in the refrigerator. More than one prediction can be made for a single hypothesis. Here is a sample prediction for the hypothesis that acid rain causes plants to grow more slowly.

Prediction: If a plant is watered with only acid rain (which has a pH of 4), then the plant will grow at half its normal rate.

3 **Test the Hypothesis** After you have formed a hypothesis and made a prediction, you should test your hypothesis. There are different ways to do this. Perhaps the most familiar way is to conduct a **controlled experiment.** A controlled experiment tests only one factor at a time. A controlled experiment has a **control group** and one or more **experimental groups.** All the factors for the control and experimental groups are the same except for one factor, which is called the **variable.** By changing only one factor, you can see the results of just that one change.

Sometimes, the nature of an investigation makes a controlled experiment impossible. For example, dinosaurs have been extinct for millions of years, and the Earth's core is surrounded by thousands of meters of rock. It would be difficult, if not impossible, to conduct controlled experiments on such things. Under such circumstances, a hypothesis may be tested by making detailed observations. Taking measurements is one way of making observations.

4 **Analyze the Results** After you have completed your experiments, made your observations, and collected your data, you must analyze all the information you have gathered. Tables and graphs are often used in this step to organize the data.

5 **Draw Conclusions** Based on the analysis of your data, you should conclude whether or not your results support your hypothesis. If your hypothesis is supported, you (or others) might want to repeat the observations or experiments to verify your results. If your hypothesis is not supported by the data, you may have to check your procedure for errors. You may even have to reject your hypothesis and make a new one. If you cannot draw a conclusion from your results, you may have to try the investigation again or carry out further observations or experiments.

Draw Conclusions

Do they support your hypothesis?

No

Yes

6 **Communicate Results** After any scientific investigation, you should report your results. By doing a written or oral report, you let others know what you have learned. They may want to repeat your investigation to see if they get the same results. Your report may even lead to another question, which in turn may lead to another investigation.

Test the Hypothesis

Analyze the Results

Communicate Results

Scientific Method in Action

The scientific method is not a "straight line" of steps. It contains loops in which several steps may be repeated over and over again, while others may not be necessary. For example, sometimes scientists will find that testing one hypothesis raises new questions and new hypotheses to be tested. And sometimes, testing the hypothesis leads directly to a conclusion. Furthermore, the steps in the scientific method are not always used in the same order. Follow the steps in the diagram below, and see how many different directions the scientific method can take you.

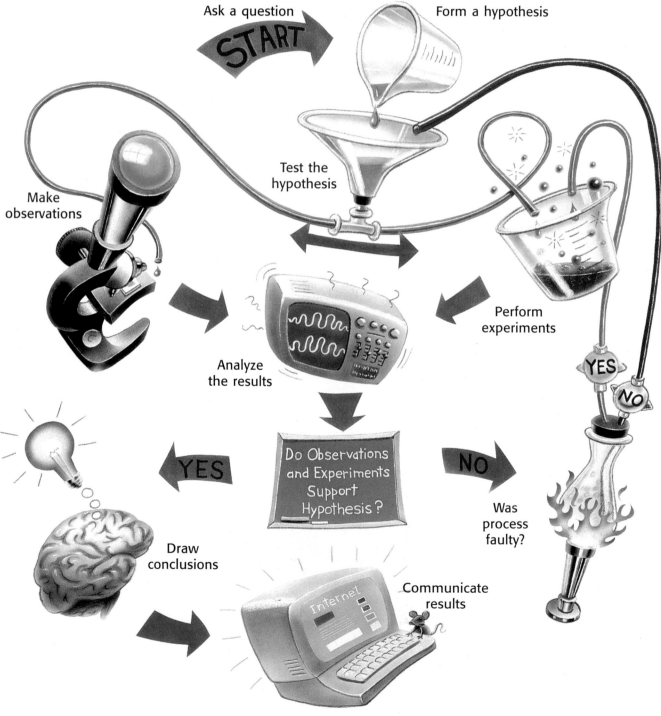

Ask a question

START

Form a hypothesis

Test the hypothesis

Make observations

Perform experiments

Analyze the results

YES

NO

YES

Do Observations and Experiments Support Hypothesis?

NO

Was process faulty?

Draw conclusions

Communicate results

Internet

Making Charts and Graphs

Circle Graphs

A circle graph, or pie chart, shows how each group of data relates to all of the data. Each part of the circle represents a category of the data. The entire circle represents all of the data. For example, a biologist studying a hardwood forest in Wisconsin found that there were five different types of trees. The data table at right summarizes the biologist's findings.

Wisconsin Hardwood Trees	
Type of tree	**Number found**
Oak	600
Maple	750
Beech	300
Birch	1,200
Hickory	150
Total	3,000

How to Make a Circle Graph

1 In order to make a circle graph of this data, first find the percentage of each type of tree. To do this, divide the number of individual trees by the total number of trees and multiply by 100.

$$\frac{600 \text{ oak}}{3,000 \text{ trees}} \times 100 = 20\%$$

$$\frac{750 \text{ maple}}{3,000 \text{ trees}} \times 100 = 25\%$$

$$\frac{300 \text{ beech}}{3,000 \text{ trees}} \times 100 = 10\%$$

$$\frac{1,200 \text{ birch}}{3,000 \text{ trees}} \times 100 = 40\%$$

$$\frac{150 \text{ hickory}}{3,000 \text{ trees}} \times 100 = 5\%$$

2 Now determine the size of the pie shapes that make up the chart. Do this by multiplying each percentage by 360°. Remember that a circle contains 360°.

$20\% \times 360° = 72°$ $25\% \times 360° = 90°$
$10\% \times 360° = 36°$ $40\% \times 360° = 144°$
$5\% \times 360° = 18°$

3 Then check that the sum of the percentages is 100 and the sum of the degrees is 360.

$20\% + 25\% + 10\% + 40\% + 5\% = 100\%$
$72° + 90° + 36° + 144° + 18° = 360°$

4 Use a compass to draw a circle and mark its center.

5 Then use a protractor to draw angles of 72°, 90°, 36°, 144°, and 18° in the circle.

6 Finally, label each part of the graph, and choose an appropriate title.

A Community of Wisconsin Hardwood Trees

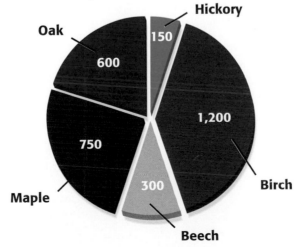

Population of Appleton, 1900–2000	
Year	Population
1900	1,800
1920	2,500
1940	3,200
1960	3,900
1980	4,600
2000	5,300

Line Graphs

Line graphs are most often used to demonstrate continuous change. For example, Mr. Smith's science class analyzed the population records for their hometown, Appleton, between 1900 and 2000. Examine the data at left.

Because the year and the population change, they are the *variables*. The population is determined by, or dependent on, the year. Therefore, the population is called the **dependent variable**, and the year is called the **independent variable**. Each set of data is called a **data pair**. To prepare a line graph, data pairs must first be organized in a table like the one at left.

How to Make a Line Graph

1 Place the independent variable along the horizontal (*x*) axis. Place the dependent variable along the vertical (*y*) axis.

2 Label the *x*-axis "Year" and the *y*-axis "Population." Look at your largest and smallest values for the population. Determine a scale for the *y*-axis that will provide enough space to show these values. You must use the same scale for the entire length of the axis. Find an appropriate scale for the *x*-axis too.

3 Choose reasonable starting points for each axis.

4 Plot the data pairs as accurately as possible.

5 Choose a title that accurately represents the data.

Population of Appleton, 1900–2000

(Line graph: y-axis labeled "Population" with values 0, 1,000, 2,000, 3,000, 4,000, 5,000, 6,000. x-axis labeled "Year" with values 1900, 1920, 1940, 1960, 1980, 2000. A straight line rises from about 1,800 at 1900 to about 5,300 at 2000.)

How to Determine Slope

Slope is the ratio of the change in the *y*-axis to the change in the *x*-axis, or "rise over run."

1 Choose two points on the line graph. For example, the population of Appleton in 2000 was 5,300 people. Therefore, you can define point *a* as (2000, 5,300). In 1900, the population was 1,800 people. Define point *b* as (1900, 1,800).

2 Find the change in the *y*-axis.
(*y* at point *a*) − (*y* at point *b*)
5,300 people − 1,800 people = 3,500 people

3 Find the change in the *x*-axis.
(*x* at point *a*) − (*x* at point *b*)
2000 − 1900 = 100 years

4 Calculate the slope of the graph by dividing the change in *y* by the change in *x*.

$$\text{slope} = \frac{\text{change in } y}{\text{change in } x}$$

$$\text{slope} = \frac{3,500 \text{ people}}{100 \text{ years}}$$

$$\text{slope} = 35 \text{ people per year}$$

In this example, the population in Appleton increased by a fixed amount each year. The graph of this data is a straight line. Therefore, the relationship is **linear.** When the graph of a set of data is not a straight line, the relationship is **nonlinear.**

Using Algebra to Determine Slope

The equation in step 4 may also be arranged to be:

$$y = kx$$

where y represents the change in the y-axis, k represents the slope, and x represents the change in the x-axis.

$$\text{slope} = \frac{\text{change in } y}{\text{change in } x}$$

$$k = \frac{y}{x}$$

$$k \times x = \frac{y \times x}{x}$$

$$kx = y$$

Bar Graphs

Bar graphs are used to demonstrate change that is not continuous. These graphs can be used to indicate trends when the data are taken over a long period of time. A meteorologist gathered the precipitation records at right for Hartford, Connecticut, for April 1–15, 1996, and used a bar graph to represent the data.

Precipitation in Hartford, Connecticut April 1–15, 1996

Date	Precipitation (cm)	Date	Precipitation (cm)
April 1	0.5	April 9	0.25
April 2	1.25	April 10	0.0
April 3	0.0	April 11	1.0
April 4	0.0	April 12	0.0
April 5	0.0	April 13	0.25
April 6	0.0	April 14	0.0
April 7	0.0	April 15	6.50
April 8	1.75		

How to Make a Bar Graph

❶ Use an appropriate scale and a reasonable starting point for each axis.

❷ Label the axes, and plot the data.

❸ Choose a title that accurately represents the data.

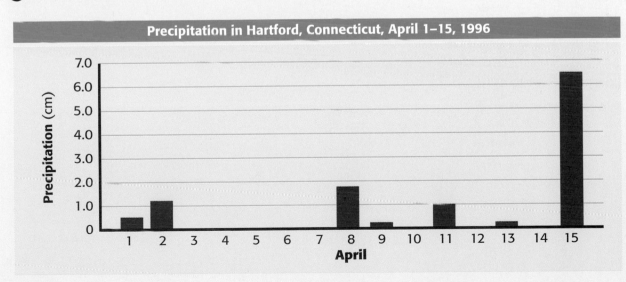

Precipitation in Hartford, Connecticut, April 1–15, 1996

The Six Kingdoms

Kingdom Archaebacteria

The organisms in this kingdom are single-celled prokaryotes.

Archaebacteria		
Group	**Examples**	**Characteristics**
Methanogens	*Methanococcus*	found in soil, swamps, the digestive tract of mammals; produce methane gas; can't live in oxygen
Thermophiles	*Sulpholobus*	found in extremely hot environments; require sulphur, can't live in oxygen
Halophiles	*Halococcus*	found in environments with very high salt content, such as the Dead Sea; nearly all can live in oxygen

Kingdom Eubacteria

There are more than 4,000 named species in this kingdom of single-celled prokaryotes.

Eubacteria		
Group	**Examples**	**Characteristics**
Bacilli	*Escherichia coli*	rod-shaped; free-living, symbiotic, or parasitic; some can fix nitrogen; some cause disease
Cocci	*Streptococcus*	spherical-shaped, disease-causing; can form spores to resist unfavorable environments
Spirilla	*Treponema*	spiral-shaped; responsible for several serious illnesses, such as syphilis and Lyme disease

Kingdom Protista

The organisms in this kingdom are eukaryotes. There are single-celled and multicellular representatives.

Protists		
Group	**Examples**	**Characteristics**
Sacodines	*Amoeba*	radiolarians; single-celled consumers
Ciliates	*Paramecium*	single-celled consumers
Flagellates	*Trypanosoma*	single-celled parasites
Sporozoans	*Plasmodium*	single-celled parasites
Euglenas	*Euglena*	single-celled; photosynthesize
Diatoms	*Pinnularia*	most are single-celled; photosynthesize
Dinoflagellates	*Gymnodinium*	single-celled; some photosynthesize
Algae	*Volvox*, coral algae	4 phyla; single- or many-celled; photosynthesize
Slime molds	*Physarum*	single- or many-celled; consumers or decomposers
Water molds	powdery mildew	single- or many-celled, parasites or decomposers

Kingdom Fungi

There are single-celled and multicellular eukaryotes in this kingdom. There are four major groups of fungi.

Fungi		
Group	**Examples**	**Characteristics**
Threadlike fungi	bread mold	spherical; decomposers
Sac fungi	yeast, morels	saclike; parasites and decomposers
Club fungi	mushrooms, rusts, smuts	club-shaped; parasites and decomposers
Lichens	British soldier	symbiotic with algae

Kingdom Plantae

The organisms in this kingdom are multicellular eukaryotes. They have specialized organ systems for different life processes. They are classified in divisions instead of phyla.

Plants		
Group	**Examples**	**Characteristics**
Bryophytes	mosses, liverworts	reproduce by spores
Club mosses	*Lycopodium,* ground pine	reproduce by spores
Horsetails	rushes	reproduce by spores
Ferns	spleenworts, sensitive fern	reproduce by spores
Conifers	pines, spruces, firs	reproduce by seeds; cones
Cycads	*Zamia*	reproduce by seeds
Gnetophytes	*Welwitschia*	reproduce by seeds
Ginkgoes	*Ginkgo*	reproduce by seeds
Angiosperms	all flowering plants	reproduce by seeds; flowers

Kingdom Animalia

This kingdom contains multicellular eukaryotes. They have specialized tissues and complex organ systems.

Animals		
Group	**Examples**	**Characteristics**
Sponges	glass sponges	no symmetry or segmentation; aquatic
Cnidarians	jellyfish, coral	radial symmetry; aquatic
Flatworms	planaria, tapeworms, flukes	bilateral symmetry; organ systems
Roundworms	*Trichina,* hookworms	bilateral symmetry; organ systems
Annelids	earthworms, leeches	bilateral symmetry; organ systems
Mollusks	snails, octopuses	bilateral symmetry; organ systems
Echinoderms	sea stars, sand dollars	radial symmetry; organ systems
Arthropods	insects, spiders, lobsters	bilateral symmetry; organ systems
Chordates	fish, amphibians, reptiles, birds, mammals	bilateral symmetry; complex organ systems

Using the Microscope

Parts of the Compound Light Microscope

- The **ocular lens** magnifies the image 10×.

- The **low-power objective** magnifies the image 10×.

- The **high-power objective** magnifies the image either 40× or 43×.

- The **revolving nosepiece** holds the objectives and can be turned to change from one magnification to the other.

- The **body tube** maintains the correct distance between the ocular lens and objectives.

- The **coarse-adjustment knob** moves the body tube up and down to allow focusing of the image.

- The **fine-adjustment knob** moves the body tube slightly to bring the image into sharper focus.

- The **stage** supports a slide.

- **Stage clips** hold the slide in place for viewing.

- The **diaphragm** controls the amount of light coming through the stage.

- The light source provides a **light** for viewing the slide.

- The **arm** supports the body tube.

- The **base** supports the microscope.

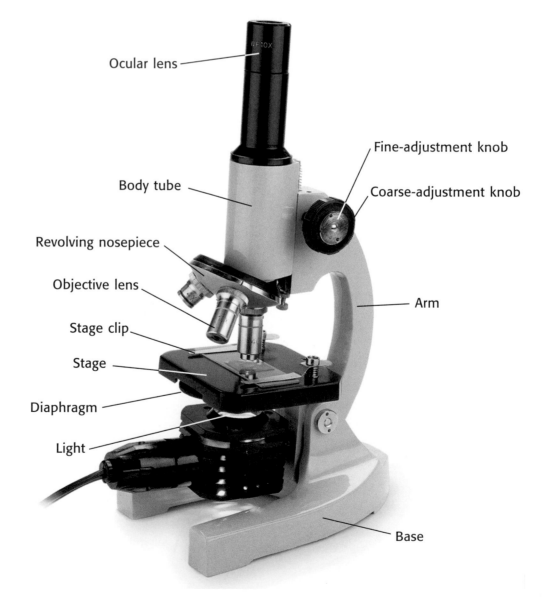

Ocular lens

Fine-adjustment knob

Body tube

Coarse-adjustment knob

Revolving nosepiece

Objective lens

Arm

Stage clip

Stage

Diaphragm

Light

Base

Proper Use of the Compound Light Microscope

1 Carry the microscope to your lab table using both hands. Place one hand beneath the base, and use the other hand to hold the arm of the microscope. Hold the microscope close to your body while moving it to your lab table.

2 Place the microscope on the lab table at least 5 cm from the edge of the table.

3 Check to see what type of light source is used by your microscope. If the microscope has a lamp, plug it in, making sure that the cord is out of the way. If the microscope has a mirror, adjust it to reflect light through the hole in the stage.
Caution: If your microscope has a mirror, do not use direct sunlight as a light source. Direct sunlight can damage your eyes.

4 Always begin work with the low-power objective in line with the body tube. Adjust the revolving nosepiece.

5 Place a prepared slide over the hole in the stage. Secure the slide with the stage clips.

6 Look through the ocular lens. Move the diaphragm to adjust the amount of light coming through the stage.

7 Look at the stage from eye level. Slowly turn the coarse adjustment to lower the objective until it almost touches the slide. Do not allow the objective to touch the slide.

8 Look through the ocular lens. Turn the coarse adjustment to raise the low-power objective until the image is in focus. Always focus by raising the objective away from the slide. *Never focus the objective downward.* Use the fine adjustment to sharpen the focus. Keep both eyes open while viewing a slide.

9 Make sure that the image is exactly in the center of your field of vision. Then switch to the high-power objective. Focus the image, using only the fine adjustment. *Never use the coarse adjustment at high power.*

10 When you are finished using the microscope, remove the slide. Clean the ocular lens and objective lenses with lens paper. Return the microscope to its storage area. Remember, you should use both hands to carry the microscope.

Making a Wet Mount

1 Use lens paper to clean a glass slide and a coverslip.

2 Place the specimen you wish to observe in the center of the slide.

3 Using a medicine dropper, place one drop of water on the specimen.

4 Hold the coverslip at the edge of the water and at a 45° angle to the slide. Make sure that the water runs along the edge of the coverslip.

5 Lower the coverslip slowly to avoid trapping air bubbles.

6 Water might evaporate from the slide as you work. Add more water to keep the specimen fresh. Place the tip of the medicine dropper next to the edge of the coverslip. Add a drop of water. (You can also use this method to add stain or solutions to a wet mount.) Remove excess water from the slide by using the corner of a paper towel as a blotter. Do not lift the coverslip to add or remove water.

Glossary

A

absolute dating determining the age of an object or event in years, usually by measuring the amount of unstable atoms in the sample (133)

active transport the movement of particles through proteins in the cell membrane against the direction of diffusion; requires cells to use energy (36)

adaptation a characteristic that helps an organism survive in its environment (104)

adenine (AD uh NEEN) one of the four bases that combine with sugar and phospate to form a nucleotide subunit of DNA; adenine pairs with thymine (80)

alleles different forms of a single gene (61)

anaerobic describes an organism that does not need oxygen (139)

Animalia the classification kingdom containing complex, multicellular organisms that lack cell walls, are usually able to move around, and possess nervous systems that help them be aware of and react to their surroundings (171)

Archaebacteria (AHR kee bak TIR ee uh) a classification kingdom containing bacteria that thrive in extreme environments (167)

australopithecine (ah STRA loh PITH uh seen) an early hominid that evolved more than 3.6 million years ago (146)

B

bacteria extremely small, single-celled organisms without a nucleus; prokaryotic cells (14, 167)

binary fission the simple cell division in which one cell splits into two; used by bacteria (42)

C

cell cycle the life cycle of a cell; in eukaryotes it consists of chromosome duplication, mitosis, and cytokinesis (42)

cell membrane a phospholipid layer that covers a cell's surface and acts as a barrier between the inside of a cell and the cell's environment (11)

cell wall a structure that surrounds the cell membrane of some cells and provides strength and support to the cell membrane (17)

cellular respiration the process of producing ATP in the cell from oxygen and glucose; releases carbon dioxide and water (39)

Cenozoic era the period in the geologic time scale beginning about 65 million years ago and continuing until the present day (143)

centromere the region that holds chromatids together when a chromosome is duplicated (43)

chlorophyll a green pigment in chloroplasts that absorbs light energy for photosynthesis (19)

chloroplast an organelle found in plant and algae cells where photosynthesis occurs (19)

chromatids identical chromosome copies (43)

chromosome a coiled structure of DNA and protein that forms in the cell nucleus during cell division (42)

class the level of classification after phylum; the organisms in all phyla are sorted into classes (161)

classification the arrangement of organisms into orderly groups based on their similarities and presumed evolutionary relationships (160)

community all of the populations of different species that live and interact in an area (8)

cytokinesis (SIET oh ki NEE sis) the process in which cytoplasm divides after mitosis (45)

cytoplasm (SIET oh PLAZ uhm) cellular fluid surrounding a cell's organelles (11)

cytosine (SIET oh SEEN) one of the four bases that combine with sugar and phosphate to form a nucleotide subunit of DNA; cytosine pairs with guanine (80)

D

dichotomous key (die KAWT uh muhs) an aid to identifying unknown organisms that consists of several pairs of descriptive statements; of each pair of statements, only one will apply to the unknown organism, and that statement will lead to another set of statements, and so on, until the unknown organism can be identified (164)

diffusion the movement of particles from an area where their concentration is high to an area where their concentration is low (34)

DNA deoxyribonucleic (dee AHKS ee RIE boh noo KLEE ik) acid; hereditary material that controls all the activities of a cell, contains the information to make new cells, and provides instructions for making proteins (11, 80)

dominant trait the trait observed when at least one dominant allele for a characteristic is inherited (59)

E

ecosystem a community of organisms and their nonliving environment (8)

endocytosis (EN doh sie TOH sis) the process in which a cell membrane surrounds a particle and encloses it in a vesicle to bring it into the cell (37)

endoplasmic reticulum (EN doh PLAZ mik ri TIK yuh luhm) a membrane-covered cell organelle that produces lipids, breaks down drugs and other substances, and packages proteins for delivery out of the cell (18)

Eubacteria (YOO bak TIR ee uh) a classification kingdom containing mostly free-living bacteria found in many varied environments (167)

eukaryotic cell (eukaryote) (yoo KER ee OHT) a cell that contains a central nucleus and a complicated internal structure (15, 140)

evolution the process by which populations accumulate inherited changes over time (105)

exocytosis (EK soh sie TOH sis) the process used to remove large particles from a cell; during exocytosis, a vesicle containing the particles fuses with the cell membrane (37)

extinct describes a species of organism that has died out completely (135)

F

family the level of classification after order; the organisms in all orders are sorted into families (161)

fermentation the breakdown of sugars to make ATP in the absence of oxygen (39)

fossil the solidified remains or imprints of a once-living organism (106, 132)

fossil record a historical sequence of life indicated by fossils found in layers of the Earth's crust (106)

Fungi a kingdom of complex organisms that obtain food by breaking down other substances in their surroundings and absorbing the nutrients (170)

G

generation time the period between the birth of one generation and the birth of the next generation (118)

genes segments of DNA that carry hereditary instructions and are passed from parent to offspring; located on chromosomes (61)

genotype the inherited combination of alleles (61)

genus the level of classification after family; the organisms in all families are sorted into genera (161)

geologic time scale the division of Earth's history into distinct intervals of time (134)

Golgi complex the cell organelle that modifies, packages, and transports materials out of the cell (20)

guanine (GWAH NEEN) one of the four bases that combine with sugar and phosphate to form a nucleotide subunit of DNA; guanine pairs with cytosine (80)

H

heredity the passing of traits from parent to offspring (56)

hominid the family referring specifically to humans and several extinct, humanlike species, some of which were human ancestors (145)

homologous (hoh MAHL uh guhs) **chromosomes** chromosomes with matching information (43)

K

kingdom the most general of the seven levels of classification (161)

lysosome a special vesicle in a cell that digests food particles, wastes, and foreign invaders (22)

M

meiosis (mie OH sis) cell division that produces sex cells (65)

Mesozoic era the period in the geologic time scale beginning about 248 million years ago and ending about 65 million years ago (142)

mitochondria (MIET oh KAHN dree uh) cell organelles surrounded by two membranes that break down food molecules to make ATP (19)

mitosis nuclear division in eukaryotic cells in which each cell receives a copy of the original chromosomes (43)

multicellular made of many cells (7)

mutagen anything that can damage or cause changes in DNA (90)

mutation a change in the order of the bases in an organism's DNA; deletion, insertion, or substitution (90, 117)

N

natural selection the process by which organisms with favorable traits survive and reproduce at a higher rate than organisms without the favorable trait (116)

Neanderthal a species of hominid that lived in Europe and western Asia from 230,000 years ago to about 30,000 years ago (148)

nucleotide a subunit of DNA consisting of a sugar, a phosphate, and one of four nitrogenous bases (80)

nucleus the membrane-covered organelle found in eukaryotic cells; contains the cell's DNA and serves as a control center for the cell (14)

O

order the level of classification after class; the organisms in all the classes are sorted into orders (161)

organ a combination of two or more tissues that work together to perform a specific function in the body (5)

organ system a group of organs that works together to perform body functions (6)

organelle (OHR guh NEL) a structure within a cell, sometimes surrounded by a membrane (11)

organism anything that can independently carry out life processes (7)

osmosis the diffusion of water across a cell membrane (35)

P

Paleozoic era the period in the geologic time scale beginning about 570 million years ago and ending about 248 million years ago (141)

passive transport the diffusion of particles through proteins in the cell membrane from areas where the concentration of particles is high to areas where the concentration of particles is low (36)

pedigree a diagram of family history used for tracing a trait through several generations (92)

phenotype an organism's inherited appearance (61)

photosynthesis (FOHT oh SIN thuh sis) the process by which plants capture light energy from the sun and convert it into sugar (38, 140)

phylum the level of classification after kingdom; the organisms from all the kingdoms are sorted into several phyla (161)

Plantae the kingdom that contains plants—complex, multicellular organisms that are usually green and use the sun's energy to make sugar by photosynthesis (169)

plate tectonics the study of the forces that drive the movement of pieces of Earth's crust around the surface of the planet (137)

population a group of individuals of the same species that live together in the same area at the same time (7)

Precambrian time the period in the geologic time scale beginning when Earth originated, 4.6 billion years ago, and ending when complex organisms appeared, about 540 million years ago (138)

primate a type of mammal that includes humans, apes, and monkeys; typically distinguished by opposable thumbs and binocular vision (144)

probability the mathematical chance that an event will occur (62)

prokaryotic cell (prokaryote) (proh KER ee OHT) a cell that does not have a nucleus or any other membrane-covered organelles; also called a bacterium (14, 139)

prosimian the first primate ancestors; *also* a group of living primates that includes lorises and lemurs (146)

Protista a kingdom of eukaryotic single-celled or simple, multicellular organisms; kingdom Protista contains all eukaryotes that are not plants, animals, or fungi (168)

R

recessive trait a trait that is apparent only when two recessive alleles for the same characteristic are inherited (59)

relative dating determining whether an event or object, such as a fossil, is older or younger than other events or objects (133)

ribosome a small organelle in cells where proteins are made from amino acids (18, 89)

S

sediment fine particles of sand, dust, or mud that are deposited over time by wind or water (132)

selective breeding the breeding of organisms that have a certain desired trait (114)

sex cell an egg or sperm; a sex cell carries half the number of chromosomes found in other body cells (64)

sex chromosomes the chromosomes that carry genes that determine the sex of offspring (69)

speciation the process by which two populations of the same species become so different that they can no longer interbreed (120)

species the most specific of the seven levels of classification; characterized by a group of organisms that can mate with one another to produce fertile offspring (104, 161)

T

taxonomy the science of identifying, classifying, and naming living things (162)

thymine one of the four bases that combine with sugar and phosphate to form a nucleotide subunit of DNA; thymine pairs with adenine (80)

tissue a group of similar cells that work together to perform a specific job in the body (5)

trait a distinguishing quality that can be passed from one generation to another (114)

true-breeding plant a plant that always produces offspring with the same traits as the parent(s) (58)

U

unicellular made of a single cell (7)

V

vacuole (VAK yoo OHL) a large membrane-covered structure found in plant cells that serves as a storage container for water and other liquids (21)

vesicle a membrane-covered compartment in a eukaryotic cell that forms when part of the cell membrane surrounds an object and pinches off (21)

vestigial structure (ves TIJ ee uhl) the remnant of a once-useful anatomical structure (107)

Index

Boldface numbers refer to an illustration on that page.

Credits

Abbreviations used: (t) top, (c) center, (b) bottom, (l) left, (r) right, (bkgd) background

ILLUSTRATIONS

All illustrations, unless otherwise noted below by Holt, Rinehart and Winston.

Table of Contents: p. iv, Morgan-Cain & Associates; vi(b), John White/The Neis Group.

Scope and Sequence: T11, Paul DiMare, T13, Dan Stuckenschneider/Uhl Studios, Inc.

Chapter One Page 6 (br), Christy Krames; p. 6 (c), Michael Woods/Morgan-Cain & Associates; p. 7 (cl), Morgan-Cain & Associates; p. 7 (c), Morgan-Cain & Associates; p. 7 (cr), Christy Krames; p. 8 (br), Yuan Lee; p. 10 (bl), David Merrell/Suzanne Craig Represents Inc.; p. 12 (c), Morgan-Cain & Associates; p. 12 (tl), Terry Kovalcik; p. 13 (bc), Terry Kovalcik; p. 13 (cr), Morgan-Cain & Associates; p. 14 (br), Morgan-Cain & Associates; p. 15 (tr), Morgan-Cain & Associates; p. 16, Morgan-Cain & Associates; p. 17, Morgan-Cain & Associates; p. 18, Morgan-Cain & Associates; p. 19, Morgan-Cain & Associates; p. 20, Morgan-Cain & Associates; p. 21, Morgan-Cain & Associates; p. 22, Morgan-Cain & Associates; p. 23, Morgan-Cain & Associates; p. 29, Morgan-Cain & Associates.

Chapter Two p. 35 (tr), Stephen Durke/Washington Artists; p. 36 (bl,br), Morgan-Cain & Associates; p. 36 (tl), Terry Kovalcik; p. 37 (c), Morgan-Cain & Associates; p. 38 (bl), Morgan-Cain & Associates; p. 39, Morgan-Cain & Associates; p. 40 (tl), Robin Carter; p. 40 (cl), Morgan-Cain & Associates; p. 40 (bl), Morgan-Cain & Associates; p. 40 (cr), Morgan-Cain & Associates; p. 40 (br), Morgan-Cain & Associates; p. 44 (l), Alexander & Turner ; p. 51 (cr), Morgan-Cain & Associates.

Chapter Three Page 57 (b), Mike Weplo/Das Group; p. 58, John White/The Neis Group; p. 59, John White/The Neis Group; p. 60, John White/The Neis Group; p. 61, John White/The Neis Group; p. 65 (r), Alexander & Turner; p. 66 (l), Alexander & Turner; p. 67 (r) Alexander & Turner; p. 68, Alexander & Turner; p. 69 (bc), Alexander & Turner; p. 69 (br), Rob Schuster/Hankins and Tegenborg; p. 69 (cr), Blake Thornton/Rita Marie; p. 73 (cr), Blake Thornton/Rita Marie; p. 74, John White/The Neis Group; p. 75 (bl), John White/The Neis Group.

Chapter Four p. 80, Rob Schuster/Hankins and Tegenborg; p. 82 (c), Alexander & Turner; p. 82 (tl), Marty Roper/Planet Rep; p. 83 (cl), Alexander & Turner; p. 84, Morgan-Cain & Associates; p. 85 (r), Grey Geisler; p. 86 (cl), John White/The Neis Group; p. 88-89, Rob Schuster/Hankins and Tegenborg; p. 90 (tl), Rob Schuster/Hankins and Tegenborg; p. 91 (b) Rob Schuster/Hankins and Tegenborg; p. 96 Alexander & Turner; 97, Rob Schuster/Hankins and Tegenborg.

Chapter Five p. 105, Steve Roberts, p. 107 (tr), Ross, Culbert and Lavery; p. 107 (b), Rob Wood/Wood, Ronsaville, Harlin; p. 108-109, Rob Wood/Wood, Ronsaville, Harlin; p. 110, Christy Krames; p. 111 (l), Sarah Woods; p. 111 (tr), David Beck; p. 111 (cr), Frank Ordaz/Dimension; p. 113 (tr), Tony Morse/Ivy Glick; p. 113 (b), John White/The Neis Group; p. 115, Ross, Culbert and Lavery; p. 116 (r), Will Nelson/Sweet Reps; p. 118 (c), Carlyn Iverson; p. 118 (bl), Frank Ordaz/Dimension; p. 120 (c), Mike Weplo/Das Group; p. 120 (bl), Will Nelson/Sweet Reps; p. 121 (c), Carlyn Iverson; p. 124 (tc), Rob Wood/Wood, Ronsaville, Harlin; p. 124 (br), Christy Krames; p. 125, Carlyn Iverson; p. 127 (tr), Ross, Culbert and Lavery; p. 128 (tl), Carlyn Iverson.

Chapter Six p. 132 (b), Mike Weplo/Das Group; p. 133 (cr), Mike Weplo/Das Group; p. 133 (br), Rob Schuster/Hankins and Tegenborg; p. 134, Barbara Hoopes-Ambler; p. 135, John White/The Neis Group; p. 136, MapQuest.com; p. 137 (tr), MapQuest.com; p. 137 (br), Walter Stuart; p. 139, John White/The Neis Group; p. 140, Craig Attebery/Jeff Lavaty Artist Agent; p. 141, Barbara Hoopes-Ambler; p. 142, Barbara Hoopes-Ambler; p. 143 (tr), John White/The Neis Group; p. 144 (bl), Todd Buck; p. 144 (br), Will Nelson/Sweet Reps; p. 145, Christy Krames; p. 152, Barbara Hoopes-Ambler; p. 155 (tr), John White/The Neis Group; p. 155 (tr), John White/The Neis Group; p. 155 (tr), John White/The Neis Group; p. 155 (tr), John White/The Neis Group; p. 155 (tr), John White/The Neis Group; p. 156 (br), Greg Harris.

Chapter Seven p. 161 (bear, blue jay, earthworm), Michael Woods/Morgan-Cain & Associates; p. 161 (boy), Frank Ordaz/Dimension; p. 161 (whale), Graham Allen; p. 161 (lynx), David Ashby; p. 161 (cat, lion), Will Nelson/Sweet Reps; p. 162 (tl), Will Nelson/Sweet Reps; p. 162 (bear, platypus), Michael Woods/Morgan-Cain & Associates; p. 162 (cat, lion), Will Nelson/Sweet Reps; p. 163 (b), John White/The Neis Group; p. 163 (tr), Blake Thornton/Rita Marie; p. 164 (c), Marty Roper/Planet Rep; p. 164 (bl), John White/The Neis Group; p. 165 (br), Cy Baker/WAA; p. 165 (tl), John White/The Neis Group; p. 165 (tr), John White/The Neis Group; p. 174, John White/The Neis Group; p. 176 (cr), Marty Roper/Planet Rep; p. 177, (lemur), Will Nelson/Sweet Reps; p. 177 (baboon), Graham Allen; p. 177 (chimpanzee), Michael Woods/Morgan-Cain & Associates; p. 177 (human), Frank Ordaz; p. 178 (bl), John White/The Neis Group; p. 178 (tr), Barbara Hoopes-Ambler.Nelson/Sweet

LabBook p. 184 (tl), David Merrell/Suzanne Craig Represents Inc.; p. 184 (cr), Rob Schuster/Hankins and Tegenborg; p. 188 (br), Kip Carter; p. 190 (br), Keith Locke; p. 191 (cr), Keith Locke; p. 192, Rob Schuster/Hankins and Tegenborg; p. 193 (cr), Rob Schuster/Hankins and Tegenborg.

Appendix p. 196 (t), Terry Guyer; p. 200 (b), Mark Mille/Sharon Langley.

PHOTOGRAPHY

Cover and Title page: Dr. Dennis Kunkel/Phototake

Feature Borders: Unless otherwise noted below, all images copyright ©2001 PhotoDisc/HRW. "Across the Sciences" 30, 52, 156, all images by HRW; "Careers" 157, sand bkgd and Saturn, Corbis Images; DNA, Morgan Cain & Associates; scuba gear, ©1997 Radlund & Associates for Artville; "Eye on the Environment" 128, clouds and sea in bkgd, HRW; bkgd grass, red eyed frog, Corbis Images; hawks, pelican, Animals Animals/Earth Scenes; rat, Visuals Unlimited/John Grelach; endangered flower, Dan Suzio/Photo Researchers, Inc.; "Health Watch" 77, dumbbell, Sam Dudgeon/HRW Photo; aloe vera, EKG, Victoria Smith/HRW Photo; basketball, ©1997 Radlund & Associates for Artville; shoes, bubbles, Greg Geisler; "Scientific Debate" 100, 178, Sam Dudgeon/HRW Photo; "Science Fiction" 53, 101, 129, saucers, Ian Christopher/Greg Geisler; book, HRW; bkgd telescope, Dave Cutler Studio, Inc./SIS; "Science Technology and Society" 76, robot, Greg Geisler; "Weird Science" 179, mite, David Burder/Stone; atom balls, J/B Woolsey Associates; walking stick, turtle, EclectiCollection.

Table of Contents: p. iv(cl), Bonnie Jacobs/Southern Methodist University; p. v(t), Dr. Tony Brian & David Parker/Science Photo Library/Photo Researchers, Inc.; p. v(br), Runk/Schoenberger/Grant Heilman; p. v(bl), Sam Dudgeon/HRW Photo; p. iv(bl), Ken Lucas; p. vi(t) Robert Brons/BPS/Stone; p. vi(c), Visuals Unlimited/ Sherman Thomson; p. vii(tl), Visuals Unlimited/Doug Sokell; vii(tr), Visuals Unlimited/K. G. Murti; p. vii(cl), Visuals Unlimited/D. M. Phillips; p. vii(bl), Biophoto Associates/ Science Source/Photo Researchers, Inc.; p. vii(br), CNRI/Science Photo Library/Photo Researchers, Inc.

Scope and Sequence: T8(l), Lee F. Snyder/Photo Researchers, Inc.; T8(r), Stephen Dalton/Photo Researchers, Inc.; T10, E. R. Degginger/Color-Pic, Inc., T12(l), Rob Matheson/The Stock Market

Master Materials List: T26(bl, br), Image ©2001 PhotoDisc; T27(cl, bc), Image ©2001 PhotoDisc

Chapter One: pp. 2-3 Dennis Kunkel/Phototake 3 HRW Photo; p. 4(cl), Image Copyright ©2001 Photodisc, Inc.; p. 4(bl, bcl, bcr), Dr. Yorgos Nikas/Science Photo Library/Photo Researchers, Inc.; p. 4(br), Lennart Nilsson; p. 5(tc), Visuals Unlimited/ Fred Hossler; p. 5(tl), National Cancer Institute/Science Photo Library/ Photo Researchers, Inc.; p. 5(tr), GW Willis/BPS/Stone; p. 5(cr), Visuals Unlimited/G. Shih and R. Kessel; p. 7(tc), Visuals Unlimited/Michael Abbey; p. 7(tr), Robert Brons/BPS/ Stone; p. 7(tl), David M. Phillips/Photo Researchers, Inc.; p. 7(b), E.S. Ross; p. 8(t), Joe McDonald/DRK Photo; p. 9(cl, c), C.C. Lockwood/DRK Photo; p. 9(b), Visuals Unlimited/Kevin Collins; p. 9(br), Leonard Lessin/Peter Arnold; p. 10(tl), Visuals Unlimited/Doug Sokell; p. 10(tr), Visuals Unlimited/K. G. Murti; p. 10(cl), Visuals Unlimited/D. M. Phillips; p. 11(br), Biophoto Associates/Science Source/Photo Researchers, Inc.; p. 11(tr), Dr. Petit/Rapho/Liaison International; p. 13 AP/Wide World Photos; p. 21(tr), Biology Media/Photo Researchers, Inc.; p. 24(tl, tc) Runk/ Schoenberger/Grant Heilman; p. 24(tr) Michael Abbey/Photo Researchers, Inc.; p. 24(bl) Runk/Schoenberger/Grant Heilmanp. 26(tr), Robert Brons/BPS/Stone; p. 26(c), Joe McDonald/DRK Photo; p. 28 Biophoto Associates/Science Source/Photo Researchers, Inc.; p. 30(l), Hans Reinhard/Bruce Coleman; p. 30(tr), Andrew Syred/ Stone; p. 31 Dr. Smith/University of Akron.

Chapter Two: pp. 32-33 Walker/Science Source/Photo Researchers, Inc.; p. 33 HRW Photo; p. 35(br), Visuals Unlimited/David M. Philips ; p. 37(tr), Photo Researchers, Inc.; p. 37(cr), Birgit H. Satir; p. 39 Runk/Schoenberger/Grant Heilman; p. 42 CNRI/ Science Photo Library/Photo Researchers, Inc.; p. 43(tr), L. Willatt, East Anglian Regional Genetics Service/Science Photo Library/Photo Researchers, Inc.; p. 43(br), Biophoto Associates/Photo Researchers, Inc.; p. 44(all), Ed Reschke/Peter Arnold; p. 45(cl), Visuals Unlimited/R. Calentine; p. 45(tr, cr), Biology Media/Photo Researchers, Inc.; p. 40(tc), Visuals Unlimited/Stanley Flegler; p. 48(cr) Runk Schoenberger/Grant Heilman; p. 49 Ed Reschke/Peter Arnold; p. 50 CNRI/Science Photo Library/Photo Researchers, Inc.; p. 51(cl, c), Biophoto Associates/Science Source/Photo Researchers, Inc.; p. 52 Lee D. Simons/Science Source/Photo Researchers, Inc.

Chapter Three: pp. 54-55 Carr Clifton/Mindon Pictures; p. 55 HRW Photo; p. 56(c), Frans Lanting/Minden Pictures; p. 56(br), Corbis; p. 57 Runk/Schoenberger/Grant Heilman Photography; p. 63(br), Image Copyright ©2001 Photodisc, Inc.; p. 63(tr), Gerard Lacz/Animals Animals; p. 64(cl), Phototake/CNRI/Phototake NYC; p. 64(bc), Biophoto Associates/Photo Researchers, Inc.; p. 69 Phototake/CNRI/Phototake NYC; p. 72 Frans Lanting/Minden Pictures; p. 76 Hank Morgan/Rainbow; p. 77(t, r), Dr. F. R. Turner, Biology Dept., Indiana University.

Chapter Four: pp. 78-79 Will & Deni McIntyre/Photo Researchers, Inc.; p. 79(t) HRW Photo; p. 79(bl) Leonard Lessin/Peter Arnold; p. 79(bc) Reprinted from "The Science of Fingerprints" courtesy of the FBI; p. 79(br) Archive Photos; p. 81(tr), Science Photo Library/Photo Researchers, Inc.; p. 81(br), Archive Photos; p. 83 Dr. Gopal Murti/Science Photo Library/Photo Researchers, Inc.; p. 84(cl), Phil Jude/Science Photo Library/Photo Researcher, Inc.; p. 85(cl), Biophoto Associates/Photo Researchers, Inc.; p. 85(tl), J.R. Paulson & U.K. Laemmli/University of Geneva; p. 85(bl), Dan McCoy/Rainbow; p. 86(br), Lawrence Migdale/Photo Researchers, Inc.; p. 91(br, cr), Jackie Lewin/Royal Free Hospital/Science Photo Library/Photo Researchers, Inc.; p. 93(cl), Remi Benali and Stephen Ferry/Gamma-Liaison; p. 93(tr), Visuals Unlimited/Science Visuals Unlimited/Keith Wood; p. 95 Victoria Smith/HRW Photo; p. 98 Kenneth Eward/Science Source/Photo Researchers, Inc.; p. 99 Remi Benali and Stephen Ferry/Gamma-Liaison; p. 100 Volker Steger/Peter Arnold

Chapter Five: pp. 102-103 Jeff Rotman/Stone; p. 103 HRW Photo; p. 104(cr), Gail Shumway/FPG International; p. 104(cl), Doug Wechsler/Animals Animals; p. 106(cl), Ken Lucas; p. 106(cr), John Cancalosi/ Tom Stack & Associates; p. 111(br), Visuals Unlimited/H.W. Robison; p. 112(b), Christopher Ralling; p. 112(bl), William E. Ferguson; p. 114(tr), Jeanne White/Photo Researchers, Inc.; p. 114(tl), Baines Photo; p. 114(br), Robert Pearcy/Animals Animals; p. 114(cl), John Daniels/DANI2/Bruce Coleman, Inc.; p. 114(bc), Dennis and Catherine Quinn; p. 114(bl), Yann Arthus-Bertrand/Corbis; p. 114(cr), Fritz Prenzel/Animals Animals; p. 115(tl), Library of Congress/Corbis; p. 117(tr), Image Copyright ©2001 Photodisc, Inc.; p. 119(l, r), M.W. Tweedie/Photo Researchers, Inc.; p. 126 Ken Lucas; p. 127(bl), Breck P. Kent/Animals Animals; p. 127(bc), Pat & Tom Leeson/Photo Researchers, Inc.; p. 128(tr), Doug Wilson/Westlight.

continued on page 216

Self-Check Answers

Chapter 1—Cells: The Basic Units of Life

Page 11: Cells need DNA to control cell processes and to make new cells.

Page 14: 1. The surface-to-volume ratio decreases as the cell size increases. 2. A eukaryotic cell has a nucleus and membrane-covered organelles.

Page 18: Cell walls surround the cell membranes of some cells. All cells have cell membranes, but not all cells have cell walls. Cell walls give structure to some cells.

Chapter 2—The Cell in Action

Page 35: In pure water, the grape would absorb water and swell up. In water mixed with a large amount of sugar, the grape would lose water and shrink.

Page 43: After duplication, there are four chromatids—two from each of the homologous chromosomes.

Chapter 3—Heredity

Page 67: 1. four 2. two 3. They make copies of themselves once. They divide twice. 4. Two, or half the number of chromosomes in the parent, are present at the end of meiosis. After mitosis, there would be four chromosomes, the same number as in the parent cell.

Chapter 4—Genes and Gene Technology

Page 83: TGGATCAAC

Page 89: 1. 1000 amino acids 2. DNA codes for proteins. Your flesh is composed of proteins, and the way those proteins are constructed and combined influences much about the way you look.

Chapter 5—The Evolution of Living Things

Page 119: The population of light-colored moths would increase.

Chapter 6—The History of Life on Earth

Page 135: 5 g, 2.5 g

Page 141: b, c, d, a

Chapter 7—Classification

Page 168: 1. The two kingdoms of bacteria are different from all other kingdoms because bacteria are prokaryotes—single-celled organisms that have no nucleus. 2. The organisms in the kingdom Protista are all eukaryotes.

Credits (continued)

Chapter Six: pp. 130-131 Reuters Newmedia, Inc./CORBIS; p. 131 HRW Photo p. 132 Louie Psihoyos/Matrix; p. 138 SuperStock; p. 139 Visuals Unlimited/NMSM; p. 140 M. Abbey/Photo Researchers, Inc.; p. 144(cr), Daniel J. Cox/Stone; p. 144(c), Art Wolfe/Stone; p. 146(bl), John Reader/Science Photo Library/Photo Researchers, Inc.; p. 146(tl), Daniel J. Cox/Gamma-Liaison; p. 147(tr), David Brill; p. 147(br), John Gurche; p. 148(bl), John Reader/Science Photo Library/Photo Researchers, Inc.; p. 148(bl), E.R. Degginger/Bruce Coleman; p. 148(tl, br), Neanderthal Museum; p. 149 David Brill/National Geographic Society Image Collection; p. 153 Renee Lynn/Photo Researchers, Inc.; p. 154 John Reader/Science Photo Library/Photo Researchers, Inc.; p. 156(c), Thomas W. Martin, APSA/Photo Researchers, Inc.; p. 157(tl, b), Bonnie Jacobs/Southern Methodist University

Chapter Seven: pp. 158-159 Frans Lanting/Minden Pictures; p. 159 HRW Photo; p. 160 Ethnobotany of the Chacabo Indians, Beni, Bolivia, Advances in Economic Botany/The New York Botanical Gardens; p. 162(tl), Library of Congress/Corbis; p. 166 Biophoto Associates/Photo Researchers, Inc.; p. 167(tr), Sherrie Jones/Photo Researchers, Inc.; p. 167(bl, bc), Dr. Tony Brian & David Parker/Science Photo Library/ Photo Researchers, Inc.; p. 168(tl), Visuals Unlimited/M.Abbey; p. 168(cl), Visuals Unlimited/Stanley Flegler; p. 168(br), Chuck Davis/Stone; p. 169(c), Corbis Images; p. 169(b), Art Wolfe/Stone; p. 170(tl), Robert Maier; p. 170(c), Visuals Unlimited/Sherman Thomson; p. 170(br), Visuals Unlimited/Richard Thom; p. 171(cr), Telegraph Colour Library 1997/FPG; p. 171(tr), SuperStock; p. 171(cl), G. Randall/FPG; p. 171(c), SuperStock; p. 175 Robert Maier; p. 179 Peter Funch

Labook: "LabBook Header": "L", Corbis Images, "a", Letraset-Phototone, "b" and "B", HRW, "o" and "k", Images Copyright ©2001 PhotoDisc, Inc. 680(tc), Scott Van Osdol/HRW Photo; p. 181(cl), Michelle Bridwell/HRW Photo; p. 181(br), Image Copyright ©2001 Photodisc, Inc.; p. 182(bl), Stephanie Morris/HRW Photo; p.183(tr), Jana Birchum/HRW Photo; p. 183(b), Peter Van Steen/HRW Photo; p. 193(tr), Jana Burchum/HRW Photo; p. 193(b), Peter Van Steen/HRW Photo; p. 197(tl), Peter Van Steen/HRW Photo.

Appendix: p. 206 CENCO

Sam Dudgeon/HRW Photos: p,viii-1, 24(cl), 34, 41, 46, 70, 84, 87, 150, 151, 180(bl), 181(bc), 183(tl), 185, 186, 187, 193(tl), 197(br)

John Langford/HRW Photos: p. 39 ,48(cr), 8, 181(tr), p. 8(cr, br)

Acknowledgements continued from page iii.

Alyson Mike
Science Teacher
East Valley Middle School
East Helena, Montana

Donna Norwood
Science Teacher and Dept. Chair
Monroe Middle School
Charlotte, North Carolina

James B. Pulley
Former Science Teacher
Liberty High School
Liberty, Missouri

Terry J. Rakes
Science Teacher
Elmwood Junior High School
Rogers, Arkansas

Elizabeth Rustad
Science Teacher
Crane Middle School
Yuma, Arizona

Debra A. Sampson
Science Teacher
Booker T. Washington Middle School
Elgin, Texas

Charles Schindler
Curriculum Advisor
San Bernardino City Unified Schools
San Bernardino, California

Bert J. Sherwood
Science Teacher
Socorro Middle School
El Paso, Texas

Patricia McFarlane Soto
Science Teacher and Dept. Chair
G. W. Carver Middle School
Miami, Florida

David M. Sparks
Science Teacher
Redwater Junior High School
Redwater, Texas

Elizabeth Truax
Science Teacher
Lewiston-Porter Central School
Lewiston, New York

Ivora Washington
Science Teacher and Dept. Chair
Hyattsville Middle School
Washington, D.C.

Elsie N. Waynes
Science Teacher and Dept. Chair
R. H. Terrell Junior High School
Washington, D.C.

Nancy Wesorick
Science and Math Teacher
Sunset Middle School
Longmont, Colorado

Alexis S. Wright
Middle School Science Coordinator
Rye Country Day School
Rye, New York

John Zambo
Science Teacher
E. Ustach Middle School
Modesto, California

Gordon Zibelman
Science Teacher
Drexell Hill Middle School
Drexell Hill, Pennsylvania